W9-BZW-389

PENGUIN BOOKS

READ THE BEATLES

Born in Glasgow, Scotland, June Skinner Sawyers has written extensively about music, travel, history, and popular culture. She contributes regularly to the *Chicago Tribune* and the *San Francisco Chronicle* and is an adjunct lecturer at the Newberry Library in Chicago. She is the author of numerous books, including *Celtic Music: A Complete Guide* and *Tougher Than the Rest: The 100 Best Bruce Springsteen Songs,* and has edited several literary and music anthologies, including *Racing in the Street: The Bruce Springsteen Reader; Dreams of Elsewhere: The Selected Travel Writings of Robert Louis Stevenson; The Greenwich Village Reader;* and *The Road North: 300 Years of Classic Scottish Travel Writing.* She lives in Chicago.

READ THE BEATLES

Classic and New Writings on the Beatles, Their Legacy, and Why They Still Matter

FOREWORD BY ASTRID KIRCHHERR

EDITED BY

June Skinner Sawyers

PENGUIN BOOKS

PENGUIN BOOKS
Published by the Penguin Group
Penguin Group (USA) Inc., 375 Hudson Street, New York, New York 10014, U.S.A.
Penguin Group (Canada), 90 Eglinton Avenue East, Suite 700, Toronto,
Ontario, Canada M4P 2Y3 (a division of Pearson Penguin Canada Inc.)
Penguin Books Ltd, 80 Strand, London WC2R 0RL, England
Penguin Ireland, 25 St Stephen's Green, Dublin 2, Ireland (a division of Penguin Books Ltd)
Penguin Group (Australia), 250 Camberwell Road, Camberwell,
Victoria 3124, Australia (a division of Pearson Australia Group Pty Ltd)
Penguin Books India Pvt Ltd, 11 Community Centre,
Panchsheel Park, New Delhi - 110 017, India
Penguin Group (NZ), cnr Airborne and Rosedale Roads, Albany,
Auckland 1310, New Zealand (a division of Pearson New Zealand Ltd)
Penguin Books (South Africa) (Pty) Ltd, 24 Sturdee Avenue,
Rosebank, Johannesburg 2196, South Africa

Penguin Books Ltd, Registered Offices:
80 Strand, London WC2R 0RL, England

First published in Penguin Books 2006

1   3   5   7   9   10   8   6   4   2

Copyright © June Skinner Sawyers, 2006
All rights reserved

Maps by Amelia Janes

Pages 353–56 constitute an extension of this copyright page.

LIBRARY OF CONGRESS CATALOGING-IN-PUBLICATION DATA
Read the Beatles : classic and new writings on the Beatles, their legacy, and
why they still matter / edited by June Skinner Sawyers ; foreword by Astrid Kirchherr.
p.   cm.
Includes index.
ISBN 0-14-303732-3
1. Beatles.   2. Rock musicians—England—Biography.
I. Sawyers, June Skinner, 1957–
ML421.B4R42 2006
782.42166092'2—dc22
[B]   2006043799

Printed in the United States of America
Set in New Caledonia
Designed by Alice Sorensen

Except in the United States of America, this book is sold subject to the condition
that it shall not, by way of trade or otherwise, be lent, resold, hired out, or otherwise
circulated without the publisher's prior consent in any form of binding or cover other
than that in which it is published and without a similar condition including this
condition being imposed on the subsequent purchaser.

The scanning, uploading, and distribution of this book via the Internet or via any
other means without the permission of the publisher is illegal and punishable by law.
Please purchase only authorized electronic editions, and do not participate in or encourage
electronic piracy of copyrighted materials. Your support of the author's rights is appreciated.

To the people of Liverpool—
past, present, and future

"I awoke one morning and found myself famous."
—Lord Byron after the publication of *Childe Harold's Pilgrimage*, 1812

Contents

■

Part One ■ TOGETHER

Part Two ■ APART

FOUR ■ Ringo Starr: Acting Naturally

FIVE ■ A Way of Remembering:
Why the Beatles Still Matter

Foreword

When I first met the Beatles in the Kaiserkeller in Hamburg, it was immediately clear to me that they were something very special. I had no idea, however, that in just a few years they would become the most successful band of all time.

Their unbelievable stage presence struck me with tremendous power. Their musicality, their good looks, and their spot-on humor—I had never experienced anything like it. We went to hear John, Paul, George, Stu, and Pete every time we could—first in the Kaiserkeller, and later at the Top Ten Club on the Reeperbahn and the legendary Star-Club. They attracted us like human magnets.

As we got to know each other better and spent most of our free time together, I became deeply impressed by their intelligence, their civility, their charm, and their immense curiosity and open-mindedness.

Stuart and I fell in love with each other, and he left the band to study art in Hamburg. Paul took over on bass. And we all continued to spend endless hours contemplating the meaning of life.

We were all very similar: We had, on the one hand, our group of French-influenced German friends in Hamburg, the so-called Existentialists, and, on the other, the American-influenced Beatles. Because it was a relatively short time after the end of the Second World War and because we were citizens of two nations that had recently been enemies, we faced each other at first with a few prejudices and misconceptions. John, Paul, George, Stu, and Pete, for example, would have been more likely to expect a strapping, red-cheeked young maiden with straw-blond braids and a dirndl dress than me—a self-assured, short-haired young photographer wearing a leather suit and driving my own convertible. We, on the other hand, remembered the "Tommies"—British soldiers—who had occupied Hamburg in 1945.

These prejudices soon evaporated and led to a give-and-take that was as intense as it gets. We had so many common interests—music, literature, film, and art; we talked heatedly about God and the world.

Of course, the Beatles wanted to hit it big, and they did everything they could by practicing and honing their repertoire as much as possible.

George dreamed of being as famous as the Shadows, who were popular in Europe at the time, so that he could buy his father, a bus driver, his own bus. John wanted to be bigger than Elvis.

As the Beatles eclipsed their own idols, the world itself began to change under their influence, even beyond the realm of pop culture, which they themselves had shaped so significantly. They gave young people more confidence and showed them, by example, how to be more critical and more individual. With their wonderful, distinctive personalities, they taught youth how to be different, how to stand apart from the crowd, and how to dare, to experiment, and to assert themselves with humor, intelligence, and tolerance—this and much more. At the high point of their careers, with Ringo on drums, they summed up the spirit of an entire generation in their simple, incisive, and direct way: All you need is love.

It is an honor for me to be able to write the foreword for this book. I am happy to have experienced all of the positive things my friends have brought about. I am also happy that new generations turn to them again and again. Their music has long been "classical" music; it has become folk music in the best possible sense.

And I am sad that Stu, John, and George left us so early. They had so much more to give to the world.

Astrid Kirchherr
Hamburg
April 12, 2006

Acknowledgments

Any book about the Beatles involves the assistance of many people. In particular, I wish to thank the following: Amelia Janes for her excellent maps of Liverpool; my eagle-eyed editor David Cashion and his resourceful assistant, Karen M. Anderson, who made the often time-consuming process of hunting down permissions and dealing with the subsequent paperwork less arduous; to Lynn Tews, project manager, at the Permissions Group, Inc., who helped with last-minute legal wrangles; my agent Scott Mendel; Elizabeth M. Solaro for the translation of Astrid Kirchherr's foreword, originally written in German; Anthony DeCurtis for his kindness and spirit above and beyond the call of official duty; David Schmitt at *Playboy* magazine who made it possible to reprint an excerpt from the seminal John Lennon–Yoko Ono interview when I had given up hope; Colin Hall for showing this former Glaswegian parts of Liverpool that I never would have seen without him; and to the people of Liverpool itself, especially Mara Salami at Mersey Partnership; Dave Jones at Cavern City Tours; guide extraordinaire and native Liverpudlian Jackie Spencer at Live@pool Tours; the staff of the Beatles Story museum at Albert Dock, especially Jerry Goldman; and Graham Paisley and Dave Peters at St. Peter's Church in Woolton, where it all began those many years ago in 1957. Theresa Albini accompanied me on my journey to Liverpool and was equally impressed with the city and its friendly people. Malcolm Caldwell, poet Dana Gioia, musician Jon Langford, Beatles chronicler Mark Lewisohn, Andrew O'Hagan, and Luc Sante were asked to contribute original pieces but, alas, time and other commitments got in the way—I thank them nevertheless. A special nod as well to Ulf Krüger, Astrid Kirchherr's manager, for his gracious assistance. Anyone interested in the Beatles and the Hamburg connection should consider Ms. Kirchherr's Web site, www.center-of-beat.com.

Chronology

February 18, 1933   Yoko Ono is born in Tokyo.

September 10, 1939   Cynthia Powell is born in Blackpool.

June 23, 1940   Stuart Sutcliffe is born in Edinburgh.

July 7, 1940   Richard Starkey is born in the front room of 9 Madryn Street, Liverpool, a Victorian terraced house.

October 9, 1940   John Winston Lennon is born at Oxford St. Maternity Hospital in Liverpool.

June 18, 1942   James Paul McCartney is born at Walton Hospital, Rice Lane, in Liverpool.

February 25, 1943   George Harrison is born at 12 Arnold Grove, a two-up, two-down terraced house built in the 1890s, in the Wavertree section of Liverpool.

January 16, 1957   Alan Synter opens the jazz-themed Cavern Club on Mathew Street in a seedy warehouse district of Liverpool. Inspired by the Parisian jazz club, Le Caveau Français, the short-lived jazz theme soon changes to skiffle, and then to rock.

May 1957   Lennon forms the Quarry Men.

June 22, 1957   The Quarry Men make their public debut at a street carnival on Rosebery Street in Liverpool.

July 6, 1957   Ivan Vaughan introduces fifteen-year-old Paul McCartney to John Lennon at the garden fête, St. Peter's Church, Woolton, Liverpool.

August 7, 1957   The Quarry Men skiffle group, led by John Lennon but sans Paul McCartney (who was at a Boy Scout summer camp) and George Harrison (who hadn't joined yet), makes its Cavern Club debut.

February 6, 1958   George Harrison joins the Quarry Men.

July 15, 1958   Julia Lennon dies after being struck by a vehicle driven by an off-duty police officer outside Aunt Mimi's Menlove Avenue house in Liverpool. Eventually, the officer goes to trial but is acquitted.

August 29, 1959   The Quarry Men play on opening night in the basement of the Casbah coffee club, a teenage social club, in West Derby, Liverpool. Run by Mona Best, Pete Best's mother, the group played there forty-four times.

May 1960   The Silver Beetles audition for Larry Parnes at the Blue Angel in Liverpool, receiving their first break. Passing the audition, they are hired to be the backing band for Johnny Gentle on a nine-day tour of Scotland, making stops at Alloa, Inverness, Fraserburgh, Keith, Forres, Nairn, and Peterhead.

May 25, 1960   Rory Storm and the Hurricanes, with Ringo Starr on drums, make their debut at the Cavern Club.

May 30, 1960   The Silver Beetles make their debut at the Jacaranda coffee bar on Slater Street in Liverpool.

June 2, 1960   The Beatles perform their first "professional" engagement at Neston Institute in Liverpool.

August 17–October 3, 1960   The Beatles play two clubs in Hamburg: the Indra and the Kaiserkeller.

November 21, 1960   George Harrison is deported from Germany for being underage and not having a work permit.

Late November 1960   Astrid Kirchherr gets engaged to Stuart Sutcliffe.

December 27, 1960   Considered the turning point in the Beatles career and the birthplace of Beatlemania, the Beatles perform at the Town Hall Ballroom in Litherland, Liverpool.

January 1961   Stuart Sutcliffe returns to England.

February 21, 1961   The Beatles play their first gig—a lunchtime session—at the Cavern Club in Liverpool. Their pay? A whopping £5. They make their evening debut a month later, on March 21.

April 1–July 1, 1961   The Beatles play thirteen weeks at the Top Ten Club on the Reeperbahn in Hamburg.

June 1961   The Beatles record with producer Bert Kaempfert in Hamburg, backing Tony Sheridan on five songs: two standards, "My Bonnie Lies Over the Ocean" and "When the Saints Go Marching In," Sheridan's "Why (Can't You Love Me Again)," Hank Snow's "Nobody's Child," and Jimmy Reed's "Take Out Some Insurance on Me, Baby." They also make two recordings without Sheridan, "Ain't She Sweet" and "Cry for a Shadow."

Late June 1961   Stuart Sutcliffe leaves the band at the end of the month to study art and stay in Hamburg.

July 2, 1961   The Beatles return to Liverpool, without Stuart Sutcliffe.

July 6, 1961   The first issue of *Mersey Beat*, the Liverpool music newspaper, is published. Lennon contributes the article "Being a Short Diversion on the Dubious Origins of the Beatles."

September 1, 1961   Sutcliffe begins his studies at the Staatliche Hochschule für bildende Künste (University of Fine Arts) under Eduardo Paolozzi.

October 23, 1961   "My Bonnie" is released in Germany, reaching No. 32 on the German hit parade.

November 9, 1961   Brian Epstein attends a lunchtime performance by the Beatles at the Cavern Club.

December 10, 1961   Brian Epstein agrees to become the Beatles' manager.

January 1, 1962   The Beatles make their first formal audition for a British record company at Decca Studios, Broadhurst Gardens, in London, where they tape fifteen songs: "Like Dreamers Do," "Money (That's What I Want)," "Till There Was You," "The Sheik of Araby," "To Know Her Is to Love Her," "Take Good Care of My Baby," "Memphis, Tennessee," "Sure to Fall (In Love with You)," "Hello Little Girl," "Three Cool Cats," "Crying, Waiting, Hoping," "Love of the Loved," "September in the Rain," "Besame Mucho," and "Searchin'."

April 1962   The Star-Club opens in Hamburg.

April 10, 1962   Twenty-one-year-old Stuart Sutcliffe dies of a brain hemorrhage in Hamburg while en route to the hospital. His body is returned to Liverpool in May.

April 13–May 31, 1962   The Beatles spend seven weeks at the Star-Club in Hamburg.

June 4, 1962   The Beatles sign a recording contract with Parlophone, a division of EMI.

June 6, 1962   The Beatles make their first visit to EMI Studios, 3 Abbey Road, in St. John's Wood, London, recording four songs: "Besame Mucho," "Love Me Do," "P.S. I Love You," and "Ask Me Why."

June 24, 1962   The Beatles make their final appearance at the Casbah coffee club, which closes at the end of the month.

August 16, 1962   Drummer Pete Best is fired.

August 18, 1962   Ringo Starr makes his first appearance with the Beatles at Hulme Hall, a Tudor-style village hall in Port Sunlight, on the Wirral peninsula across the Mersey from Liverpool.

August 23, 1962   John Lennon marries Cynthia Powell at Mount Pleasant Register Office in Liverpool.

September 11, 1962   After three separate trips to EMI Studios, the Beatles finish recording their first single, "Love Me Do"/"P.S. I Love You," with session drummer Andy White replacing Ringo Starr on the drums.

October 5, 1962 "Love Me Do"/"P.S. I Love You" is released as a single in the U.K.

November 1–14, 1962 The Beatles return to the Star-Club in Hamburg for a brief tour. They perform on a bill with Little Richard.

November 26, 1962 The Beatles return to EMI Studios to record their second single, "Please Please Me"/"Ask Me Why."

December 18–31, 1962 The Beatles make their final visit to Hamburg, playing at the Star-Club for thirteen nights.

January 1963 The Beatles play their second tour of Scotland—and their first tour as headliners—stopping at Elgin, Dingwall, Bridge of Allan, and Aberdeen and making an appearance on a children's television show in Glasgow.

February 11, 1963 The Beatles record their entire album, the fourteen-track *Please Please Me,* in one day at EMI Studios.

March 22, 1963 *Please Please Me* is released in Britain.

April 8, 1963 John Charles Julian Lennon is born to John and Cynthia Lennon at Sefton General Hospital, Liverpool.

April 18, 1963 The Beatles make their first appearance at the Royal Albert Hall in London.

August 3, 1963 After nearly three hundred performances, the Beatles make their final appearance at the Cavern Club.

September 11, 1963 The Beatles begin work on their second album, *With the Beatles,* at EMI Studios.

October 1963 The Beatles begin their Swedish concert tour.

October 13, 1963 The first twinges of Beatlemania emerge when the Beatles perform on *Sunday Night at the London Palladium* on British television.

January 20, 1964 *Meet the Beatles,* the first Beatles album in the United States, is released.

February 9, 1964 The Beatles perform live in front of an audience of 728 people on *The Ed Sullivan Show* in New York City. An estimated 73 million people in the United States watch as the band performs five songs: "All My Loving," "Till There Was You," "She Loves You," "I Saw Her Standing There," and "I Want to Hold Your Hand." The show also features singer/banjoist Tesse O'Shea, the New York cast of *Oliver* starring Georgia Brown and future Monkee Davy Jones, and impressionist Frank Gorshin.

February 11, 1964 The Beatles give their first concert in North America at the Washington Coliseum in Washington, D.C.

February 12, 1964   The Beatles give two thirty-four-minute shows at Carnegie Hall in New York City, at 7:45 and 11:15 P.M.

February 16, 1964   The Beatles make their second live appearance on *The Ed Sullivan Show* from the Deauville Hotel in Miami Beach. An estimated 70 million people watch as they perform "She Loves You," "This Boy," "All My Loving," "I Saw Her Standing There," "From Me to You," and "I Want to Hold Your Hand."

March 2, 1964   Shooting on *A Hard Day's Night* begins. Filming continues on and off until late April. The locations include Marylebone station in London; the Turks Head pub in St. Margaret's; Twickenham Film Studios; Gatwick Airport South in Surrey; Scala Theatre in London; River Thames towpath in Kew, Surrey; Hammersmith Odeon cinema in London; Thornbury Playing Fields in Isleworth; and Edgehill Road in West Ealing.

March 23, 1964   John Lennon's first book, *In His Own Write,* is published.

April 4, 1964   The Beatles occupy all five top positions on *Billboard*'s Top Pop Singles chart.

June 4, 1964   The Beatles twenty-seven-day world tour begins in Copenhagen. Other stops on the tour include Hillegom and Blokker in the Netherlands; Kowloon in Hong Kong; Adelaide, Melbourne, Sydney, and Brisbane in Australia; and Wellington, Auckland, Dunedin, and Christchurch in New Zealand. In Melbourne alone, some 250,000 people—reportedly the largest number of Australians ever assembled in one place at one time—line the streets.

July 6, 1964   The Beatles attend the world premiere of *A Hard Day's Night* at the London Pavilion cinema in Piccadilly Circus.

July 28–29, 1964   The Beatles return to Sweden for a brief second tour.

August 11, 1964   The Beatles begin recording *Beatles for Sale* at EMI Studios.

August 19–September 20, 1964   The Beatles begin their first full-fledged North American tour with their first stop at the Cow Palace in San Francisco, followed by the Convention Center in Las Vegas; the Coliseum in Seattle; Empire Stadium in Vancouver; the Hollywood Bowl in Los Angeles; Red Rocks Amphitheatre in Denver; Cincinnati Gardens in Cincinnati; Forest Hills Tennis Stadium in Queens, New York; Convention Hall in Atlantic City, New Jersey; Convention Hall in Philadelphia; Indiana State Fair Coliseum in Indianapolis; Milwaukee Arena in Milwaukee; International Amphitheatre in Chicago; Olympia Stadium in Detroit; Maple Leaf Gardens in Toronto; the Forum in Montreal; Gator Bowl in Jacksonville, Florida; Boston Garden in Boston; Civic Center in Baltimore; Civic Arena in Pittsburgh; Public Auditorium in Cleveland; City Park Stadium in New Orleans; Municipal Stadium in Kansas City, Missouri;

Dallas Memorial Auditorium in Dallas; and the Paramount Theatre in New York City.

September 6, 1964   Halfway through their first American tour the Beatles made public in a statement to the press their feelings toward segregation: "We will not appear unless Negroes are allowed to sit anywhere," referring to reports that blacks were confined to balconies at public events.

October 19–21, 1964   The Beatles perform three consecutive nights in Scotland in Edinburgh, Dundee, and Glasgow.

February 1965   Shooting of *Help!* begins in the Bahamas. Other locations include Austria and Salisbury Plain in Wiltshire.

February 11, 1965   Ringo Starr marries Maureen Cox.

June 12, 1965   The Beatles are created Members of the Order of the British Empire (MBEs) by Queen Elizabeth. Not everyone is pleased, though—some soldiers return their medals in protest.

June 14, 1965   Paul McCartney begins recording "Yesterday" at EMI Studios.

June 24, 1965   John Lennon's second book, *A Spaniard in the Works*, is published.

June 24–27 and 30, 1965   The Beatles perform in Milan, Genoa, and Rome in Italy and in Nice in France.

July 2–3, 1965   The Beatles perform in bullrings in Madrid and Barcelona, Spain.

July 29, 1965   The premiere of *Help!* takes place in London; it opens in New York on August 23.

August 11, 1965   Race riots in Watts, an African-American neighborhood of Los Angeles, leave thirty-four dead.

August 15–31, 1965   The Beatles start their second North American tour, performing their first concert at Shea Stadium in New York. More than 55,600 people attend (including Mick Jagger and Keith Richards, as well as Steve Van Zandt and Meryl Streep), creating a new world record for a pop concert. Other locations on the tour are Maple Leaf Gardens in Toronto; Atlanta Stadium in Atlanta; Sam Houston Coliseum in Houston; Comiskey Park in Chicago; Metropolitan Stadium in Minneapolis; Memorial Coliseum in Portland, Oregon; Balboa Stadium in San Diego; the Hollywood Bowl in Los Angeles; and ending at the Cow Palace in San Francisco.

October 12, 1965   The Beatles begin recording *Rubber Soul* at EMI Studios.

October 26, 1965 The Beatles receive their MBEs from the queen at Buckingham Palace.

November 27, 1965 The first of Ken Kesey's so-called acid tests is held in Santa Cruz, California.

December 3, 1965 The Beatles begin their last British tour with stops in Glasgow, Newcastle, Liverpool, Manchester, Sheffield, Birmingham, London, and Cardiff.

January 21, 1966 George Harrison marries Pattie Boyd.

March 4, 1966 Lennon grants an interview with Maureen Cleave of the London *Evening Standard,* and makes a controversial statement about the Beatles being more popular than Jesus.

April 6, 1966 Recording on *Revolver* begins at EMI Studios.

April 8, 1966 The cover of *Time* asks, "Is God Dead?"

June 5, 1966 The Beatles return to *The Ed Sullivan Show* with a taped appearance, introducing two music videos, "Rain" and "Paperback Writer." On subsequent shows, the Beatles introduce other videos, including "Hello Goodbye," "Penny Lane," "Strawberry Fields Forever," "Two of Us," and "Let It Be."

June 24–26, 1966 The Beatles perform in Munich, Essen, and Hamburg.

June 30–July 2, 1966 The Beatles perform five shows in the Nippon Budokan Hall in Tokyo, becoming the first rock band to perform there.

July 4, 1966 The Beatles perform twice—for 30,000 in the afternoon and 50,000 in the evening—at Rizal Memorial Football Stadium in Manila. The next day riots break out over a supposed snub of Imelda Marcos by the group.

July 29, 1966 *Datebook,* an American teen magazine, reprints the Maureen Cleave interview. Radio stations throughout the American South—the so-called Bible Belt—burn Beatles' records.

August 11–12, 1966 Lennon apologizes for the furor over his remarks at a press conference in Chicago.

August 12–29, 1966 The Beatles begin their final concert tour at the International Amphitheatre in Chicago. The other venues are Olympia Stadium in Detroit; Cleveland Stadium in Cleveland; D.C. Stadium in Washington, D.C.; John F. Kennedy Stadium in Philadelphia; Maple Leaf Gardens in Toronto; Suffolk Downs Racetrack in Boston; Mid-South Coliseum in Memphis; Crosley Field in Cincinnati; Busch Stadium in St. Louis; Shea Stadium in New York; the Coliseum in Seattle; and Dodger Stadium in Los Angeles. The Beatles perform their last concert at Candlestick Park in San Francisco on August 29.

September 1966   Shooting of *How I Won the War,* with Lennon in the role of Pvt. Gripweed, begins in West Germany.

November 9, 1966   John Lennon meets Yoko Ono at the Indica Gallery in London during a private preview of her show, *Unfinished Paintings and Objects.*

November 24, 1966   The Beatles begin recording *Sgt. Pepper's Lonely Hearts Club Band.*

March 30, 1967   The cover of *Sgt. Pepper,* designed by pop artist Peter Blake, is shot at photographer Michael Cooper's studio in the Chelsea section of London. It consists of a montage of fifty-seven photographs, nine waxwork models, and, of course, the Beatles themselves.

June 1, 1967   *Sgt. Pepper's Lonely Hearts Club Band* is released in Britain.

June 2, 1967   *Sgt. Pepper* is released in the United States.

June 16–18, 1967   Monterey Pop is held in California.

June 25, 1967   The Beatles perform "All You Need Is Love" for the *Our World* television special, the first television special to be broadcast worldwide. An estimated 400 million people (some sources say as many as 700 million) watch. Singing backup are Eric Clapton and members of the Rolling Stones and the Who.

July 7, 1967   *Time* runs a cover story on "The Hippies: Philosophy of a Sub-Culture."

July 12, 1967   Race riots leave twenty-six dead and fifteen hundred injured in Newark, New Jersey.

July 23–27, 1967   Race riots in Detroit leave forty-three dead and two thousand injured.

July 24, 1967   A full-page ad in the London *Times* urges the legalization of marijuana in Britain. All four Beatles sign it.

August 25, 1967   The Beatles travel from Euston Station in London to Bangor, Wales, to attend a weekend seminar on meditation by the Maharishi Mahesh Yogi.

August 27, 1967   Brian Epstein dies of a drug overdose in his flat at 24 Chapel Street, Belgravia, London. The death is officially ruled accidental.

November 9, 1967   *Rolling Stone* publishes its first issue.

January 1968   The Beatles launch Apple Corps, which includes a recording studio, a record label (Apple Records), a film division, and a boutique. In addition to Beatles records, Apple releases albums by James Taylor, Mary Hopkin, Billy Preston, Ravi Shankar, and others.

March 31, 1968   Lyndon Baines Johnson announces that he will not run for re-election.

April 4, 1968   Martin Luther King, Jr., is assassinated by James Earl Ray in Memphis, triggering weeks of rioting and looting across the United States.

May 3, 1968   Leftist student protesters in France attempt to topple the government of Charles de Gaulle.

May 14, 1968   John Lennon and Paul McCartney appear on *The Tonight Show,* the first appearance either makes on an American television talk show, to announce the formation of Apple Corps. The guest host is baseball player Joe Garagiola, who, inexplicably, seems at a loss for words during the interview.

July 1, 1968   Lennon's first art exhibition, *You Are Here,* opens at the Robert Fraser Gallery in London.

July 17, 1968   *Yellow Submarine* stages its world premiere.

August 22, 1968   Cynthia Lennon sues John for divorce on grounds of adultery.

August 26–29, 1968   The Democratic National Convention is held in Chicago; antiwar demonstrators and police clash.

September 6, 1968   Eric Clapton plays solo guitar on "While My Guitar Gently Weeps" during the recording of the White Album at EMI Studios, the first time a non-Beatle musician plays on a Beatles studio recording.

October 18, 1968   Police raid Ringo Starr's flat at 34 Montagu Square, London, where Lennon and Yoko temporarily are staying and discover 219 grams of cannabis.

November 21, 1968   Yoko has a miscarriage.

November 25, 1968   *The Beatles* (better known as the White Album) is released in the United States.

November 28, 1968   In London, Lennon pleads guilty to possession of marijuana.

November 29, 1968   Lennon and Ono's first album together, *Unfinished Music No. 1: Two Virgins,* is released.

January 30, 1969   In their last public performance, the Beatles perform "Get Back," "Don't Let Me Down," "I've Got a Feeling," and "The One After 909" in a forty-two-minute lunchtime concert on the rooftop of the Apple Corps building. A portion of the performance appears in the *Let It Be* film.

March 12, 1969   Paul McCartney and Linda Eastman marry in London.

March 20, 1969   John Lennon and Yoko Ono marry in Gibraltar.

March 25–31, 1969   John and Yoko stage their first "bed-in" for peace in Room 902 of the Amsterdam Hilton.

May 9, 1969   John and Yoko's second album, *Unfinished Music No. 2: Life with the Lions,* is released.

May 16, 1969   Lennon's application for an American visa is rejected because of his drug conviction in November 1968.

May 26–June 2, 1969   John and Yoko stage their second, and final, "bed-in" for peace in Room 1742 of the Hôtel Reine-Elizabeth in Montreal.

July 1, 1969   Recording on the Beatles' final studio album, *Abbey Road,* begins at the EMI Studios.

July 4, 1969   "Give Peace a Chance," Lennon's first solo single, is released.

July 20, 1969   Neil Armstrong becomes the first man to walk on the moon.

August 9, 1969   Five people, including actress Sharon Tate, are murdered by the Manson family in Los Angeles. Manson gives two reasons for the murder spree: the Book of Revelations and the White Album.

August 15, 1969   Woodstock Music and Art Fair takes place in Bethel, New York, attracting some 450,000 people.

August 20, 1969   The last Beatles studio session at Abbey Road, featuring all four band members, takes place; the last song they record is, appropriately, "The End."

September 13, 1969   The Plastic Ono Band stages its concert debut at Varsity Stadium, University of Toronto.

September 23, 1969   Rumors that "Paul is dead" circulate.

October 12, 1969   Yoko suffers her second miscarriage.

October 15, 1969   Moratorium Day, a nationwide protest against the Vietnam War, prompts more than a quarter of a million people to congregate in Washington, D.C., the largest antiwar rally ever.

October 27, 1969   Ringo begins recording *Sentimental Journey* at EMI Studios, becoming the first Beatle to record a solo studio album.

November 25, 1969   Lennon returns his MBE medal to the Queen. He includes a note with the medal, which states: "Your Majesty, I am returning my MBE in protest against Britain's involvement in the Nigeria-Biafra thing, against our support of America in Vietnam, and against 'Cold Turkey' slipping down in the charts. With love, John Lennon."

December 12, 1969 The *Plastic Ono Band—Live Peace in Toronto* is released on Apple.

January 1970 Lennon's solo single, "Instant Karma," is released.

April 10, 1970 The Beatles officially break up.

April 17, 1970 Paul McCartney releases his first solo album, *McCartney*.

May 8, 1970 The album *Let It Be* is released in Britain.

May 13, 1970 The film *Let It Be* opens in New York. It opens in London and Liverpool a week later, on May 20.

November 1970 George Harrison becomes the first Beatle to release a solo record, the mammoth three-album set *All Things Must Pass,* prompting Richard Williams in *Melody Maker* to proclaim the event as "the rock equivalent of the shock felt by pre-war moviegoers when Garbo first opened her mouth in a talkie: 'Garbo talks!—Harrison is free!'"

December 11, 1970 *Plastic Ono Band,* Lennon's first solo album, is released.

August 1, 1971 George Harrison's Concert for Bangladesh, to raise funds for the victims of the Pakistani civil war, is held at Madison Square Garden in New York. Among the participants are Ravi Shankar, Billy Preston, Eric Clapton, Leon Russell, a surprise appearance from Bob Dylan, and the always reliable Ringo Starr, who sings "It Don't Come Easy." The concert raises more than $200,000 for UNICEF.

October 9, 1971 Lennon's album *Imagine* is released.

December 11, 1971 John and Yoko perform at a benefit rally, attended by 15,000 people, in Ann Arbor, Michigan, to support John Sinclair, writer and founder of the White Panther Party. Sinclair had been sentenced to nearly a decade in prison for possession of two marijuana cigarettes.

February 14–18, 1972 John and Yoko cohost the *Mike Douglas Show* on American television.

March 16, 1972 John and Yoko are served with deportation notices because of his 1968 drug conviction in London.

March 1973 Despite protests from fans, the Cavern Club is demolished. A replica is later rebuilt using the bricks from the original building. Today, it is a crucial part of the revitalized Mathew Street scene.

March 23, 1973 Lennon is ordered to leave the United States within sixty days; Yoko is granted permanent residency status.

September 7–8, 1974   The first Beatlefest (now called the Fest for Beatles Fans) is held at the Commodore Hotel in New York by founder Mark Lapidos. Lapidos met with John Lennon five months earlier and shared with him his idea of holding a Beatles fan convention, complete with movies, special guests, live music, flea markets, discussions, and even look-alike and sound-alike contests. All the Beatles donate items for a charity raffle. Lennon is especially supportive ("I'm all for it. I'm a Beatles fan, too!").

November 16, 1974   Lennon's single, "Whatever Gets You through the Night," tops the *Billboard* charts.

January 9, 1975   The Beatles partnership is dissolved in the London High Court.

October 7, 1975   The New York State Supreme Court reverses Lennon's deportation order.

October 9, 1975   Sean Ono Lennon is born in New York.

February 23–25, 1976   George Harrison is sued by Bright Tunes Music, which owns the copyright for the 1963 Chiffons hit, "He's So Fine," charging that Harrison lifted the melody and arrangement of the song for "My Sweet Lord." The court finds Harrison guilty of "subconscious plagiarism" and orders him to pay the plaintiff more than a half million dollars.

April 1, 1976   Freddie Lennon, John's father, dies in Brighton General Hospital in England.

July 27, 1976   Lennon's application to become a resident alien is approved at a hearing in New York.

September 29, 1980   John and Yoko's first "comeback" interview is published in *Newsweek*.

November 17, 1980   John and Yoko's *Double Fantasy* album is released.

December 8, 1980   John Lennon is fatally shot by Mark David Chapman outside the lobby of the Dakota apartment building in New York City. He is cremated at Hartsdale Crematorium, New York.

December 27, 1980   "(Just Like) Starting Over" bolts to the top of the U.S. singles chart, staying there for five weeks.

March 29, 1981   Two thousand people attend a special memorial service for John Lennon held at the Anglican Cathedral in Liverpool.

April 16, 1981   A section of Central Park, across from the Dakota, is renamed Strawberry Fields.

May 15, 1981   George Harrison's single, "All Those Years Ago," a tribute to John, makes in into the American top ten.

June 12, 1981   Yoko releases *Seasons of Glass.* The controversial cover features Lennon's blood-spattered and shattered glasses.

August 24, 1981   Mark David Chapman is sentenced to a minimum of twenty years and a maximum of life in prison.

October 28, 1981   *Lennon,* a musical play, opens in Liverpool. It opens off-Broadway in New York the following year, but soon closes because of poor sales. It opens in London in November 1985.

February 24, 1982   Yoko, accompanied by Sean, receives the Album of the Year award for *Double Fantasy* at the Grammys, held in Los Angeles.

December 16, 1983   Polydor releases the first posthumous Lennon recording, *Heartplay: An Unfinished Dialogue.*

1984   Ringo Starr narrates the animated British children's television program, *Thomas the Tank Engine and Friends* (known as *Shining Time Station* in the United States).

January 27, 1984   Polydor releases *Milk and Honey,* the Lennon-Ono follow-up to *Double Fantasy.*

March 7, 1984   Liverpool City Council passes a resolution conferring each Beatle with the Honorary Freedom of the City award.

March 21, 1984   Yoko officially opens Strawberry Fields in Central Park. Sean, Julian, and Mayor Ed Koch also attend the ceremony.

April 25, 1984   Liverpool's first official statue of the Beatles, by sculptor John Doubleday, is unveiled at the Cavern Walks shopping center. The following day, the Cavern Walks complex officially opens.

May–September 1984   *The Art of the Beatles* exhibition runs at the Walker Art Gallery, Liverpool. The exhibition attracts some 50,000 visitors.

December 1984   The Cavern Mecca, a Liverpool museum and information center, closes.

August 10, 1985   Michael Jackson acquires ATV Music, including 260 Beatles songs, for $47.5 million.

December 2, 1985   *John and Yoko: A Love Story* premieres on American television. Mark McGann plays John; Kim Miyori, Yoko.

1986   The Beatles Festival starts in Liverpool.

October 6, 1986   Harper & Row publish the first posthumous collection of Lennon prose and poetry, *Skywriting by Word of Mouth.*

November 30, 1986   *The Dream Is Over,* a ballet based on Lennon's music and written by Christopher Bruce, is presented on the London television arts series *The South Bank Show.* It later premieres at the Sadler's Wells Theatre in London.

January 20, 1988   The Beatles are inducted into the Rock and Roll Hall of Fame.

September 30, 1988   Yoko unveils a star with Lennon's name outside the Capitol Records' Tower building along the Hollywood Walk of Fame.

October 3, 1988   Yoko's documentary, *Imagine: John Lennon,* opens in the United States; it opens in London at the end of the month.

May 1, 1990   The Beatles Story, a permanent Beatles museum, opens at the Albert Dock, Liverpool.

February 20, 1991   Yoko Ono accepts the Lifetime Achievement Award granted posthumously to John Lennon at the Grammy Awards in New York.

June 28, 1991   Paul McCartney's *Liverpool Oratorio* is performed by the Royal Liverpool Philharmonic Orchestra, with Carl Davis conducting, at Liverpool's Anglican Cathedral to celebrate the orchestra's 150th anniversary. It was here, at the age of eleven, that Paul failed an audition to sing in the choir.

January 20, 1994   John Lennon is inducted into the Rock and Roll Hall of Fame.

February 1994   The three surviving Beatles reunite to record additional music to several unfinished Lennon demos, with ELO's Jeff Lynne producing. The first new song, "Free as a Bird," premieres on November 19, 1995, as part of *The Beatles Anthology* television program on ABC in the United States and on ITV in the United Kingdom. The second new track, "Real Love," is released on March 4, 1996.

November 30, 1994   Apple Records releases a two-CD collection of early Beatles performances on the BBC, entitled *Live at the BBC.*

January 1996   The Liverpool Institute for the Performing Arts (LIPA) opens in Paul McCartney and George Harrison's old grammar school. McCartney donates £1 million from his own pocket. The queen officially opens the building on June 7, 1996.

1997   Yoko Ono establishes the John Lennon Scholarship Program, which recognizes young songwriters working in any genre between the ages of fifteen and twenty-five.

March 11, 1997   Paul McCartney is knighted.

September 25, 1997 The FBI makes public all but ten secret files on John Lennon.

April 17, 1998 Linda McCartney dies from cancer in Arizona. She is cremated and her ashes scattered in Arizona and at the family farm in England.

March 15, 1999 Paul McCartney is inducted into the Rock and Roll Hall of Fame.

October 16, 1999 McCartney's orchestral *Working Classical,* performed by the London Symphony Orchestra with the Loma Mar Quartet, premieres at the Liverpool Cathedral.

December 30, 1999 George Harrison and his family are attacked in his Friar Park estate outside London while sleeping by thirty-three-year-old Michael Abram, a paranoid schizophrenic and, ironically, fellow Liverpudlian, who is charged with breaking and entering and attempted murder. Olivia Harrison, his wife, sustains minor cuts to her forehead and wrists, but George is stabbed at least ten times and suffers a punctured right lung.

2000 The Beatles release a best-of collection, entitled *1,* that includes twenty-seven No. 1 Beatles hits. Within five weeks, it becomes the best-selling album of the year. Later in the year, the Beatles release *The Beatles Anthology,* which includes interviews with all four band members. The book goes straight to the top of *The New York Times* best-seller's list.

October 9, 2000 The world's first museum dedicated to the life of John Lennon opens on the anniversary of his sixtieth birthday in a suburb north of Tokyo. Yoko Ono, who opened the museum and donated most of the exhibits, notes that Lennon had a special place in his heart for Japan. "Japan was a very important place for John because John's son was half Japanese, but also we felt that we were somehow bridging the difference between East and West." Among the memorabilia are handwritten song lyrics, Lennon's first guitar, and a pair of his wire-rimmed glasses.

December 8, 2000 A bronze statue of John Lennon is unveiled in a Havana, Cuba, park on the twentieth anniversary of his murder in New York. Once denigrated as a decadent Westerner, the Cuban government honors the ex-Beatle as a "revolutionary" hero who was a constant victim of U.S. harassment.

September 11, 2001 Terrorist attacks take place in New York City, Washington, D.C., and Pennsylvania.

November 29, 2001 George Harrison dies from lung and brain cancer at the age of fifty-eight.

March 15, 2002 Yoko Ono officially opens a new £32.5 million passenger terminal to mark the formal renaming of Liverpool's airport to Liverpool John Lennon Airport and to unveil a bronze statue of Lennon by sculptor Tom Murphy on the upper level of the main terminal. The airport tag line seems appropriate, "Above Us Only Sky," a phrase from Lennon's classic song, "Imagine." The tag line and a self-portrait line drawing of Lennon appear everywhere, from the signs leading to the airport to the official airport carpets.

May 24–August 4, 2002   The Walker Art Gallery in Liverpool sponsors the first comprehensive exhibition in Britain of Paul McCartney's paintings.

June 11, 2002   Paul McCartney marries Heather Mills. The couple announce they are seeking a divorce in May 2006.

January 2003   Police raids in England and the Netherlands recover nearly five hundred original Beatles studio tapes, recorded during the *Let It Be* sessions.

March 2003   *The Beatles Anthology* television series is released on DVD with additional bonus material.

2004   The film, *Let It Be*, is restored and released in DVD form as *Let It Be . . . Naked*. The album of the same name was previously released in November 2003.

February 8, 2004   The Beatles receive the National Academy of Recording Arts and Sciences President's Award at the 46th Annual Grammy Awards in Los Angeles in honor of the fortieth anniversary of their arrival in the United States. Olivia Harrison represents George, Yoko Ono represents John; Paul and Ringo submit videotaped commentary.

February 24, 2004   Liverpool hosts its official George Harrison tribute concert at the Empire Theatre.

March 15, 2004   George Harrison is posthumously inducted into the Rock and Roll Hall of Fame by Tom Petty and Jeff Lynne at the Waldorf-Astoria in New York. Olivia and Dhani Harrison accept the award on George's behalf.

April 2004   Beatles chronicler Mark Lewisohn signs a deal, reportedly for seven figures, with Crown to publish a three-part Beatles biography to be published over the next decade. The first volume will concentrate on the years 1940–1963, the second volume on 1964–1967, and the third volume on 1968 to the present day.

September 2004   The FBI is ordered to release the remaining John Lennon files.

October 2004   Mark David Chapman is denied parole.

October 2004   Revolution Studios announces a new film, *All You Need Is Love*, directed by Julie Taymor in which nearly twenty Beatles songs will be used to tell the story between an American girl and an English boy in the late sixties.

November 16, 2004   Capitol releases *The Capitol Albums, Vol. 1,* the first American release of *Meet the Beatles, The Beatles Second Album, Something New,* and *Beatles '65* in a boxed-set format.

February 6, 2005   Paul McCartney performs during halftime at the Super Bowl in Jacksonville, Florida.

February 13, 2005   An all-star lineup, including Bono, Stevie Wonder, Norah Jones, Alicia Keys, Tim McGraw, and Brian Wilson, sing "Across the Universe" at the Grammy Awards held in Los Angeles to benefit tsunami victims and their families.

May 2005   Drummer Zak Starkey, son of Ringo Starr, joins Oasis for their summer 2005 concert tour.

May 31, 2005   Strawberry Field, which opened in 1936, closes after nearly seventy years of looking after Liverpool's orphan population. In 1984 Yoko Ono donated more than $120,000 to keep it open. Over the years, though, the preference for placing children with foster families reduces the need for orphanages.

July 2005   *Lennon,* a biomusical based on the life of John Lennon, opens on Broadway. It features ten actors, all portraying the singer at different points in his life. Thirty songs are featured, including two unpublished songs, "India, India" and "I Don't Want to Lose You," which Yoko Ono gave to writer-director Don Scardino. It closes on September 24 after only forty-nine performances.

July 2, 2005   Bob Geldorf organizes a series of free concerts at Hyde Park in London, at the Museum of Art in Philadelphia, at the Circus Maximus in Rome, and near the Brandenburg Gate in Berlin to raise world awareness of poverty. The London performers include Elton John, Mariah Carey, Coldplay, Madonna, R.E.M., Sting, U2, and Sir Paul McCartney.

September 16–November 29, 2005   Paul McCartney tours North America, beginning in Miami and ending in Los Angeles, and including four sold-out concerts on September 30 and October 1, 4, and 5 at New York's Madison Square Garden.

October 2005   *Variety* names the Beatles the top entertainers of the last one hundred years.

June 18, 2006   The perenially youthful Paul McCartney turns sixty-four.

June 30, 2006   Cirque de Soleil's LOVE, a live theatre production of Beatles songs, opens at the custom-built Mirage theatre in Las Vegas with Sir George Martin and his son, Giles, as music directors. It features 360° seating, panoramic video projections, and surround sound, as well as radical remixes of Beatles songs.

READ THE BEATLES

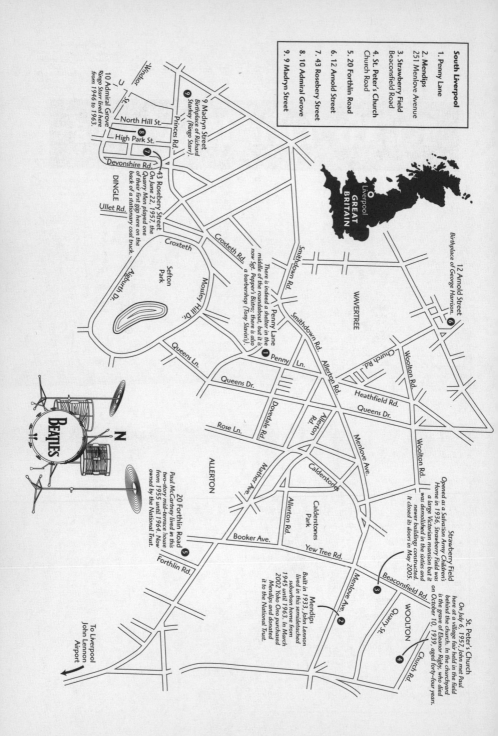

South Liverpool

1. Penny Lane
2. Mendips
   251 Menlove Avenue
3. Strawberry Field
   Beaconsfield Road
4. St. Peter's Church
   Church Road
5. 20 Forthlin Road
6. 12 Arnold Street
7. 43 Rosebery Street
8. 10 Admiral Grove
9. 9 Madryn Street

10 Admiral Grove
Ringo Starr lived here from 1946 to 1963.

9 Madryn Street
Birthplace of Richard Starkey (Ringo Starr).

43 Rosebery Street
On June 22, 1957, the Quarry Men played one of their first gigs here on the back of a stationary coal truck.

There is indeed a shelter in the middle of the roundabout, but it is now Sgt. Pepper's Bistro; there is also a barbershop (Tony Slavin's).

GREAT BRITAIN
Liverpool

12 Arnold Street
Birthplace of George Harrison

WAVERTREE

ALLERTON

DINGLE

WOOLTON

Strawberry Field
Opened as a Salvation Army Children's Home in 1936, Strawberry Field was a large Victorian mansion but it was demolished in the sixties and newer buildings constructed. It closed its doors in May 2005.

St. Peter's Church
On July 6, 1957, John met Paul here at a village fair held in the field behind the church. In the churchyard is the grave of Eleanor Rigby, who died on October 10, 1933, aged forty-four years.

Mendips
Built in 1933, John Lennon lived in this semidetached suburban home from 1945 until 1963. In March 2002 Yoko Ono purchased Mendips and donated it to the National Trust.

20 Forthlin Road
Paul McCartney lived in this two-story mid-terrace house from 1955 until 1964. Now owned by the National Trust.

To Liverpool John Lennon Airport

N

BEATLES

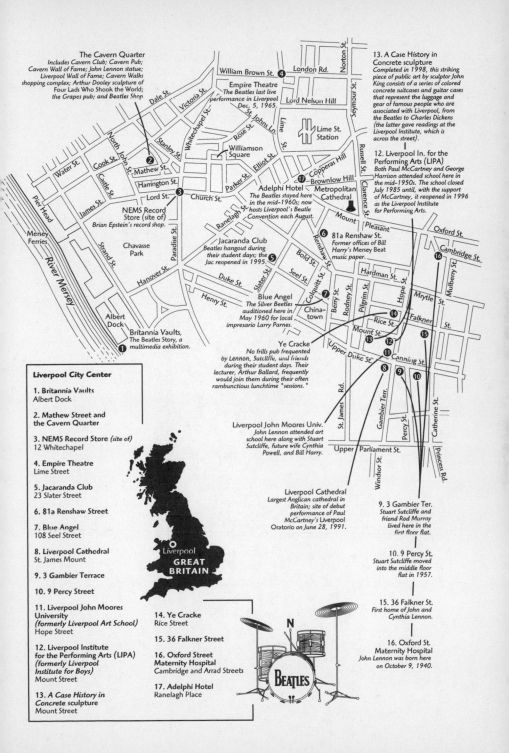

The Cavern Quarter
Includes Cavern Club; Cavern Pub; Cavern Wall of Fame; John Lennon statue; Liverpool Wall of Fame; Cavern Walks shopping complex; Arthur Dooley sculpture of Four Lads Who Shook the World; the Grapes pub; and Beatles Shop.

William Brown St. ④   London Rd.
Norton St.
Seymour St.
Lord Nelson Hill

Empire Theatre
The Beatles last live performance in Liverpool Dec. 5, 1965.

Lime St. Station

13. A Case History in Concrete sculpture
Completed in 1998, this striking piece of public art by sculptor John King consists of a series of colored concrete suitcases and guitar cases that represent the luggage and gear of famous people who are associated with Liverpool, from the Beatles to Charles Dickens (the latter gave readings at the Liverpool Institute, which is across the street).

12. Liverpool In. for the Performing Arts (LIPA)
Both Paul McCartney and George Harrison attended school here in the mid-1950s. The school closed July 1985 until, with the support of McCartney, it reopened in 1996 as the Liverpool Institute for Performing Arts.

Williamson Square

Adelphi Hotel
The Beatles stayed here in the mid-1960s; now hosts Liverpool's Beatle Convention each August.

Metropolitan Cathedral ⑰ Brownlow Hill

NEMS Record Store (site of)
Brian Epstein's record shop.

Chavasse Park

6. 81a Renshaw St.
Former offices of Bill Harry's Mersey Beat music paper.

Oxford St.
Cambridge St.

Jacaranda Club ⑤
Beatles hangout during their student days; the Jac reopened in 1995.

Mersey Ferries
River Mersey

Albert Dock

Britannia Vaults,
The Beatles Story, a multimedia exhibition. ①

Blue Angel ⑦
The Silver Beetles auditioned here in May 1960 for local impresario Larry Parnes.
China-town

Ye Cracke
No frills pub frequented by Lennon, Sutcliffe, and friends during their student days. Their lecturer, Arthur Ballard, frequently would join them during their often rambunctious lunchtime "sessions."

Liverpool John Moores Univ.
John Lennon attended art school here along with Stuart Sutcliffe, future wife Cynthia Powell, and Bill Harry.

Upper Parliament St.

Liverpool Cathedral
Largest Anglican cathedral in Britain; site of debut performance of Paul McCartney's Liverpool Oratorio on June 28, 1991.

9. 3 Gambier Ter.
Stuart Sutcliffe and friend Rod Murray lived here in the first floor flat.

10. 9 Percy St.
Stuart Sutcliffe moved into the middle floor flat in 1957.

15. 36 Falkner St.
First home of John and Cynthia Lennon.

16. Oxford St. Maternity Hospital
John Lennon was born here on October 9, 1940.

Liverpool City Center

1. Britannia Vaults
   Albert Dock

2. Mathew Street and the Cavern Quarter

3. NEMS Record Store *(site of)*
   12 Whitechapel

4. Empire Theatre
   Lime Street

5. Jacaranda Club
   23 Slater Street

6. 81a Renshaw Street

7. Blue Angel
   108 Seel Street

8. Liverpool Cathedral
   St. James Mount

9. 3 Gambier Terrace

10. 9 Percy Street

11. Liverpool John Moores University
    (formerly Liverpool Art School)
    Hope Street

12. Liverpool Institute for the Performing Arts (LIPA)
    (formerly Liverpool Institute for Boys)
    Mount Street

13. *A Case History in Concrete* sculpture
    Mount Street

14. Ye Cracke
    Rice Street

15. 36 Falkner Street

16. Oxford Street Maternity Hospital
    Cambridge and Arrad Streets

17. Adelphi Hotel
    Ranelagh Place

Liverpool
GREAT BRITAIN

N

BEATLES

Introduction

■

"We're all really the same person. We're just four parts of the one."
—Paul McCartney on the Beatles

For a band that separated thirty-five years ago, the Beatles have had a remarkably fruitful post-breakup career. Millions of people still listen to their music, some for the first time. What accounts for their remarkable longevity after all these years?

The truth is that the Beatles mean different things to different people and, perhaps most significantly, different things to different generations. What a baby boomer hears is not the same thing that a member of Generation X hears. Their music is so timeless, so full of subtle flavors and nuances, that whatever it is you wish to find, it will probably be there. For a band that never stayed still, that was constantly reinventing itself, it seems only fitting that their music has flourished for so long. The Beatles changed along with us.

They were always more than just a rock band. For whatever the reasons—and you'll read about plenty of them in this collection—they spoke to millions of people around the world on a genuinely profound level. Whether they liked it or not—and much of the time they didn't—they belonged to us and, for many, they still remain a big part of our collective unconscious.

Everywhere I go these days I seem to hear snippets of Beatles music or the songs of individual Beatles. Popping into a local restaurant, "Eight Days a Week" blares jubilantly from the loudspeakers. An hour later, just around the corner, the radio plays John Lennon's "Nobody Told Me." Is this a mere coincidence or is there another resurgence in the making? Or, perhaps more likely, is it just that the Beatles' music never really went away?

It's remarkable how certain Beatles and solo Beatle songs have become such an indelible part of our daily living. Some examples are clever, such as a recent advertisement promoting a pair of rubber boots under the tag line of "Rubber Soul." Other times, they appear under more poignant circumstances: On a spring afternoon in suburban

Chicago, someone, obviously in pain over a senseless act of violence, taped the lyrics of John Lennon's "Imagine" to a table holding bouquets of flowers as a memorial to the victims of the crime.

A significant amount of fiction—some good, most bad—has been inspired by the Beatles. There have been short stories (Robert Hemenway's "The Girl Who Sang with the Beatles"; Robert Olen Butler's "Relic," about a Vietnamese man living outside New Orleans who comes into possession of one of John Lennon's shoes), poetry (Allen Ginsberg, Philip Larkin, Paul Muldoon, Campbell McGrath, David Wojahn), and plays (Willy Russell's *John, Paul, George, Ringo, and Bert* and Norman Revill's *Dead Beat in Dakota*). Several novels look to the Beatles as literary muses. The characters in Haruki Murakami's *Norwegian Wood* (2000) constantly play Beatles songs, "Norwegian Wood" being a particular favorite. "Those guys sure knew something about the sadness of life, and gentleness," says one character. Douglas Coupland's novel *Eleanor Rigby* (2005) takes its title and inspiration from the Beatles classic of the same name.

Beatles songs appear on vanity plates (SGT PEPR, LVRITA 1, HEY JUDE, MR KITE 2). Indeed, the Beatles are so ubiquitous that even plants have been named after them (Abbey Road iris, Strawberry Fields Forever daylily, Ringo dahlia).

More than forty years after the Beatles' triumphant arrival in New York City, it's easy to forget just how derogatory and condescending the attitude of the mainstream press was toward them. To anyone who thinks the Beatles knew nothing but acclaim, it almost comes as a shock. To put it bluntly, the foursome did not make a good first impression. "Talentwise . . . the Beatles seem to be 75 percent publicity, 20 percent haircut and 5 percent lilting lament," wrote John Horn, the television critic for the *New York Herald Tribune*. "They're really a magic act that owes less to Britain than to Barnum." Worse, *The Washington Post* called the foursome "asexual and homely."

Conventional wisdom at the time considered the Beatles to be nothing but a fleeting fancy, a harmless diversion. And like all teenage fads, they, too, would soon disappear.

Some diversion. All these many years later, the books are still being published, the musicals are still being launched, the television programs are still being broadcast, the songs are still being played around the world—on the radio, in the privacy of a home, in a restaurant. And yet so many times throughout their career, doubts about their longevity persisted. John Lennon himself once said, ". . . [I]t can't last. Anyway," he added, "I'd hate to be old. Just imagine it. Who would want to listen to an eighty-year-old Beatle?"

In September 1966, when sales fell during what came to be their last concert tour, *Time* asked, "Is Beatlemania dead?" Had the novelty worn off, people wondered? Some thought so. Fewer fans waited at airports, not as many kids gathered around the hotels. Unlike the year before, Shea Stadium in New York did not sell out. The climate at the concerts had changed, too. Bomb threats, clashes between fans and police, and even death threats signaled an ominous turn. It got so bad that Paul McCartney began vomiting before going on stage when the fear became overwhelming. Within a fairly short time, the world would experience the horrors of the Manson murders, death at the Altamont music festival in California, the shooting of student protesters at Kent State, and riots during the 1968 Democratic National Convention in Chicago. In such a violent place, love was not enough.

After their last live concert in August 1966, at San Francisco's Candlestick Park, the Beatles retreated into the safety of the studio. Less than a year later, *Sgt. Pepper's Lonely Hearts Club Band* was released. Its effect on popular culture was, in a word, galvanizing. Most of the mainstream press hailed it as nothing short of a masterpiece. Hyperbole after hyperbole filled the pages of newspapers and magazines around the world. Poems have been written about it, such as Richard Foerster's "Playland." "More than Eliot or Auden," wrote Foerster, "the Beatles' songs were the poetry that spoke most directly to my adolescent soul in 1967." *Newsweek* compared the songs of Lennon and McCartney to the poetry of T. S. Eliot, while music critic Kenneth Tynan called the release of *Sgt. Pepper* "a decisive moment in the history of Western civilization." Wow. What does one do for an encore after that?

Actually, one of the most famous quotes belongs to music critic Langdon Winner, who in one paragraph captured the essence of the *Sgt. Pepper* moment: "In every city in Europe and America the stereo systems and the radio played, 'What would you think if I sang out of tune . . . Woke up, got out of bed . . . looked much older, and the bag across her shoulder . . . in the sky with diamonds, Lucy in the . . .' and everyone listened," he wrote. [See the Greil Marcus essay in this volume for the full quote.]

Whenever *Sgt. Pepper* is mentioned, inevitably the Winner comment is paraded about. I think the reason for that is because to anyone who did not experience it—and that includes a huge portion of today's population—the idea of a piece of pop music actually bringing an entire generation together seems preposterous. One cannot imagine such a thing happening in the fragmented, niche-driven marketplace of the present day.

Still, when the Beatles did break up, critics wondered if their music would endure. "Another generation soon will create new symbols to recognize itself by, which will mean little to those of us to whom the '60s meant a great deal," Dorothy Gallagher wistfully wrote in the September 1974 issue of *Redbook*. "Whether the music of the Beatles— together or separately—will survive remains to be seen. But for the rest of us the Beatles have marked our lives indelibly."

Everything, though, goes in cycles. The assassination of John Lennon in December 1980 changed the way the world looked at the Beatles. Now a Beatles reunion became impossible, and attitudes changed. The Beatles legend grew, but this time it was different because with Lennon gone, there was no turning back or, for that matter, no moving forward. The music never died, of course. Rather, new generations of listeners learned about the Beatles from their own parents. Writes Steven D. Stark in *Meet the Beatles*, "Unlike other rock figures, such as Mick Jagger or Bob Dylan, the Beatles retired close to their peak. Frozen in time and memory, they never faded before our eyes."

The fact that we are still writing about the Beatles and, more important perhaps, that millions of people are still listening to them certainly attests to their unprecedented longevity. The release of *The Beatles Anthology* in 1995 and, more recently, the Beatles compilation, *1*, in 2000, has introduced a whole new generation to their music. As remarkable as it sounds, millions of people today are listening to the Beatles for the first time. Just look at the numbers: *1* sold nearly 30 million copies worldwide and topped the *Billboard* charts when it was first released. Significantly, the biggest demographics among its buyers were not baby boomers but sixteen- to twenty-four-year olds.

"The Beatles' music is the passageway through which most young people are led from the cradle of children's songs into the world of adult music," wrote Neil Strauss in *The New York Times*. They have remained relevant to future generations partly because parents continue to hand down the music to their children. It's no coincidence that Beatles festivals hold puppet shows sung along to Beatles songs. Trivia contests are huge hits among the younger set. Indeed, some of the most knowledgeable contestants are children and preteens.

The Beatles pushed the pop song to its limits, incorporating all kinds of ideas and all types of music into their widely eclectic repertoire. Their impact has been immense, wide-ranging, and ongoing. Classic-style rock bands have looked at them for inspiration (from U2 to Cold-play), as have such power pop groups as Fountains of Wayne and Sugar Ray. You can hear echoes of the Beatles in the music of the Swedish rock band Soundtrack of Our Lives, especially the psychedelic-era *Sgt. Pepper* Beatles. The Beatles have also influenced less obvious musical styles, too, such as grunge (Kurt Cobain and Nirvana) and even hip-hop.

Hip-hop? Some may raise an eyebrow at that suggestion, given that the Beatles were often criticized for being "too white." But consider the sheer range of black artists who have covered their music over the decades. The list—and it is long—includes Jimi Hendrix, Aretha Franklin, Ben E. King, the Isley Brothers, Lou Rawls, Smokey Robinson, Stevie Wonder, Wilson Pickett, and Marvin Gaye, but also Nina Simone, Otis Redding, Ramsey Lewis, Ray Charles, Richie Havens, Sarah Vaughan, and Shirley Bassey. Of course, the Beatles, like many British bands before and since, have recorded their own renditions of R&B and Motown classics. They started their career covering such artists as Chuck Berry, Fats Domino, and Little Richard. At the press conferences during their first American tour, they made clear that African-American musicians were among their major influences. They also invited Motown stalwart Mary Wells to join them on their U.K. tour. "The Beatles were the first white artists to ever admit that they grew up on black music," said Smokey Robinson. What's more, several rap artists have gone on record as being bona fide Beatles fans. The group's groundbreaking innovations in the recording studio have not gone unnoticed within the hip-hop community. Some rappers have even called "Tomorrow Never Knows" the first electronic song. To hip-hop producer and musician Puestlove, the Beatles personified the hip-hop aesthetic: "They would lay the music down, manipulate it, fuck with it, try to push it." In other words, they tested the limits of the studio technology of their day.

Probably the most unusual coming together between the Beatles and hip-hop must be *The Grey Album* by composer-producer-deejay Danger Mouse (aka Brian Burton). In 2004, Burton remixed the White Album with rapper Jay-Z's *The Black Album,* essentially transposing bits and pieces of Beatles music into hip-hop rhythms and then integrating them with Jay-Z's vocals to create a seamless whole: the music of the

Beatles and the lyrics of Jay-Z together for the first time. Burton burned *The Grey Album* ostensibly for a few friends. Word moved fast, though, for within a month more than one million copies had been downloaded on the Internet. Burton's little underground project quickly took off and he became famous almost overnight. Moreover, *Rolling Stone* called *The Grey Album* "an ingenious hip-hop record that sounds oddly ahead of its time" while *Entertainment Weekly* called it the best album of 2004.

Following the controversy, sales of the decades-old White Album spiked.

Read the Beatles is a collection of classic and new writing that looks at the Beatles as a group and as individual solo artists. Some of the pieces are justly famous, such as "What Songs the Beatles Sang . . ." by William Mann, which ran uncredited in *The Times* (London) and was one of the earliest pieces of criticism from the mainstream press that took the band seriously. The most controversial selection must be Maureen Cleave's "How Does a Beatle Live? John Lennon Lives Like This." This was the piece where Lennon claimed that the Beatles were more popular than Jesus, uttered as an off-the-cuff remark and statement of fact rather than a boast. It barely raised an eyebrow when it was initially published in the London *Evening Standard* in early March 1966 but when it reached American shores, in the pages of a teen magazine, it caused an uproar, especially in the Bible Belt. Other important topics in Beatles history are included, from the initial giddiness of Beatlemania to the "Paul is dead" rumors to the Manson murders, from *Sgt. Pepper* to the White Album, and to the eventual demise of the most famous rock band in the world.

The book is divided into two parts. Part One, "Together," consists of six sections. Each section looks at a particular time during the Beatles relatively short performing and recording career: the early Liverpool years when they were playing in sweaty dives on Mathew Street; the rambunctious nights in Hamburg; the heady times of rampant Beatlemania, when the whole world seemed to revolve around their every move; the great middle years that were full of such triumph and turmoil; the later years when the fragile partnership between four very different men began taking its toll; and a look back at what made them special and why they still resonate so loudly today.

Part Two, "Apart," looks at the Beatles individually: John Lennon's politics, his struggles with the FBI and deportation proceedings, his tragic death; Paul McCartney's solo career; George Harrison's spirituality and his attempts to carve out his own special place in the post-Beatles world; and Ringo Starr's irrepressible spirit and often underappreciated drumming style. This section closes with original essays—some fun, some analytical, some reflective—by songwriter Wyn Cooper; singer Steve Earle; critics Anthony DeCurtis, Ashley Kahn, and Greg Kot; and writers Tom Piazza and Touré. Finally, Colin Hall, the custodian of John Lennon's childhood home as well as a music journalist, offers a unique perspective on what it is like to be the keeper of memories.

Was it luck or just chance that brought John Lennon and Paul McCartney together during the summer of 1957? What would have happened if John did not meet Paul on that fateful day in early July at the Woolton garden fête, in an open field behind the gothic spires of St. Peter's churchyard where, in an ironic twist of fate, lies the grave of a woman named Eleanor Rigby? Was it meant to be? Did destiny play its part?

We'll never know. What matters is that they did meet and, in the process, changed the course of popular music history. And for that we should be forever grateful.

Part One

■

TOGETHER

ONE

■

City on the Mersey

Jim O'Donnell

■

On a summer day on July 6, 1957, musical history was made. For it was here, at the St. Peter's Parish Church[1] garden fête in Woolton, a leafy Liverpool neighborhood, that two teenage boys met for the first time. One was John Lennon, the other Paul McCartney. Music journalist Jim O'Donnell spent many hours, days, weeks, and even years researching the Beatles and the city of Liverpool before putting pen to paper. Of course, memory can play tricks, and O'Donnell was faced with accommodating the many discrepancies and contradictions in the story of when John first met Paul.

O'Donnell meticulously reconstructs that legendary day with great care and a generosity of spirit. It reads like a novel, the "characters" come to vivid life. But O'Donnell's book also serves as a love letter of sorts to the city of Liverpool itself, the same city that struck such a deep chord in the hearts of Lennon and McCartney.

"The Afternoon Hours"

from *The Day John Met Paul*

■ IT'S 4:28 P.M. About ten minutes into the Quarry Men show, the high-spirited, high-haired teenager from Allerton, Paul McCartney, arrives on his bike at the church field. He leans the bike against a fence. The cologne of freshly baked cakes grazes his nose. There is a moderate breeze. The afternoon sky is toneless. The sun gilds the area every few minutes. The teenager wonders about the music he's hearing. It's definitely not standard fare for a church fair, at least no church fair that he has ever been to.

McCartney walks into the big open field. In today's *Liverpool Echo*, this is the teenage John Lennon's Libra horoscope: "All sorts of things come into the open today." The horoscope continues: "The whole week is good for learning where you stand and how you can best achieve your aims. A little quiet thinking out will be all to the good."

McCartney walks through the field desultorily. He's not even aware of the guitar strapped to his back; it's like a body part. In the sun, his hair seems to have brown lights in it. The Liverpool earth receives his shadow warmly.

The teenager's gaze is all over the place at once. The big brown eyes sweep the big green pasturage. His attention bounces around the fair like a glinting silver ball in a pinball machine. He hits a few bumpers, rings a few bells, picks up glimmers from the area of the stage as the band's equipment dispatches half a dozen little suns. Near the middle of the field he sees his friend Ivan Vaughan. McCartney goes over to Vaughan, a dark-haired young man with an ever-ready smile. They greet and Vaughan nods toward the music. The two of them walk over to the left side of the stage.

They shoulder their way forward until there are only a few yards of hot Liverpool aerosphere between the teenager named Lennon and the teenager named McCartney. Directly behind the trees behind Lennon is a church called St. Mary's. It's partially visible through open slashes in the trees. There is a priest at the church by the name of Father McKenzie. Lennon is singing a song called "Come Go with Me" by a five-man U.S. vocal group known as the Del Vikings. The song is the Del Vikings' first hit. It charts as high as Number 4 in America. They recorded the song in Pittsburgh while they were stationed at a local air force base. One of the air force musicians backing the group on the record is a drummer named Sgt. Peeples.

Paul McCartney, age fifteen, stands stock-still on the warm grass. He's as immobile as the black tuxed figure on the top of a wedding cake. It's 4:32 P.M. The air is toasty. The teenager hitches his thumbs in the pockets of his tight black pants. In his white jacket, he looks like one of his father's pipe cleaners sticking halfway out of a dark tobacco pouch. The wide round face turns to Lennon and locks in: a rock'n'roll radar dish picking up a signal. His eyes, not quite tea-saucer size, are transfixed on the stage. He stares intently. McCartney's brown diamond eyes mirror two John Lennons skating across their ice-watery surfaces.

He unhitches one thumb from a pocket and raises an open hand to his forehead to shield his eyes against a sudden sluice of sun. Like a sky-sailing wheel of fortune, the sun has displayed many different numbers this day, shown many different faces. The teenager's eyes land on Lennon's fingers. He fastens his mind on the guitar player at the microphone. The rest of the band—and the world—melt into the hot afternoon. His own feeling for rock'n'roll provides a musical drawbridge for him to cross the moat into Lennon's dream castle. McCartney puts the day's heat somewhere else: his facial features are frozen. Even his long-fringed eyelashes are motionless. He squints to the point where his eyebrows have a beetling cast.

The sleek, slender, slippery figure of sixteen-year-old John Lennon inclines his head toward the microphone and rips the local latitude and longitude with "Come Go with Me." He has a whipcord of a voice. This being his home field, he gives the show a little something extra. He purrs the lyric, then snarls it. The simple amplification system translates the lyric into bolts of words. In the long sculpture of his face, his mouth seems chiseled with a toenail cutter. His lips slice the words thin. The expression is half smile, half smirk.

The teenager doesn't know all the words to the song, so he makes some of them up. No one in the Quarry Men is surprised. His band-mates never know what he's going to do next when he picks up a guitar. He might do anything—and it will probably be fun. In his hands, the guitar is an exclamation point. Most of the audience doesn't know he's making up the words. Even most of the teenagers don't know it: they *hear* the lyrics, but they *understand* the drums and guitars. Besides, the singer knows how the song *feels*. He's getting that across, and that's what matters most.

With the start of each song, Lennon leaves Liverpool and lives in the music. He is nowhere but in the music. His legs are planted on the wooden scaffold; locks of hair hang over his forehead—locks to the front door of a rock'n'roll sweatshop. Adrenal sparks shoot through his back and calves and thighs. But his mind is in a castle of dreams; a velvety vertigo.

The intense, shifting, nonconformist actions of Lennon's life give form to the movement of his music. His guitar lines pour over the length of the grounds in a thin stream of silvery coins. He plays hard. To do less would be unconscionable to him. He loves the music that much. The hands are sturdy. The fingers are sure. He coils his left hand around the guitar neck in a grip like Queen Victoria's around the reins of her horse in front of St. George's Hall. This most proper of queens wouldn't approve of him at this moment, however, as he is patently not being proper; that is, he has a guitar in his hands, yet he's playing banjo chords, using only four strings. But he makes do. In a hot moment, he brandishes the guitar in the manner of a teenage toreador. In a cool mo-ment, the guitar rocks back and forth like a grandfather clock's pendu-lum. In all moments, the Lennon guitar takes a beating. His first guitar had a label on the inside that said "Guaranteed Not to Split." This is his second guitar, a better one, but Rod Davis, next to him on banjo, wouldn't be surprised if it split any second.

As Lennon plays, he tries to take the crowd's pulse—tries to put his finger on what sorts of performer actions get what sorts of audience re-actions. The light terra-cotta eyes window-shop across the multifarious English faces. The young guitarist offers a mixed bag of movements and gestures . . . and even expressions. In a single minute, his eyes stray from convivial to condemnatory to contemplative to convulsed—and back to convivial. Never do they look confused. He knows what he wants to be doing, and he's doing it.

In turn, some in the audience take *his* measure. There is a vertigi-nous sense about the singer-guitarist of both friendship and danger; of open fields and dark alleys; of a swishing blade of meadow and a switch-blade. All that anyone can tell for sure about the young Lennon is that he's working up a good sweat—the war paint of the rock musician. A patch of sweat stains the back of his shirt. His onstage heart is a heavy hammer. His mouth is spitless. He swipes his lower lip with his tongue.

The teenager is having fun. He's having a rock'n'roll field day on the big Liverpool field.

A small shed of grass away, both thumbs in the corners of his peg-legged pants pockets, another teenager is also having fun. Fifteen-year-old guitarist Paul McCartney listens for a rock'n'roll heartbeat; looks down Lennon's throat for inflammation of the lyric. He finds the older teenager's health to be solid as a rock. This may be a garden party, but McCartney can tell that the guitar player is not garden variety.

In frisking Lennon's technical knowledge, he follows the guitarist's fingers and deciphers the fact that he's playing banjo chords. In taking an inventory of Lennon's singing background, he can tell that Lennon doesn't know all the words to all the songs. The young man makes note of and accepts these limitations. But, laserlike, he transpierces the limitations—sees past the banjo chords and wrong words and comes up with other perceptions.

To start with, Lennon's creative extemporaneousness etches itself across McCartney's mind. He likes how Lennon makes up words on the spot—suffuses the music with a teenage Liverpool touch. In addition, without even knowing all the words, the guy still captures the triumph of each song.

Secondly, the fifteen-year-old is taken by the concrete actuality of the band—the simple fact of its existence in the real world. Here's a cluster of local blokes—around his own age—up on a stage playing not-half-bad rock'n'roll.

And thirdly, McCartney realizes that, for the first time in his life, he's looking at someone who cares about this crazy new music as much as he does. He knows that he and Lennon share a good friend—rock'n'roll. He can tell that they both listen to the same sounds and, more importantly, hear the same messages. And, most importantly, the music really *matters* to them.

It has been one thing for McCartney to hear the music on the radio or on records, or to see it in the movies or on stage, or even to see local bands that fool around with it. But he can tell that this guy isn't fooling around. This music means something to Lennon—and *he* means business. McCartney holds a sharp eye on this fellow who is in his own age group, in his own city, and playing his own music. It is as if Lennon is incarnating the music for McCartney—rendering the sound waves into something as real as shore waves; taking the notes McCartney hears in each ear and bringing them together into sharp focus behind his eyes, lifting the music off the radio airwaves and putting it into Liverpool air. The deeper mysteries of rock'n'roll begin to crystallize behind McCartney's long, dark brown eyelashes.

Note

1. Lennon was a member of the church's choir from the late forties until 1954. See Steve Turner, *The Gospel According to the Beatles* (Louisville, Ky.: Westminster John Knox, 2006).

Cynthia Lennon

■

In the autumn of 1957, eighteen-year-old Cynthia Powell began her studies at the Liverpool College of Art. She took courses in pottery, silversmithing, architecture, and lettering. It was during the latter class that she first set eyes on John Winston Lennon. Her first impression was not good: "I think he was the last stronghold of the Teddy Boys [young British thugs] . . . I felt that I had nothing in common with this individual and as far as I was concerned I never would. In fact he frightened me to death. The only thing that John and I had in common was that we were both blind as bats without our glasses." Even so, from that moment on, her life would never be the same. Although she wasn't Lennon's "type" (she was from "posh" Hoylake on the Wirral peninsula, across the River Mersey from Liverpool, and the somber, shy Powell didn't look anything like Lennon's ideal woman, Brigitte Bardot), they eventually married on August 23, 1962, at the registry office in Liverpool. She was pregnant with Julian.

The following excerpt from her autobiography recalls Lennon's friendship with Stuart Sutcliffe and vividly captures the excitement of Liverpool's nightlife scene in pre-Beatlemania, a time when the boys, in pre-Cavern days, were playing the Jacaranda on Slater Street, a coffee bar that reminded Cynthia of something out of Dante's *Inferno*: a hot, steamy, cramped, and airless basement. The Jac, as it is called, shut down before reopening in 1995 with, ironically, the Pete Best Band as the featured performer.

"The Liverpool Scene"

from *A Twist of Lennon*

■ AT THIS TIME John was having a wonderful time painting. Stuart's influence on him grew very strong. All his inhibitions, brought about by the discipline of Lettering, were gone and he threw himself naturally into an orgy of oil paint, sand, sawdust, in fact anything he could lay his hands on to create paintings that were truly individual. John was in his element during this period. The only dark cloud on his horizon was the Lettering exam that he knew he would have to pass at the end of the year. If he failed that he would definitely be out on his ear. If John was worried he was marvellous at concealing it.

Then Allan Williams, a young, stocky, bearded friend of Stuart's, rose out of the dust like a phoenix into the lives of John and the boys at this time. Although John was immersed in his painting, his keenest interest was still music. The boys continued to practise and perfect the numbers they had been learning, the only problem was the lack of opportunity to show off their talents. Allan Williams provided that for them in his coffee bar the Jacaranda. The Jac, as it was so fondly called by all who entered its portals, was a coffee bar famous for its bacon butties. Down the narrow stairs to the basement was another world. My first impression was that of Dante's *Inferno*. The heat, sweat and noise nearly knocked you over with their power as you struggled and shoved to descend the narrow heaving stairs.

The music that pulsated upwards, almost as if it were desperately trying to escape the stifling confines of the basement, was from a steel band. Not rock and roll, but a black steel band and they were marvellous! The atmosphere was electric—they were great and the only band of their kind in the area. Now at this point my memory fails me, but I think the boys hung around the Jac so often and pestered Allan so much that he finally weakened and let them have a blast for a night so that they could put their money and their guitars where their mouths were.

If Stuart hadn't been such a good friend of Allan's, I believe Allan would have turned a deaf ear to this request. For John was always cadging either food or money from Allan, and I'm sure he wondered what on earth he was letting himself in for. When eventually he gave in and allowed them their first public appearance, it was to a rather disgruntled audience. "Who the hell are they, Allan?"

"Rubbish!" "We want the steel band back." "God almighty, they really are bloody awful!" That's just a sample of the initial comments thrown at them by kids who later were to become their most avid fans.

Allan was soon to become a very firm supporter of the Beatles. His ears and intuition told him even in those very amateur, raw, early days that these lads definitely had something special. It wasn't their appearances that instilled this confidence in him, for there couldn't have been a scruffier group of musicians anywhere in Liverpool. And if definitely wasn't their stage presence. They didn't know what that was. In fact their foul language would have sent many a teenager's parents into a screaming fit if they had heard them in full flow.

It was a certain magic—so indefinable as to be almost non-existent at times—until they started playing their guitars and singing their harmonies. That was the moment the tingle went up the spine, the first stages of addiction. It was a very far cry from the neatness and uniformity of the Shadows, who were way up in the popularity charts at the time. So totally opposite was their image that it seemed unbelievable that the kids and teeny-boppers would take even a second look at the Beatles, never mind follow them to the ends of the earth. The only uniformity that they adhered to at that stage was in their own choice of attire. Unpressed jeans, black T-shirts and tennis plimps—usually dirty. Their hair was long and greased back at the sides but left at the front to fall casually onto their foreheads. Rough diamonds in every sense of the word compared to the Shadows' clean-cut, besuited image. They were young, rough and sexy. Their music was gutsy and raw, and with the help and guidance of Allan Williams, their limited experience was about to grow in a very exciting way.

With all the excitement of live performances I was beginning to find myself absorbed into a whole new lifestyle. John's perfect image of a woman was, I said earlier, Brigitte Bardot. I found myself fast becoming moulded into her style of dress and haircut. I had only recently gone through my change from secretary-bird to Bohemian when I met John, but under his influence another metamorphosis was taking place and this time the emphasis was on *oomph!* Long blonde hair (out came the Hiltone), tight black sweaters, tight short skirts, high-heeled pointed shoes, and to add the final touch, black fish-net stockings and suspenders. The only trouble with an outfit like that was that on many an occasion, when I had arranged to meet my beloved in Liverpool outside Lewis's store directly underneath the then controversial statue of a nude man, or outside Central Station or wherever, John would invariably turn up late and I was forever in danger of being picked up by the most unsavoury characters that Liverpool could offer.

I must have looked every inch like a Liverpool Totty—a prostitute—on the game. Attempting to look inconspicuous under those circumstances was impossible, and once again I fell prey to my own excruciating self-consciousness, until John arrived at my side, then all would be well again. If that was the way he wanted me to look then it was all right by me, but I must admit there was a shy, bespectacled, secretary-type trying to get out. It was much, much safer being inconspicuous.

When Allan took the Beatles under his wing, he also gave them the opportunity to air their talents in other dance-hall venues and clubs. John, finding home life with Mimi less than *avant garde,* decided to move into Stuart's flat with him, a decision that Mimi did her utmost to squash. But his mind was made up. He felt he had to cut the apron strings and please himself. I was to spend many a night in that flat with John—my mother believing me to be staying with Phyllis. [Phyllis McKenzie, Cynthia's best friend at the time.]

Although it was wonderful spending illicit nights away from home, we had terrible trouble trying to keep clean. It was impossible, no matter how hard we tried. The floor was filthy, in fact everything was covered with muck. If the electricity had been cut off or the supply of soap had run out we would wash in cold water and without light, emerging into the bright daylight of Liverpool and walking hand in hand to the city centre for breakfast looking, I suspect, like a couple of chimney sweeps. John didn't really care too much, but I had to return home and explain my appearance to my disbelieving mother. Oh, it was great fun! Looking like a fallen angel was one thing, but looking like a dirty fallen angel on the last train home to suburbia was quite another kettle of fish.

The lunchtime and dance-hall sessions were often very frightening experiences for me, mainly because the music lovers who followed the Beatles around were becoming more and more possessive about their chosen Beatle idol. And this, let me add, was in the very early stages of the group's career. I would accompany John on most of their gigs. Sometimes he would be petrified because he had heard on the grapevine that he was to be kicked in by the local Teds. Their Judies (Birds) were taking too much notice of the Beatles and the Teds weren't going to stand for it. The real danger areas were Bootle and Litherland town halls and Garston. All the local hard knocks would be waiting to put the boot into Lennon, McCartney, Harrison and Sutcliffe. The joy of performing was well and truly knocked out of them on those occasions and sheer unadulterated panic set in. I, on the other hand, being the only female connected with the Beatles at the beginning, was in a horribly vulnerable position. The fanatical John Lennon followers did not take kindly to me. I was a threat to their fantasies and dreams. The most dangerous place for me in those days was the ladies' loo. I honestly thought that once I had entered, I wouldn't get out again in one piece, or worse still that I would never be seen alive again. My solution to this was to keep a very low profile and keep my mouth firmly shut. I would smile in such a friendly way, and if it was necessary for me to speak I would adopt my best Liverpool accent in case they thought that I was putting on airs and graces. I was really afraid of someone picking an argument with me. I was definitely no match at all for those girls. They could have killed me as soon as look at me.

From the first appearance at the Jacaranda, John, Paul, George and Stuart went from strength to strength. They were minus a drummer, that was true, and to begin with they played with borrowed amplifiers. Allan gave them regular gigs, lunchtime sessions mainly—don't forget we were still at college or school. Everything seemed to fit in beautifully, although needless to say our academic studies took second place to the excitement of live performances. During this period Allan Williams' interests also extended to two or three other Liverpool groups. He wasn't their manager in the accepted sense, but he did help them in any way that he could, acquiring work for them in the numerous clubs and dance-halls in Liverpool and even on the other side of the water, would you believe! In recompense Allan would, at the end of the day, keep back enough expenses for his trouble. He was quite an enigmatic man, a character full of enthusiasm, ambition and boundless energy. The man, in fact, who was responsible for putting the Liverpool sounds on the map.

The Jac, as I have said, was dark, sweaty and alive, alive with sounds and God only knows what else. Office clerks, shop assistants, factory workers, students, layabouts, black, white, yellow, coffee-coloured were all squashed together in the steaming, vibrating Jacaranda melting pot. When the boys played with their borrowed amplifiers, their microphones were tied to brush handles held at the base of the so-called stage by ardent, ever-accommodating little Liverpool fans. It was a beautiful sight. Co-operation and communication held together by four scruffy young lads playing their hearts out, for peanuts. Although the idea of playing for money was important, the mere fact that they could play to an audience and create electricity between themselves and everyone else who heard their music was more than enough in those early stages to satisfy their young egos. They could begin to see the light at the end of the tunnel.

Enthusiasm and excitement mounted at the prospect of some sort of a career in the world of music. John had decided, now that he had tasted the show biz scene, that this was very definitely the life for him. All the ideas that everyone else had had for him of making an impact on the art world faded into the back of beyond with incredible rapidity, and with almost no regret at all. John's Aunt Mimi, however, was distraught and agitated at the prospect of her charge racing headlong into an unpredictable future armed only with an old guitar, with no qualifications, and virtually penniless. Her view of his future couldn't have been blacker at that time. A famous quote from Mimi was, "It's all very nice playing the guitar, John, but you will never make any money at it!" Poor Mimi's advice from the heart fell on very deaf ears, and thank goodness it did.

It was during this particular period that life at college was warming up for the end of Summer term exams. One of those exams was to be John's last chance to prove himself worthy of staying on at the college. There was a slight chance that John would scrape through, with a little help from his friends, until Allan Williams dropped a bombshell. "Lads," he said, "Larry Parnes and Billy Fury are coming up from London to hold an audition. Parnes needs a backing group for Billy on his next tour." From that moment all hell was let loose. When I saw John after he had heard this earth-shattering news you would have thought that he had won the pools. "Christ, Cyn, do you know what this means? An audition for Larry Parnes and Billy Fury. Bloody hell I don't believe it. *Christ,* it's too much. Billy Fury, just imagine it! Backing Billy Fury. Yahoo!"

Sheer unadulterated joy shone from John's face as he was relating this marvellous news to me. He was like a child who has lost a penny and found a pound note. There wasn't any doubt in John's mind at that moment that they could possibly fail this chance-of-a-lifetime audition. His optimism was boundless. The fact that none of the boys rated Billy Fury in their personal top ten didn't even enter his head. Billy Fury had made it and now they were on their way, thanks to Allan Williams. During the weeks before the audition John, Paul, George and Stuart practised until their fingers nearly dropped off. But when the full impact of the situation sank in, they began to get nervous. For a start they didn't have a drummer. Then Stuart was worried—understandably so since his new found prowess at the bass guitar left a great deal to be desired. I think for the first time they took a critical look at themselves and they really weren't sure what they could do to improve their appearance and musical standard. They realised that they had to rely on their own particular brand of magic; they couldn't *afford* to do anything else. When the fateful day finally arrived, the adrenaline was running very fast.

The boys had scouted around Liverpool for the best stand-in drummer they could find, and they were successful. They were all set. The stage clothes, instead of dirty jeans, black T-shirts and scruffy off-white plimsolls were, (wait for it) clean jeans, clean black T-shirts and scruffy off-white plimsolls. Their hair was combed and greased to perfection. To me they looked beautiful. Their faces were fresh and alive with a mixture of excitement and fear. I was so proud of them I could have cried.

At the audition, which was being held in the basement of Allan's club, The Blue Angel, the tension was mounting. The drummer was conspicuous by his absence. The boys busied themselves, tuning their guitars with shaking hands, discussing how they were going to stand, smoking ciggies as if they were about to go out of fashion, deciding what movements they should make, if any, to impress the visiting stars of entertainment and show business. They were all so innocent and young in their attitude it was lovely. It was into this scene, with a backcloth of a dingy Liverpool basement in the process of being decorated, that the VIPs eventually made their entrance. The sudden silence and atmosphere of expectation was extremely overpowering until Allan's introductions broke the spell. I think Allan was as nervous as the boys by this time and they all started talking at once. Comparisons are odious, and I was very biased at the time, but the expensively dressed suavity of the visiting stars couldn't hold a candle then to the appearance of those four lads. Billy Fury was quite to the point of being sullen throughout the ensuing proceedings. He hardly said a word, let alone showed any enthusiasm. Larry Parnes sat and listened intently to the boys as they sang and played their hearts out. I sat inconspicuously in one corner with my fingers and legs tightly crossed, watching, scrutinizing the faces of the audience for signs of disapproval or, God willing, enthusiasm.

I suppose auditioning someone is a little like buying a house. If you show enthusiasm the vendors might put the price up. As it happened the boys did not secure the job. Larry Parnes' reasoning was that Stuart's bass playing was definitely not up to performance standard, but, and it was a very big but, he was prepared to take the rest of them on. He was impressed. Following a deep discussion amongst themselves and Allan, John refused point blank. "If Stuart isn't with us then they can forget it." And that was that as far as John was concerned. His loyalty to Stuart was marvellous, and he was immediately backed up by Paul and George. Stuart, on the other hand, was feeling incredibly low. He did his utmost to dissuade them from their final decision and my heart went out to him. He felt, quite naturally, that their opportunity to make a name for themselves had been ruined by his lack of talent. Allan sat next to Stuart and suggested that he showed them his other talent, portraiture. Stuart refused at first but with more encouragement proceeded to sketch Billy Fury and Larry Parnes. Stuart always carried an old canvas bag with him containing a sketchbook and the necessary materials for on-the-spot drawings of subjects that inspired him, and which he could utilize later in his oil-painting. I can't say that Stuart was inspired at all by the subjects confronting him. He was too full of disappointment and remorse for artistic inspiration to break through, but he proceeded to work on and finish his charcoal portraits of his sitters, much to their delight and surprise.

Parnes liked the Beatles (minus Stuart) a lot and before leaving informed Allan that he would keep them in mind if anything else suitable turned up. There were other Liverpool groups taking part in this audition, groups with far more experience than the Beatles, well-established Liverpool groups. Cass and the Cassanovas, Rory Storm and the Hurricanes, Derry and the Seniors. Rory Storm had just come back from a very successful season at a Butlin's holiday camp in North Wales, and the drummer for the group was the one and only Richard Starkey, alias Ringo Starr. A mere twinkle in the Beatles' eyes at that time. I must admit that even though the turnout of the other groups was far superior to the boys' as far as clothes and equipment were concerned, like Larry Parnes I only had eyes for them.

Although there was an air of disappointment following us all around for some time, the anti-climax wasn't too bad. After all, they were instilled with a greater confidence than ever before. They had been judged the winners of that particular contest and against all odds. They couldn't be bad. What they really needed now was a steady supply of work and with it a steady supply of money for better equipment. Sad to say, though, that wasn't to be for quite a while.

■

TWO

Rock the Reeperbahn

David Wojahn

■

Quite a few poems have been written about the Beatles. David Wojahn, though, is perhaps the best-known rock and roll poet or, more accurately, the best-known poet who often uses rock as his subject. He has also composed a poem about the murder of John Lennon ("The Assassination of John Lennon as Depicted by the Madame Tussaud Wax Museum, Niagara Falls, Ontario, 1987"). Both this and the following poem are from *Mystery Train,* his fine collection of poetry, in which he uses rock to mirror American history and where everyone from Buddy Holly and Elvis Presley to Bob Dylan and Janis Joplin, and from the Rolling Stones to Brian Wilson, is represented. He once confessed, ". . . 'listening to rock and roll music started the process which made me become a poet."

Here he offers a poetic homage to the Beatles' early days in rowdy Hamburg when Pete Best was still the drummer.

"Fab Four Tour Deutschland: Hamburg, 1961"

from *Mystery Train*

"Und now Ladies und Gentlemun, *Der Peedles!*"
The emcee oozes pomade, affecting the hip American,

But the accent twists the name to sound like *needles,*
Or some Teutonic baby's body function.

The bassist begins, nodding to the drummer,
Who flaunts his movie-star good looks: Pete Best,

Grinning as the drums count four. "Roll Over
Beethoven"'s the opener. McCartney's Elvis

Posturing's too shrill, the playing sloppy,
But Lennon, stoned on Romilar, doesn't care.

Mild applause, segue into "Long Tall Sally. . . ."
One will become a baby-faced billionaire,

One a film producer, one a skewed sort of martyr,
And this one, the drummer, a Liverpool butcher.

Philip Norman

■

Considered the definitive biography of the Beatles, Philip Norman's *Shout! The Beatles in Their Generation* is a well-written and thoughtful account of the band, their lives, and their music. Norman has covered the Beatles in one form or another since 1968 when he was assigned to cover their ill-fated business venture, Apple Corps, so he knows the territory well. He has also written biographies of Elton John, Buddy Holly, and the Rolling Stones, as well as a wickedly good novel, *Everyone's Gone to the Moon,* set during the heyday of swinging '60s London.

This excerpt recalls the early days of the Beatles in Liverpool on the eve of their inaugural—and life-changing—visit to Hamburg. The German city hasn't forgotten the Liverpudlians. Hamburg is planning to erect a Beatles memorial commemorating the group's time in the city.

"The Great Freedom"

from *Shout! The Beatles in Their Generation*

■ THE SILVER BEATLES hit their lowest point in the summer of 1960. Still drummerless, they had given up trying to persuade dance promoters like Les Dodd and Sam Leach to book them. Their only regular engagement was at a strip club part-owned by Allan Williams, off Liverpool's Upper Parliament Street. Williams paid them ten shillings each to strum their guitars while a stripper named Janice grimly shed her clothes. At Janice's request, the musicians stuck to standards such as "Moonglow" and the "Harry Lime Theme," and they even gamely attempted "The Gipsy Fire Dance" from sheet music.

The New Cabaret Artistes Club was run for Williams by a West Indian named Lord Woodbine. Born in Trinidad, Woody earned a varied living as a builder and decorator, steel band musician, and freelance barman. His ennoblement—after the fashion of calypso singers—derived from a certain self-possessed grandeur as much as from the Woodbine cigarette permanently hinged on his lower lip.

Lord Woodbine ran his own club, the New Colony, in the attic and basement of a semiderelict house in Berkeley Street. The Silver Beatles played there, too, sometimes in the afternoons, while merchant seamen danced against hard-faced whores, and occasional troublemakers were pacified by the sight of the cutlass that Lord Woodbine kept under the bar.

Williams promised he would make something better happen for them soon. And Williams, by a sequence of cosmic blunders into 1,000-to-1 chances, did exactly that.

It all started when Williams returned to his coffee bar, the Jacaranda, one night and heard silence when he expected to hear the Royal Caribbean Steel Band. The entire band, he was told, had been lured away by a German theatrical agent to appear at a club in Hamburg. Down in the basement, set about by Stu Sutcliffe's voodoo murals, not a single 40-gallon steel drum remained.

To Williams, as to most Englishmen of that era, Hamburg, more than London or even Paris, was a city of breathtaking wickedness. British soldiers stationed after World War II in Germany brought back extraordinary tales of entertainments purveyed by the Reeperbahn, Hamburg's legendary cabaret district—of women wrestling in mud and sex displays involving pythons, donkeys, and other animal associates. Such things could only be whispered about in a Britain where the two-piece bathing suite was still considered rather daring.

Evidently, along with everything else, there were music clubs along the Reeperbahn. Williams's curiosity was further aroused by letters from various members of the Royal Caribbean Steel Band, showing no remorse at their sudden disappearance but telling Williams guilelessly what a great place Hamburg was and urging him to come across with some of his Liverpool beat groups to share it.

His first idea was to take the Silver Beatles with him to Hamburg on an exploratory trip, but chronic shortage of cash prevented this. Instead, he got them to make a tape recording of their music, in company with Cass and the Casanovas and a local trad jazz band, the Noel Lewis Stompers, to be played to the Hamburg impresarios.

The journey that Williams made was in every sense characteristic. Wearing a top hat and accompanied by Lord Woodbine, he took a cheap charter flight to Amsterdam, intending to proceed to West Germany by train. In one eventful night in the Dutch capital, he succeeded in drinking champagne from a chorus girl's shoe; passing Lord Woodbine off as a genuine English aristocrat; and being thrown into the street after making matador passes at a flamenco dancer with his coat.

The next evening found him in a similar state, temporarily parted from Lord Woodbine and dazzled by the overarching lights of the

Grosse Freiheit, that small but crowded tributary of the Hamburg Reeperbahn, whose name in English means "The Great Freedom."

Halfway down the Grosse Freiheit, opposite a Roman Catholic church, Williams stumbled into a downstairs club called the Kaiserkeller. He found it to be decorated in confusedly nautical style, with booths like lifeboats, barrels for tables, and a mural depicting life in the South Sea Isles. On a tiny central space several hundred people danced while an Indonesian group performed Elvis Presley songs in German.

Williams demanded to speak to the proprietor and, after some delay, was shown into the presence of a short, broad-chested man with a quiff of sandy hair, a turned-up nose, and a disabled leg that little inhibited his movements. Before the conversation had progressed far a waiter came in to report a disturbance in the club area. Williams, through the open door, saw a squad of waiters systematically working over a solitary customer. Snatching from his desk drawers a long ebony cosh, the proprietor left the room with an agile, hopping gait, to lend them a hand.

The talk then resumed on amiable lines. Allan Williams introduced himself as the manager of the world's best rock 'n' roll groups. The Kaiserkeller's owner, whose name was Bruno Koschmider, inquired if they were as good as Tommy Steele. Williams assured him they were better than Elvis Presley. For proof he brought out the tape he had made of the Silver Beatles and others. But when it was played on Herr Koschmider's tape recorder, nothing could be heard but scrabble and screech. Somebody back in Liverpool had blundered.

Having failed, as he thought, to convert Hamburg's Reeperbahn to Liverpool beat music, Allan Williams returned to being a functionary of the great Larry Parnes. The Silver Beatles—or plain Beatles, as they now defiantly called themselves—receded somewhat in Williams's mind. His chief property was the rhythm-and-blues group Derry and the Seniors, which Parnes had promised work in a summer show at Blackpool. The entire band, in expectation of this, gave up their jobs to turn professional. Then, at the last minute, a letter arrived on elaborately crested Parnes notepaper canceling the engagement.

An enraged deputation led by Howie Casey, the Seniors' sax player, confronted Williams at his Blue Angel Club in Seel Street. Casey was a youth of powerful build, and Williams promised hastily to find them some alternative work. In sheer desperation, he packed the entire five-piece group and their equipment into his Jaguar and headed for the only place he could think of where work for a rock 'n' roll band might magically exist. He was taking them, he said, to the famous 2i's coffee bar in London. There, in the home of skiffle, where Tommy Steele had first been discovered, something or other must surely turn up.

Fortune now smiled upon the agitated Welshman to the ludicrous, implausible extent that Fortune sometimes does. Upon entering the 2i's, whom should he see first but a small, barrel-chested West German gentleman with a quiff of sandy hair, a turned-up nose, and a disabled leg not at the moment noticeable. It was Herr Bruno Koschmider, proprietor of the Kaiserkeller club in Grosse Freiheit, Hamburg.

Koschmider, it transpired, had been deeply impressed by Williams's visit to his establishment, playing unintelligible tapes and boasting of rock 'n' roll groups better than Elvis. Not long after Williams's dispirited return to Liverpool, Herr Koschmider had decided to visit England and hear these wonderful groups for himself. Naturally, however, it was not Liverpool he visited, but London, and the famous 2i's coffee bar.

He had already paid one visit to the 2i's and had signed up a solo singer, Tony Sheridan, to appear at the Kaiserkeller. Sheridan in fact was a gifted performer, temporarily down on his luck. At the Kaiserkeller, he had been such a sensation that Bruno Koschmider had decided to sack his Indonesian Elvis impersonators and go over completely to English rock 'n' roll. He was thus at the 2i's a second time, hoping to hire another English group. He had not yet done so when Derry and the Seniors walked in.

It was the work of a few minutes for Williams to get Derry and the Seniors up and playing on the 2i's stage. Despite having had nothing to eat but some stale cake, they performed so well that Bruno Koschmider booked them for his Kaiserkeller club on the spot. They would receive thirty marks each per day—about twenty pounds a week—with travel expenses and accommodation found. A contract was drafted with the help of a German waiter from the adjacent Heaven and Hell coffee bar.

Derry and the Seniors set off by train from Liverpool to Hamburg with five pounds between them and no work permits. If challenged, Allan Williams said, the four tough-looking Liverpool boys and their black lead singer should pretend to be students on vacation. The story did not convince German frontier officials, and at Osnabruck the entire group was ordered off the train and held in custody until Bruno Koschmider could be contacted to vouch for them.

The next news to reach Williams was a great deal better. Derry and the Seniors, together with Tony Sheridan and his band, were a hit at Herr Koschmider's Kaiserkeller. Together with rapturous postcards from various musicians, a letter arrived from Koschmider himself, asking

Williams to send across a third group to play in another of Koschmider's clubs, the Indra.

The group Williams wanted to send was Rory Storm and the Hurricanes. They, however, were already committed to a summer season at Butlin's Skegness holiday camp. Gerry and the Pacemakers, his second choice, did not fancy going abroad. So Allan Williams, rather reluctantly, wrote to Bruno Koschmider, telling him to expect a group called the Beatles.

Shortly afterward, a letter of protest arrived from the Seniors' lead singer, Derry Wilkie. It would spoil things for everyone, Derry said, if Allan Williams sent over "a bum group like the Beatles."

The offer came when John Lennon's art college career was approaching the point of collapse. He had recently sat—or rather half-sat—the exam by which his past three years' work would be assessed. The test paper in lettering, his weakest subject, was supposed to have been completed in May, while the Beatles were touring Scotland with Johnny Gentle. Cynthia, John's girlfriend, had risked her own college career by doing the paper for him, racked by pains from a grumbling appendix, under a single lightbulb at the Gambier Terrace flat.

And yet, for all John's inexhaustible laziness, there were still glimpses of brilliance, in his cartoons and poster designs, which made Arthur Ballard, his tutor, think him worth defending. In Ballard's view, the only logical place for John was the newly opened faculty of design: unfortunately, however, he could not convince the relevant department head. "I had a row with the fellow in the end," Ballard says. "I told him if he couldn't accept an eccentric like John, he ought to be teaching in Sunday school. Then I heard from Cyn that it didn't matter because John was going to Hamburg. He'd told everyone he'd be getting a hundred pounds a week."

For Stu Sutcliffe the break with college was more serious, coming as it did at the start of a year's postgraduate teacher training. Stu at first turned down the Hamburg trip; then John and the others talked him into it. The college subsequently indicated it was willing to accept him on the teaching course as a late entrant.

Paul McCartney obtained his father's consent with typical diplomacy and circuitousness. With A-level exams now past, he technically had no further school commitments. His English teacher, Dusty Durband, was in fact one of the first to hear of the Hamburg offer, just before the Institute broke up for the summer. Mr. Durband was skeptical. "As far as

I knew, Paul was going on, as his father wished, to teacher-training college. When he told me about Hamburg, I said, 'Just who do you want to be, Paul? Tommy Steele?' He just grinned and said, 'No, but I feel like giving it a try.'"

Jim McCartney, when told the big news at last, faced a united front consisting of Paul, his brother Michael, and Allan Williams, who came up to Forthlin Road to assure him the arrangements were all aboveboard. Though full of misgivings, Jim felt that if Paul were allowed this one jaunt he might the sooner return to his senses, and to college. He let Paul go at the price of only a minimal pep talk about being careful and eating regular meals.

George Harrison, though even now only just seventeen, encountered the least opposition from his family. With his father and elder brothers he had achieved the status of working man, and was as such entitled to command of his own affairs. The quiet, hardworking Harrison family, besides, had produced its share of travelers. As well as Harry and his sea voyages, there was Louise, George's grown-up sister, now married to an American and living in St. Louis. Germany, by contrast, seemed not too distant; if the Harrisons knew of the Reeperbahn's reputation, they were prepared to trust in George's level head. His mother made him promise to write, and baked him a tin of homemade scones for the journey.

One big worry spoiled the collective excitement. It was the same old plaguing worry—they still had no drummer. What would do as backing for a stripper in Upper Parliament Street would not do, Allan Williams told them forcefully, for a big-time, luxurious Hamburg nightspot like the Indra Club. The contract with Herr Koschmider specified a full instrumental complement. If the Beatles could not provide one, the gig must be given to someone else.

They had been searching, in fact, ever since Tommy Moore had deserted them to return to his forklift truck at Garston bottle works. The only replacement they had been able to find was a boy called Norman Chapman whom they had overheard one night, practicing on Slater Street in a room above the National Cash Register Company. Norman played a few dates with them, happily enough, but then had to join one of the last batches of young Britons drafted into the Army.

Lately, for want of anything better, the Beatles had gone back to playing at the Casbah, Mona Best's cellar club in Hayman's Green. They had not been there since they were called the Quarry Men and had walked out over the docking of fifteen shillings from their night's fee.

To their surprise, they found the Casbah thriving. Ken Browne, the bespectacled ex–Quarry Man, now led his own group, the Black Jacks, with Mrs. Best's son, Peter, on drums. The Black Jacks were among the most popular groups in that district, drawing even larger crowds to the Casbah than did big names like Rory Storm and the Hurricanes.

Pete Best had just left Liverpool Collegiate Grammar School with abundant GCE passes and athletic distinctions but not so clear-cut a plan as hitherto to go on to teacher-training college. The taciturn, good-looking boy, to his mother's surprise, announced instead that he wanted to become a professional drummer. Mrs. Best, ever ready to encourage and invigorate, helped him raise the deposit on a brand-new drum set that he had long been admiring in the music department at Blackler's.

That decision taken, nothing much seemed to happen. The Black Jacks were due to disband because Ken Browne was about to move away from Liverpool. No other group had offered Pete a job as drummer, nor was he one to push himself. For several weeks, he sat around at home all day, and at night went downstairs into the club to watch this other group Mo was now booking. Whenever he came in, a little desperate sigh used to run around the girls on the nearer benches.

The Beatles, too, had noticed Pete Best. More specifically, they had noticed his glittering new drum set. Five weeks after leaving school Pete was rung up by Paul McCartney and asked if he would like to join them for a two-month club engagement in Hamburg. The question, really, was superfluous. Pete Best said he would.

They were to travel to Hamburg by road. Allan Williams had offered to drive them there himself, not in his Jaguar but in a battered cream-and-green Austin minibus that he had acquired for his Liverpool enterprises. Williams, thinking he might as well make a party of it, invited also along his Chinese wife, Beryl, his brother-in-law, Barry Chang, and his West Indian business associate, Lord Woodbine. On their way through London they were to pick up a tenth passenger, the waiter from the Heaven and Hell coffee bar, who was returning to Hamburg to become Bruno Koschmider's interpreter.

None of the five Beatles had ever been abroad before. John Lennon, indeed, only acquired a passport within a few days of setting off. Their preparations, even so, were not elaborate. Williams advanced them fifteen pounds to buy new black crewneck sweaters from Marks and Spencer and some extra pairs of tennis shoes. For a stage uniform they now had little short high-buttoning jackets of houndstooth check. Their luggage was the family type, hauled out from under spare-room beds. Paul also brought along a new, very cheap, solid guitar and a tiny Elpico amplifier to go with the one that, strictly speaking, still belonged to the art college. George had the tin of homemade scones his mother had baked for him.

Only one parent was outside the Jacaranda to see them off. Millie Sutcliffe, having said good-bye to Stu at home, followed him down to Slater Street secretly and stood in a shop doorway, watching while the van was loaded and its sides were embellished with a legend, THE BEATLES, in cutout paper letters stuck on with flour and water paste. For some reason, Mrs. Sutcliffe could not stop herself from crying.

At Newhaven, where they were to embark for the Hook of Holland, the dockers at first refused to load the top-heavy conveyance aboard its appointed cross-Channel steamer. John talked them into it just a few moments before sailing time. The English coast receded amid a chorus of "Bye Bye Blackbird" from the Anglo-Chinese party clustered at the stern rail.

In Holland next morning the minibus surfaced among crowds of students on bicycles, some of whom leaned against its tattered sides for support. Williams shared the driving with Lord Woodbine while Beryl, perched on the overheating gearbox, acted as navigator. The five Beatles, Barry Chang, and the German waiter, Herr Steiner, occupied the rear, cut off by a wall of luggage and utensils for cooking along the way. As they headed off across Europe, some more fitful singing broke out.

Like Derry and the Seniors before them, the Beatles were without the necessary German work permits. At the frontier, they, too, planned to pose as students on vacation. They had not proceeded far into Holland before Williams began to doubt if they would get even that far. During a brief stop at Arnhem John emerged from a shop with a mouth organ that, in Lord Woodbine's words, "he'd picked up to look at and forgotten to put back."

The halt is commemorated by a snapshot that Barry Chang, Williams's Chinese brother-in-law, took at the Arnhem Memorial to the dead of World War II. Paul, in a turned-up lumberjack collar, sits with Pete Best and George in front of a marble plinth inscribed with the epitaph "Their Names Liveth For Ever More." John is missing from the group; he had refused to get out of the van.

❖   ❖   ❖

They expected a city like Liverpool, and this, in a sense, they found. There was the same river, broad like the Mersey but, unlike the Mersey, crowded with ships and with shipyards beyond that seemed to grow out of lush forests. There was the same overhead railway that Liverpool had recently lost, although nothing resembling the same tired cityscape beneath. Not the bomb sites and garbage, but tree-lined boulevards, seamless with prosperity; chic shops and ships' chandlers and cafés filled with well-dressed, unscarred, confident people. There was a glimpse of the dark-spired City Hall, and of the Alster lake, set about by glass-walled banks and press buildings, and traversed by elegant swans. What was said inside Allan Williams's minibus that August evening would be echoed many times afterward in varying tones of disbelief: Wasn't this the country that had *lost* the war?

The journey from the West German frontier had been rich in incident. At one point, they were almost run down by a tram, in whose rails Lord Woodbine had accidentally jammed the minibus's front wheels. Allan Williams, taking over as driver on the outskirts of Hamburg, had immediately rammed a small sedan.

They arrived on the Reeperbahn just as neon lights were beginning to eclipse the fairground palings of the nightclubs and their painted, acrobatic nudes. Spotting the narrow road junction, where an *imbiss* belched out fumes of *frikadellen* and *currywurst*, Allan Williams remembered where he was. They turned left into Grosse Freiheit, welcomed by overarching illuminations and the stare of predatory eyes.

Even John Lennon, with his fondness for human curiosities, had not expected an employer quite like Bruno Koschmider. The figure that hopped out of the Kaiserkeller to greet them had begun life in a circus, working as a clown, fire-eater, acrobat, and illusionist with fifty small cage-birds hidden in his coat. His dwarfish stature; his large, elaborately coiffured head; his turned-up nose and quick, stumping gait, all made even John not quite like to laugh. Bruno, for his part, was unimpressed by the look of his new employees: "They were dressed in bad clothes—cheap shirts, trousers that were not clean. Their fingernails were dirty."

If Bruno was somewhat disconcerting, his Kaiserkeller club brought much reassurance. The exterior portico bore, in large letters, the name DERRY AND THE SENIORS VON LIVERPOOL. A glimpse inside, on the way to Koschmider's office, showed what seemed a vast meadow of tables and side booths, shaped like lifeboats, around the stage and miniature dance floor. The Beatles, their spirits reviving, began to laugh and cuff one another, saying this was all right, wasn't it? Allan Williams reminded them that they were not booked to play here but in one of Herr Koschmider's other clubs, the Indra.

Further along the Grosse Freiheit, beyond St. Joseph's Catholic church, the illuminations dwindled into a region of plain-fronted bordellos interspersed with private houses where elderly *hausfraus* still set potted plants on the upper window ledges. Here, under a neon sign shaped like an elephant, was to be found the Indra Club. Bruno Koschmider led the way downstairs into a small cellar cabaret, gloomy, shabby, and at that moment occupied by only two customers. Down here, for the next eight weeks, the Beatles would be expected to play for four and a half hours each weeknight and six hours on Saturdays and Sundays.

Koschmider next conducted them to the living quarters provided under the terms of his contract with Allan Williams. Across the road from the Indra he operated a small cinema, the Bambi Kino, that varied the general diet of flesh by showing corny old gangster movies and Westerns. The Beatles' lodgings were one filthy room and two windowless cubbyholes immediately behind—and in booming earshot of the cinema screen. The only washing facilities were the cinema toilets, from the communal vestibule of which an old woman attendant stared at them grimly over her saucer of tips.

It was some consolation to meet up with Derry and the Seniors and to learn that, despite munificent billing outside the Kaiserkeller, Liverpool's famous R&B group were also having to sleep rough. "Bruno gave us one little bed between five of us," Howie Casey, the sax player, says. "I'd been sleeping on that, covered by a flag, and the other lads slept on chairs set two together. The waiters used to lock us inside the club each night."

The Bambi Kino was not a great deal worse than the cellar of Lord Woodbine's New Colony Club or the Gambier Terrace flat back home in Liverpool. Paul and Pete Best took a cubbyhole each while John, Stu, and George flopped down in the larger room. All five were soon asleep, untroubled by the sounds of gunfire and police sirens that wafted through the grimy wall from the cinema screen.

Their first night's playing at the Indra was a severe letdown. Half a dozen people sat and watched them indifferently from tables with red-shaded lamps. The clientele, mainly prostitutes and their customers, showed little enthusiasm for Carl Perkins's "Honey Don't" or Chuck Berry's "Too Much Monkey Business." The club also bore a curse in the form of an old woman living upstairs who continually phoned police headquarters on the Reeperbahn to complain about the noise. Bruno Koschmider, not wishing for that kind of trouble, hissed at them to turn even their feeble amplifiers down.

Allan and Beryl Williams, Barry Chang, and Lord Woodbine remained in Hamburg throughout that inaugural week. Williams, himself comfortably ensconced in a small hotel, did what he could to improve the Beatles' living quarters—it was at his urgent insistence that Bruno provided blankets for their beds. Beryl shopped in the city center with her brother, and Lord Woodbine, as usual, remained worried by nothing. He sang calypsos at the Kaiserkeller and, one night, grew so affected by its libations that he attempted to dive into the South Sea Islands mural.

Williams, in his conscientious moments, worried about the club he had committed his charges to, and about their plainly evinced hatred of it. On their opening night they had played the entire four-and-a-half-hour stretch mutinously still and huddled-up. "Come on, boys!" Williams exhorted them from the bar. "Make it a show, boys!" Bruno Koschmider took up the phrase, clapping his large, flat hands. "Mak show, boys," he would cry. "Mak show, Beatles! Mak show!"

John's answer was to launch himself into writhings and shimmyings that were a grotesque parody of Gene Vincent at the Boxing Stadium show. Down the street at the Kaiserkeller word began to spread of this other group *von* Liverpool who leapt around the stage like monkeys and stamped their feet deafeningly on the stage. They were stamping out the rhythm to help their new drummer, Pete Best, and also to goad the old woman upstairs.

Before long, the rival groups from the Kaiserkeller had come up to the Indra to see them. Howie Casey was astonished at the improvement since their audition as the Silver Beatles in front of Larry Parnes. "That day, they'd seemed embarrassed about how bad they were," Howie says. "You could tell something had happened to them in the meantime. They'd turned into a good stomping band."

Derry and the Seniors brought with them a wide-eyed, curly-haired youth whom all the Beatles—George especially—regarded with awe. Born Anthony Esmond Sheridan McGinnity, he was better known as Tony Sheridan, a singer and inspired solo guitarist with many appearances to his credit on the *Oh Boy!* television show. His talent, however, was accompanied by habits too blithely erratic to suit the rock 'n' roll star-makers. When Bruno Koschmider hired him he had been sacked from *Oh Boy!* and most other engagements, and was playing at the 2i's coffee bar for one pound a night. Even now, the British police were hard on his trail due to various installment plan irregularities.

Anthony Esmond steered the Beatles, past beckoning doorway touts, for an insider's tour of the Reeperbahn's peculiar delights. They saw the women who grappled in mud, cheered on by an audience tied into a protective communal bib. They visited the Roxy Bar and met ravishing hostesses with tinkling laughs and undisguisably male biceps and breastbones. Two streets away, where a wooden fence forbade entry to all under eighteen, their companions steered them through the Herbertstrasse, past red-lit shop windows containing whores in every type of fancy dress, all ages from nymphet to scolding granny, smiling or scowling forth, gossiping with one another, reading, knitting, listlessly examining their own frilly garters or spooning up bowls of soup.

The other initiation was into beer. For beer, damp gold, foam piling under thin metal bar taps, had never been more plentiful. Derry and the Seniors, when they first opened at the Kaiserkeller, had been allowed beer ad lib in breaks between performing. Though Koschmider had hastily withdrawn this privilege, the nightly allowance still seemed vast to five boys who, at home in Liverpool, had often been hard put to scrape up the price of a half-pint each. Then there were the drinks pressed on them by customers at the Indra, the drinks that would be sent up to them onstage while they played. It became nothing unusual for a whole crate of beer to be shoved at their feet by well-wishers whose size and potential truculence underlined the necessity of finishing every bottle.

Sex was easily available. Here you did not chase it, as in Liverpool, and clutch at it furtively in cold shop doors. Here it came after you, putting strong arms round you, mincing no words; it was unabashed, expert—indeed, professional. For even the most cynical whores found it piquant to have an innocent boy from Liverpool—to lure and buy as a change from being, eternally, bait and merchandise.

The Freiheit provided an abundance of everything but sleep. Sheridan and the other musicians already knew a way to get by without it, just as the barmaids and whores and bouncers and pickpockets did. Someone in the early days had discovered Preludin, a brand of German slimming tablet that, while removing appetite, also roused the metabolism to goggle-eyed hyperactivity. Soon the Beatles—all but Pete Best— were gobbling "Prellys" by the tubeful each night. As the pills took effect they dried up the saliva, increasing the desire for beer.

Now the Beatles needed no exhortation to "mak show." John, in particular, began to go berserk onstage, prancing and groveling in imitation
of any rock 'n' roller or movie monster his dazzled mind could summon
up. The fact that their audience could not understand a word they said
provoked John into cries of "*Sieg Heil!*" and "Fucking Nazis!" to which
the audience invariably responded by laughing and clapping. Bruno
Koschmider, who had spent the war in a panzer division, was not so
amused.

At 5:00 or 6:00 A.M.—according to subsequent adventures—they
would stagger back along the sunny Freiheit, past doorway touts un-
sleepingly active. Behind the Bambi Kino they would collapse into their
squalid beds for the two or three hours' sleep that were possible before
the day's first picture show. Sometimes it would be gunfire on the screen
that jolted them awake, or the voice of George Raft or Edward G.
Robinson.

Hounded into consciousness, they would dash to the cinema toilets
while the basins were still clean. Rosa, the female custodian, for all her
outward grimness, kept clean towels for them, and odds and ends of
soap. "She thought we were all mad," Pete Best says. "She'd shout
things at us—*verrucht* [wicked] and *beknaakt*—but she'd be laughing.
We called her 'Mutti.'"

There were now five or six hours to be disposed of before they began
playing and drinking again. At the Gretel and Alphons or Willi's Bar, the
Freiheit's two most tolerant cafés, they would breakfast on cornflakes or
chicken soup, the only food that their dehydrated frames could endure.
They would then drift round the corner, through the stench of *frikadelli*
and last night's vomit, to the shop on the main Reeperbahn that fascinated John Lennon especially with its display of switchblades, bayonets,
coshes, swords, brass knuckle-dusters, and teargas pistols.

If not too devastatingly hung over they might catch a tram into central
Hamburg and stroll on the elegant boulevards, looking at the clothes and
the perfumes, the elaborate bakers and confectioners, the radios and tape
recorders and occasional displays of imported American guitars, saxo-
phones, and drums. Since their wages, paid out by Bruno on a Thursday,
seldom lasted more than twenty-four hours, such expeditions were usually limited to gazing and wishing. John, however, blew every pfenning he
had on a new guitar, an American Rickenbacker "short arm."

The daylight hours improved considerably after someone, walking on
the dockside, discovered Hamburg's long-established branch of the
British Sailors' Society, a refuge for mariners ashore in foreign ports.

Jim Hawke, the resident manager, was a hefty Londoner who had entered Hamburg with the first invading Allied troops and had subsequently done duty as a guard at the Nuremburg trials. In 1960, he and his German wife, Lilo, had been in charge of the Hamburg branch only a few months. Already, as it happened, they had met Stu Sutcliffe's father, still then a second engineer with the Booth shipping line.

Hawke, a tenderhearted man under his stern exterior, granted the same privileges to Liverpool musicians as to sailors far from home. Most attractive from the Beatles' point of view were the English breakfasts, cooked by an elderly German woman, Frau Prill, who knew the secret of frying real English chips. "They never seemed to have any money," Hawke said. "You could see them carefully counting out the coins. They always had what was the cheapest—steak, egg, and chips, which I put on for two marks 80 (about twenty-five pence). And big half-liter tankards of milk. Some days they'd have an Oxo cube beaten up in milk.

"They were never any trouble—I wouldn't have stood for it in any case. Just nice, quiet, well-behaved lads, they seemed. They didn't even smoke then. They'd sit and play draughts [checkers] or go upstairs for a game of ping-pong with my daughter, Monica. In the room through the bar we had an old piano that had come from the British forces. They used that, or John and Paul did, to help them write their songs. We had a library as well. I'd leave a bag of books for them on the table in front of the settee they always used. They liked reading, but they never took any of the books away. They said they couldn't read very easily where they were staying.

"They'd come in about eleven in the morning and stay until three or four in the afternoon. They'd be quite subdued. I'd look over from the bar and see the five of them, always round that same table, not talking—just staring into space. I've seen the same look on men who've been away at sea in tankers for a long time. Not with it, if you know what I mean."

THREE

The Early Years: Rampant Beatlemania! 1960–1964

Bob Spitz

∎

It's hard to know exactly when Beatlemania began, but December 27, 1960, is claimed by more than a few observers as being as good a date as any. On that historic night, the Beatles, after returning from Hamburg, performed at the Town Hall Ballroom in Litherland on the northern outskirts of Liverpool. They were paid £6, considerably less than what they were used to getting on the continent. The lineup that night consisted of John Lennon, Paul McCartney, George Harrison, Pete Best, and Chas Newby. Cavern Club deejay Bob Wooler introduced them to the unsuspecting crowd. Spitz describes what happened next.

from *The Beatles: The Biography*

■ THE HOUSE WAS FULL, framed in hazy silhouette—not a fleet of drunken sailors, like in Hamburg, but local teenagers, many of whom they had gone to school with. Wooler busied himself with preparations, but between the second and third records of the intermission (there was a rule: three songs between sets, no more, to avoid the possibility of fights), he walked over to deliver some last-minute advice. "I'll announce you," he hastened to tell them, "then go straight into a number as soon as the curtain opens." He watched the recognition register on the boys' faces but noted a faint disapproval in their manner. So be it, he thought.

Out front, they could hear the overheated crowd, its attention span slipping away. The throng of teenagers wanted action. They had danced distractedly between acts; the records were no substitute for the real thing, and now, in the rambling fade, their liquid laughter and stridence signaled an excitement that sought to condense into impatience. Besides, there was a general curiosity about the next band, which had been added at the eleventh hour and was advertised as being "Direct from Hamburg." A German act. It would be interesting, from the pitch of their accents and their delivery, to see how they contrasted with the sharpness of Liverpool's top bands.

The hall was packed with teenagers, many of whom had gathered at card tables along both sidewalls to await the next act. The majority were attired in what was respectfully called "fancy dress" for what remained of the holiday festivities. The well-scrubbed boys, whose dark suits were also their school uniforms, looked stiff and self-conscious, while girls, sheathed in tight calf-length skirts and white shirts, paraded gaily to and from the upstairs bathroom, applying last-minute retouches to their makeup. Those who danced drifted casually across the big, open dance floor, keeping an eye on the stage as the band shuffled into place behind the curtain. Promptly, amps crackled in resistance: John and George plugged into a shared Truvoice that saw them through infancy, while Paul switched on his trusty seafoam green Ampigo. The audience stirred and half turned while Bob Wooler crooned into an open mike: "And now, everybody, the band you've been waiting for. Direct from Hamburg—"

But before he got their name out, Paul McCartney jumped the gun and, in a raw, shrill burst as the curtain swung open, hollered: *"I'm gonna tell Aunt Mary / 'bout Uncle John / he said he had the mis'ry / buthegotalotoffun . . ."*

Oh, baby! The aimless shuffle stopped dead in its tracks. The reaction of the audience was so unexpected that Wooler had failed, in the first few seconds, to take note of it. Part of the reason was the shocking explosion that shook the hall. A whomp of bass drum accompanied each quarter note beat with terrific force. The first one struck after Paul screamed, *"Tell,"* so that the charge ricocheted wildly off the walls. There was a second on *Mary,* and then another, then a terrible volley that had the familiar *bam-bam-bam* of a Messerschmitt wreaking all hell on a local target: an assault innocent of madness. The pounding came in rhythmic waves and once it started, it did not stop. There was nowhere to take cover on the open floor. All heads snapped forward and stared wild-eyed at the deafening ambush. The music crashing around them was discernibly a species of rock 'n roll but played unlike they had ever heard it before. *Oh ba-by, yeahhhhhh / now ba-by, woooooo . . .* It was convulsive, ugly, frightening, and visceral in the way it touched off frenzy in the crowd.

The band's physical appearance created another commotion. For a tense moment, the crowd just stared, awestruck, trying to take in the whole disturbing scene. Four of the musicians were dressed in the black suits they'd bought at the Texas Shop in Hamburg: beautiful cracked-leather jackets with padded shoulders and artificial sheepskin lining that proved sweltering under the lights, black T-shirts, and silky skintight pants. With instruments slung low across their bodies, they looked like a teenage-rebel fantasy come to life. Nor could anyone take his eyes off the rude cowboy boots with flat, chopped heels that each man wore, especially John Lennon's, which were ornate Twin Eagles, emblazoned with birds carved on both the front and back and outlined with white stitching.

"I'd never seen any band look like this before," says Dave Foreshaw, a Liverpool promoter, who gazed on the spectacle in utter astonishment. "I thought: 'What are they? *Who* are they?'"

As if someone had flashed a prearranged cue, the entire crowd rushed the stage, pressing feverishly toward the footlights. Impetuous girls and boys alike abandoned their social proprieties to a purely emotional response. Everyone had stopped dancing; there were now a total gravitation toward the stage. Sensing that a fight had broken out, Brian Kelly rushed inside with several bouncers in tow. The promoter experienced a moment of real panic. According to Bob Wooler, "Long afterwards, [Kelly] told me they were seconds away from using brute force when he finally realized what the fuss was about."

The band, too, arrived at the same conclusion and began working the crowd into a sweat. They turned up the juice and tore into a wild jam. Drawing upon stage antics they'd devised while in Germany, they twisted and jerked their bodies with indignant energy. John and George proceeded to lunge around like snapping dogs and stomp loudly on the bandstand in time to the music. (Newby, forced to watch Harrison's hands for chord changes, joined in the fun at irregular intervals, although to his dismay, the lack of decent cowboy boots made his part in the clowning "far less effective.") "It was just so different," recalls Bill Ashton, an apprentice fitter for British Rail, who sang part-time as Billy Kramer with a band called the Coasters and had come to Litherland to size up the "foreign" competition. "To act that way onstage and make that kind of sound—I was absolutely staggered."

Like everyone else, Kramer was used to bands that patterned themselves after Cliff Richard and the Shadows, England's top rock 'n roll act and practitioners of smooth, carefully tended choreography. Up till then, everyone had followed in the Shadows' dainty footsteps. This band, however, was a beast of a different nature. According to Dave Foreshaw, "Normally, [popular Liverpool bands such as] the Remo Four or the Dominoes would come on and . . . perform in a polite, orderly way. This band's performance attacked the crowd. They [played] aggressively and with a lot less respect. They just *attacked* them!" And when John Lennon stepped to the mike and challenged the crowd to "get your knickers down!" the audience, in a state of unconscious, indiscriminate euphoria, screamed and raised their arms in delight.

Brian Kelly, especially, perceived a seismic shift in the landscape and moved fast to contain it by posting bouncers at the doors to prohibit rival promoters like Foreshaw from poaching his bounty. But it was too late for such empty measures. The house erupted in hysteria as the band concluded its half-hour set with a rousing version of "What'd I Say," in which Paul McCartney jackknifed through the crowd, whipping the kids into rapturous confrontation. Over the last wild applause, Bob Wooler managed to say, "That was fantastic, fellas," but it was doubtful anyone paid much attention to him. They were too busy trying to connect with what had just gone down on that stage, what had turned their little Christmas dance into a full-scale epiphany.

This much was inevitable: the band had somehow squeezed every nerve of the local rock 'n roll scene, and that scene would never be the same. In the wall of grinding sound and the veil of black leather, they had staked their claim to history. And in that instant, they had become the Beatles.

On December 1, 1963, in *The New York Times Magazine,* Frederick Lewis described the Beatles music as "basically rock 'n' roll, but less formalized, slightly more inventive. Their act, which includes much adlibbing between numbers, is both hilarious and outrageous." According to Lewis, their appeal was strongest among females between the ages of ten and thirty, but it "affects all social classes and all levels of intelligence." The media's attitude toward the Beatles early on, though, was actually more disparaging, dismissive, and disapproving. A few weeks earlier, the following uncredited article in *Newsweek* was one of the first pieces in the United States to comment on the social and cultural phenomena that came to be known as Beatlemania.

"Beatlemania"

Newsweek

November 18, 1963

THEY WEAR SHEEP-DOG BANGS, collarless jackets, and drainpipe trousers. One plays left-handed guitar, two have falsetto voices, one wishes he were a businessman, and all four sing . . . and sing . . . and sing.

They are the Beatles, and the sound of their music is one of the most persistent noises heard over England since the air-raid sirens were dismantled. This year they have sold 2.5 million recordings of their own compositions, songs like "She Loves You," "Love Me Do," and "Please, Please Me." Their theater appearances drew 5,000 screaming fans and a police riot squad in Manchester; 4,000 began queueing up at 3 A.M. in Newcastle-upon-Tyne; and 2,000 teenage girls squealed their hearts out as they besieged bobbies outside the sold-out London Palladium. "This is Beatlemania," said the Daily Mail, and added plaintively: "Where will it all lead?"

LIVERPUDLIANS: The Beatles are four young men (aged 21–23) who bellow a sort of rock-'n'-roll music, play guitars, beat drums, and figure to earn $280,000 this year. Their leader is John Lennon, a Liverpudlian like the others, and the only one of the group who is married. He writes most of their songs in collaboration with Paul McCartney, once an English Lit major. The guitarist is George Harrison who claims to be a Segovia fan, and the drummer is Ringo Starr, nicknamed for the four rings he wears.

Little more than a year ago, the Beatles were doing well to split $60 a week in a succession of sleazy clubs on the Liverpool waterfront. Then came an engagement in a Hamburg, Germany, strip joint, where their ability to play loud enough to be heard over their enthusiastic audiences and their effective presentation of the "Liverpool Sound," also known as the "Mersey Sound" (named after the oily river that flows through Liverpool), brought them to the attention of British billing agents. Somehow—and no one can explain exactly how—the Beatles, rather than 200 similar groups, clicked. "Everybody's trying to figure what suddenly makes a group go," says drummer Starr. "Sometimes I try to figure it out, too."

'OH DEARIE ME': Beatle music is high-pitched, loud beyond reason, and stupefyingly repetitive. Like rock 'n' roll, to which it is closely allied, it is even more effective to watch than to hear. They prance, skip, and turn in circles; Beatles have even been known to kiss their guitars. The style, certainly, is their own. "They don't gyrate around like Elvis," says one young girl. "They stamp about and shake and, oh dearie me, they just send the joy out to you."

Offstage, the Beatles are rather quieter, but not much different from their performing selves. Their suits tend toward leather and suede, their conversation is mostly shop, and they enjoy discussing Beatles, Ltd., the corporation they hope will keep them in whatever "beatles" eat in their old age. Last week the boys reached the pinnacle—a command performance before royalty at London's Prince of Wales Theater. Sharing the bill with Marlene Dietrich, Flanders & Swann, and other top acts, the Beatles were at their noisy best. Queen Mother Elizabeth found them lovable—"so young, fresh, and vital," and Lord Snowden offered to photograph them. But the boys were unawed. "People in the cheaper seats, please clap," Lennon told the audience. "The rest of you just rattle your jewelry."

William Mann

■

Here is the famous piece by William Mann celebrating the musical prowess of the Beatles. It was also very much ahead of its time—Mann wrote the uncredited piece for *The Times* in London in late 1963, during the height of Beatlemania in Britain but a few months before the Beatles crossed over to American shores.

"What Songs the Beatles Sang . . ."

The Times (London)
December 23, 1963

■ THE OUTSTANDING ENGLISH COMPOSERS of 1963 must seem to have been John Lennon and Paul McCartney, the talented young musicians from Liverpool whose songs have been sweeping the country since last Christmas, whether performed by their own group, the Beatles, or by the numerous other teams of English troubadours that they also supply with songs.

I am not concerned here with the social phenomenon of Beatlemania, which finds expression in handbags, balloons and other articles bearing the likenesses of the loved ones, or in the hysterical screaming of young girls whenever the Beatle Quartet performs in public, but with the musical phenomenon. For several decades, in fact since the decline of the music-hall, England has taken her popular songs from the United States, either directly or by mimicry. But the songs of Lennon and McCartney are distinctly indigenous in character, the most imaginative and inventive examples of a style that has been developing on Merseyside during the past few years. And there is a nice, rather flattering irony in the news that the Beatles have now become prime favourites in America, too.

The strength of character in pop songs seems, and quite understandably, to be determined usually by the number of composers involved; when three or four people are required to make the original tunesmith's work publicly presentable it is unlikely to retain much individuality or to wear very well. The virtue of the Beatles' repertory is that, apparently,

they do it themselves; three of the four are composers, they are versa-
tile instrumentalists, and when they do borrow a song from another
repertory, their treatment is idiosyncratic—as when Paul McCartney
sings "Till There Was You" from *The Music Man,* a cool, easy, tasteful
version of this ballad, quite without artificial sentimentality.

Their noisy items are the ones that arouse teenagers' excitement.
Glutinous crooning is generally out of fashion these days, and even a song
about "Misery" sounds fundamentally quite cheerful; the slow, sad song
about "This Boy," which features prominently in Beatle programmes, is
expressively unusual for its lugubrious music, but harmonically it is one of
their most intriguing, with its chains of pandiationic clusters, and the sentiment is acceptable because voiced cleanly and crisply. But harmonic interest is typical of their quicker songs, too, and one gets the impression
that they think simultaneously of harmony and melody, so firmly are the
major tonic sevenths and ninths built into their tunes, and the flat submediant key switches, so natural is the Aeolian cadence at the end of
"Not a Second Time" (the chord progression which ends Mahler's *Song
of the Earth*).

Those submediant switches from C major into A-flat major, and to a
lesser extent mediant ones (e.g., the octave ascent in the famous "I
Want to Hold Your Hand") are a trademark of Lennon-McCartney
songs—they do not figure much in other pop repertories, or in the
Beatles' arrangements of borrowed material—and show signs of becoming a mannerism. The other trademark of their compositions is a
firm and purposeful bass line with a musical life of its own; how Lennon
and McCartney divide their creative responsibilities I have yet to discover, but it is perhaps significant that Paul is the bass guitarist of the
group. It may also be significant that George Harrison's song "Don't
Bother Me" is harmonically a good deal more primitive, though it is
nicely enough presented.

I suppose it is the sheer loudness of the music that appeals to Beatle
admirers (there is something to be heard even through the squeals) and
many parents must have cursed the electric guitar's amplification this
Christmas—how fresh and euphonious the ordinary guitars sound in
the Beatles' version of "Till There Was You"—but parents who are still
managing to survive the decibels and, after copious repetition over several months, still deriving some musical pleasure from the overhearing,
do so because there is a good deal of variety—oh, so welcome in pop
music—about what they sing.

The autocratic but not by any means ungrammatical attitude to tonality (closer to, say, Peter Maxwell Davies's carols in *O Magnum Mysterium* than to Gershwin or Loewe or even Lionel Bart); the exhilarating and often quasi-instrumental vocal duetting, sometimes in scat or in falsetto, behind the melodic line; the melismas with altered vowels ("I saw her yesterday-ee-ay") which have not quite become mannered, and the discreet, sometimes subtle, varieties of instrumentation—a suspicion of piano or organ, a few bars of mouth-organ obbligato, an excursion on the claves or maracas; the translation of African Blues or American western idioms (in "Baby, It's You," the Magyar 8/8 metre, too) into tough, sensitive Merseyside.

These are some of the qualities that make one wonder with interest what the Beatles, and particularly Lennon and McCartney, will do next, and if America will spoil them or hold on to them, and if their next record will wear as well as the others. They have brought a distinctive and exhilarating flavour into a genre of music that was in danger of ceasing to be music at all.

Martin Goldsmith

■

As most everyone knows, rock and roll history was made on February 7, 1964, when the Beatles "invaded" America, a scant three months after the Kennedy assassination. During their whirlwind two-week visit, they appeared twice on *The Ed Sullivan Show,* and played two concerts at Carnegie Hall and one concert in Washington, D.C.

As proof that the Beatles are an indelible part of Western history, Martin Goldsmith's *The Beatles Come to America* is part of John Wiley & Sons Turning Points series, where contemporary writers look at "the defining events of our time." Other titles cover such topics as Columbus in the New World, Jackie Robinson and the integration of baseball, the fall of the Berlin Wall, D-Day, and Abraham Lincoln and the Emancipation Proclamation. The Beatles, then, share some rather heady company.

In the following excerpt, Goldsmith looks at the song, "I Want to Hold Your Hand," that introduced Americans to the Beatles.

from *The Beatles Come to America*

■ IT WAS, AND REMAINS, a great song, a joyous, reassuring sentiment riding gently atop an exuberantly beautiful melody. And it will always be Our Song, the song that, more than any other, introduced us Americans to the Beatles. I think it is safe to say that all of us who call upon our first memories of hearing the band on the radio think of December 1963 and January 1964 and hear, playing sweetly in our mind's ear, "I Want to Hold Your Hand."

"I remember when we got the chord that made that song," recalled John Lennon near the end of his life. "We were in Jane Asher's house, downstairs in the cellar, playing on the piano at the same time, and we had 'Oh, you-u-u . . . got that something . . .' And Paul hits this chord and I turn to him and say, 'That's it! Do that again!' In those days, we really used to absolutely write like that—both playing into each other's noses."

But the song is so much more than a single chord, of course. The words may be simple, but they express tender longing and the heartfelt magic of human touch in a sentiment both innocent and profoundly worldly. And the music—"It's beautiful, the kind of song I like to sing," said John—underscores the meaning of the words with an artistry of which master melodist Franz Schubert would be proud.

The song opens with a series of five descending phrases:

1. Oh, yeah I'll (E down to B)

2. Tell you something (C up to D then down to A)

3. I think you'll understand (B down to F-sharp)

4. When I (again E down to B)

5. Say that something (again C to D down to A)

It's only then, after establishing that downward flowing line, that the melody leaps up an entire octave to land joyfully on the word "hand," the punchline of the song. The first lines are all breathless anticipation, and when the central idea of the lover's message is delivered, it comes bursting out in a manner that transcends everything that's come before. It's simple, direct, and utterly magical, the essence of lasting art.

There's a hush at the start of the bridge ("And when I touch you I feel happy inside") that leads to an exuberance made all the more explosive because of that hush: "It's such a feeling that my love I can't hide, I can't hide, I can't hide!" John's and Paul's voices achieve a gleeful and glorious harmony at the climax.

The end of the song offers new harmonic delights, as a brand-new chord is unveiled just before the title line is repeated for the last time and new vocal harmonies grace the final expression of "hold your hand." And as if all that were not enough, two sets of triplets broaden out the rhythm under the last word before the final cadence arrives. The very effort of stopping such a runaway train of emotion helps us realize what an exhilarating ride it has been.

Those triplets point to another, more subterranean reason that "I Want to Hold Your Hand" may have had such a profound effect on the American consciousness, or subconsciousness. A triple meter accompanies the emotional climax of the song, the (thrice) repeated ejaculations of the phrase "I can't hide." That same meter serves as the song's introduction, hammered out by John's and George's ringing guitars. Only a little more than a month before, another triple rhythm had been at the heavy heart of the Dead March played by the muffled drums that accompanied President Kennedy's caisson on its solemn march through the streets of Washington. I can still close my eyes and summon an image of the black-and-white telecast of the funeral, and the soundtrack of the broadcast is that slow and stately triple meter.

Rhythm is the strongest and most elemental connection we have to music. Is it possible that the joyful triple meter heard right at the outset, then again at the song's high point, and finally at the very end somehow registered with us as we struggled to throw off the gloom of November 1963, and we subconsciously heard "I Want to Hold Your Hand" not only as an offered gesture of love but also as a gentle reminder that life goes on after death? Did the song connect a painful past to a hopeful future? Were there extramusical forces at work?

In my hometown of St. Louis, my top-40 radio station of choice, KXOK, could have had a jump on its competitors. The afternoon drive-time DJ, Don "Stinky" Shaffer, received a phone call one day in the fall of 1963 from a woman with an English accent who identified herself as living in southern Illinois, well within the reach of KXOK's signal. She told Shaffer that she'd married an American GI and had come to live in America, but that her younger brother was back in England and a member of a very popular band. She offered to drive to St. Louis and play her brother's record for him. Shaffer warily agreed, and the next afternoon the woman arrived at the studio, bearing an advanced pressing of her brother's latest hit single, not yet even released in the United Kingdom. She played the record for Shaffer and KXOK's operations director Bud Cannell. Shaffer recalls thinking the record sounded like "country music with a British accent" and assured the woman that the record wouldn't work for the KXOK audience. So Louise Harrison Caldwell went home to Illinois and KXOK missed out on the chance to introduce her brother George's band's "I Want to Hold Your Hand" to America.

Within weeks, another American radio station would claim that honor, and the entire country would begin to experience "such a feeling."

Paul Johnson

■

Not everyone was enamored with the Beatles. This provocative piece by Paul Johnson originally ran in the February 28, 1964, issue of the *New Statesman,* at a time when Britain was in the throes of Beatlemania and just when the Beatles had captured the heart of America. Johnson, though, was not impressed. Appalled by the "new cult of youth," he criticized the vacuity of the teenagers he witnessed on the television screen ("here apparently, is a collective portrait of a generation enslaved by a commercial machine") and abhorred a new cultural movement where actually hearing the music during a performance becomes almost unnecessary.

"The Menace of Beatlism"

New Statesman
February 28, 1964

■ MR WILLIAM DEEDES is an Old Harrovian, a member of the cabinet and the minister in charge of the government's information services. Mr Deedes, it will be remembered, was one of those five ministers who interviewed Mr Profumo on that fateful night and were convinced by him that he had not slept with Miss Keeler. Now any public relations man, even a grand one who sits in the cabinet, can use a touch of credulity; but even so I remember thinking at the time: "If Deedes can believe that, he'll believe anything." And indeed he does! Listen to him on the subject of The Beatles:

> They herald a cultural movement among the young which may become part of the history of our time . . . For those with eyes to see it, something important and heartening is happening here. The young are rejecting some of the sloppy standards of their elders, by which far too much of our output has been governed in recent years . . . they have discerned dimly that in a world of automation, declining craftsmanship and increased leisure, something of this kind is essential to restore the human instinct to excel at something and the human faculty of discrimination.

Incredible as it may seem, this was not an elaborate attempt at whimsy, but a serious address, delivered to a meeting of the City of London Young Conservatives, and heard in respectful silence. Not a voice was raised to point out that the Emperor wasn't wearing a stitch. The Beatles phenomenon, in fact, illustrates one of my favourite maxims: that if something becomes big enough and popular enough—and especially commercially profitable enough—solemn men will not be lacking to invest it with virtues. So long as The Beatles were just another successful showbiz team the pillars of society could afford to ignore them, beyond bestowing the indulgent accolade of a slot in the Royal Variety Performance. But then came the shock announcement that they were earning £6,250,000 a year—and, almost simultaneously, they got the stamp of approval from America.

This was quite a different matter: at once they became not only part of the export trade but an electorally valuable property. Sir Alec Home promptly claimed credit for them, and was as promptly accused by Mr Wilson of political clothes-stealing. Conservative candidates have been officially advised to mention them whenever possible in their speeches. The Queen expressed concern about the length of Ringo's hair. Young diplomats at our Washington embassy fought for their autographs. A reporter described them as "superb ambassadors for Britain." It is true that the Bishop of Woolwich has not yet asked them to participate in one of his services, but the invitation cannot be long delayed. And, while waiting for the definitive analysis of their cultural significance by Messrs Raymond Williams and Richard Hoggart we have Mr Deedes' contribution on behalf of the cabinet.

Of course, our society has long been brainwashed in preparation for this apotheosis of inanity. For more than two decades now, more and more intellectuals have turned their backs on their trade and begun to worship at the shrine of "pop culture." Nowadays, if you confess that you don't know the difference between Dizzy Gillespie and Fats Waller (and, what is more, don't care) you are liable to be accused of being a fascist.

To buttress their intellectual self-esteem, these treasonable clerks have evolved an elaborate cultural mythology about jazz, which purports to distinguish between various periods, tendencies and schools. The subject has been smeared with a respectable veneer of academic scholarship, so that now you can overhear grown men, who have been expensively educated, engage in heated argument on the respective techniques of Charlie Parker and Duke Ellington. You can see writers

of distinction, whose grey hairs testify to years spent in the cultural vine-
yard, squatting on the bare boards of malodorous caverns, while through
the haze of smoke, sweat and cheap cosmetics comes the monotonous
braying of savage instruments.

One might, I suppose, attribute such intellectual treachery to the
fact that, in jazz circles, morals are easy, sex is cheap and there is a permissive attitude to the horrors of narcotics. Men are, alas, sometimes
willing to debauch their intellects for such rewards. But I doubt if this
is the real reason. The growing public approval of anti-culture is itself,
I think, a reflection of the new cult of youth. Bewildered by a rapidly
changing society, excessively fearful of becoming out of date, our leaders are increasingly turning to young people as guides and mentors—or,
to vary the metaphor, as geiger-counters to guard them against the per-
ils of mental obsolescence. If youth likes jazz, then it must be good, and
clever men must rationalise this preference in intellectually respectable
language. Indeed, whatever youth likes must be good: the supreme
crime, in politics and culture alike, is not to be "with it." Even the most
unlikely mascots of the Establishment are now drifting with the current:
Mr Henry Brooke, for instance, finds himself appointing to the latest
Home Office committee the indispensable teenager, who has, what is
more, the additional merit of being a delinquent.

Before I am denounced as a reactionary fuddy-duddy, let us pause an
instant and see exactly what we mean by this "youth." Both TV channels
now run weekly programmes in which popular records are played to
teenagers and judged. While the music is performed, the cameras
linger savagely over the faces of the audience. What a bottomless chasm
of vacuity they reveal! The huge faces, bloated with cheap confectionery
and smeared with chain-store makeup, the open, sagging mouths and
glazed eyes, the hands mindlessly drumming in time to the music, the
broken stiletto heels, the shoddy, sterotyped, "with-it" clothes: here
apparently, is a collective portrait of a generation enslaved by a commercial machine. Leaving a TV studio recently, I stumbled into the
exodus from one of these sessions. How pathetic and listless they
seemed: young girls, hardly any more than 16, dressed as adults and already lined up as fodder for exploitation. Their eyes came to life only
when one of their grotesque idols—scarcely older than they—made a
brief appearance, before a man in a camel-hair coat hustled him into
a car. Behind this image of "youth," there are, evidently, some shrewd
older folk at work.

And what of the "culture" which is served up to these pitiable victims? According to Mr Deedes, "the aim of The Beatles and their rivals is first class of its kind. Failure to attain it is spotted and criticised ruthlessly by their many highly-discriminating critics." I wonder if Mr Deedes has ever taken the trouble to listen to any of this music? On the Saturday TV shows, the merits of the new records are discussed by panels of "experts," many of whom seem barely more literate or articulate than the moronic ranks facing them. They are asked to judge each record a "hit" or a "miss," but seem incapable of explaining why they have reached their verdict. Occasionally one of the "experts" betrays some slight acquaintance with the elementals of music and makes what is awesomely described as a "technical" point: but when such merit is identified in a record, this is usually found to be a reason for its certain commercial failure.

In any case, merit has nothing to do with it. The teenager comes not to hear but to participate in a ritual, a collective grovelling to gods who are themselves blind and empty. "Throughout the performance," wrote one observer, "it was impossible to hear anything above the squealing except the beat of Ringo's drums." Here, indeed, is "a new cultural movement: music which not only cannot be heard but does not *need* to be heard. As such I have no doubt that it is, in truth, "first class of its kind."

If The Beatles and their like were in fact what the youth of Britain wanted, one might well despair. I refuse to believe it—and so I think will any other intelligent person who casts his or her mind back far enough. What were we doing at 16? I remember the drudgery of Greek prose and the calculus, but I can also remember reading the whole of Shakespeare and Marlowe, writing poems and plays and stories. It is a marvellous age, an age of intense mental energy and discovery. Almost every week one found a fresh idol—Milton, Wagner, Debussy, Matisse, El Greco, Proust—some, indeed, to be subsequently toppled from the pantheon, but all springing from the mainstream of European culture. At 16, I and my friends heard our first performance of Beethoven's Ninth Symphony; I can remember the excitement even today. We would not have wasted 30 seconds of our precious time on The Beatles and their ilk.

Are teenagers different today? Of course not. Those who flock round The Beatles, who scream themselves into hysteria, whose vacant faces flicker over the TV screen, are the least fortunate of their generation, the dull, the idle, the failures: their existence, in such large numbers, far from being a cause for ministerial congratulation, is a fearful indictment of our education system, which in 10 years of schooling can scarcely raise them to literacy. What Mr Deedes fails to perceive is that the core of the teenage group—the boys and girls who will be the real leaders and creators of society tomorrow—never go near a pop concert. They are, to put it simply, too busy. They are educating themselves. They are in the process of inheriting the culture which, despite Beatlism or any other mass-produced mental opiate, will continue to shape our civilisation. To use Mr Deedes' own phrase, though not in the sense he meant it, they are indeed "rejecting some of the sloppy standards of their elders." Of course, if many of these elders in responsible positions surrender to the Gadarene Complex and seek to elevate the worst things in our society into the best, their task will be made more difficult. But I believe that, despite the antics of cabinet ministers with election nerves, they will succeed.

Andrew Sarris

■

Artistic expectations for the Beatles' first movie were not particularly high. It's easy to forget that the initial reaction to the Beatles, especially in the United States, was one of derision. During their first visit, in February 1964, an editorial in the *Washington Star* described their musical talent as "minimal. Their weird hair style is merely a combination of the beehive and the Hamlet . . . hairdo. We have never produced a Shakespeare. But we never produced a Beatle, either." So the acclaim given *A Hard Day's Night* was all the more impressive. Andrew Sarris's review, which is reprinted below, called it "the *Citizen Kane* of jukebox musicals" as well as "a movie that works on every level for every kind of audience." Busley Crowther in *The New York Times* called it "a whale of a comedy" even though he couldn't tell the four musicians apart except for Ringo ("the big-nosed one"). The Beatles were even being favorably compared to the Marx Brothers.

Shot quickly and cheaply in black and white, *A Hard Day's Night* was a precursor to the later ubiquitous rock videos, and its pseudo-documentary style influenced later generations of directors. Filming began on March 2, 1964, and ended on April 24 on a residential street, Edgehill Road, in West Ealing, London. The film made its northern premiere less than three months later, in Liverpool, on Friday, July 10. It made its London debut on July 6.

"A Hard Day's Night"

The Village Voice
August 27, 1964

■ *A Hard Day's Night* is a particularly pleasant surprise in a year so full of unexpectedly unpleasant surprises. I have no idea who is the most responsible—director Richard Lester or screenwriter Alun Owen or the Messrs John Lennon, Paul McCartney, George Harrison, and Ringo Starr, better known collectively as The Beatles. Perhaps it was all a happy accident, and the lightning of inspiration will never strike again in the same spot. The fact remains that *A Hard Day's Night* has turned out to be the *Citizen Kane* of jukebox musicals, the brilliant crystallisation of such diverse cultural particles as the pop movie, rock 'n' roll, *cinéma vérité*, the *nouvelle vague*, free cinema, the affectedly hand-held camera, frenzied cutting, the cult of the sexless subadolescent, the semi-documentary, and studied spontaneity. So help me, I resisted The Beatles as long as I could. As a cab driver acquaintance observed, "So what's new about The Beatles? Didn't you ever hear of Ish Kabibble?" Alas, I had. I kept looking for openings to put down The Beatles. Some of their sly crows' humour at the expense of a Colonel Blimp character in a train compartment is a bit too deliberate. "I fought the war for people like you," sez he. "Bet you're sorry you won," sez they. Old Osborne ooze, sez I. But just previously, the fruitiest looking of the four predators had looked up enticingly at the bug-eyed Blimp and whimpered "Give us a kiss." Depravity of such honest frankness is worth a hundred pseudo-literary exercises like *Becket*.

Stylistically, *A Hard Day's Night* is everything Tony Richardson's version of *Tom Jones* tried to be and wasn't. Thematically, it is everything Peter Brook's version of *Lord of the Flies* tried to be and wasn't. Fielding's satiric gusto is coupled here with Golding's primordial evil, and the strain hardly shows. I could have done with a bit less of a false sabre-toothed, rattling wreck of an old man tagged with sickeningly repetitious irony as a "clean" old man. The pop movie mannerisms of the inane running joke about one of the boys' managers being sensitively shorter than the other might have been dispensed with at no great loss.

The foregoing are trifling reservations, however, about a movie that works on every level for every kind of audience. The open-field helicopter-shot sequence of The Beatles on a spree is one of the most exhilarating expressions of high spirits I have seen on screen. The razor-slashing wit of the dialogue must be heard to be believed and appreciated. One as horribly addicted to alliteration as this otherwise sensible scribe can hardly resist a line like "Ringo's drums loom large in his legend."

I must say I enjoyed even the music enormously, possibly because I have not yet been traumatised by transistors into open rebellion against the "top 40" and such. (I just heard "Hello, Dolly" for the first time the other day, and the lyrics had been changed to "Hello, Lyndon.") Nevertheless I think there is a tendency to underrate rock 'n' roll because the lyrics look so silly in cold print. I would make two points here. First, it is unfair to compare R&R with Gershwin, Rodgers, Porter, Kern, *et al.*, as if all pre-R&R music from Tin Pan Alley was an uninterrupted flow of melodiousness. This is the familiar fallacy of nostalgia. I remember too much brassy noise from the big-band era to be stricken by the incursions of R&R. I like the songs The Beatles sing despite the banality of the lyrics, but the words in R&R only mask the poundingly ritualistic meaning of the beat. It is in the beat that the passion and togetherness is most movingly expressed, and it is the beat that the kids in the audience pick up with their shrieks as they drown out the words they have already heard a thousand times. To watch The Beatles in action with their constituents is to watch the kind of direct theatre that went out with Aristophanes, or perhaps even the Australian bushman. There is an empathy there that a million Lincoln Center Repertory companies cannot duplicate. Towards the end of *A Hard Day's Night* I began to understand the mystique of The Beatles. Lester's crane shot facing the audience from behind The Beatles established the emotional unity of the performers and their audience. It is a beautifully Bazinian deep-focus shot of hysteria to a slow beat punctuated by the kind of zoom shots I have always deplored in theory but must now admire in practice. Let's face it. My critical theories and preconceptions are all shook up, and I am profoundly grateful to The Beatles for such pleasurable softening of hardening aesthetic arteries.

As to what The Beatles "mean," I hesitate to speculate. The trouble with sociological analysis is that it is unconcerned with aesthetic values. *A Hard Day's Night* could have been a complete stinker of a movie and still be reasonably "meaningful." I like The Beatles in this moment in film history not merely because they mean something but rather because they express effectively a great many aspects of modernity that have converged inspiredly in their personalities. When I speak affectionately of their depravity, I am not commenting on their private lives, about which I know less than nothing. The wedding ring on Ringo's finger startles a great many people as a subtle Pirandellian switch from a character like Dopey of the Seven Dwarfs to a performer who chooses to project an ambiguous identity. It hardly matters. When we are 14 we learn to our dismay that all celebrities are depraved and that the he-man actor we so admired would rather date a mongoose than a girl. Then at 15 we learn that all humanity is depraved in one way or another and Albert Schweitzer gets his kicks by not squashing flies. Then at 16 we realise that it doesn't matter how depraved we all are; all that matters is the mask we put on our depravity, the image we choose to project to the world once we have lost our innocence irrevocably. There is too much of a tendency to tear away the masks in order to probe for the truth beneath. But why stop with the masks? Why not tear away the flesh as well and gaze upon the grinning skeletons lurking in all of us?

Consequently, what interests me about The Beatles is not what they are but what they choose to express. Their Ish Kabibble hairdos, for example, serve two functions. They become unique as a group and interchangeable as individuals. Except for Ringo, the favourite of the fans, the other three Beatles tend to get lost in the shuffle. And yet each is a distinctly personable individual behind their collective façade of androgynous selflessness—a façade appropriate, incidentally, to the undifferentiated sexuality of their sub-adolescent fans. The Beatles are not merely objects, however. A frequent refrain of their middle-aged admirers is that The Beatles don't take themselves too seriously. They take themselves seriously enough, all right; it is their middle-aged admirers and detractors they don't take too seriously. The Beatles are a sly bunch of anti-Establishment anarchists, but they are too slick to tip their hand to the authorities. People who have watched them handle their fans and the press tell me that they make Sinatra and his clan look like a bunch of rubes at a county fair. Of course, they have been shrewdly promoted, and a great deal of the hysteria surrounding them has been rigged with classic fakery and exaggeration. They may not be worth a paragraph in six months, but right now their entertaining message seems to be that everyone is "people," Beatles and squealing sub-adolescents as much as Negroes and women and so-called senior citizens, and that however much alike "people" may look in a group or a mass or stereotype, there is in each soul a unique and irreducible individuality.

Gloria Steinem

■

In December 1964, the Beatles were, in the words of Gloria Steinem, "the single biggest attraction in the world." Everyone wanted a piece of them. The question on most minds at the time was, would they last? The consensus seemed to be the same: a resounding *no.* The Beatles were a fad, and like every fad, their reign would eventually end.

Toward the conclusion of their 1964 North American concert tour, the Beatles were holed up in a motel at Kennedy International Airport (several Manhattan hotels already had turned them down). Steinem, a young and aggressive reporter from *Cosmopolitan,* was determined to interview the one Beatle, John Lennon, who seemed to have the best chance of a future after the tumult of fame ended. He was the literary Beatle, after all. After being told by a policeman to move on ("We got orders, lady. No press"), Steinem persisted—she wouldn't take no for an answer—and in the early dawn hours managed to get a one-on-one interview with her elusive prey.

"Beatle with a Future"

Cosmopolitan
December 1964

■ IN BRITAIN, THE BEATLES outdraw Queen Elizabeth. In America, they attract bigger crowds than the President and Elizabeth Taylor combined. All over Europe and even in Hong Kong, teenagers turn out in droves whether or not they understand the lyrics. The Beatles have become, quite literally, the single biggest attraction in the world.

Show business experts disagree on the sociology or psychology or simple merchandising behind this success, but they agree on one thing: like every craze from the hula-hoop to the ancient Celts' habit of painting themselves blue, it must come to an end, and probably an abrupt one. At ages 21 to 24, they don't seem to have thought about the problem much, but under pressure of constant questions from reporters, they have come up with a few clues. George Harrison, the youngest Beatle and the only one who shows any interest in the business side of their career, might produce records for other pop music stars. Paul McCartney— at 22, the Beatle with the best looks and on-stage personality—is likely to continue a show business career as a solo. Ringo Starr (born Richard Starkey), the oldest of the four and the prototype of a non-verbal pop musician, hasn't voiced a preference for anything but a future of playing the drums and tossing his eyebrow-length hair. Only John Lennon, 24 and the one married Beatle, has shown signs of a talent outside the hot-house world of musical fadism and teenage worship: he has written a book titled *In His Own Write*—a slender, whimsical collection of anecdotes, poems and Thurber-like drawings—that is in its seventh printing here.

. . . The difficulty of getting to The Beatles at all (one London colum-nist claimed he had had less trouble interviewing De Gaulle) plus Lennon's extreme reluctance to talk to strangers (he cares, explained [Brian] Epstein, "not a fig or a damn or a button for anyone save a tight, close-guarded clique of less than a dozen") have kept him a mystery. Yet he continues to be spoken of as "the Beatle who will last," "the intellec-tual one" and "a popular hero who, like Sinatra, gained fame through teenage adulation, but can keep it through talent."

Will he last?

There is no sure answer, but an observation of the odd world The Beatles inhabit, a few hours with that "close-guarded clique" and some words from Mr. Lennon himself offer a few clues.

By the end of their recent, 32-day American tour, The Beatles had given concerts in 24 cities, grossed a record $2 million, spent two days relaxing on their first American ranch, flown back to New York via care-fully guarded chartered plane ("like," as one reporter put it, "a troop movement in wartime or a shipment of gold to Fort Knox"), been spir-ited by helicopter and car into Manhattan's Paramount Theatre, and were getting ready for their last chore before returning to London: a half-hour performance as the climax of a show benefitting United Cerebral Palsy and Retarded Infants Services, Inc.

Tickets were expensive . . . but the theatre was sold out and scream-ing, non-ticket-holding fans had forced police to set up barricades near the Paramount at nine o'clock in the morning.

Those fans—the thousands of weeping, screeching girls—surrounded the theatre completely, and wading through them was a process so slow that it was possible to interview a few on the way. Most of them seemed to be lank-haired, single-minded, under 16 and carrying homemade placards ("I Love You, Ringo," "If You Can't Marry Me, George Please Just *Look* at Me"), record jackets to be autographed or photographs of their favorite. (Feather Schwartz, ex-secretary of The Beatles fan club of America, discovered that the average Beatle fan is 13 to 17 years old, of middle-class background, white, Christian, a B-minus student, weighs 105 to 140 pounds, owns a transistor radio with an earplug attachment and has Beatle photographs plastered all over her room.) One girl paused in her effort to climb over a five-foot-high police barricade to tell me that she was "crazy wild about John" because he was "utterly fab." Another said she was "passionately in love with Ringo," and had saved $25 of her allowance to get there from Pennsylvania. Tears were streaming down her face; she had yelled herself hoarse at passing taxis, unaware that her beloved had entered the Paramount secretly, two hours before. Would she go out with Ringo if he asked her? Would she like to marry him? She looked startled. "I don't think so," she said. "I hardly know him."

When I finally reached a harried policeman, he was turning away a pretty blonde with a letter of accreditation from a high school newspaper in New Jersey. He turned away my press credentials with the same: "We got orders, lady. No press," and shoved me back into the crowd. A girl with braces on her teeth and a life-size picture of John pinned to her chest was sympathetic. "They turned away a guy who said he was from *The New York Times*," she said soothingly; "and boy was *he* mad."

Forty-five minutes and several pleadings later, a policeman let me in the stage door ("OK lady, I guess you're too persistent to be a nut") and warned me I was on my own. That left only five flights of stairs, six policemen and three private guards between me and Bess Coleman, the representative of The Beatles' New York office who was very apologetic ("I told all the policemen I saw to let you through but there are *so many*") and assured me that my interview with John Lennon was set.

Miss Coleman ushered me into a room where I was to wait and left me with its assorted occupants: a blonde girl with her hair in purple plastic curlers, four men with black suits and briefcases, a young man in corduroy pants and Beatle-length hair and a pretty matron in a cocktail dress. I walked to the window and looked down. A roar like the distant sound of an Army–Navy football game came up from the crowd five storeys below. "You better not stand there, honey," the blonde girl said kindly. "They go crazy when they see somebody, *anybody*. The police told us to stay away from the windows." The pretty matron introduced herself as a writer for a national women's magazine. She had been on most of the month-long tour, she said, but had not yet been able to interview one of The Beatles: if I got to see John, might she sit in and listen? I told her she was welcome to come if it turned out to be a public interview, but that I hoped to talk with him privately. The Beatle-haired young man—identified by the matron as Neil Aspinall, The Beatles' road manager—broke his consultation with the men in black suits and smiled. "Well, then," he said with a Liverpudlian lilt, "we're very optimistic now, aren't we?"

In the hall, while looking for reassurance and Miss Coleman, I discovered two more roomsful of waiting people, glimpsed Ed Sullivan disappearing into a third, answered a ringing pay phone ("Please tell Paul McCartney that he doesn't know me but I'm very pretty and I'll be in the first booth at the Astor drugstore after the show") and was given a paper cup filled with The Beatles' favorite drink, an equal-parts combination of warm Coca-Cola and Scotch. The Beatles, Miss Coleman assured me, were much too exhausted to see anyone before the show; would I mind waiting until afterward? She introduced me to a reed-thin, shirt-sleeved young man named Derek Taylor—head of publicity and public relations for The Beatles—sat us down in the room, now deserted by everyone but the matron, and asked Taylor to turn the other way while she changed her dress.

Eyes to the wall, Taylor explained that they were all exhausted from the long tour of one-night stands and sleeping only on the chartered plane ("In Kansas City, we stayed in a hotel; the next day the manager was offered $750 for one of The Beatles' sheets"), and that the two-day ranch vacation ("The Beatles rode and fished and stayed up all night playing poker") hadn't helped much. Though the ranch was 13,000 acres in the middle of Missouri and "surrounded by the tiniest hamlets," local disc jockeys had learned of The Beatles' presence. By midnight of the first day, all roads to the ranch were jammed and carloads of teenagers had arrived from St. Louis. And, though Neil Aspinall had learned by experience how to move The Beatles ("The plane stops at the end of the runway; we use special cars and drivers to bash up to hotel and theatre entrances, sometimes we use tunnels. . . . There's really no precedent for this sort of thing"), Ringo had had his shirt torn off, and Brian Epstein was once nearly pushed in front of an oncoming train.

. . . It was time for The Beatles' performance. Everyone crowded into the hall, looking expectantly at the room in which The Beatles had been "incommunicado" and "resting," the same room into which I had seen Ed Sullivan disappear. Paul McCartney came out first, looking soft-faced and vulnerable as a choirboy. George Harrison and Ringo Starr followed animated and laughing. John Lennon moved quickly behind them, but his face was stoic and aloof behind his dark glasses (the face that inspired a London journalist to write, "It has the fear-neither-God-nor-man quality of a Renaissance painter's aristocrat"). Behind Lennon came three chic young girls, two brunettes and a blonde, in their late teens or early twenties. McCartney jerked his head toward them as he got in the elevator and told some of his staff members to "look after the birds now, won't ya."

I turned to Derek Taylor, about to comment that—what with Ed Sullivan and these three—The Beatles hadn't been so incommunicado after all, but Taylor was already looking harassed and apologetic. "Look," he said. "You've got to be patient with them. If you just come to the party they're having afterwards at the hotel, I'm sure John will talk to you." We were challenged by a policeman but Taylor showed a lapel pass and we got to the elevator. "You'll be more sure of getting to The Beatles," he said helpfully, "if you stick with the birds."

The Beatles' entourage crowded together in the wings, and I talked to the birds. Were they working for The Beatles or interviewing them? No, they were just friends. "We met The Beatles at a press conference in Philadelphia," said the pretty blonde, "that's where we're from." Two of them wore wool suits with short culotte skirts. They all looked as if they had stepped from the pages of a teenage fashion magazine, and one carried a comb and hairbrush which she used frequently and passed around to the others. "Well, two of us had met them," corrected the friendly blonde, "and this time we brought along a friend."

Out in the dark, crowded theatre, we stood by the apron of the stage and watched the show: sobs, shouts and piercing screams ("I'm over here, Ringo. *Please!*") drowned out all but an occasional drumbeat. Girls were hanging precariously from the two large balconies and standing on the arms of their chairs. Behind me, a woman held her six-year-old on her shoulders and four girls with linked arms were jumping up and down in time to the music and crying.

Taylor stood next to me and tapped my arm just before each chorus of screams reached a crescendo. "You can always tell," he explained calmly. "It happens just after one of them tosses his hair or lifts his guitar." What about the strange, firecracker bursts of light? Was that part of the lighting effect? "No," he smiled. "It's the flashes from everyone taking pictures." Three overweight, poorly dressed girls were sobbing and calling out as they pressed against us, and a fourth girl with an exceedingly large nose was waving a banner that said, "Georgie, You Are My Dream." "Sometimes," said Taylor, "when we pick a few girls to come in and get autographs, we pick pretty ones like those." He nodded at the birds who were watching the stage with secret smiles. "But I usually try to pick the ones with braces on their teeth and acne. Meeting a Beatle helps. And they can impress their friends."

Ringo tossed his hair, and a fresh wave of screams went up. Paul smiled and looked endearing. John lifted his guitar, setting off more screams, but he sang without smiling ("That's because," fellow Liverpudlian Neil Aspinall had once explained to a reporter, "he's giving you his soul when he sings"). The crush was so great that our arms were pinned to our sides, but a path suddenly cleared as if by magic, and the slim, elegant figure of Brian Epstein—the 30-year-old mastermind behind The Beatles' success—strode to the end of it, leaving a lingering trail of shaving scent. The girl with the banner had been pushed out of the way. "I don't *like* Englishmen," she said, and resumed her screaming. The three birds, who never screamed, looked at her with curiosity. One began idly to brush her hair with her eyes glued to the stage. "How do you like The Beatles?" the blonde shouted into my ear. "Fine," I said. "Just fine."

The Beatles were leaving for London early the next morning. That, plus the fact that several Manhattan hotels had turned them down, brought them to the Riviera Motor Inn at Kennedy Airport. The rooms were small, barely big enough for a bureau, twin beds and a television set but they had commandeered a whole floor and there were policemen guarding the halls. Our room was jammed with carts of Scotch and Coca-Cola, trays of sandwiches and two photographers, the young ladies from Philadelphia, a tall girl who had followed The Beatles from San Francisco, several journalists who had been on the Beatle tour, a pretty airline stewardess in a very lowcut dress who was acting as hostess, and, occasionally, Neil Aspinall and Derek Taylor. Two of The Beatles were in other rooms, but Ringo Starr and Lennon were in the one adjoining us with the door locked. It was opened only to admit Aspinall, Taylor, one or two other selected young men and liquor.

At three o'clock, I had still not seen a Beatle, but I had spent two hours interviewing the entourage, who told me some facts of Lennon's life. . . . Everyone agreed on one thing: Lennon was certainly the most talented in diverse ways, and therefore the most likely to succeed creatively even after the Beatle craze was over. As Epstein had written in his autobiography, "Had there been no Beatles and no Epstein participation, John would have emerged from the mass of population as a man to reckon with." "He's untutored," said Taylor, "but he's a natural writer. He loves the sound of words. He's an original."

The door to the next room opened and Taylor, who seemed to remember everybody else's problems in spite of his own exhaustion ("I'm worried about him," confided the matron, "he's slept hardly at all for five days"), ushered me in and introduced me. It was 4 A.M. and the small group—Lennon, Ringo, American folk singer Bob Dylan, Dylan's manager, the tall girl from San Francisco, photographer Bob Freeman who designed the titles of The Beatles' movies and Lennon's book, and an unidentified, bearded journalist—were in the combined grip of fatigue and a crisis involving Brian Epstein. Taylor, it seemed, had told The Beatles that Epstein had refused to let the three birds ride in his limousine, and Epstein was furious at Taylor.

Lennon received me calmly ("Oh, I know about that article") and went on giving desultory advice to Taylor on the care and handling of Epstein. ("He's all right, but he doesn't understand people having a few laughs, not even me laughs with me wife.") The conversation dwindled into silence. Would Lennon come with me for an interview? "Oh, well now, I don't have anything to say. My friends and those other articles will tell you all." The voice was musical, but the face behind the sunglasses was impervious.

Wouldn't he like to set the record straight, to check the information I already had? "No, I don't think so." Silence. The tall girl leaned over to Lennon and told him that his skin was looking mottled again. "I know," he said and looked embarrassed. "It's nerves."

The phone rang several times and no one answered. I picked it up. A Princess Mary somebody-or-other was calling from a phone booth. Could she please speak to a Beatle? I asked Lennon if he would like to speak to the Princess. "No," he said. I hung up.

Taylor came back from a conference with Aspinall about whether or not he should leave his post as publicity chief and go back to being a newspaperman ("The Beatles are fine," said Taylor, "but their life is unbearable") and asked Lennon if there wasn't something he could do about Paul who had barricaded his door and gone to bed without saying goodbye to his friend from Philly. "She's rather upset," Taylor explained. "After all, Paul did make a big thing of her and now he won't even say goodbye." "Look," Lennon said patiently, "Paul is Paul and nothing's going to change him." Ringo, in a purple silk shirt with white polka dots, shifted his weight mournfully. "Always worrying about people," he said.

The phone rang again. The Princess, now at her home phone and reduced to saying that she was a friend of The Animals, hoped very much she could speak with The Beatles and invite them to an island hotel. "No," said Lennon, "hang up." "Don't answer the phone," counselled the bearded journalist. "You can't answer all the calls around here, you'd go crazy."

Wouldn't Lennon answer any interview questions at all? "I don't think so," he said and addressed the journalist. "You ought to get out of your hotel room, see a little more of our country, beautiful monuments and all that. See the Statue of Liberace." It was a good imitation of an interview, and we all laughed. "Statue of Liberace is good," said Bob Freeman. "Is that the first time you've used that?"

At that point, Lennon was staring into his drink. Ringo observed meditatively that he didn't see why policemen had to stand right in front of the door, and that in one hotel, the police had stolen souvenirs from their rooms. More silence. It was 5 A.M.

I told Lennon that I understood how tired he must be of answering questions, and began to say goodbye. He looked surprised. Aspinall came back, explaining comfortingly to Taylor that Brian Epstein had once slapped him, but that was just one of the manager's moods that had to be understood. . . . "Listen," said Freeman kindly, nodding towards me, "she's all right. She's a friend of friends." The effect on Lennon was as magical as an OK from the Mafia. He smiled for the first time, and told me not to leave. "But she's the press," Ringo muttered skeptically. "You see," said Taylor reasonably, "they've been exploited so much that it's hard for them to trust anyone."

Would Lennon like to write another book?

"I would, but you can't plan it. I just put things down and stuff them in my pockets until I have enough."

Had he been influenced by the authors he was compared to?

"I mean to read Joyce but I never have. I got a laugh from all those intellectuals saying I was like him. I've read some Thurber stories though. And *Alice in Wonderland*."

We checked a few biographical details and discussed their second movie, which they plan to begin in February. ("I wouldn't write the script for it. I wouldn't know how.") He now lives just outside London with his wife and infant son. He owns a Rolls-Royce. (How does it feel? "Great!") He likes America and doesn't like New Zealand. He loves the Crazy Gang kind of comedy, and he adores Peter Sellers. (It's true that he improvised some of the first film's dialogue, including the interchange between an Old School Britisher and a Beatle. Britisher: "I fought the war for your sort." Beatle: "And aren't you sorry now.") He has no plans to retire while the money is coming in, unless the life should become unbearable. What about reports that, since the Establishment has accepted them, British teenagers have gone on to other groups? "That's all the same. We'll just be us." He is enthusiastic about rival groups. The Rolling Stones and The Animals. How much money has he made? "A lot." Has success changed him? "Yes, it's made me richer." Does he aspire to change socially? "No, I'm from Liverpool."

Would he like to be a writer?

"I don't know. I guess so. I write what I think of, when I think of it."

Was he surprised by his good reviews?

"Yes, I love those hellishly intellectual things they say, but I'd keep on writing whether they said them or not."

What will he do when there are no more Beatles?

"That's the question everybody asks us, but I'll tell you this. I know this thing can't last. I'm saving the money. And I've got a lot of things I want to do."

I thanked Taylor who, having made the decision to quit the life of The Beatles and become a newspaperman again, looked relieved and, for the first time, cheerful.

I thanked Lennon, who looked worried, and said, "I hope you're as true as you seem."

I said goodbye to the three birds who still sat in the adjoining room. Two were stretched out on the bed and a third was applying eye shadow. ("Women," Lennon had once told a reporter, "should be obscene and not heard.") They smiled their Mona Lisa smiles.

A fat policeman, yawning and red-eyed, said goodbye to me.

Outside it was dawn, but four girls were sitting patiently on the curbstone. Had I seen The Beatles, had I touched them? I said yes. A girl in an outgrown raincoat stretched out a Beatle photograph. "Here," she said. "Sign this for me."

Larry Kane

■

It was 1964 and the Beatles were doing thirty-two shows in twenty-five cities in thirty-one days. It was the first major rock-and-roll concert tour in the history of popular music, and Larry Kane was the only American journalist who would travel on both the 1964 and 1965 Beatles' North American tours. At the time, Kane was news director of WFUN radio in Miami. Like most journalists of the day, he thought the Beatles were nothing more than a fad—an extremely popular fad, admittedly—and that, like all fads, they would quickly disappear. Things got off to a rocky start—Lennon was particularly prickly toward Kane—but slowly the four young men began to open up and reveal themselves as ordinary human beings living under extraordinary circumstances.

During a concert at Philadelphia's Convention Hall, Kane surveyed the crowd of screaming youngsters more closely. What was going on offstage was just as interesting as what was happening onstage. Perhaps more so. In reality, it could have been any stop on the Beatles' tour. The same scene was repeated over and over again wherever they performed. The kids, he concluded, were "on a natural high, in an altered state of focused obsession."[1] How significant were the Beatles to those teenagers who experienced these now historic concerts? Apparently, more than one can imagine. Or, as one teenager said about seeing the Beatles at the Baltimore Civic Center on September 13, 1964, "Other than the birth of my children, it was the single most important highlight of my life."

"A Stranger in the Bedroom"

from *Ticket to Ride:*
Inside the Beatles' 1964 Tour
That Changed the World

■ THE BIRTHPLACE OF AMERICAN liberty, Philadelphia, was having a bad summer. Riots had broken out in North Philadelphia—a devastating example of the racial divide that was tearing through America. With the Beatles and their fans arriving, Philadelphia's tough and brassy police department wasn't taking any chances. Neither was Brian Epstein.

The increased caution began before we even arrived in the city.

The Beatles used a surprising ruse to get them out of their Atlantic City hotel: a fish truck. It worked well. The truck carried them about five miles east of Atlantic City, where they joined the bus caravan away from the shore and into the City of Brotherly Love. Looking out the bus windows, I saw the famed Philadelphia Highway Patrol, an elite force of motorcycle cops, protecting us at the front, rear and both sides, giving us presidential-level security in a city just torched by violence.

Strangely, we did not drive toward the center of the city. Instead, the roar of the motorcycles came to an end in an underground garage at the Philadelphia Convention Center, where the concert was scheduled for later that night. Oddly, the garage was empty. Imagine—the Philadelphia police department had reserved an entire municipal garage for the safety of the Beatles. While the cleanup from the riots was still underway, the city government wanted to give the Beatles a fab experience in Philly. But they didn't yet know that this experience would last only five hours. Once again, as he had in Vancouver, Epstein had cancelled the group's reservations at the exclusive Warwick Hotel in Center City Philadelphia. It would be a night of rock-and-roll—rock at the concert, and roll down the runway and up into the air toward Indianapolis.

As the Beatles settled into a small dressing room, I worried about a dark cloud that was suddenly and strangely hanging over the tour. Psychic Jeane Dixon had forecast the week before that the Beatles' plane would crash on the flight out of Philadelphia. Lennon had asked me about it. With a frown and a shrug, I said, "Are you kidding?" John joked about the fearful forecast but told me quietly that he obsessed about the fatal flight of Buddy Holly.

Like a virus, the fright spread throughout the traveling party, even prompting George to make a phone call to Dixon. Everyone wanted to know, "What did she say?" George said she was "reassuring," saying that it was okay to fly.

Dixon was a newsmaker—she had forecast the death of JFK—and her alleged vision was making all the gossip columns. I normally wouldn't have introduced the subject of her dire prediction to the Beatles, but since it was already on everybody's minds, I went ahead and asked George to comment.

KANE: George, we've been hearing things, and reading about this woman who's predicting a plane disaster.

HARRISON: Uh, normally I just take it with a laugh and a smile and a pinch of salt. Thinking, you know, she's off her head. But, y'know, it's not a nice thing to say, especially when you're flying almost every day. But, just hope for the best, and keep a stiff upper head, and away we go. If you crash, you crash. When your number's up, that's it.

I instantly felt sleazy asking the question during down time in the garage in Philadelphia. In doing so, I raised his anxiety level, not to mention mine. This was the first time I had asked the wrong question at the wrong time. I felt dirty. George handled it well, but it wasn't my best moment.

It was time to clean up my act, as well as my travel-weary body. Art Schreiber joined me for a fast cab ride to the Warwick Hotel, where we freshened up in the rooms we had paid for but would barely use. In the cab, I had gotten my first glimpse of Philadelphia, unaware that in a few years I would begin a long career there. The city was greener than any city I'd ever seen. And hotter. What I would later remember about the concert at the Philadelphia Convention Hall was the heat, the overwhelming security and the spirit of the fans.

Thirteen thousand crazed Philadelphians packed the hall, some in balconies, most on the floor. And the hall was ornate. As I looked around, I recalled that this was the same convention hall where both Democratic and Republican parties gathered in conventions in 1948, nominating President Harry Truman and Republican challenger Thomas Dewey. The place was truly historical. Within an hour, it would become hysterical.

Hy Lit, a popular local deejay, was getting ready to introduce the band from the stage when I noticed some girls in the first few rows taking off their jewelry. When the Beatles arrived on stage, a new flying token of adoration also arrived: jewelry of all sorts, including bracelets, necklaces and—don't forget Ringo—lots of rings. The gems were accompanied by jellybeans, of course, which the Beatles eventually stomped on, primarily for safety reasons since the heat and dripping perspiration was already causing a slippery stage. The main arena was so hot, in fact, that I was beginning to feel sick to my stomach.

Moving quickly to the side corridor, I watched Philadelphia's police hauling away unruly fans. The kids were not cooperating, and neither were some parents. As one brave policeman hauled away her child, a mother screamed in anguish, "Get your goddamned hands off my kid, you punk." The cop, by this point blushing red from his inability to contain this little Dennis the Menace, dropped the child to the floor and said, "He's yours!" The policeman looked at me with a sympathetic glare and, realizing from my tape recorder that I was a newsman, sighed, "This is tough."

That episode mirrored a difficult situation that I experienced in all the venues. Police officers, aware of their responsibilities but wary of manhandling fun-loving children, were severely conflicted. It was a game of dare, and while the police protected the Beatles, it was almost impossible for them to protect themselves from the onrushing crowds, or to protect the crowds from themselves.

Veteran *Philadelphia Daily News* reporter Rose DeWolf was covering the story. Rose remembers: "If those guys were singing songs, I didn't know it. The screaming was endless, but the kids were cute and so were the Beatles. I was in the front row with other reporters, and minutes after the concert got underway, started pulling jellybeans and marshmallows from my hair. The marshmallows had messages written on them to the Beatles. Believe me, the real show wasn't just the Beatles. The show was the kids in the audience!"

During that show, I also found that the conduct and behavior of the fans was getting more of my attention than the music. Moving back from the corridor into the main hall, I surveyed the situation: Girls and some boys close together, standing, screaming, moaning, groaning, ripping at their hair, pushing, shoving, falling on the floor and crying, real tears streaming down hundreds of faces, smearing their mascara and lipstick, and mothers and fathers hiding in the back, some of them dancing to the music.

For the first time, I started wondering whether these kids were in a state of trance. What was making them go? Was this part of a bigger picture? Was there no love in their lives, or were they just "'tweeners" trapped in a time warp, caught between fantasy and reality, stuck between puberty and adulthood?

When Paul sang "I Saw Her Standing There," a girl would look at the stage and stare at Paul, her eyes fixed, no blinking, in order to make it appear that he was singing to her: "I saw YOU standing there."

Tina Camma, a Philadelphia teenager on that night, remembers:

"I became a huge Beatles fan on the night when I first watched them on the *Ed Sullivan Show* in 1964. Imagine my surprise when my aunt and uncle asked me if I would like to see the Beatles in person at their first Philadelphia concert. I couldn't say 'yes' fast enough. My uncle purchased three tickets for my cousin Nancy, her cousin Diane and me. At that time, the ticket price was $5.50, but my uncle paid a scalper the hefty sum of $35.00 per ticket. To this day, I have saved my ticket stub (Center Orchestra F-Q-seat 1)!

"My heart was pounding as we approached the entrance thinking that I was *really* going to see the Beatles, and especially Paul, my favorite. You could feel the electricity in the air.

"After what seemed an eternity, the Beatles were finally introduced, and they were right in front of me. The first song they sang was 'If I Fell.' I was sure that Paul was singing directly to me! Of course, you couldn't hear a word they sang since there was so much screaming by excited fans—including myself! Everyone stood on their chairs for the *entire* concert. At the conclusion of the concert, I had no voice.

"It was a night I will never forget!"

Tina Camma believed, like so many others at every show, that Paul was singing to her. To this reporter, the connection between fan and Beatle was an extraordinary phenomenon, a special link that traveled beyond idolatry and entered the world of one-to-one personal chemistry and communion. Unfortunately for those thousands of girls, the relationship between them and their favorite Beatle was always a one-way street.

Still, the mixture of the music and the musicians and the reaction to both was amazing. The experts can spend decades figuring that puzzle out, but there's one thing I know for sure—there were no hallucinatory drugs on those premises to cause this phenomenon. It was a little early in the sixties for that. Those kids were simply on a natural high, in an altered state of focused obsession.

Another obsession—that nasty forecast of an aircraft calamity—remained on our minds as we took a long post-concert bus ride to the North Philadelphia airport, the smaller of the city's two airstrips. As Beatles and company boarded the plane, the atmosphere was markedly different from that on previous flights. Neil Aspinall, the Beatles' protector and friend, and a typically serious man, was even more intense than usual. Lennon looked perturbed. Even Clarence Frogman Henry, a cheerful man who had taken the place of the Righteous Brothers as one of the opening acts, looked dour.

The flight to Indianapolis was subdued, but thankfully it was also short and uneventful. Art Schreiber, master journalist and Washington correspondent during the JFK assassination in November 1963, took it in stride, leaning over and saying to me, "Well, if shit happens, the headline will read, 'Beatles perish in crash along with unidentified reporters.' We'll just be a damn footnote to history." Art made me laugh, along with John Lennon. Traveling down the aisle later, John broke out a big smile and said, "So how are the nameless, faceless, unidentified new whores doing tonight?"

Uninfluenced by our anxiety, the Electra had a smooth-as-silk landing in Indianapolis. This airline's date with disaster would have to wait another two years. As far as Jeane Dixon goes, she gained world fame as official astrologer and psychic to First Lady Nancy Reagan in the eighties. Who knows how much she, like the Beatles, shaped history, but on that night of September 2, 1964, she was dead wrong. And that was a very good thing.

Note

1. American humorist Jean Shepherd made similar observations in *Playboy*, commenting on their unprecedented popularity: "In two years they had become a phenomenon that had somehow transcended stardom—or even showbiz. They were mythical beings, inspiring a fanaticism bordering on religious ecstasy among millions all over the world. I began to have the uncomfortable feeling," he concludes, "that all this fervor had nothing whatsoever to do with entertainment, or with talent, or even with the Beatles themselves. I began to feel that they were the catalyst of a sudden world madness that would have burst upon us whether they had come on the scene or not." Despite the carnival atmosphere, Shepherd is impressed that they manage "somehow to remain remarkably human, totally unlike the Kewpies created by fandom and the press." Or, as Louis Menand once wrote, "[T]hey were the only people around who did not think that the supreme joy of human life was to touch a Beatle. They become one another's reality check." Louis Menand, "When They Were Fab," *The New Yorker*, October 16 and 23, 2000.

FOUR

The Middle Years:
A Day in the Life
1965–1967

Greil Marcus

■

Some moments stand out in our collective memory. Many of us will always remember where we were when we heard that JFK was assassinated or Neil Armstrong took the first steps on the moon. In musical history, one of those moments must be the first time the Beatles appeared on *The Ed Sullivan Show* in February 1964. After that night, everything changed.

At the time, Greil Marcus was a college student in California. Bored by the music coming from the radio, he was blown away by these four young men from Liverpool with the unusual hair who had the nerve to sing in their native English accents ("I didn't know they had rock & roll in England," Marcus writes).

In this piece, Marcus describes the impact of the Beatles' appearance as a "pop explosion," that is, "an irresistible cultural upheaval that cuts across lines of class and race." The Beatles were all things to all people. They affected our quality of life, deepening it, sharpening it. The release of *Sgt. Pepper's Lonely Hearts Club Band* in 1967 was the apotheosis of the Beatles as a worldwide cultural phenomenon. And then, three years later, it was all over.

"Another Version of the Chair"

from *The Rolling Stone Illustrated History of Rock and Roll*

■ ON FEBRUARY 9TH, 1964, I was in college in California, a rock & roll fan with creeping amnesia. I remembered Chuck Berry but not the guitar solo in "Johnny B. Goode." The excitement, the sense of being caught up in something much bigger than one's own private taste, had disappeared from rock years before. There was still good stuff on the radio—there had been "Heat Wave" by a group called Martha and the Vandellas the summer before, "Be True to Your School" by the Beach Boys a few months after that, and even "On Broadway" by the Drifters—but in 1963 all of it seemed drowned out by Jimmy Gilmer's "Sugar Shack," the Number One song of the year and perhaps the worst excuse for itself rock & roll had yet produced. Rock & roll—the radio—felt dull and stupid, a dead end.

There had been an item in the paper that day about a British rock & roll group that was to appear on *The Ed Sullivan Show* that night: "The Beatles" (a photo too—were those wigs, or what?). I was curious—I didn't know they had rock & roll in England—so I went down to a commons room where there was a TV set, expecting an argument from whoever was there about which channel to watch.

Four hundred people sat transfixed as the Beatles sang "I Want to Hold Your Hand," and when the song was over the crowd exploded. People looked at the faces (and the hair) of John, Paul, George and Ringo and said Yes (and who could have predicted that a few extra inches of hair would suddenly seem so right, so necessary? Brian Epstein?); they heard the Beatles' sound and said Yes to that too. What was going on? And where had all those people come from?

Back at the radio I caught "I Saw Her Standing There" and was instantly convinced it was the most exciting rock & roll I'd ever heard (with Paul's one-two-three-*fuck!* opening—how in the world did they expect to get away with that?). Someone from down the hall appeared with a copy of the actual record—you could just go out and *buy* this stuff?—and announced with great fake solemnity that it was the first 45 he'd purchased since "All Shook Up." Someone else—who played a twelve-string guitar and as far as I knew listened to nothing but Odetta—began to muse that "even as a generation had been brought together by the Five Satins' 'In the Still of the Nite,' it could be that it would be brought together again—by the Beatles." He really talked like that; what was more amazing, he talked like that when a few hours before he had never heard of the Beatles.

The next weeks went by in a blur. People began to grow their hair (one acquaintance argued with great vehemence that it was physically impossible for male hair—at least, *normal* male hair—to grow to Beatle length); some affected British (or, when they could pull it off, Liverpool) accents. A friend got his hands on a British Beatles album unavailable in the United States and made a considerable amount of money charging people for the chance to hear John Lennon sing "Money (That's What I Want)" at two bucks a shot. Excitement wasn't in the air; it *was* the air.

A few days after that first performance on the Sullivan show I spent the evening with some friends in a cafe in my hometown. It was, or anyway had been, a folk club. This night one heard only *Meet the Beatles*. The music, snaking through the dark, suddenly spooky room, was instantly recognizable and like nothing we had ever heard. It was joyous, threatening, absurd, arrogant, determined, innocent and tough, and it drew the line of which Dylan was to speak: "This was something that never happened before."

It was, as Lester Bangs says in his survey of the British Invasion, not simply a matter of music, but of event. Dylan had heard the Beatles in New York before his Colorado revelation; I had first heard them on the radio in early 1963, when "Please Please Me" was released in the United States, liked the record, disliked the followup, then forgot the group altogether. It was only in the context of the Beatles' event that their music was perceived for what it was.

The event was a pop explosion; the second, and thus far the last, that rock & roll has produced.

A pop explosion is an irresistible cultural upheaval that cuts across lines of class and race (in terms of sources, if not allegiance), and, most crucially, divides society itself by age. The surface of daily life (walk, talk, dress, symbolism, heroes, family affairs) is affected with such force that deep and substantive changes in the way large numbers of people think and act take place. Pop explosions must link up with, and accelerate, broad shifts in sexual behavior, economic aspirations and political beliefs; a pervasive sense of chaos, such as that which hit England in 1963 with the Profumo scandal, and the United States in the mid-Sixties with the civil rights movement, the Kennedy assassination, and later the Vietnam War, doesn't hurt.

Now, it has been argued, by British critic George Melly, that a pop explosion merely "turns revolt into a style" (poet Thom Gunn's line on Elvis, originally), but in fact pop explosions can provide the enthusiasm, the optimism and the group identity that make mass political participation possible. A pop explosion is more than a change in style even if it is far less than a revolution, though it can look like either one—depending on who is looking, and when. (Not that "changing the world" in the political sense of the term is never a "goal" of a pop explosion, if such an event can be said to have a goal beyond good times; still, a pop explosion changes the world by affecting the moment, which means that the world retains the capacity to change back, momentarily.)

Enormous energy—the energy of frustration, desire, repression, adolescence, sex, ambition—finds an object in a pop explosion, and that energy is focused on, organized by and released by a single, holistic cultural entity. This entity must itself be capable of easy, instantaneous and varied imitation and extension, in a thousand ways at once; it must embody, suggest, affirm and legitimize new possibilities on all fronts even as it outstrips them. This is a fancy way of saying that the capacity for fad must be utterly profound.

And, at its heart, a pop explosion attaches the individual to a group—the fan to an audience, the solitary to a generation—in essence, *forms* a group and creates new loyalties—while at the same time it increases one's ability to respond to a particular pop artifact, or a thousand of them, with an intensity that verges on lunacy. Ringo's shout of "All right, George!" just before the guitar break in "Boys" becomes a matter of indefinable and indefensible significance; styles on Carnaby Street outdo the pace of the pop charts and change literally by the hour. Yet within it all is some principle of shape, of continuity, of value.

This principle was the Beatles. As was so often pointed out in the mid-Sixties, the sum of the Beatles was greater than the parts, but the parts were so distinctive and attractive that the group itself could be all things to all people, more or less. You did not have to love them all to love the group, and this was why the Beatles became bigger than Elvis; this was what had never happened before. And so it began. The past was felt to dissolve, the future was conceivable only as an expansion of the present, and the present was defined absolutely by its expansive novelty. Towering above Bob Dylan, the Rolling Stones, a score of British groups, American groups, Mary Quant, the Who, whatever and whoever sprung up day by day, the Beatles seemed not only to symbolize but to contain it all—to make history by anticipating it.

The first pop explosion, beginning in 1955 and 1956, began to yield to normalcy by about 1957. The Beatles' event, beyond all expectations save perhaps their own, intensified not only in momentum but in magnetism; reaching more and more people with greater and greater mythic and emotional power, for at least four years. The Beatles affected not only the feel but the quality of life: They deepened it, sharpened it, brightened it, not merely as a factor in the cultural scheme, but as a presence.

Their event reached its height, and in many ways its effective end, with the release of *Sgt. Pepper* on June 2nd, 1967. For months rumors had swept the pop world that the Beatles were engaged in a historic project that would sum up, and transcend, all that had been accomplished in the previous four years. In February a single, "Penny Lane" b/w "Strawberry Fields Forever," was released (if this extraordinary music was merely a taste of what the Beatles were up to, what would the album be like?) and then, in the spring, tapes leaked out. A strange, maddening song called "A Day in the Life Of" was played on the radio and quickly withdrawn. Tension and speculation grew. It was said (correctly) that the new LP had taken 700 hours to record, as opposed to twelve hours for the Beatles first; that it included astonishingly experimental techniques, huge orchestras, hundred-voice choirs. Stories began to appear not only in the pop press but in the daily papers. The record, unheard, was everywhere.

Then the announcement was made. The record would be released for airplay on Sunday midnight, one week before appearing in the stores; any station putting the disc on the air even one minute before the assigned time would find all forthcoming prerelease airing privileges forever withheld. The fact that many stations habitually went off the air at Sunday midnight in order to service their transmitters, was of no consequence—or perhaps, from the perspective of Brian Epstein and the Beatles, it was a challenge. At any rate, the stations stayed on. They played the record all night and all the next day, vying to see which station could play it the longest, putting in calls to John and Paul in London that never went through, tracking every last second of the endless final chord of "A Day in the Life" (no "Of," as it turned out), generating an unprecedented sense of public euphoria, excitement, satisfaction and joy.

Almost immediately, *Sgt. Pepper* was certified as proof that the Beatles' music—or at least this album—was Art. But what mattered was the conscious creation of the event—the way in which the summing-up-the-spirit-of-the-times style of the music (which for the most part has not survived its time) was perfectly congruent with the organizing-the-spirit-of-the-times manner in which the album was released and received. Which is to say that *Sgt. Pepper,* as the most brilliantly orchestrated manipulation of a cultural audience in pop history, was nothing less than a small pop explosion in and of itself. The music was not great art; the event, in its intensification of the ability to respond, was.

"The closest Western Civilization has come to unity since the Congress of Vienna in 1815 was the week the *Sgt. Pepper* album was released," Langdon Winner wrote in 1968. "In every city in Europe and America the stereo systems and the radio played, 'What would you think if I sang out of tune . . . Woke up, got out of bed . . . looked much older, and the bag across her shoulder . . . in the sky with diamonds, Lucy in the . . .' and everyone listened. At the time I happened to be driving across country on Interstate 80. In each city where I stopped for gas or food—Laramie, Ogallala, Moline, South Bend—the melodies wafted in from some far-off transistor radio or portable hi-fi. It was the most amazing thing I've ever heard. For a brief while the irreparably fragmented consciousness of the West was unified, at least in the minds of the young."

And so it seemed as if the world really did turn around the Beatles, even if the truth was that this music, as opposed to this event, represented that point at which the Beatles began to be formed more by the times than the other way around. In the next few months Brian Epstein would die, and the Beatles, who had unified the young, would themselves begin to fragment—anticipating, as usual, the fragmentation that in years to come would separate the audience they had created. Still, if *Sgt. Pepper* was an ending, it was an ending that has never been matched. It was perhaps in the nature of the game that it would be all downhill from there.

Allen Ginsberg

■

There have been numerous poems written about or inspired by the Beatles. During the Beatles' 1965 concert tour of North America, Allen Ginsberg was in attendance when the band performed twice on August 22 at the Memorial Coliseum in Portland, Oregon. What he saw was repeated across both the United States and Canada—the deafening roar of the crowd, and the police lined up to shield the four musicians from overzealous fans. Here are his piquant observations, written down several days after the shows.

"Portland Coliseum"

from *Collected Poems 1947–1980*

A brown piano in diamond
   white spotlight
Leviathan auditorium
   iron rib wired
   hanging organs, vox
      black battery
A single whistling sound of
   ten thousand children's
      larynxes asinging
      pierce the ears
   and flowing up the belly
   bliss the moment arrived

Apparition, four brown English
   jacket christhair boys
Goofed Ringo battling bright
   white drums
Silent George hair patient
   Soul horse
Short black-skulled Paul
   with thin guitar
Lennon the Captain, his mouth

a triangular smile,
all jump together to End
    some tearful memory song
    ancient-two years,
    The million children
    the thousand worlds
bounce in their seats, bash
    each other's sides, press
    legs together nervous
Scream again & claphand
    become one Animal
    in the New World Auditorium
    —hands waving myriad
        snakes of thought
    screetch beyond hearing

while a line of police with
    folded arms stands
Sentry to contain the red
    sweatered ecstasy
    that rises upward to the
        wired roof.

August 27, 1965

Maureen Cleave

■

There have been many important pieces written about the Beatles over the years, but Maureen Cleave's portrait of John Lennon that originally ran in the London *Evening Standard* has to be the most incendiary.[1] At least, that was the effect it had in the United States, especially in the American South, when its contents were reprinted some five months later in the American teen magazine *Datebook* on the eve of the Beatles' American tour.

In Cleave's profile, Lennon comes across as curiously detached from the outside world as he lives an isolated existence surrounded by "wooded hills and stockbrokers" in a mock Tudor house on the outskirts of London. He watches movies and television programs, sleeps at will, and adds to a growing number of possessions. The statement on established religion that upset so many people in the United States, that indeed instigated a firestorm of controversy, is uttered matter of factly, almost as an aside ("Christianity will go. It will vanish and shrink . . . we're more popular than Jesus now"). No one, least of all Lennon, could have predicted the reaction. Radio stations across the country invited listeners to burn Beatles records. According to Beatles' biographer Philip Norman, their music was banned from thirty-five American radio stations. In addition, Spain and the Vatican denounced Lennon and South Africa banned Beatles music from the radio.

Ironically, Lennon was right on a more profound level. The Beatles, after all, *had* become a religion for millions of people around the world. On tour in Australia in 1964, press agent Derek Taylor observed the chilling vision of countless outstretched hands along the motorcade route, handicapped people throwing away their crutches at the mere sight of the boys, as if their presence could cure them of their ills. "The only thing left for the Beatles is to go on a healing tour," he told *The Saturday Evening Post*. Writes Devin McKinney in *Magic Circles: The Beatles in Dream and History*, "That the Beatles were, to many, the Christs of their time remained an open secret waiting to be announced. . . . There had been teen idols before; there had never been the Beatles."

The pressure was so bad that Lennon felt compelled to apologize at a press conference in Chicago on August 11 and again on August 12 from the Beatles' suite in the now defunct Astor Tower hotel. Noticeably shaken, he answered the reporter's questions as the cameras rolled. Here is an excerpt from the first press conference.

JOHN: If I had said television is more popular than Jesus, I might have got away with it. You know, but as I just happened to be talking to a friend, I used the word "Beatles" as a remote thing—not as what "I" think as Beatles—as those other Beatles like other people see us. I just said "they" are having more influence on kids and things than anything else, including Jesus. But I said it that way which is the wrong way. Yap yap.

Q: Some teenagers have repeated your statement—"I like the Beatles more than Jesus Christ." What do you think about that?

JOHN: Well, originally I was pointing out that fact in reference to England—that we meant more to kids than Jesus did, or religion, at that time. I wasn't knocking it or putting it down, I was just saying it as a fact. . . . I'm not saying that we're better, or greater, or comparing us with Jesus Christ as a person or God as a thing or whatever it is, you know. I just said what I said and it was wrong, or was taken wrong. And now it's all this.

Q: There have been threats against your life, there have been record burnings, you've been banned from some radio stations—Does this bother you?

JOHN: Well, it worries me.

Q: Is this an attempt to raise your flagging popularity?

JOHN: I could think of a much easier way . . .

Q: Are you sorry you said it?

JOHN: I am. Yes, you know, even though I never meant what people think I meant by it. I'm still sorry I opened my mouth.

The second press conference continued along the same theme.

Q: A disc jockey in Birmingham, Alabama, who really started most of the repercussions, has demanded an apology from you.

JOHN: He can have it, you know. I apologize to him if he's upset and he really means it, you know, I'm sorry. I'm sorry I said it for the mess it's made. But I never meant it as a lousy or anti-religious thing, or anything, you know, and I can't say anymore than that. There's nothing else to say really, you know—no more words.

PAUL: The thing is that they seem to think that by saying that, you know, John's getting at them. But he isn't at all, you know. It's just a straight comment on something, which may be right and may be wrong, but he's gotta answer as he feels honestly, you know. And if they think that for him to say that is wrong then they don't believe in free speech, you know. And I thought everyone here did.

Q: Was there as much repercussion and reaction to your statements throughout Europe and other countries of the world as there was here in America?

GEORGE: No.

The Vatican City newspaper *L'Osservatore Romano* accepted Lennon's apology the next day, on August 13. In an editorial, the paper noted, "It cannot be denied that there is some foundation to the latest observations of John Lennon about atheism or the distraction of many people. And so the matter is closed."
Here is the article that started all the ruckus.

"How Does a Beatle Live?
John Lennon Lives Like This"

London *Evening Standard*
March 4, 1966

■ IT WAS THIS time three years ago that The Beatles first grew famous. Ever since then, observers have anxiously tried to gauge whether their fame was on the wax or on the wane; they foretold the fall of the old Beatles, they searched diligently for the new Beatles (which was as pointless as looking for the new Big Ben).

At last they have given up; The Beatles' fame is beyond question. It has nothing to do with whether they are rude or polite, married or unmarried, 25 or 45; whether they appear on *Top of the Pops* or do not appear on *Top of the Pops*. They are well above any position even a Rolling Stone might jostle for. They are famous in a way the Queen is famous. When John Lennon's Rolls-Royce, with its black wheels and its black windows, goes past, people say: "It's the Queen," or "It's The Beatles." With her they share the security of a stable life at the top. They all tick over in the public esteem—she in Buckingham Palace, they in the Weybridge–Esher area. Only Paul remains in London.

The Weybridge community consists of the three married Beatles; they live there among the wooded hills and the stockbrokers. They have not worked since Christmas and their existence is secluded and curiously timeless. "What day is it?" John Lennon asks with interest when you ring up with news from outside. The fans are still at the gates but The Beatles see only each other. They are better friends than ever before.

Ringo and his wife, Maureen, may drop in on John and Cyn; John may drop in on Ringo; George and Pattie may drop in on John and Cyn and they might all go round to Ringo's, by car of course. Outdoors is for holidays.

They watch films, they play rowdy games of Buccaneer; they watch television till it goes off, often playing records at the same time. They while away the small hours of the morning making mad tapes. Bedtimes and mealtimes have no meaning as such. "We've never had time before to do anything but just be Beatles," John Lennon said.

He is much the same as he was before. He still peers down his nose, arrogant as an eagle, although contact lenses have righted the short sight that originally caused the expression. He looks more like Henry VIII than ever now that his face has filled out—he is just as imperious, just as unpredictable, indolent, disorganised, childish, vague, charming and quick-witted. He is still easy-going, still tough as hell. "You never asked after Fred Lennon," he said, disappointed. (Fred is his father; he emerged after they got famous.) "He was here a few weeks ago. It was only the second time in my life I'd seen him—I showed him the door." He went on cheerfully: "I wasn't having *him* in the house."

His enthusiasm is undiminished and he insists on its being shared. George has put him on to this Indian music. "You're not listening, are you?" he shouts after 20 minutes of the record. "It's amazing this—so cool. Don't the Indians appear cool to you? Are you listening? This music is thousands of years old; it makes me laugh, the British going over there and telling them what to do. Quite amazing." And he switched on the television set.

Experience has sown few seeds of doubt in him: not that his mind is closed, but it's closed round whatever he believes at the time. "Christianity will go," he said. "It will vanish and shrink. I needn't argue about that; I'm right and I will be proved right. We're more popular than Jesus now; I don't know which will go first—rock 'n' roll or Christianity. Jesus was all right but his disciples were thick and ordinary. It's them twisting it that ruins it for me." He is reading extensively about religion.

He shops in lightning swoops on Asprey's these days and there is some fine wine in his cellar, but he is still quite unselfconscious. He is far too lazy to keep up appearances, even if he had worked out what the appearances should be—which he has not.

He is now 25. He lives in a large, heavily panelled, heavily carpeted, mock Tudor house set on a hill with his wife Cynthia and his son Julian. There is a cat called after his aunt Mimi, and a purple dining room. Julian is three; he may be sent to the Lycée in London. "Seems the only place for him in his position," said his father, surveying him dispassionately. "I feel sorry for him, though. I couldn't stand ugly people even when I was five. Lots of the ugly ones are foreign, aren't they?"

We did a speedy tour of the house, Julian panting along behind, clutching a large porcelain Siamese cat. John swept past the objects in which he had lost interest: "That's Sidney" (a suit of armour); "That's a hobby I had for a week" (a room full of model racing cars); "Cyn won't let me get rid of that" (a fruit machine). In the sitting room are eight little green boxes with winking red lights; he bought them as Christmas presents but never got round to giving them away. They wink for a year; one imagines him sitting there till next Christmas, surrounded by the little winking boxes.

He pauses over objects he still fancies; a huge altar crucifix of a Roman Catholic nature with IHS on it; a pair of crutches, a present from George; an enormous Bible he bought in Chester; his gorilla suit.

"I thought I might need a gorilla suit," he said; he seemed sad about it. "I've only worn it twice. I thought I might pop it on in the summer and drive around in the Ferrari. We were all going to get them and drive round in them but I was the only one who did. I've been thinking about it and if I didn't wear the head it would make an amazing fur coat—with legs, you see. I would like a fur coat but I've never run into any."

One feels that his possessions—to which he adds daily—have got the upper hand; all the tape recorders, the five television sets, the cars, the telephones of which he knows not a single number. The moment he approaches a switch it fuses; six of the winking boxes, guaranteed to last till next Christmas, have gone funny already. His cars—the Rolls, the Mini-Cooper (black wheels, black windows), the Ferrari (being painted black)—puzzle him. Then there's the swimming pool, the trees sloping away beneath it. "Nothing like what I ordered," he said resignedly. He wanted the bottom to be a mirror. "It's an amazing household," he said. "None of my gadgets really work except the gorilla suit—that's the only suit that fits me."

He is very keen on books, will always ask what is good to read. He buys quantities of books and these are kept tidily in a special room. He has Swift, Tennyson, Huxley, Orwell, costly leather-bound editions of Tolstoy, Oscar Wilde. Then there's *Little Women,* all the *William* books from his childhood; and some unexpected volumes such as *Forty-One Years in India,* by Field Marshal Lord Roberts, and *Curiosities of Natural History,* by Francis T. Buckland. This last—with its chapter headings "Ear-less Cats," "Wooden-Legged People," "The Immortal Harvey's Mother"—is right up his street.

He approaches reading with a lively interest untempered by too much formal education. "I've read millions of books," he said, "that's why I seem to know things." He is obsessed by Celts. "I have decided I am a Celt," he said. "I am on Boadicea's side—all those bloody blue-eyed blondes chopping people up. I have an awful feeling wishing I was there—not there with scabs and sores but there through *reading* about it. The books don't give you more than a paragraph about how they *lived;* I have to imagine that."

He can sleep almost indefinitely, is probably the laziest person in England. "*Physically* lazy," he said. "I don't mind writing or reading or watching or speaking, but sex is the only physical thing I can be bothered with any more." Occasionally he is driven to London in the Rolls by an ex-Welsh guardsman called Anthony; Anthony has a moustache that intrigues him.

The day I visited him he had been invited to lunch in London, about which he was rather excited. "Do you know how long lunch lasts?" he asked. "I've never been to lunch before. I went to Lyons the other day and had egg and chips and a cup of tea. The waiters kept looking and saying: 'No, it *isn't* him, it *can't* be him.'"

He settled himself into the car and demonstrated the television, the folding bed, the refrigerator, the writing desk, the telephone. He has spent many fruitless hours on that telephone. "I only once got through to a person," he said, "and they were out."

Anthony had spent the weekend in Wales. John asked if they'd kept a welcome for him in the hillside and Anthony said they had. They discussed the possibility of an extension for the telephone. We had to call at the doctor's because John had a bit of sea urchin in his toe. "Don't want to be like Dorothy Dandridge," he said, "dying of a splinter 50 years later." He added reassuringly that he had washed the foot in question.

We bowled along in a costly fashion through the countryside. "Famous and loaded" is how he describes himself now. "They keep telling me I'm all right for money but then I think I may have spent it all by the time I'm 40 so I keep going. That's why I started selling my cars; then I changed my mind and got them all back and a new one too.

"I want the money just to *be* rich. The only other way of getting it is to be born rich. If you have money, that's power without having to be powerful. I often think that it's all a big conspiracy, that the winners are the Government and people like us who've got the money. That joke about keeping the workers ignorant is still true; that's what they said about the Tories and the landowners and that; then Labour were meant to educate the workers but they don't seem to be doing that any more."

He has a morbid horror of stupid people: "Famous and loaded as I am, I still have to meet soft people. If often comes into my mind that I'm not really rich. There are *really* rich people but I don't know where they are."

He finds being famous quite easy, confirming one's suspicion that The Beatles had been leading up to this all their lives. "Everybody thinks they *would* have been famous if only they'd had the Latin and that. So when it happens it comes naturally. You remember your old grannie saying soft things like: 'You'll make it with that voice.'" Not, he added, that he had any old grannies.

He got to the doctor 2¾ hours early and to lunch on time but in the wrong place. He bought a giant compendium of games for Asprey's but having opened it he could not, of course, shut it again. He wondered what else he should buy. He went to Brian Epstein's office. "Any presents?" he asked eagerly; he observed that there was nothing like getting things free. He tried on the attractive Miss Hanson's spectacles.

The rumour came through that a Beatle had been sighted walking down Oxford Street! He brightened. "One of the others must be out," he said, as though speaking of an escaped bear. "We only let them out one at a time," said the attractive Miss Hanson firmly.

He said that to live and have a laugh were the things to do; but was that enough for the restless spirit?

"Weybridge," he said, "won't do at all. I'm just stopping at it, like a bus stop. Bankers and stockbrokers live there; they can add figures and Weybridge is what they live in and they think it's the end, they really do. I think of it every day—me in my Hansel and Gretel house. I'll take my time; I'll get my *real* house when I know what I want.

"You see, there's something else I'm going to do, something I must do—only I don't know what it is. That's why I go round painting and taping and drawing and writing and that, because it may be one of them. All I know is, this isn't *it* for me."

Anthony got him and the compendium into the car and drove him home with the television flickering in the soothing darkness while the Londoners outside rushed home from work.

Note

1. Cleave, a trusted journalist within Beatles circles, wrote what Beatles historian Mark Lewisohn calls the first important piece of journalism—it ran in the London *Evening Standard* in early 1963 after the release of "Please Please Me." See Mark Lewisohn, "I Wanna Be Your Fan," in "1,000 Days of Beatlemania," *Mojo*, 2002.

William Mann

■

William Mann was the classical music writer for *The Times* (London). He also, most famously, is credited for being the first music critic from the mainstream press to write positively on the Beatles, back in late 1963. Here, a few years down the road, he again rhapsodizes about the Fab Four with the release of *Sgt. Pepper's Lonely Hearts Club Band*. "Any of these songs," he writes, "is more genuinely creative than anything currently to be heard on pop radio stations."

"The Beatles Revive Hopes of Progress in Pop Music"

The Times (London)

May 29, 1967

■ A FEW SATURDAYS ago, on *Juke Box Jury*, Paul Jones let fall a remark about the depressing state of pop music; the programme's compère, David Jacobs, countered, a trace primly, that some people considered the pop scene to be in unusually healthy condition. My sympathies at the time were firmly with Mr Jones. The quantity of nondescript songs then figuring in the hit parade was sad even when one admits that dozens of boring creations have to be sifted, in every field of art always, before something of real quality is discovered. The picture looks much more gay now that The Beatles have produced their new LP, *Sgt. Peppers' Lonely Hearts Club Band*. In fact it has not looked so cheerful since their last LP *Revolver*. After listening to *Sgt. Pepper*, I have been reflecting on what happened to pop music in the meantime, and some not unhealthy and quite interesting trends do emerge; if they are connected with these two LPs and with the excellent intervening Beatles single, "Penny Lane" and "Strawberry Fields," that is hardly to be wondered at.

Pop music in the last few months, as for the last 12 years or more, has been dominated by ballads and beat music, and not all are or have been pot-boilers. There has also been a progressive broadening or interest in genres that could appeal without necessarily dragging pop through the artistic mire: oriental sounds, folk music, creative revivals of pop classics, novelty numbers and in particular vaudeville as a style, creative raids on classical styles and idioms, and looting (not always just vulture-like) of earlier experiments by the most progressive groups. Spur-ring these varied developments is the recognition that popularity has many faces.

The younger teenagers of 1963 who fell like hungry travellers upon the Merseyside Beat are now much older and more sophisticated, and more experienced in adult ways. Pop music still has to cater for them and for the distinctive characteristics they have by now assumed. Mod, rocker, intellectual, rebel, permissive, careerist, all get comfort or inspi-ration from different music, and The Beatles have held their supremacy because they can dip into all these inkwells with equally eloquent re-sults. There is still a faithful pop following among the generations who cut their teeth on Tommy Steele, Alma Cogan, Vera Lynn, Bing Crosby and George Formby, to go no farther back. And since 1963 a new generation of young people has arrived, demanding (or maybe only enthusiastically accepting) the pop music appropriate to its own age.

One can imagine a new pop group deciding cold-bloodedly to con-centrate commercially on appealing to one of these age-groups. The creators of The Monkees do not deny having done so and even virtuoso pop musicians are galled by the success of a group that was brought, Frankenstein-fashion, into being without reference to musical talents. Their songs are carefully modelled on early Beatle style uncreatively but skilfully manipulated. Their first single, "Last train to Clarksville," flopped in Britain at first but zoomed up the charts as soon as The Mon-kees began to appear in weekly short films on television (the manner of presentation heavily indebted to *A Hard Day's Night*). Just now The Monkees are idols of the pre-teenage generation and are not quite de-spised by those approaching O-levels. This has been their year, in the absence of anything more remarkable, and the showmanship involved has to be admired, if not the musical artistry. I suspect that their songs were written by a computer fed with the first two Beatle LPs and *The Oxford Book of Nursery Rhymes*.

It has also been a period of nursery lyrics. The Lennon–McCartney "Yellow submarine" set the ball rolling and of late we have had no end of songs whose words bring out the delayed adolescence in all of us: The Alan Price Set's "Simon Smith and his dancing bear," Manfred Mann's "Ha-ha said the clown," Sandie Shaw's "Puppet on a string" (which alarmingly, though to the delight of unmusical patriots, won the Euro-vision Song Contest), The Hollies' "Lullaby for Tim," Dave Clark's

"Tabitha Twitchit." All these encourage separatists in their belief that pop music is strictly for the pre-adolescent—not to mention [David Bowie's] heavy-handedly facetious number about a laughing gnome which was ecstatically plugged for several weeks by the pirate stations but steadfastly remained the flop it deserved to be.

The words of songs are as important as the music: Monteverdi, Schumann, Wolf, Britten have all accepted this belief to their advantage, and pop music has benefited whenever composers have done likewise. The Moon–June syndrome is nowadays frowned on. There were skilful, imaginative lyrics in the 1930s (think of Ira Gershwin and, earlier, of "St James's Infirmary Blues"). But the importance of the lyric in modern pop songs owes more to Bob Dylan than to anybody. Dylan was part of the protest folksong movement, and though nowadays this is in abeyance and Dylan a sick man slowly on the mend, with only a very pop number about a leopardskin hat to keep his laurels green, his influence on the content of pop lyrics is still strong: think of The Bee Gees' "New York mining disaster 1941" (music essentially early Beatles), and The Animals "When I was young," and Cat Stevens's "Matthew and son" of a while back. Social comment is helpful to a pop song, and some of these have deservedly done well in the charts. The sneering lazy Dylan voice, and the folksong ballad type of tune he favours, are still much copied. Folksong is very much a part of pop, as is testified by the success of The Dubliners' "Seven drunken nights" (a favourite Irish closing-time number) and, on a slightly different wavelength, the Russian-derived "OK" of Dave Dee, Dozy, Beaky, Mick and Tich.

Folksong as an ingredient of pop is an exhumation of the past (paralleled in straight music by the new popularity among concertgoers of preclassical music, and in art by the resurgence of *Art nouveau*), and in the past 12 months there has been an even more prevalent revival of the 1920s vaudeville number. "Winchester Cathedral," by the New Vaudeville Band, set it going last September. Since then we have had "Peek-a-boo" and "Finchley Central," and The Kinks, who had already moved into the contemporary satire sphere, have lately jumped into vaudeville with their very likable "Waterloo sunset" (part of a place-names cult, connected with "Penny Lane," perhaps with "A nightingale sang in Berkeley Square" and even "Let's all go down the Strand" or "Basin Street Blues").

The idea of reviving vaudeville is rather artificial, not to say escapist, but it accords with a certain camp trend in fashions and in decorative art. It may be thought by some people no more odd than the revitalised honky-tonk and boogie-woogie of some Rolling Stones numbers in their recent turncoat LP, *Between the Buttons* (which includes one ultra-camp song, "A strange thing happened to me yesterday"). And there is the rare but often appealing grope back to classical or baroque musical language, as in the Alberti string figuration of The Beatles' "Eleanor Rigby" (another song with a powerful lyric) and the new, distinctly Bach-derived "Whiter shade of pale" by Procol Harum (whose name is supposedly Latin, even if it should be "procul") which has its pop parentage in some Animals numbers and is very beautiful indeed. There is the growing allure of oriental, at present chiefly Indian, music initiated by George Harrison of The Beatles, taken up by The Rolling Stones and nowadays quite common as an accompanying texture (like the revival of the harpsichord a few years ago). From The Beatles also came the current preoccupation with more or less disciplined whorls of electronically manipulated clusters of sound, famous through "Tomorrow never knows" but audible on all sides, and adopted in concerts by several groups spectacularly as well as audibly. In some records by The Righteous Brothers and The Walker Brothers, and in some of Jimi Hendrix's songs, it is just an all-too-generalised effect. But in "Strawberry Fields," and The Stones' "Paint it black," it was poetically and precisely applied. The vogue word for this is psychedelic music.

There remain the beat-songs and ballads. Beat music has, by natural evolution, become more varied and occasionally more subtle than it used to be. It is no longer fettered to unchanging two or four in a bar, nor need it be harmonised entirely diatonically in root positions; the bass-line can be vivid, like the words, but usually is not. Most groups are content to put over something enthusiastic and with a big, noisy sound, though The Rolling Stones, The Hollies, The Moody Blues, Manfred Mann, The Who (these last two groups for the moment less actively) have shown, like The Beatles, that beat music can be as diverse as any other sort. Ballads are the despair of forward-looking pop students. Not that they are irredeemable: there are cool ballads, and ballads with a vital pulse, and ballads with distinctive tunes or interesting words. But again and monotonously again, the sticky, sweaty, vacuous ballad reaches to the melting hearts of housewives who prefer the lowest when they hear it, and accordingly it soars to the top like a jetplane made of golden syrup.

There is hope for all these pop genres, and *Sgt. Pepper's Lonely Hearts Club Band* provides it in abundance. Two of the tracks are quasi-ballad:

"Fixing a hole" is cool, anti-romantic, harmonically a little like the earlier "Yesterday" and "Michelle"; "She's leaving home" is a slow waltz reminiscent of old musical comedy but with a classically slanted accompaniment for harp and string quartet [*sic*], and with ironical words about a minor domestic tragedy (the texts, which are of consistently lively poetic interest, are printed in full on the back cover). There is a neat vaudeville number "When I'm sixty-four," which comments pointedly on this old-time vogue and its relevance for modern beat song. George Harrison's "Within you without you" carries the manner of Indian music farther into pop than ever before though the tune of the song is recognisably mixolydian; there are hints of Indian atmosphere in some of the other songs (which are all by Lennon and McCartney).

Psychedelia can be diagnosed in the fanciful lyric and intriguing asymmetrical music of "Lucy in the sky," as well as in the sound effects of "Lovely Rita" (she is a parking meter warden), and the hurricane glissandi of "A day in the life" which has been banned by the BBC for its ambivalent references to drug-taking—though if anything on the record is going to encourage dope it is surely the "tangerine trees and marmalade skies" and the "girl with kaleidoscope eyes" in "Lucy in the sky" which contains none of these whoosh noises. I greatly enjoy the five-bar phrases of "Good morning good morning" which is something like a novelty number; and the tidy simplicity and shapely bass-line of "A little help from my friends," the only track that would have been conceivable in pop songs five years ago.

Any of these songs is more genuinely creative than anything currently to be heard on pop radio stations, but in relationship to what other groups have been doing lately *Sgt. Pepper* is chiefly significant as constructive criticism, a sort of pop music master class examining trends and correcting or tidying up inconsistencies and undisciplined work, here and there suggesting a line worth following. The one new exploration is the showband manner of the title song, its reprise, and its interval song, "Being for the benefit of Mr Kite." These three give a certain shape and integrity to the two sides, and if the unity is slightly specious the idea is, I think, new to popsong LPs, which are usually unconnected anthologies, and it is worth pursuing. Sooner or later some group will take the next logical step and produce an LP which is a popsong-cycle, a Tin Pan Alley *Dichterliebe*. Whether or not the remains of Schumann and Heine turn in their graves at this description depends on the artistry of the compiler.

Richard Goldstein

■

It has been called the most famous album in the history of popular music. It is certainly among the most written about. It is still being written about. Agree or disagree, in November 2003, *Rolling Stone* magazine ranked the five hundred greatest albums of all time, with *Sgt. Pepper's Lonely Hearts Club Band* heading the list. Calling it the most important rock and roll album ever made by the greatest rock and roll band of all time, the editors praised its fearlessness, audacity, and creativity. It was released on June 1, 1967, in Britain and the following day in the United States. Critics argued about its merits in the pages of the national press, including Richard Goldstein, the music critic for *The New York Times.* Not everyone was unanimous in their praise of the album, however. Goldstein called *Sgt. Pepper* "fraudulent," prompting an outpouring of support for the band and the album from both fans and rival critics alike. Tom Philips in *The Village Voice* countered by calling *Sgt. Pepper* "the most ambitious and most successful record album ever issued." The following is Goldstein's review of *Sgt. Pepper,* which originally appeared in the June 18, 1967, issue of *The New York Times.*

"We Still Need the Beatles, but . . ."

New York Times

June 18, 1967

■ THE BEATLES SPENT an unprecedented four months and $100,000 on their new album, "Sergeant Pepper's Lonely Hearts Club Band" (Capitol SMAS 2653, mono and stereo). Like fathers-to-be, they kept a close watch on each stage of its gestation. For they are no longer merely superstars. Hailed as progenitors of a Pop advant garde, they have been idolized as the most creative members of their generation. The pressure to create an album that is complex, profound and innovative must have been staggering. So they retired to the electric sanctity of their recording studio, dispensing with their adoring audience, and the shrieking inspiration it can provide.

The finished product reached the record racks last week; the Beatles had supervised even the album cover—a mind-blowing collage of famous and obscure people, plants and artifact. The 12 new compositions in the album are as elaborately conceived as the cover. The sound is a pastiche of dissonance and lushness. The mood is mellow, even nostalgic. But, like the cover, the over-all effect is busy, hip and cluttered.

Like an over-attended child "Sergeant Pepper" is spoiled. It reeks of horns and harps, harmonica quartets, assorted animal noises and a 41-piece orchestra. On at least one cut, the Beatles are not heard at all instrumentally. Sometimes this elaborate musical propwork succeeds in projecting mood. The "Sergeant Pepper" theme is brassy and vaudevillian. "She's Leaving Home," a melodramatic domestic saga, flows on a cloud of heavenly strings. And, in what is becoming a Beatle tradition, George Harrison unveils his latest excursion into curry and karma, to the saucy accompaniment of three tambouras, a dilruba, a tabla, a sitar, a table harp, three cellos and eight violins.

Harrison's song, "Within You and Without You," is a good place to begin dissecting "Sergeant Pepper." Though it is among the strongest cuts, its flaws are distressingly typical of the album as a whole. Compared with "Love You To" (Harrison's contribution to "Revolver"), this melody shows an expanded consciousness of Indian ragas. Harrison's voice, hovering midway between song and prayer chant, oozes over the melody like melted cheese. On sitar and tamboura, he achieves a remarkable Pop synthesis. Because his raga motifs are not mere embellishments but are imbedded into the very structure of the song, "Within You and Without You" appears seamless. It stretches, but fits.

What a pity, then, that Harrison's lyrics are dismal and dull. "Love You To" exploded with a passionate sutra quality, but "Within You and Without You" resurrects the very clichés the Beatles helped bury: "With our love/ We could save the world/ If they only knew." All the minor scales in the Orient wouldn't make "Within You Without You" profound.

The obsession with production, coupled with a surprising shoddiness in composition, permeates the entire album. There is nothing beautiful on "Sergeant Pepper." Nothing is real and there is nothing to get hung about. The Lennon raunchiness has become mere caprice in "Being for the Benefit of Mr. Kite." Paul McCartney's soaring Pop magnificats have become merely politely profound. "She's Leaving Home" preserves all the orchestrated grandeur of "Eleanor Rigby," but its framework is emaciated. This tale of a provincial lass who walks out on a repressed home life, leaving parents sobbing in her wake, is simply no match for those stately swirling strings. Where "Eleanor Rigby" compressed tragedy into poignant detail, "She's Leaving Home" is uninspired narrative, and nothing more. By the third depressing hearing, it begins to sound like an immense put-on.

There certainly are elements of burlesque in a composition like "When I'm 64," which poses the crucial question: "Will you still need me/ Will you still feed me/ When I'm 64?" But the dominant tone is not mockery; this is a fantasy retirement, overflowing with grandchildren, gardening and a modest cottage on the Isle of Wight. The Beatles sing, "We shall scrimp and save" with utter reverence. It is a strange fairy tale, oddly sad because it is so far from the composers' reality. But even here, an honest vision is ruined by the background which seeks to enhance it.

"Lucy in the Sky with Diamonds" is an engaging curio, but nothing more. It is drenched in reverb, echo and other studio distortions. Tone overtakes meaning and we are lost in electronic meandering. The best Beatle melodies are simple if original progressions braced with pungent lyrics. Even their most radical compositions retain a sense of unity.

But for the first time, the Beatles have given us an album of special effects, dazzling but ultimately fraudulent. And for the first time, it is not exploration which we sense, but consolidation. There is a touch of the Jefferson Airplane, a dab of Beach Boys vibrations, and a generous pat of gymnastics from The Who.

The one evident touch of originality appears in the structure of the album itself. The Beatles have shortened the "banding" between cuts so that one song seems to run into the next. This produces the possibility of a Pop symphony or oratorio, with distinct but related movements. Unfortunately, there is no apparent thematic development in the placing of cuts, except for the effective juxtaposition of opposing musical styles. At best, the songs are only vaguely related.

With one important exception, "Sergeant Pepper" is precious but devoid of gems. "A Day in the Life" is such a radical departure from the spirit of the album that it almost deserves its peninsular position (following the reprise of the "Sergeant Pepper" theme, it comes almost as an afterthought). It has nothing to do with posturing or put-on. It is a deadly earnest excursion in emotive music with a chilling lyric. Its orchestration is dissonant but sparse, and its mood is not whimsical nostalgia but irony.

With it, the Beatles have produced a glimpse of modern city life that is terrifying. It stands as one of the most important Lennon-McCartney compositions, and it is a historic Pop event.

"A Day in the Life" starts in a description of suicide. With the same conciseness displayed in "Eleanor Rigby," the protagonist begins: "I read the news today, oh boy." This mild interjection is the first hint of his disillusionment; compared with what is to follow, it is supremely ironic. "I saw the photograph," he continues, in the voice of a melancholy choir boy:

> *He blew his mind out in a car*
> *He didn't notice that the lights had changed*

"A Day in the Life" could never make the Top 40, although it may influence a great many songs which do. Its lyric is sure to bring a sudden surge of Pop tragedy. The aimless, T. S. Eliot–like crowd, forever confronting pain and turning away, may well become a common symbol. And its narrator, subdued by the totality of his despair, may reappear in countless compositions as the silent, withdrawn hero.

Musically, there are already indications that the intense atonality of "A Day in the Life" is a key to the sound of 1967. Electronic-rock, with its aim of staggering an audience, has arrived in half-a-dozen important new releases. None of these songs has the controlled intensity of "A Day in the Life," but the willingness of many restrained musicians to "let go" means that serious aleatory-pop may be on the way.

Ultimately, however, it is the uproar over the alleged influence of drugs on the Beatles which may prevent "A Day in the Life" from reaching the mass audience. The song's refrain, "I'd like to turn you on," has rankled disk jockeys supersensitive to "hidden subversion" in rock 'n' roll. In fact, a case can be made within the very structure of "A Day in the Life" for the belief that the Beatles—like so many Pop composers—are aware of the highs and lows of consciousness.

The song is built on a series of tense, melancholic passages, followed by soaring releases. In the opening stanza, for instance, John's voice comes near to cracking with despair. But after the invitation, "I'd like to turn you on," the Beatles have inserted an extraordinary atonal thrust which is shocking, even painful, to the ears. But it brilliantly encases the song and, if the refrain preceding it suggests turning on, the crescendo parallels a drug-induced "rush."

The bridge begins in a staccato crossfire. We feel the narrator rising, dressing and commuting by rote. The music is nervous with the dissonance of cabaret jazz. A percussive drum melts into a panting railroad chug. Then

Found my way upstairs and had a smoke
Somebody spoke and I went into a dream

The words fade into a chant of free spacious chords, like the initial marijuana "buzz." But the tone becomes mysterious and then ominous. Deep strings take us on a Wagnerian descent and we are back to the original blues theme, and the original declaration, "I read the news today, oh boy."

Actually, it is difficult to see why the BBC banned "A Day in the Life," because its message is, quite clearly, the flight from banality. It describes a profound reality, but it certainly does not glorify it. And its conclusion, though magnificent, seems to represent a negation of self. The song ends on one low, resonant note that is sustained for 40 seconds. Having achieved the absolute peace of nullification, the narrator is beyond melancholy. But there is something brooding and irrevocable about his calm. It sounds like destruction.

What a shame that "A Day in the Life" is only a coda to an otherwise undistinguished collection of work. We need the Beatles, not as cloistered composers, but as companions. And they need us. In substituting the studio conservatory for an audience, they have ceased being folk artists, and the change is what makes their new album a monologue.

Christopher Porterfield

■

In this *Time* magazine cover story, staffer Christopher Porterfield praises the Fab Four for their desire to change, grow, and experiment. Whereas other musicians were content to repeat themselves ad nauseam, the Beatles, he writes, "are creating the most original, expressive and musically interesting sounds being heard in pop music." He then acknowledges that "serious musicians" are listening to them, including composer Ned Rorem and conductor Leonard Bernstein. In other words, the Beatles were doing what no other popular artist had done before: turning pop music into art.

"Pop Music: The Messengers"

Time

September 22, 1967

■ THE COVER ON a new LP album called *Sgt. Pepper's Lonely Hearts Club Band* is a photomontage of a crowd gathered round a grave. And a curious crowd it is: Marilyn Monroe is there, so are Karl Marx, Edgar Allan Poe, Albert Einstein, Lawrence of Arabia, Mae West, Sonny Liston, and eight Beatles.

Eight? Well, four of them, standing around looking like wax dummies, are indeed wax models of the Beatles as most people remember them: nicely brushed long hair, dark suits, faces like sassy choirboys. The other four Beatles are very much alive: thin, hippie-looking, mustachioed, bedecked in bright, bizarre uniforms. Though their expressions seem subdued, their eyes glint with a new awareness tinged with a little of the old mischief. As for the grave in the foreground: it has THE BEATLES spelled out in flowers trimmed with marijuana plants.

With characteristic self-mockery, the Beatles are proclaiming that they have snuffed out their old selves to make room for the new Beatles incarnate. And there is some truth to it. Without having lost any of the genial anarchism with which they helped revolutionize the life style of young people in Britain, Europe and the U.S., they have moved on to a higher artistic plateau.

CUNNING COLLAGES. Rich and secure enough to go on repeating themselves—or to do nothing at all—they have exercised a compulsion for growth, change and experimentation. Messengers from beyond rock 'n' roll, they are creating the most original, expressive and musically interesting sounds being heard in pop music. They are leading an evolution in which the best of current post-rock sounds are becoming something that pop music has never been before: an art form. "Serious musicians" are listening to them and marking their work as a historic departure in the progress of music—any music.

Ned Rorem, composer of some of the best of today's art songs, says: "They are colleagues of mine, speaking the same language with different accents." In fact, he adds, the Beatles' haunting composition, *She's Leaving Home*—one of 12 songs in the *Sgt. Pepper* album—"is equal to any song that Schubert ever wrote." [The Rorem essay appears in this volume.] Conductor Leonard Bernstein's appreciation is just as high; he cites Schumann. As Musicologist Henry Pleasants says: "The Beatles are where music is right now."

Like all good popular artists, the Beatles have a talent for distilling the moods of their time. Gilbert and Sullivan's frolics limned the pomposities of the Victorian British Empah; Cole Porter's urbanities were wonderful tonics for the hung-over '30s; Rodgers and Hammerstein's ballads reflected the sentiment and seriousness of the World War II era. Today the Beatles' cunning collages piece together scraps of tension between the generations, the loneliness of the dislocated '60s, and the bitter sweets of young love in any age. At the same time, their sensitivity to the absurd is sharper than ever.

CHEERFUL SKEWERING. By contrast, their early music had exuberance and an occasional oasis of unexpected harmony, but otherwise blended monotonously into the parched badlands of rock. *I Want to Hold Your Hand*, the Beatles' biggest hit single—it has sold 5,000,000 copies since 1963—was a cliché boy-girl lyric and a simple tune hammered onto the regulation *aaba* pop-song structure. But the boys found their conventional sound and juvenile verses stultifying. Says Paul McCartney: "We didn't like the idea of people going onstage and being very unreal and doing sickly songs. We felt that people would like it more, and we would like it more, if there was some—reality."

Thus it was that the group's chief lyricist, John Lennon, began tuning in on U.S. Folk Singer Bob Dylan (*The Times They Are A-Changin'*); it wasn't Dylan's sullen anger about life that Lennon found appealing so much as the striving to "tell it like it is." Gradually, the Beatles' work began to tell it too. Their 1965 song, *Nowhere Man* ("Doesn't have a point of view, knows not where he's going to"), asked: "Isn't he a bit like you and me?" Last year's *Paperback Writer* cheerfully skewered the craven commercialism of the hack.

An even sharper departure from Big Beat banalities came as Tunesmith McCartney began exhibiting an unsuspected lyrical gift. In 1965, he crooned the loveliest of his ballads, *Yesterday*, to the accompaniment of a string octet—a novel and effective backing that gave birth to an entire new genre, baroque-rock. Still another form, raga-rock, had its origins after George Harrison flipped over Indian music, studied with Indian sitar Virtuoso Ravi Shankar, and introduced a brief sitar motif on the 1965 recording *Norwegian Wood.* Now everybody's making with the sitar.

COPPING OUT, PLUGGING IN. Meanwhile, the growing sophistication of the Beatles' outlook found expression in a series of sharply observed vignettes of English life. The most poignant was last year's *Eleanor Rigby,* who

> *Waits at the window, wearing the face*
> *that she keeps in a jar by the door . . .*
> *Father McKenzie writing the words of a*
> *sermon that no one will hear . . .*

Fantasy took flight in their songs, from *Yellow Submarine*'s childlike picture of a carefree existence beneath the waves to the vastly more complex and ominous vision in *Strawberry Fields Forever* of a retreat from uncertainty into a psychedelic cop-out:

> *It's getting hard to be someone but it all works*
> *out, it doesn't matter much to me.*
> *Let me take you down, 'cause I'm going to*
> *strawberry fields.*

Moreover, *Strawberry Fields,* with its four separate meters, freewheeling modulations and titillating tonal trappings, showed that the Beatles had flowered as musicians. They learned to bend and stretch the pop-song mold, enriched their harmonic palette with modal colors, mixed in cross-rhythms, and pinched the classical devices of composers from Bach to Stockhausen. They supplemented their guitar sound with strings, baroque trumpets, even a calliope. With the help of their engineer, arranger and record producer, George Martin, they plugged into a galaxy of space-age electronic effects, achieved partly through a mixture of tapes run backward and at various speeds.

PSYCHIC SHIVERS. All the successes of the past two years were a foreshadowing of *Sgt. Pepper*, which more than anything else dramatizes, note for note, word for word, the brilliance of the new Beatles. In three months, it has sold a staggering 2,500,000 copies—each a guaranteed package of psychic shivers. Loosely strung together on a scheme that plays the younger and older generations off against each other, it sizzles with musical montage, tricky electronics and sleight-of-hand lyrics that range between 1920s ricky-tick and 1960s raga. *A Day in the Life*, for example, is by all odds the most disturbingly beautiful song the group has ever produced. The narrator's mechanical progress through the day ("Dragged a comb across my head, found my way downstairs") is tensely counterpointed with lapses into reverie and with chilling tableaux of frustration and despair:

> *I read the news today, oh boy,*
> *About a lucky man who made the grade . . .*
> *He blew his mind out in a car.*

At the end, the refrain, "I'd love to turn you on," leads to a hair-raising chromatic crescendo by a full orchestra and a final blurred chord that is sustained for 40 seconds, like a trance of escape, or perhaps resignation.

It's a long way from "I want to hold your hand" to "I'd love to turn you on." In between, the Beatles kept their cool, even when they were decorated by the Queen. They managed to retain the antic charm that had helped make them the rage of Britain and that sparkled on millions of TV screens in February 1964, when America got its first glimpse of them live on the *Ed Sullivan Show*. Only once did they show a serious lapse in taste: the cover of their 1966 album *Yesterday and Today* was a photograph of the four wearing butcher's smocks and laden with chunks of raw meat and the bodies of decapitated dolls. Reaction in the U.S. was so violent that Capital Records pulled it off the market, explaining that it was a misguided attempt at "pop-art satire."

PILGRIMAGE TO LIVERPOOL. Now that the Beatles' music is growing more complex and challenging, they are losing some younger fans. Teeny-boppers, most of whom would rather shriek up than freak out, are turning off at *A Day in the Life,* doubling back through *Strawberry Fields* and returning to predictably cute 1964-model Beatles—in the form of such blatantly aping groups as the Monkees.

On the other hand, the youngsters who were the original Beatlemaniacs are themselves older now, and dig the Beatles on a less hysterical level. Two years ago, Kathy Dreyfuss of Los Angeles went on a pilgrimage to the Beatles' home town of Liverpool with her mother. "I was such a screaming fan I couldn't eat or sleep," says Kathy, looking back from the very earnest vantage point of 16. "I realize now I was submerging all my problems in the Beatles. I still like them, but it isn't such a madness. Now their songs are about the things I think about—the world, love, drugs, the way things are."

In exchange for the teeny-boppers, the new Beatles have captivated a different and much more responsive audience. "Suddenly," says George Harrison, "we find that all the people who thought they were beyond the Beatles are fans." That includes not only college students but parents, professors, even business executives.

HARDY MINORITY. Considering that the Beatles' trademark is off-beat irreverence, their effect on mature audiences is oddly amusing. If the teeny-boppers made the Beatles plaster gods, many adults make them pop prophets, and tend to theorize solemnly, instead of seriously, about their significance. The Rev. B. Davie Napier, dean of the chapel at Stanford University, says that "no entity hits as many sensitive people as these guys do." Napier, who has dwelt in past sermons on *Yellow Submarine* and *Eleanor Rigby,* is convinced that *Sgt. Pepper* "lays bare the stark loneliness and terror of these lonely times," and he plans to focus on the album in an address to freshman students. Atlanta Psychiatrist Tom Leland says that the Beatles "are speaking in an existential way about the meaninglessness of actuality." There is even a womb's-eye view. Chicago Psychiatrist Ner Littner believes that the Beatles' "strong beat seems to awaken echoes of significant early experiences such as the fetal intrauterine serenity that repetitively reverberates to the mother's heartbeat."

Other over-interpreters include the listeners who—like literary critics dissecting a sonnet—ferret out indirect references in Beatle lyrics and persist in catching a whiff of drugs in such innocuous songs as *Yellow Submarine.* And there is still the hardy minority that insists on viewing the Beatles as the great put-on of the century.

DERIVATIVE MEWING. Not so long ago, the pop scene was going nowhere. Rock 'n' roll had catapulted into the bestseller charts in the

1950s on the chugging riffs of Bill Haley and His Comets (*Rock Around the Clock*) and the rhythmic caterwauling of Elvis Presley. But even they were bleached-out copies of the vibrant, earthy rhythm-and-blues sung in the subculture of Negro music. Until the early 1960s, rock 'n' roll went through a doldrum of derivative mewing by white singers, with only occasional breakthroughs by such Negroes as Ray Charles and Fats Domino.

The Beatles, along with other British groups—the Rolling Stones, the Animals—revitalized rock by closely imitating (and frankly crediting) such Negro originators of the style as Muddy Waters, Chuck Berry and Bo Diddley. Soon the Negro "soul sound" surged into the white mass market. The old-line blues merchants have enjoyed a revival, and a younger, slicker breed of rhythm-and-blues singers—notably Lou Rawls, Aretha Franklin, Diana Ross and the Supremes—have taken up commanding positions on the sales charts. "Until the Beatles exposed the origins, the white kids didn't know anything about the music," says Veteran Blues Shouter Waters, 52. "Now they've learned it was in their backyard all the time."

As the Beatles moved on, absorbing and extending Bob Dylan's folk-rock hybrid and sowing innovations of their own, they were like musical Johnny Appleseeds; wherever they went, they left flourishing fields for other groups to cultivate. "They were saying, 'If you want to get better, here's the route,'" says Art Garfunkel, 25, half of the folk-rock duo, Simon and Garfunkel. Nowadays, according to independent Record Producer Charlie Greene, 28, "no matter how hard anybody tries, no matter how good they are, almost everything they do is a cop on the Beatles." Yet the Beatles' example is not limiting but liberating, as other rock musicians have attested with generous praise. Says hefty Cass Elliot of The Mamas and The Papas: "They're untouchable."

Today, the rock scene has shifted from England back to the U.S., and particularly to the West Coast (some San Franciscans are calling their city the Liverpool of the U.S.). There, as elsewhere in the States, rock is currently in the midst of a huge syncretic surge toward a new idiom— and the Beatles' wildly eclectic spirit hovers over it all. As the Lovin' Spoonful's songwriter, John Sebastian, says: "Here we are in the middle of the mulch."

Blues, folk, country and western, ragas, psychedelic light and sound effects, swatches of Mahler, jazzlike improvisations—all are spaded into the mulch by such vital and imaginative groups as the Doors, the Grateful

Dead, the Jefferson Airplane, the Paul Butterfield Blues Band, the Byrds and the new British trio, the Cream. Like the Beatles, most of these groups write their own music and thereby try not only to arrive at their own peculiar mixture of elements, but also to stamp their identity on whatever they do.

HIPPIE ANTHEM. None has so far matched the distinctiveness and power of the Beatles' mixture—which, after all, is responsible for having boosted them into their supramusical status. Thus their flirtation with drugs and the dropout attitude behind songs like *A Day in the Life* disturbs many fans, not to mention worried parents. The whole *Sgt. Pepper* album is "drenched in drugs," as the editor of a London music magazine puts it. One track features Drummer Ringo Starr quavering, "I get high with a little help from my friends." Another number, *Lucy in the Sky with Diamonds,* evokes a drug-induced hallucination, and even the initials of the title spell out LSD, though the Beatles plead sheer coincidence.

The overall theme of drugs is no coincidence, however. All four Beatles have admitted taking LSD at least occasionally. Yet it is not clear whether their songs are meant to proselytize on behalf of drugs or simply to deal with them as a subject of the moment. In the most recent Beatle pronouncement about LSD Paul McCartney said. "I don't recommend it. It can open a few doors, but it's not any answer. You get the answers yourself."

Some segments of the Beatles' audience read messages into the songs that may never have been intended. The hippie brigade, for example, has adopted as an anthem of sorts *She's Leaving Home,* which tells of a runaway girl whose parents gave her everything money could buy but no happiness. "Man, that's the story of the hippies," says one of them. A 15-year-old boy who left home to become a hippie interprets the Beatles' songs as a put-down of his parents: "They're saying all the things I always wanted to say to my parents and their freaky friends."

BLOWING AWAY COBWEBS. Even the Beatles' nonmusical utterances tend to take on the tone and weight of social prophecy. "Only Hitler ever duplicated their power over crowds," says Sid Bernstein, who organized their three New York concerts. "I'm convinced they could sway a presidential election if they wanted to." If that is far-fetched, the fact remains that when the Beatles talk—about drugs, the war in Viet Nam, religion—millions listen, and this is a new situation in the pop music world.

It is not altogether a bad situation, either. And it could be worse.

At least the fact that nobody ever bothered to ask Elvis Presley about anything indicates a certain level of discrimination. In any case, callow as their ideas sometimes are, the Beatles exemplify a refreshing distrust of authority, disdain for conventions and impatience with hypocrisy. "I think they're on to something," says their friend Richard Lester, 35, who directed their two films. "They are more inclined to blow away the cobwebs than my contemporaries."

Kids sense a quality of defiant honesty in the Beatles and admire their freedom and open-mindedness; they see them as peers who are in a position to try anything, and who can be relied on to tell it to them straight—and to tell them what they want to hear. As for the parents who are targets of the Beatles' satirical gibes, they seem to be able to take a large number of direct hits and still come up smiling. Says Chicago Public Relations Man Water Robinson, 39, father of three boys: "The Beatles are explorers, trusty advance scouts. I like them to report to my kids."

WITHIN THE MAZE. Characteristically, the Beatles are uncomfortable on their pedestals and soapboxes. They have always insisted, as Paul McCartney says, that "the fan at my gate knows really that she's equal to me, and I take care to tell her that." John Lennon's remark that "we're more popular than Jesus," which set off an anti-Beatle furor last year, was not a boast but an expression of disgust. Though he phrased it ineptly, he was posing the question: What kind of world is it that makes more fuss over a pop cult than over religion?

To discourage fuss, the Beatles lead their private lives within a maze of high hedges and walls, security guards and secret telephone numbers. Even John Lennon's art-nouveau Rolls-Royce, painted with a rainbow of swirling floral patterns on a bright yellow background, has smoked one-way glass in the side and rear windows to keep the curious from peeking in. The boys make occasional outings to such London nightspots as The Bag of Nails and The Speakeasy, but must plan them with a military eye for the element of surprise and a ready path of retreat in case they are mobbed. Only in the past few months has it become possible for them to walk through the city like ordinary mortals. Ringo Starr explains the fine points of the art: "If you're not dodging and running, you don't get people excited. If you take it cool and just trot about, they leave you."

Otherwise the Beatles live in a style that is quietly luxurious—as well it might be, considering their income from records, films, television appearances, song publishing and copyright royalties, and assorted tie-ins with Beatle merchandise. The most conservative estimates put the net worth of Harrison and Starr at $3,000,000 each and of Lennon and McCartney at $4,000,000 (because of their extra earnings as songwriters). The figures could easily be twice as high.

STOCKBROKER BELT. The three married Beatles and their look-alike wives own large homes in Weybridge, part of the suburban "stockbroker belt," 40 minutes from London. John, 26, his wife Cynthia, a former art student, and their four-year-old son Julian, live in a Tudor mansion with a swimming pool. Like the other Beatles, John has a taste for outlandishly gaudy outfits custom-tailored in brocades, silks and the like, for gadgets (five TV sets, uncounted tape recorders and cameras), and eccentric collections (a huge altar cross, a suit of armor called Sidney).

Down the hill from John is Sunny Heights, the 15-room tile-and-stucco digs where Ringo, 27, wallows in domesticity with Wife Maureen, a former Liverpool hairdresser, and Sons Zak, 2, and month-old Jason. Ringo, who never practices drums between Beatle performances, has made his place the group's unofficial clubhouse; on the spacious grounds are a treehouse and an old air-raid shelter, and indoors an elaborate bar named The Flying Cow.

George, 24, the newest Beatle husband (he married London Model Patti Boyd early last year), lives nearby in a big white bungalow. He and his friends are daubing the outside walls with colorful cartoons, flowers and abstract designs, some in fluorescent paint that shines in the daylight. Unlike Ringo, he practices a great deal, and his music room is strewn with 12 guitars.

Bachelor Paul, 25 (his favorite "bird" is 21-year-old Actress Jane Asher), is a movie addict, loves "the look of London," tools around town in a spiffy blue Aston Martin DB 5. He lives in a high-walled house in the city's prosperous St. John's Wood neighborhood—oddly furnished, for a Beatle, in a tastefully quaint style, including an old fashioned lace tablecloth on the dining room table—and has daily bouts of "bashing" at the piano, which he has never quite learned to play.

VICTORIAN SHADOWS. The Beatles keep in touch constantly, bounding in and out of each other's homes like members of a single large family—which, in a sense, they are. Their friendship is an extraordinarily intimate and empathetic bond. When all four are together, even close friends like Mick Jagger of the Rolling Stones sense invisible barriers thrown up between themselves and outsiders. "We're still our own best friends," each says.

With good reason. Not only are they welded together by the sheer fact of being the Beatles, but they also share a common lower-middle-class background in the sooty, Victorian shadows of Liverpool. Paul, the son of a cotton salesman, and John, who was raised by an aunt after his father deserted the family, were playing together as early as 1955. George, whose father was a bus driver, joined them in 1958. Two years later they met Ringo (born Richard Starkey), a docker's son. Their families were dubious about musical careers. "If Paul had listened to me," says Jim McCartney wryly, "he would have been a teacher." But the boys persisted. Besides the musical satisfaction, playing in a band was a way to be somebody—especially with the local girls—to make some money and exert their nonconformity. And after they linked up with Brian Epstein, the elegant would-be actor and son of a wealthy Liverpool furniture retailer, it was a way to get out of Liverpool. Epstein shrewdly piloted their career until his death last month at 32 (TIME, Sept. 8).*

So tightly knit is the quartet that a leading idea for their next movie is to present them as separate manifestations of a single person. They constitute a four-way plug-in personality, each sparking the circuit in his own way. Paul, outgoing and talkative, spreads a sheen of charm; he is the smoother-over, the explainer, as pleasingly facile at life as he is at composing melodies. George, once the least visible of the group, now focuses his energies on Indian music and philosophy; an occasional contributor to the Beatle songbook, he is the most accomplished instrumentalist of the lot (he has always played lead guitar).

Ringo, a thoroughly unpretentious fellow, is also the most innately comic temperament; he is the catalyst, and also the deflator, of the crew. Most mysterious of all—and possibly most important—is John, the creative mainspring, who has lately grown strangely brooding and withdrawn; he is more thoughtful and tough-minded than the others, reads voraciously. His telephone is usually answered by a tape-recorded voice, asking the caller to leave a message. But Lennon rarely returns calls, instead, so the story goes, plays the tapes over and over with maniacal glee.

RECIPE FOR ORCHESTRA. Since the Beatles gave up touring a year ago, each has had more freedom to tackle individual pursuits. John has a major acting assignment in the forthcoming Richard Lester film called *How I Won the War;* Paul tried his hand at a movie sound track

---

* A coroner's report attributed his death to an accidental "incautious" overdose of sleeping tablets.

and wrote a fine score for the current release, *The Family Way.* But their most rewarding activity is still as a group—making records.

They have transformed themselves from a "live" performing team to an experimental laboratory group, and they have staked out the recording studio as their own electronic rumpus room. To achieve the weird effects on *Sgt. Pepper,* they spent as much as 20 hours on a song, often working through the night. The startling crescendo in *A Day in the Life* illustrates their bold, erratic, but strikingly successful method. Says Paul: "Once we'd written the main bit of the music, we thought, now look, there's a little gap there; and we said oh, how about an orchestra? Yes, that'll be nice. And if we do have an orchestra, are we going to write them a pseudoclassical thing, which has been done better by people who know how to make it sound like that—or are we going to do it like we write songs? Take a guess and use instinct. So we said, right, what we'll do to save all the arranging, we'll take the whole orchestra as one instrument. And we just wrote it down like a cooking recipe: 24 bars; on the ninth bar, the orchestra will take off, and it will go from its lowest note to its highest note."

The 41-piece orchestra, as it turned out, consisted mostly of members of the New Philharmonia, who had trouble following the recipe. Unaccustomed to ad-libbing, they had to be cajoled by John and Paul, who threaded among the musicians, urging them to play at different tempos and to please try not to stay together. Partly as a result of filling that "gap," the *Sgt. Pepper* album cost three months of work and $56,000—which is about as much as it costs to record five albums for London's New Philharmonia Orchestra.

SOUND PICTURES. Such recording practices are early steps in a brand-new field. George Martin, the producer whose technical midwifery is helping to make the steps possible, likens them to the shift from representational painting to abstractionism. "Until recently," he says, "the aim has been to reproduce sounds as realistically as possible. Now we are working with pure sound. We are building sound pictures."

In fact, some observers predict that "sound pictures" may prove to be the medium through which the Beatles—and the more adventurous rock groups in their wake—can merge with "classical" contemporary music. Already, says Robert Tusler, who teaches 20th century music at U.C.L.A., "the Beatles have taken over many of the electronic concepts in music that have been worked on by the German composers of the Cologne group. They've made an enormous contribution to electronic music."

Whatever else it comes to, the Beatles' approach to recording *Sgt. Pepper* will serve as a model for future sessions. And the boys themselves will be commanding more and more of the technical operations. "We haven't pushed George Martin out of the engineers' booth," says McCartney, "but we've become equals. The music has more to do with electronics now than ever before. To do those things a few years ago was a bit immoral. But electronics is no longer immoral."

In their other enterprises, too, the Beatles are reaching out for total artistic autonomy. They are talking about directing their next film themselves. Last week they careened through the southwest English countryside filming *Magical Mystery Tour,* an hour-long TV special, for worldwide broadcast during the Christmas season. They are not only providing the music but writing, directing, producing and financing as well. When it is wrapped up to their satisfaction, they will offer it to the highest bidder. And they have already written songs—later this year they may do a full score—for a forthcoming cartoon based on *Yellow Submarine.*

FILLING THE GAP. Unlike the occasional celebrity who grows to believe his own publicity and uses it as a license, the Beatles have maintained their good humor and, apart from toying with drugs, their exemplary behavior. But fame and instant millions also have a way of inflicting private agonies on public personalities. The Beatles' current solution is spiritualism, specifically "transcendental meditation," as propounded by Maharishi Mahesh Yogi, 56, a tiny, cherubic seer with shoulder-length locks. The yogi, unfortunately, is somewhat less than lucid when it comes to describing his insights. Two 30-minute sessions of transcendental meditation a day, he says, enable a person to perceive the divinity within himself. "It is the direct, simple and natural way of coming to That." What's That? Replies Maharishi: "I am That, you are That, all this is That."

That's good enough for John, Paul, Ringo and George, who plan to take two months off to study with Maharishi at his Academy of Meditation in Shankaracharya, Kashmir.

"The four of us," explains Ringo, "have had the most hectic lives. We have got almost anything money can buy. But when you can do that, the things you buy mean nothing after a time. You look for something else, for a new experience. It's like your Dad going to the boozer and you want to find out what the taste of drink is like. We have found something now which fills the gap. Since meeting His Holiness, I feel great."

The feeling is mutual. Says His Holiness: "I can bring them up as very practical philosophers of their age. They can do a great deal for the youth which they lead." Precisely what marvels the yogi has in store for his disciples is a good question. Yet for openers he has persuaded the Beatles to renounce drugs. Paul claims that he now realizes that taking drugs was "like taking an aspirin without having a headache." Says John: "If we'd met Maharishi before we had taken LSD, we wouldn't have needed to take it." Skeptics notwithstanding, the Beatles could well be on to something fruitful again, which may find expression in who knows what strange new musical forms.

And what, after all, could be a more fitting philosophy than transcendentalism for the Beatles, who have repeatedly transcended the constricting identities foisted on them by press and public, whose whole career has been a transcendent, heel-clicking leap right over pop music's high Himalayas? On the basis of what they have achieved so far, it would be rash to dispute George when he says: "We haven't really started yet. We've only just discovered what we can do as musicians, what thresholds we can cross. The future stretches out beyond our imagination."

Robert Christgau

■

There was much give and take in the mainstream press about the merits of *Sgt. Pepper.* One of the most public of arguments was between Richard Goldstein, the best known pop critic in the United States at the time, in *The New York Times* (reprinted in this volume) and Robert Christgau in *Esquire* magazine. Goldstein panned the album; Christgau, on the other hand, praised it. The public outrage at Goldstein's negative review was so strong that Tom Phillips published a rebuttal (also in the *Times*) while Goldstein, feeling he had to defend himself, responded in the *Village Voice.* This carping among music critics—and Beatles fans—indicates just how strongly people felt, how possessive they were, toward the Beatles at the time. It was fine to criticize other musicians, but not the Beatles. That's when it became personal.

"Secular Music"

Esquire
December 1967

■ IN CASE YOU'VE been in New Guinea or something, you ought to be told that the Beatles have a new album out. It is called *Sgt. Pepper's Lonely Hearts Club Band,* and even before its release on June 2 it was the subject of all kinds of published and unpublished rumors. Afterward, the information barrage was overwhelming. Capital Records sent out an extraordinary feature, spiced with terms like "modals," "atonality," and—egad—"bowels" and casting aspersions upon the "Tin Pan Alley–spawned lyrical cliché." There were stories in *Life* (in which Paul McCartney, to the surprise of no one and the shock of quite a few, revealed that he had sampled the dreaded lysergic acid diethylamide; he was seconded quickly by John and George, but Ringo, lovely Ringo, has remained silent), *Time* (in which George Martin, the group's producer, who has a degree in music and is thus permitted to be a genius, was singled out as the brains of the operation), and *Newsweek* (in which the former kings of rock and roll were compared, unpejoratively and in order, to Alfred Lord Tennyson, Edith Sitwell, Charlie Chaplin, Donald Barthelme, Harold Pinter, and T. S. Eliot—and *not* Elvis Presley or even Bob Dylan). The trades bristled with excited little pieces that always

seemed to contain the word "artistic." And in *The New York Times*
Richard Goldstein put the album down and was almost lynched.

Goldstein, who has had his own story in *Newsweek,* is the best-known
critic of pop in the country. Like any rising star, he engendered the inevitable *ressentiment,* always masquerading, of course, as contempt for
the phony, the sellout, etc. I often disagree with Goldstein, but a sellout
he is not. He is unfailingly honest and about as malevolent as Winnie-
the-Pooh. There are very few "pop critics" who can match him even
occasionally for incisiveness, perspective, and wit. Goldstein was disappointed with *Sgt. Pepper.* After an initial moment of panic, I wasn't. In
fact, I was exalted by it, although a little of that has worn off. Which is
just the point. Goldstein may have been wrong, but he wasn't that wrong.
Sgt. Pepper is not the world's most perfect work of art. But that is what
the Beatles' fans have come to assume their idols must produce.

It all started in December, 1965, when they released *Rubber Soul,* an
album that for innovation, tightness, and lyrical intelligence was about
twice as good as anything they or anyone else (except maybe the Stones)
had done previously. In June, 1966, Capitol followed with *The Beatles—
"Yesterday" . . . and Today,* comprising both sides of three singles plus
extra cuts from the English versions of *Rubber Soul* and *Revolver.* The
Beatles (perhaps as a metaphor for this hodgepodge, which was not released in England) provided a cover that depicted Our Boys in bloody
butcher aprons, surrounded by hunks of meat and dismembered doll.
The powers yowled, the cover was replaced at a reported cost of
$250,000, and then in August the American *Revolver* went on sale. That
did it. *Revolver* was twice as good and four times as startling as *Rubber
Soul,* with sound effects, Oriental drones, jazz bands, transcendentalist
lyrics, all kinds of rhythmic and harmonic surprises, and a filter that
made John Lennon sound like God singing through a foghorn.

Partly because the ten-month gap between *Revolver* and *Sgt. Pepper*
was so unprecedented, the album was awaited in much the same spirit
as installments of Dickens must have been a century ago. Everyone was
a little edgy: Could they do it again? The answer: yes and no. *Sgt. Pepper* is a consolidation, more intricate than *Revolver* but not more sub-
stantial. Part of Goldstein's mistake, I think, has been to allow all the
filters and reverbs and orchestral effects and overdubs to deafen him to
the stuff underneath, which was pretty nice, and to fall victim to over-
anticipation. Although Goldstein still insists he was right, I attribute his
review to a failure of nerve.

Plus, perhaps, a predilection for folk music. *Sgt. Pepper,* four months in gestation, is the epitome of studio rock, and Goldstein wasn't entirely wrong when he accused it of being "busy, hip and cluttered." It contains nothing as lovely as "In My Life" on *Rubber Soul* or "Here, There and Everywhere" on *Revolver.* But no one seems to care. The week after Goldstein's review appeared, *Cash Box* listed *Sgt. Pepper* as the best-selling album in the country, a position it has occupied all summer.

Meanwhile, Goldstein himself has become a storm center. The *Voice,* his home base, published a rebuttal by a guy named Tom Phillips, who works for the *Times.* (Now who's square?) Goldstein responded with a *Voice* defense of his review. (Title: "I Lost My Cool Through the New York Times.") Paul Williams, of *Crawdaddy,* complained that Goldstein "got hung up on his own integrity and attempted to judge what he admittedly [sic] did not understand." (What have *you* done for rock this week?) And the *Times* was deluged with letters, many abusive and every last one in disagreement, the largest response to a music review in its history.

The letters are a fascinating testimony to what the Beatles mean to their fans. The correspondents are divided about equally between adolescents and young adults, with age often volunteered as a credential. Needless to say, Goldstein is frequently accused of being Old. (For the record, he is twenty-three. And I am twenty-five.) One common complaint was that Goldstein missed the acronymic implications of a lush little fantasy called "Lucy in the Sky with Diamonds." (Singers on a trip with pretensions?) Even more common is the indignant avowal that George Harrison's "Within You Without You" did not, as Goldstein averred, "resurrect the very clichés the Beatles helped bury," and that "Lucy in the Sky with Diamonds," as Sherry Brody, of Brooklyn, put it, "is not like other songs by stupid groups that say I love you and junk like that." (I hope I don't sound condescending. Miss Brody's letter is not only charming—she signs, "Please write back!"—but every bit as perceptive as many of its more ambitious competitors.) Of course, the clichés in "WYWY" to which Goldstein was referring were not "I love you and junk like that." They were "self-discovery" and "universal love," the kind of homilies that used to make the Beatles giggle, but that Harrison now seems to take seriously.

"WYWY" provided the most convenient launching pad for the textual analyses that almost everyone felt compelled to send off. One writer claimed that a book by William R. Shears (Ringo's persona on the record is "Billy Shears"), called *Here It Is,* is full of illuminating cross-references. A high-school freshman invoked the album as an example of "tmesis—the appearance of a poem to do credit to its words." Many saw the album as "an attack on middle-class values." Some writers were sure the Beatles had arrived at their current synthesis because, to quote a Juilliard student, "they have refused to prostitute themselves for their fans." But others insisted that *Sgt. Pepper* was "for the people."

The genius of the Beatles can be found in those last two contradictory suggestions, because both are true. Few of their old fans could have anticipated their present course or wished for it. Yet the Beatles have continued to please more of the old-timers than anyone but they—and the old-timers themselves—could have hoped. They really started the whole long-haired hippie business four years ago, and who knows whether they developed with it or it developed with them? All those pages of analysis are a gauge of how important the Beatles have become to . . . *us.*

One song on *Sgt. Pepper,* "Being for the Benefit of Mr. Kite," seems to me deliberately one-dimensional, nothing more than a description of a traveling circus. It fits beautifully into the album, which is a kind of long vaudeville show, but I feel almost certain it has no "meaning." Yet one girl, "age fifteen," writes that it presents "life as an eerie perverted circus." Is this sad? silly? horrifying? contemptible? From an adult it might be all four, but from a fifteen-year-old it is simply moving. A good Lennon-McCartney song is sufficiently cryptic to speak to the needs of whoever listens. If a fifteen-year-old finds life "an eerie perverted circus"—and for a fifteen-year-old that is an important perception—then that's what "Being for the Benefit of Mr. Kite" can just as well be about. If you've just discovered universal love, you have reason to find "Within You Without You" "great poetry." It really doesn't matter; if you're wrong, you're right.

One of the nice things the Beatles do for those of us who love them is charge commonplace English with meaning. I want to hold your hand. It's getting better all the time. Yeah, yeah, yeah. "Fixing a Hole," to which I alluded just above, is full of such suggestive phrases. I'll resist temptation and quote only five lines: "And it really doesn't matter if I'm wrong I'm right/ Where I belong I'm right/ Where I belong./ See the people standing there who disagree and never win/ And wonder why they don't get in my door."* This passage not only indicates the

* "Fixing a Hole" by Lennon/McCartney copyright © 1967 Northern Songs Limited. Used by permission. All rights reserved. International copyright secured.

interesting things the Beatles are doing with rhyme, skewing their stanzas and dispensing almost completely with traditional song form. It also serves as a gnomic reminder of the limitations of criticism. Allow me to fall into its trap by providing my own paraphrase, viz.: "In matters of interpretation, the important thing is not whether you're 'wrong' or 'right' but whether you are faithful to your own peculiar stance in the world. Those who insist upon absolute rectitude of their opinions will never attain my state of enlightenment."

Well, there it is; I've finally done it. Pompous right? Sorry, I'm just not John Lennon. But like everyone else, I feel compelled to make Our Boys My Boys. The first thirty times I heard "Fixing a Hole," I just listened and enjoyed it, keeping time, singing along, confident that it was obscure beyond my power to investigate. Then I noticed that all the interpreters were shying away from that song, or making an obvious botch of it, and I couldn't resist the challenge. Now, after several false starts that had me convinced for a while, I think I've got it. It's not surprising that their ideas are so much like my own. That's what they're saying, isn't it?

For, just like Sherry Brody, I have my own Beatles. As far as I'm concerned, "Fixing a Hole" is not like other songs by stupid groups that say I am alienated and junk like that. And I have other prejudices. I can't believe that the Beatles indulge in the simplistic kind of symbolism that turns a yellow submarine into a Nembutal or a banana—it is just a yellow submarine, damn it, an obvious elaboration of John's submarine fixation, first revealed in *A Hard Day's Night*. I think they want their meanings to be absorbed on an instinctual level, just as their new, complex music can be absorbed on a sensual level. I don't think they much care whether *Sgt. Pepper* is Great Art or some other moldy fig. And I think they are inordinately fond (in a rather recondite way) of what I call the real world. They want to turn us on, all right—to everything in that world and in ourselves.

What else could a journalist think?

Ned Rorem

∎

One of the most famous critical pieces published about the Beatles is the following essay by classical composer Ned Rorem. Written in 1967 and originally published on January 18, 1968, in *The New York Review of Books*, it celebrates the music of the Beatles. Rorem not only explains why their music is superior (memorable melodies, "infectious freshness") to their contemporaries, he even compares them favorably to the composers of the great era of song, that is, Monteverdi, Schumann, and Poulenc. Their music appealed to all ages "at all levels." Decades later, in 2000, writer and critic Andrew O'Hagan pointed out that he still was commenting on the Beatles. In *Lies* (Counterpoint), he wrote, "All art dates from the moment it was made. Some dates well, some badly. Giotto, *Le Sacre,* the Beatles date well. Beethoven's Ninth, Lautrec, the Rolling Stones date badly."

Other "serious" music critics wrote about the Beatles during this period (including *The Times* (London) music critic William Mann, an early supporter, musicologist Wilfrid Mellers, and later Leonard Bernstein, Aaron Copland, and John Cage), but Rorem was among the first highly respected composers to come out strongly on their behalf.

"The Beatles"

The New York Review of Books
January 18, 1968

∎ I NEVER GO to classical concerts anymore, and I don't know anyone who does. It's hard still to care whether some virtuoso tonight will perform the *Moonlight* Sonata a bit better or a bit worse than another virtuoso performed it last night.

I do often attend what used to be called avant-garde recitals, though seldom with delight, and inevitably I look around and wonder: What am I doing here? What am I learning? Where are the poets and painters and even composers who used to flock to these things? Well, perhaps what I'm doing here is a duty, keeping an ear on my profession so as to justify the joys of resentment, to steal an idea or two, or just to show charity toward some friend on the program. But I learn less and less. Meanwhile the absent artists are home playing records; they are *reacting* again, finally, to something they no longer find at concerts.

Reacting to what? To the Beatles, of course—the Beatles, whose arrival has proved one of the healthiest events in music since 1950, a fact which no one sensitive can fail to perceive to some degree. By healthy I mean alive and inspired—two adjectives long out of use. By music I include not only the general areas of jazz, but those expressions subsumed in the categories of chamber, opera, symphonic: in short, all music. And by sensitive I understand not the cultivated listening ability of elite Music Lovers so much as instinctive judgment. (There *are* still people who exclaim: "What's a nice musician like you putting us on about the Beatles for?" They are the same who at this late date take theater more seriously than movies and go to symphony concerts because Pop insults their intelligence, unaware that the situation is now precisely reversed.) As to what occurred around 1950, that will be the starting concern of this brief essay, an essay with a primarily musical approach. Most of the literary copy devoted to the Beatles extols the timely daring of the group's lyrics while skirting the essential, the music. Poetry may be the egg from which the nightingale is hatched, though in the last analysis the nightingale must come first.

My "musical approach" will be that of what once was termed the long-hair composer, somewhat disillusioned, nourished at the conservatory yet exposed all his life (as is any American, of necessity) to jazz. It will not pretend to a total appraisal, only to the fact that I and my colleagues have been happily torn from a long antiseptic nap by the energy of rock, principally as embodied in the Beatles. Naturally I've grown curious about this energy. What are its origins? What need does it fill? Why should the Beatles—who seem to be the best of a good thing, who in fact are far superior to all the other groups who pretend to copy them, most of which are nevertheless American and perpetuating what once was an essentially American thing—why should the Beatles have erupted from *Liverpool?* Could it be true, as Nat Hentoff suggests, that they "turned millions of American adolescents onto what had been here hurting all the time . . . but the young here never did want it raw so they absorbed it through the British filter"? Do the Beatles hurt indeed? And are they really so new? Does their attraction, be it pain or pleasure, stem from their words—or even from what's called their *sound*—or quite plainly from their tunes? Those are the questions, more or less in order, that I'd like to examine.

Around 1940, after a rather undifferentiated puberty, American music came into its own. Composers burgeoned over the land which, then deprived of foreign fertilizer, began producing an identifiably native fruit.

By the war's end we had cultivated a crop worthy of export, for every branch of the musical tree was thriving: symphonies of all shapes were being ground out in dozens; opera concepts were transplanting themselves into midwestern towns; and, for consideration here, vocal soloists were everywhere making themselves heard. On one side were Sinatra, Horne, Holiday, stylists of a high order, gorgeously performing material whose musical value (when not derived from the twenties of Gershwin or Porter) was nevertheless middling and whose literary content was dim. On the other side were specialized concert singers—Frijsh, Fairbank and Tangeman—who, though vocally dubious, still created a new brand of sound by persuading certain youngish composers to make singable songs based on texts of quality.

By 1950 the export was well under way. But our effervescence soon flattened when we realized that no one abroad cared much. Jazz, of course, had always been an attraction in the Europe that dismissed American "serious" music as not very serious; Europe, after all, was also reawakening after two numb decades under Hitler's shadow. But that awakening was into the past, namely into the dodecaphonic system which in America had atrophied, and in Germany had been forgotten by the war. This device (no, not a device but a way of thinking, a philosophy) was being revitalized not in the Germany where it had all begun, but in France, of all places! By 1950 Pierre Boulez had single-handedly cleared the path and set the tone that music would follow for the next decade throughout the world. And America took the cue, allowing her new-found individuality to dissolve into what ultimately became the bandwagon of International Academicism.

This turn of events surprised no one more than everyone, namely our most personal and famous composers. The lean melodism conscientiously forged by Aaron Copland, which had become the accepted American Style, was now tossed out by the young. The complicated romantic Tueton soup in which music had wallowed for a century was, in the twenties, reacted against either by the Spartan purification of a Satie or a Thomson (wherefrom Copland's "Americanism") or by the laughing iconoclasm of Dada which—though primarily, like Surrealism, a painters' and poets' medium—was musically exemplified in certain works of *Les Six*. Now in the fifties complex systems were revived, literally with a vengeance by certain of the middle-aged (Elliott Carter, Milton Babbitt, Arthur Berger, etc.) whom fame had bypassed during the Coplandesque forties, and by the young in general. If Dada randomness was reanimated by John Cage, this time with a straight face, Copland himself now chose to become re-engaged in serial formality, also with a straight face, as though intimidated by those deadly serious composers half his age.

These "serious" youngsters, in keeping with the times, were understandably more geared to practical concerns of science than to "superfluous" considerations of Self-Expression. When they wrote for the human voice (which they did less and less) it was treated not as an interpreter of poetry—nor even necessarily of words—but as a mechanism, often electronically revamped. Verse itself was no longer married *to* the music, or even framed *by* the music, but was illustrated *through* the music. And there was little use left for live singers.

Live singers themselves, at least those of formal training, weren't interested anyway. Modern music was too difficult. Besides it had no audience, and neither anymore did the classical song recital so beloved in the already distant years of Teyte and Lehmann. Young singers were lured away from *lieder,* from *la mélodie,* and from their own American "art song," until not one specialist remained. They had all been seduced by the big money and hopeful celebrity of grand opera. Even today the few exceptions are European: Schwarzkopf, Souzay, Fischer-Dieskau. Our accurate Bethany Beardslee certainly makes no money, while her excellent West Coast counterpart Marni Nixon, now does movie dubbing and musical comedy. But most modern song specialists have awful voices and give vanity concerts for invited guests.

Elsewhere was developing the Progressive, or Cool, jazz of Brubeck and Kenton and Mulligan, a rarefied expression that permitted neither song nor dance. The Hit Parade was defunct, Negro stylists out of jobs and vulgar vocalists of college bands in low esteem. Song was out.

Meanwhile the wall separating so-called classical from so-called jazz was crumbling, as each division sought somehow to join with and rejuvenate the other. Yet the need for "communication" so widely lamented today seemed to be satisfied less through music—any music—than through other outlets, particularly movies. Movies, in becoming accepted as a fine art, turned out to be the one medium which could depict most articulately the inarticulateness of today, even to intellectuals. Whereas the intellectualization of music had ironically alienated the intellectual and has not much interest for anyone else. Stravinsky, for example, may be a household word, but in fact little that he composed since 1930, and virtually nothing since 1950, is in the concert repertory anywhere. Stravinsky's recent music is heard exclusively when accom-

panied by the visuals of Balanchine, when performing biannually by
Robert Craft (the presence of the master himself at these performances
being the drawing card), or when conducted by the composer on Columbia Records with whom he has an exclusive contract.

I and a handful of songwriting friends (Paul Bowles, Daniel Pink-
ham, William Flanagan, David Diamond), who began in the forties, I
consider as having come in at the end, as having attempted the irrelevant resuscitation of a creature with sleeping sickness. Most of us have
written depressingly few songs lately, and those few emerged less from
driving need than from ever rarer commissions extended by die-hard
specialists. Since there's little money, publication, recording, performance or even concern for songs, our youthful enthusiasm for that most
gently urgent of mediums has, alas, pretty much dampened.

But if the once-thriving Art of Song has lain dormant since the war,
indications now show it restirring in all corners of the world—which is
not the same world that put it to bed. As a result, when Song really becomes wide awake again (the sleep has been nourishing), its composition and interpretation will be of a quite different order and for a quite
different public.

Since big-time vocalists like Leontyne Price are, for economic reasons, no longer principally occupied with miniature forms, and since
"serious" composers like Stockhausen are, for scientific reasons, no
longer principally occupied with human utterances (of which singing is
the most primitive and hence the most expressive), and since a master
like Stravinsky (who anyway was never famed for his solo vocal works)
seems only to be heard when seen, the artful tradition of great song has
been transferred from elite domains to the Beatles and their offshoots
who represent—as any non-specialized intellectual will tell you—the
finest communicable music of our time.

This music was already sprouting a decade ago through such innocent male sex symbols as Presley in America and Johnny Halliday in
France, both of whom were then caricatured by the English in a movie
called *Expresso Bongo,* a precursor of *Privilege,* about a none-too-
bright rock singer. These young soloists (still functioning and making
lots of money) were the parents of more sophisticated, more *committed,*
soloists like Dylan and Donovan, who in turn spawned a horde of masculine offspring including twins (Simon and Garfunkel, the most cultured),
quintuplets (Country Joe & The Fish, the most exotic), sextuplets (The
Association, the most nostalgic), even septuplets (Mothers of Invention,

the most madly satirical). With much less frequency were born female descendants such as Janis Ian or Bobbie Gentry (each of whom has produced one, and only one, good song—and who may be forgotten or immortal by the time this is read) and the trio of Supremes. Unlike their "grandparents," all these groups, plus some twenty other fairly good ones, write most of their own material, thus combining the traditions of twelfth-century troubadours, sixteenth-century madrigalists, and eighteenth-century musical artisans who were always composer-performers—in short, combining all sung expression (except opera) as it was before the twentieth century.

For this expression one must now employ (as I have been doing here) the straightforward word *Song,* as opposed to the misleading *lieder* which applies just to German repertory, or the pretentious *art song* which no longer applies to anything. (The only designation in English that ever really distinguished "serious art song" from what used to be named "pop tune" was "recital song.") Now, since pop tunes as once performed by such as Billie Holiday and the Big Bands during an epoch not merely dormant but dead are heard not only in nightclub and theater but in recital and concert, and since those tunes are as good as—if not better than—anything "serious" being composed today, the best cover-all term is simply *Song.* The only sub-categories are Good and Bad. Curiously, it is not through the suave innovations of our sophisticated composers that music is regaining health, but from the old-fashioned lung exercise of gangs of kids.

That the best of these gangs should have come from England is unimportant; they could have come from Arkansas. The Beatles' world is just another part of the undifferentiated International Academicism wherein the question is to be Better rather than Different. It seems to me that their attraction has little to do with (as Hentoff implied) "what had been here hurting," but on the contrary with enjoyment.

No sooner does Susan Sontag explain that "the new sensibility takes a rather dim view of pleasure" than we discover her "new" sensibility growing stale. Her allusion was to a breed of suspiciously articulate composers—suspicious because they spend more time in glib justification than in composition—and who denigrate the *liking* of music, the *bodily* liking of it. Indeed, one doesn't "like" Boulez, does one? To like is not their consideration; to comprehend is. But surely fun is the very core of the Beatles' musically contagious expression: the Japanese, the Poles (who ignore poetic subject matter of suicide and bombs) love them as much as their English-speaking fans; and surely that expression, by the very spontaneous timeliness of its nature, is something Sontag must approve of. The Beatles are antidote to the new (read "old") sensibility, and intellectuals are allowed to admit, without disgrace, that they like this music.

The Beatles are good even though everyone knows they're good, i.e., in spite of those claims of the Under Thirties about their filling a new sociological need like Civil Rights and LSD. Our need for them is neither sociological nor new, but artistic and old, specifically a *renewal*, a renewal of pleasure. All other arts in the past decade have to an extent felt this renewal; but music was not only the last of man's "useless" expressions to develop historically, it is also the last to evolve within any given generation—even when, as today, a generation endures a maximum of five years (that brief span wherein "the new sensibility" was caught).

Why are the Beatles superior? It is easy to say that most of their competition (like most everything everywhere) is junk; more important, their betterness is consistent: each of the songs from their latest three albums is memorable. The best of these memorable tunes—and the best is a large percentage ("Here, There and Everywhere," Good Day Sunshine," "Michelle," "Norwegian Wood" are already classics)—compare with those by composers from great eras of song: Monteverdi, Schumann, Poulenc.

Good melody—even perfect melody—can be both defined and taught, as indeed can the other three "dimensions" of music: rhythm, harmony, counterpoint (although rhythm is the only one that can exist alone). Melody may be described thus: a series of notes of varying pitch and length, which evolve into a recognizable musical shape. In the case of a melody (*tune* means the same thing) which is set to words, the musical line will flow in curves relating to the verse that propels it inevitably toward a "high" point, usually called climax, and thence to the moment of culmination. The *inevitable* element is what makes the melody good— or perfect. But perfection can be sterile, as witness the thousands of thirty-two bar models turned out yesterday in Tin Pan Alley, or today by, say, Jefferson Airplane. Can we really recall such tunes when divorced from their words?

Superior melody results from the same recipe, with the difference that certain of the ingredients are blessed with the Distortion of Genius. The Beatles' words often go against the music (the crushing poetry that opens "A Day in the Life" intoned to the blandest of tunes), even as

Martha Graham's music often contradicts her dance (she gyrates hysterically to utter silence, or stands motionless while all hell breaks loose in the pit). Because the Beatles pervert with naturalness they usually build solid structures, whereas their rivals pervert with affectation, aping the gargoyles but not the cathedral.

The unexpected in itself, of course, is no virtue, though all great works seem to contain it. For instance, to cite as examples only the above four songs: "Here, There and Everywhere" would seem at mid-hearing to be no more than a charming college show ballad, but once concluded it has grown immediately memorable. Why? Because of the minute harmonic shift on the words "wave of her hand," as surprising, yet as satisfyingly *right* as that in a Monteverdi madrigal like "A un giro sol." The notation of the hyper-exuberant rhythms in "Good Day Sunshine" was as aggravatingly elusive to me as some by Charles Ives, until I realized it was made by *triplets over the bar;* the "surprise" here was that the Beatles had made so simple a process *sound* so complex to a professional ear, and yet (by a third convolution) be instantly imitable by any amateur "with a beat." "Michelle" changes key on the very second measure (which is also the second word): in itself this is "allowed"— Poulenc often did it, and certainly he was the most derivative and correct composer who ever lived; the point is that he *chose* to do it on just the second measure, and that the choice worked. Genius doesn't lie in not being derivative, but in making right choices instead of wrong ones. As for "Norwegian Wood," again it is the arch of the tune—a movement growing increasingly disjunct, an inverted pyramid formed by a zigzag—which proves the song unique and memorable, rather than merely original.

The Beatles' superiority, of course, is finally as elusive as Mozart's to Clementi: they spoke skillfully the same tonal language, but only Mozart spoke it with the added magic of genius. Who will define such magic? The public, in realizing this superiority, is right, though not, as usual, for the wrong reason—as it was, say, ten years ago with *Lolita*. For while *Lolita* was accepted pretty much as just a naughty novel, the Beatles can legitimately be absorbed by all ages on all levels: one is allowed to dance or smoke or even have a funeral (playwright Joe Orton's in London) while listening to this music. The same public when discussing the Beatles does not do so by relating them to others, but by relating them to aspects of themselves, as though they were the self-contained definition of an entire movement, or as though in their so-brief career they had (which is true), like Picasso or Stravinsky, already passed through and dispensed with several "periods." For example, no sooner was the *Sergeant Pepper* album released than a quiver of argument was set off as to whether it was inferior to their previous album *Revolver,* or to *Rubber Soul.* The Beatles, so to speak, had sired themselves. But was "Eleanor Rigby" their mother or daughter? was "Michelle" their grandmother or granddaughter? and was the She of "She's Leaving Home" perhaps a sister, since she was the most recently born, or a wife?

And what's this one hears about their sound, those psychedelic effects produced from orchestration "breakthroughs" presumably inspired by Paul McCartney's leanings toward Stockhausen and electronics? Well, as first demonstrated in "Tomorrow Never Knows" and "Strawberry Fields," the sound proves less involved with content than color, more with glamour than construction. McCartney's composition has not been affected by these "innovations" which are instrumental tricks glossily surrounding the composition. Nor is any aspect of that composition itself more "progressive" than the Big Bands of yore, or the Cool groups of yesterday. The harmony at its boldest, as with the insistent dissonances of "I Want to Tell You," is basically Impressionist and never more advanced than the Ravel of *Chansons Madécasses.* The rhythm gets extremely fancy, as in "Good Day Sunshine," but nearly always falls within a ¾ measure simpler than the simplest Bartók of fifty years ago. The melodies, such as "Fixing a Hole" or "Michelle," are exquisitely etched, but evolve from standard modes—those with the lowered thirds and sevenths of the Blues. The counterpoint when strict, as in parts of "She's Leaving Home," is no more complex than "Three Blind Mice," and when free, as in "Got to Get You into My Life," has the freedom of Hindemith—which is really Bach without the problems, meaning without the working out of the solutions presented by the rigors of eighteenth-century part-writing (The Supremes, not to mention instrumentalists like Ornette Coleman, go much farther out than the Beatles in this domain.) As for the overall form, the songs of *Sergeant Pepper* are mostly less complicated than those of previous albums which, themselves, seldom adventured beyond a basic verse/chorus structure. It is not in innovation that Paul McCartney's originality lies, but in superiority. It remains to be seen how, if ever, he deals with more spacious forms. But of that miniature scene, Song, he is a modern master. As such he is the Beatles' most significant member.

The lyrics, or rather the poems, of John Lennon have been psychoanalyzed beyond recognition. They are indeed clever, touching, appropriately timely and (which is most important) well mated with the tunes. Yet without the tunes, are they really all that much better than the words of, say, Cole Porter or Marc Blitzstein? Certainly Blitzstein's music succeeds in spite of the dated commentary of his words, and Porter's songs remain beautiful with no words at all. We are often told (for instance by Korall in *Saturday Review*) that the Beatles "are shouting about important things," but are these things any more pertinent than "Strange Fruit" yesterday or "Miss Otis Regrets" the day before? Was Peggy Lee's crooning "Where or When" less psychedelic than "Lucy in the Sky"? And even if they are, could that be what makes the Beatles good? While the film *Privilege* portrays a rock singer so subversive he requires total control, the fact is, as Gene Lee puts it, that "thus far no rock group, not even the entire rock movement put together, has made a government nervous, as Gilbert and Sullivan did." Even if, in a pinch, poems can be successfully political, no music can be proved to "signify" anything, neither protest, nor love, nor even bubbling fountains, nothing. John Lennon's words do indeed not only expose current problems ("A Day in the Life") but suggest solutions ("Fixing a Hole"); and the music—which is presumably set to the verse, not vice versa—works fine. But that music is stronger; and, like the slow and meterless Gregorian Chant which altered the "meaning" of the rapid and ribald street chanties it stemmed from, Lennon's words do or don't matter according to how they're sung.

With Billic Holiday it was not so much the song as her way with the song; like Piaf she could make mediocrity seem masterful. With the Beatles it's the song itself, not necessarily their way—like Schubert whom even a monster can't destroy. "Michelle," for example, remains as lovely but becomes more clearly projected when performed by a "real" singer like Cathy Berberian. Her diction (and the diction of nearly anyone) is better than theirs, at least to non-Cockney ears.[1] Even if the words did not come second, the Beatles oblige you to judge the music first, by virtue of their blurred enunciation.

As for George Harrison's excursions into India, they seem the least persuasive aspect of the more recent Beatle language. Like McCartney with electronics, Harrison seems to have adopted only the frosting; but in pretending to have adopted also the structure, his two big pieces, "Love You To" and "Within You Without You," end up not hypnotic, merely sprawling. Harrison's orientalism is undoubtedly sincere but sounds as fake as the pentatonicism of Country Joe & The Fish. Debussy, like all his cohorts, was profoundly influenced by the Balinese exhibits at the Paris World's Fair of 1900, which inspired his *Pagodes* and *Lindaraja*. These pieces were as persuasive in the same genre as were the concert works many decades later by Henry Cowell or Harry Partch or even Peggy Glanville-Hicks. But whereas these sophisticated musicians without concern for "authenticity" translated Eastern sound effects into Western jargons and then spoke those jargons with controlled formality, Harrison still flounders for faithful meaning where it just won't work: good will and "inspiration" will never provide him with the background—the birthright—which of necessity produced the music he would emulate.

Ringo Starr's projects, when not involved with his comrades, are unknown, though he does seem to be learning to sing with what is quite literally an unutterable charm. Nor have I seen John Lennon's war movie. Thus far, however, when the Beatles are a conjointly creative process (even more than as a performing unit) they are at their most enticing.

Just as today my own composition springs more from pristine necessity than driving inspiration (I compose what I want to hear because no one else is doing it), so I listen—sifting and waiting—only to what I need. What I need now seems less embodied in newness than in nostalgia: how many thrilling experiences do we get per year anyway, after a certain age? Such nostalgia appears most clearly engendered by the Beatles. There isn't much more to say, since structurally they're not interesting to analyze: they've added nothing new, simply brought back excitement. The excitement originates (other than, of course, from their talent) in their absolutely insolent—hence innocent—unification of music's disparate components—that is, in using the most conservative devices of harmony, counterpoint, rhythm, melody, orchestration, and making them blend with an infectious freshness. (Parenthetically, their latest, "I Am the Walrus," seems a bit worrisome, more contrived, less "inspired" than anything hitherto. Though the texture may be Vaughan Williams with a Bebop superimposition and all very pretty, the final effect becomes parody of self-parody, the artist's realest danger. Though probably even the holy Beatles must be permitted an occasional stillborn child.)

The Beatles have, so to speak, brought *fiction* back to music, supplanting criticism. No, they aren't new, but as tuneful as the thirties with the same exuberance of futility that Bessie Smith employed. They have removed sterile martyrdom from art, revived the sensual. Their sweetness lies in that they doubtless couldn't care less about these pedantic explications.

If (and here's a big If) music at its most healthy is the creative reaction of, and stimulation for, the body, and at its most decadent is the creative reaction of and stimulation for the intellect—if, indeed, health is a desirable feature of art, and if, as I believe, the Beatles exemplify this feature, then we have reached (strange though it may seem as coincidence with our planet's final years) a new and golden renaissance of song.

Note

1. To American ears, in those early days at least, Cockney and Liverpudlian accents seemed the same, which led writer Andrew O'Hagan, years later, to observe that calling the Beatles Cockneys "thrilled the denizens of East London but caused chaos in the affections of Liverpudlians everywhere." See Andrew O'Hagan," Back in the US of A," *The New York Review of Books*, May 27, 2004.

■

FIVE

Hello, Goodbye
1968–1970

Jon Wiener

■

It now seems so long ago, but in the spring of 1968, many college campuses across America were on fire. Students seized campus buildings, protesting the war in Vietnam and racial politics. Following the assassination of Martin Luther King, Jr., in Memphis, riots broke out in a dozen or so American cities. Meanwhile, across the Atlantic, students in Paris engaged in violent street battles with the police. The Western world, or so it seemed, was on the brink of revolution.

During all this turmoil, the first version of "Revolution" was recorded on May 30 at the Abbey Road Studios in London. In this excerpt from *Come Together: John Lennon in His Time,* Jon Wiener follows public reaction to the release of the Beatles' single, "Revolution," during the summer of 1968. In contrast to the Rolling Stones' "Street Fighting Man," which advocated revolution, the Beatles seemed ambivalent, hedging their bets and wanting it both ways. Not surprisingly, the New Left and counterculture press responded negatively to the song, but *Time* magazine, again not surprisingly, but for different reasons, found it "exhilarating."

Writes Wiener, "The song marked John's decision that he had political responsibilities, and that he ought to fulfill them in his music. That was a momentous decision, much more significant than the lyrics of the song."

"May '68: Rock against Revolution"

from *Come Together: John Lennon in His Time*

■ IN THE SPRING of 1968 Europe's radical youth took to the streets with new energy. It would also be a season of revolutionary transformation in John's personal life. Those who visited John at home with Cynthia early that spring found him deeply depressed. Cynthia thought "it had something to do with student riots."

Thousands of students demonstrated in February in West Berlin, supporting the Vietnamese National Liberation Front and protesting the attempted assassination of New Left leader Rudi Dutschke. The next month in London, a huge march on the American embassy in Grosvenor Square was dispersed by riot police on horseback, a shocking display of official violence. And on May 6 students began their historic uprising in Paris. These waves of revolutionary politics washed into John's life, at home in Weybridge. May '68 brought his personal liberation: he spent his first night with Yoko Ono.

Since he had met her in 1966, he had wanted to collaborate with her on art projects. In May '68, while students were fighting in the streets of Paris and Cynthia was out of town, John invited Yoko to his home. "We were very shy together at first," she recalled. They spent the night making electronic music on John's bank of tape recorders. Everyone else thought his absorption with abstract sound was weird. "Then," he said, "we just made love right there in that little studio."

"She's me in drag," he answered when interviewers asked what attracted him to her. The Liverpool rock-and-roller thought he was the same person as the Japanese avant-garde artist; it was a breathtaking statement. It revealed how alienated he had become from his identity as a Beatle. John and Yoko were inseparable beginning in May '68.

Before May '68, liberal social theorists had proclaimed that bureaucratic capitalism and the consumer society had resolved the fundamental social conflicts and made radical politics obsolete. The students of Paris challenged that. They began by rebelling against bureaucracy in the university, fighting massive street battles with the police. As students overturned state authority in the universities, workers overturned capitalist power in the factories. Two weeks after the student rebellion began, ten million workers had joined a general strike; they occupied their factories, just as students had occupied the universities. What had seemed a stable and prosperous capitalist society had been brought to the brink of revolution. Historian Mark Poster wrote, "The monstrous spectacle of meaningless toil and passive consumption gave way to an exhilarating, joyous festival." The slogans of May included "It is forbidden to forbid," "A cop lives in each of us; we must kill him," and "Power to the imagination," an idea John would later turn into the song "Imagine."

John followed the May events closely in the papers and on television. In a great failure of intellect and imagination, he accepted the view that the most important feature of the May events was the violence of the students. He opposed it as a matter of principle. He knew the violence of the American war in Vietnam remained the most important political issue, and he went on American television on May 22 to denounce it as "insanity." But he also decided to declare his separation from the revolutionaries in the streets of Paris and elsewhere. He wrote a song in India when he "had this, you know, 'God will save us' feeling about it," he said later in *Lennon Remembers*. The first version of "Revolution" was recorded on May 30 at Abbey Road studios.

The events John was thinking about had begun earlier that year, when radicals and reactionaries alike had been stunned by the unprecedented victory of the Vietnamese National Liberation Front. The Tet offensive had coordinated surprise attacks on every major Vietnamese city. NLF troops penetrated the compound of the American embassy in Saigon, shattering whatever hope the American public still held that the United States could win its war. Grassroots antiwar sentiment, mobilized around the candidacy of Senator Eugene McCarthy in the Democratic presidential primaries, forced LBJ to declare he would not seek reelection.

In New York City, students at Columbia University seized campus buildings, protesting the university's expansion into neighboring Harlem; a thousand club-swinging policemen drove them out. Martin Luther King was assassinated in Memphis; ghetto riots broke out in a dozen cities. Students held antiwar demonstrations at two hundred colleges and universities.

The Yippies called on all young people opposed to the war to gather in Chicago in August at the Democratic national convention. Most movement leaders opposed that demonstration, arguing that the plan was irresponsible and provocative. None of the rock stars who had been invited attended except Phil Ochs and Country Joe and the Fish. Most potential demonstrators stayed away. Fewer than ten thousand showed up, while hundreds of thousands had attended mobilizations in New York and Washington, D.C. On the eve of the convention it looked like the demonstrations would be a failure.

A police riot made the demonstrations historic. Mayor Richard Daley put twelve thousand police on twelve-hour shifts, had twelve thousand more National Guardsmen and Army troops called up, armed them with rifles, bazookas, and flamethrowers, and ordered them to shoot to kill. Theodore White later wrote that Hubert Humphrey was "nominated in a sea of blood." The Rolling Stones released "Street Fighting Man," in which Jagger sang about the time being right for revolution; it was immediately banned from the airwaves in Chicago and Berkeley. And the new Beatles single came out, addressing the New Left directly, written and sung by John: "You say you want a revolution. . . ."

The New Left and counterculture press responded immediately. The Berkeley *Barb* wrote with typical excess, "'Revolution' sounds like the hawk plank adopted in the Chicago convention of the Democratic Death Party." "Hubert Humphrey couldn't have said it better," Jon Landau agreed. *Ramparts* called the song a "betrayal"; the *New Left Review* called it "a lamentable petty bourgeois cry of fear." Robert Christgau wrote in the *Village Voice,* "It is puritanical to expect musicians, or anyone else, to hew to the proper line. But it is reasonable to request that they not go out of their way to oppose it. Lennon has, and it takes much of the pleasure out of their music for me."

Ramparts objected to two lines in particular. It quoted from the chorus, where John said he knew it was going to be "all right," and commented, "Well, it isn't. You *know* it's *not* gonna be all right." It also criticized John's lines "You say you want a contribution," where he states he won't give "money for people with minds that hate." "They've gotten so far from thinking of 'contribution' to a political cause as meaning what they can do as artists that they conceive of their role essentially as that of millionaires," *Ramparts* declared. The magazine had a point, with which John would soon agree when he began to contribute to the peace movement as an artist.

John's song suggested he wouldn't support a revolution until he could see "the plan." His radical critics objected to that. The movement did not have a plan, in the sense that political parties with central committees did. The movement did have a project: liberation, self-emancipation, participatory democracy. The plan was that people should take part in making the decisions that affect their lives. The plan was to break out of the system that required official plans, and instead to liberate the imagination. At the time John couldn't see this project, but he would within the year.

"Revolution" was a message song, and "the words of a message song just lie on the floor," Greil Marcus wrote at the time. But there was "a message in the music which is ultimately more powerful than anyone's words"—something the political critics of John's "Revolution" had missed. "There is freedom and movement in music, even as there is sterility and repression in the lyrics," Marcus wrote. "The music doesn't say 'cool it' or 'don't fight the cops.' . . . The music dodges the message and comes out in front."

Time devoted an entire article to the song, something it had never done before. It reported to its readers that the Beatles had criticized "radical activists the world over," and that the whole thing was "exhilarating."

John hinted that his position was not so firmly antagonistic to the left in the second version of the song, released on the "White Album" (officially titled *The Beatles*) two months after the single. In subsequent interviews he explained that the single version had been produced the way Paul wanted it, while the album version was done John's way—slower, so that the words could be understood better. And John's way had one significant change in the words: after he sang "When you talk about destruction / Don't you know that you can count me out," he added "in." The "in" was omitted from the lyrics printed on the sleeve but was perfectly clear on the record, sung with equal emphasis to the "out." "I put in both because I wasn't sure," he said. Already John was revealing some ambivalence about his relationship to the New Left—and on precisely the issue that separated the radicals most sharply from the "all you need is love" world view the Beatles had done so much to promote.

The song marked John's decision that he had political responsibilities, and that he ought to fulfill them in his music. That was a momentous decision, much more significant than the lyrics of the song. Some of the issues he raised in the song were, in any case, legitimate. He was concerned about the nature and extent of the destruction advocated by revolutionaries, he wanted to know how they envisioned future society, and he seemed to say that the politics of Maoist students were self-defeating: they weren't "gonna make it with anyone, anyhow." But he took these genuine problems of revolutionary morality and strategy as an excuse for abandoning politics altogether and substituting in its place a quest for personal liberation: "free your mind instead." More than anything else, this argument aroused the radicals' anger.

Some on the left defended "Revolution." The SDS newspaper at Cornell University said John was right to reject radicals with "minds that hate," and praised the Beatles for consistently advocating "pacifist idealism" in the face of increasing violence both in the world and among leftists. "You can argue about the effectiveness of non-violence as a tactic, but it would be absurd to claim that it is a conservative notion. . . . The Beatles want to change the world, and they are doing what they can."

Then there was the issue of the "shoo-be-do-wahs" with which Paul and George answered John's "You know it's gonna be—." The Beatles are not fools, Michael Wood argued in *Commonweal*. They know it's absurd to say "it's gonna be all right." The "shoo-be-do-wahs" suggest "they mean that statements about whether it is or isn't are all part of that political crap they dislike so much"—a cogent interpretation.

Jonathan Cott pushed John on the same question in a *Rolling Stone* interview later that year. He asked what John would say to a black person who tried to "free his mind" but found that racist institutions still oppressed him. "That's why I did the 'out and in' bit," John answered. "I don't know what I'd be doing if I was in his position. I don't think I'd be so meek and mild. I just don't know."

John revealed more about his political thinking in the electronic collage "Revolution 9," also recorded in May '68. He later explained that he thought he was "painting in sound a picture of revolution": no melody, no words, no chords, no singing, nobody playing instruments—and, as Christgau and Picarella point out, "for eight minutes of an album officially titled *The Beatles*, there were no Beatles." The whole thing sounded frightening, chaotic, inhuman. John had no sense that a revolution could liberate people's creative energy, free them from old forms of oppression, forge a new community. No wonder he wanted to "see the plan."

At least nineteen cover versions of "Revolution" have been released in the United States, including one by the Columbia Musical Treasury Orchestra, a Hawaiian guitar version by Santo and Johnny (whose "Sleep Walk" spent three weeks in the Number One slot in September 1959), and one by the Chords (could they be the same Chords who sang the original "Sh-Boom"?).

More interesting than any of these was Nina Simone's musical answer to John's song. A black jazz singer, she had worked hard for the civil rights movement and had written her own personal protest song, "Mississippi—Goddamn!" She had R&B hits in the mid-sixties with "I Put a Spell on You," "Don't Let Me Be Misunderstood," and "Young, Gifted, and Black." Her reply to John, also titled "Revolution," had a similar musical and lyrical structure to his song. She told him that if he wanted to sing about revolution, he would have to "clean" his "brain." John had told revolutionaries to count him out of any destruction; she sang about destroying oppression and injustice, and declared that the Constitution, which John defended, would have to be changed. A year later in *Lennon Remembers* John said he thought Nina Simone's answer was "very good," that he "enjoyed somebody who reacted immediately to what I had said."

Despite its significance for the New Left, "Revolution" never was a great hit. Paul had worried from the beginning that it needed to be made more commercial to succeed. His pop instincts were correct. The song does not appear on the official list of Beatles' million sellers. It peaked in the charts at Number Twelve. Part of the problem was that it was the B side of Paul's "Hey Jude," which became the biggest Beatles hit in history and drowned out "Revolution" in the fall of 1968. The masses of Beatles fans were not terribly interested in "Revolution." Many must have ignored the words and danced to the beat. Others misunderstood it: one Cleveland disc jockey introduced it by remarking that the song "calls for a reevaluation of our entire society." For the left, however, the song confirmed their worst suspicions: the Fab Four were the good boys of rock, rock's liberals.

John's "Revolution" aroused the interest not only of the left but also of the far right. William Buckley paid mocking tribute to its message in his syndicated column, and was promptly attacked by the John Birch Society—from the right. According to the Birch Society's magazine, "The Beatles are simply telling the Maoists that Fabian gradualism is working, and that the Maoists might blow it all by getting the public excited before things are ready for 'revolution'—'it's gonna be all right.' In short, 'Revolution' takes the Moscow line against Trotskyites and the Progressive Labor Party, based on Lenin's *Leftwing Extremism:* [sic] *An Infantile Disorder.*" As final evidence for this interpretation, the Birchers were urged to listen to the other key pro-Soviet statement on the White Album, "Back in the U.S.S.R."

Vincent Bugliosi
with Curt Gentry

■

For a band that believed so much in the transforming qualities of peace and love, it is strangely ironic that death and murder have followed the Beatles through much of their short existence, as well as many years after their breakup. Death threats during their concert tours, the assassination of John Lennon, the attempted murder of George Harrison are obvious examples. But the most chilling violent episodes associated with the Beatles must be the Manson murders.

When Charles Manson first heard the Beatles, he was incarcerated at a penitentiary in Washington State—by that time he had already spent half his life in and out of juvenile detention halls. Manson felt deeply that the Beatles' music carried a message: "to give up our egos." By early 1969, Manson had become obsessed with listening to the White Album and reading the Book of Revelation. What he took away from the music of the Beatles was a vision, a prophecy, of nightmarish proportions: "This music is bringing on the revolution, the unorganized overthrow of the Establishment." To Manson, it was also a premonition of a pending race war that was soon to engulf the world.

In Manson's warped mind, "Helter Skelter," a frenzied example of hard rock and ostensibly a song about an English playground slide in an amusement park, became something else altogether: a call for annihilation. On August 9, 1969, in Los Angeles, Manson's cohorts murdered Steven Parent, Voytek Frykowski, Abigail Folger, Jay Sebring, and, most famously, the very pregnant Sharon Tate, the actress-wife of director Roman Polanski. The following night, they attacked again, this time killing Leno and Rosemary LaBianca. One of the messages they left behind, written in blood on the refrigerator door, was a misspelled "HEALTER SHELTER." When the murderers eventually were caught and brought to trial, the exhibits included a copy of the White Album.

from *Helter Skelter:*
The True Story of the Manson Murders

■ IT WAS PAUL WATKINS who finally supplied the missing link in Manson's motive for the murders. Yet, if I hadn't talked to [Gregg] Jakobson and [Brooks] Poston, I might have missed its importance, for it was from all three, Gregg, Brooks, and Paul, that I obtained the keys to understanding (1) Charles Manson's unique interpretation of the Book of Revelation, and (2) his decidedly curious and complex attitude toward the English musical group the Beatles.

Several persons had told me Manson was fond of quoting from the Bible, particularly the ninth chapter of Revelation. Once Charlie had handed Jakobson a Bible, already open to the chapter, and, while he read it, supplied his own interpretation of the verses. With only one exception, which will be noted, what Gregg told me tallied with what I later heard from Poston and Watkins.

The "four angels" were the Beatles, whom Manson considered "leaders, spokesmen, prophets," according to Gregg. The line "And he opened the bottomless pit . . . And there came out of the smoke locusts upon the earth; and unto them was given power . . ." was still another reference to the English group, Gregg said. Locusts—Beatles—one and the same. "Their faces were as the faces of men," yet "they had hair as the hair of women." An obvious reference to the long-haired musicians. Out of the mouths of the four angels "issued fire and brimstone." Gregg: "This referred to the spoken words, the lyrics of the Beatles' songs, the power that came out of their mouths."

Their "breastplates of iron," Poston added, were their electric guitars. Their shapes "like unto horses prepared unto battle" were the dune buggies. The "horsemen who numbered two hundred thousand thousand," and who would roam the earth spreading destruction, were the motorcyclists.

"And it was commanded them that they should not hurt the grass of the earth, neither any green thing, neither any tree; but only those men which have not the seal of God in their foreheads." I wondered about that seal on the forehead. How did Manson interpret that? I asked Jakobson.

"It was all subjective," Gregg replied. "He said there would be a mark on people." Charlie had never told him exactly what the mark would be, only that he, Charlie, "would be able to tell, he would know," and that "the mark would designate whether they were with him or against him." With Charlie, it was either one or the other, Gregg said; "there was no middle road."

One verse spoke of worshipping demons and idols of gold and silver and bronze. Manson said that referred to the material worship of the establishment: of automobiles, houses, money.

Q. "Directing your attention to Verse 15, which reads: 'And the four angels were loosed, which were prepared for an hour, and a day, and a month, and a year, for to slay the third part of men.' Did he say what that meant?"

A. "He said that those were the people who would die in Helter Skelter . . . one third of mankind . . . the white race."

I now knew I was on the right track.

Only on one point did Jakobson's recollection of Manson's interpretation differ from that of the others. The first verse of Revelation 9 refers to a fifth angel; the chapter ends, however, referring to only four. Originally there were five Beatles, Gregg explained, one of whom, Stuart Sutcliffe, had died in Germany in 1962.

Poston and Watkins—who, unlike Jakobson, were members of the Family—interpreted this much differently. Verse I reads: "And the fifth angel sounded, and I saw a star fall from heaven unto the earth: and to him was given the key of the bottomless pit."

To members of the Family the identity of that fifth angel of the bottomless pit, was never in doubt. It was Charlie.

Verse II reads: "And they had a king over them, which is the angel of the bottomless pit, whose name in the Hebrew tongue is Abaddon, but in the Greek tongue hath his name Apollyon."

The king also had a Latin name, which, though it appears in the Catholic Douay Version, was inadvertently omitted by the translators of the King James version. It was Exterminans.

Exterminans, t/n Charles Manson.

As far as Jakobson, Watkins, and Poston knew, Manson placed no special meaning on the last verse of Revelation 9. But I found myself thinking of it often in the months ahead:

"Neither repented they of their murders, nor of their sorceries, nor of their fornication, nor of their thefts."

"The important thing to remember about Revelation 9," Gregg told me, "is that Charlie believed this was happening *now*, not in the future. It's going to begin now and it's time to choose sides . . . either that or flee with him to the desert."

According to Jakobson, Manson believed "the Beatles were spokesmen. They were speaking to Charlie, through their songs, letting him know from across the ocean that this is what was going to go down. He believed this firmly . . . He considered their songs prophecy, especially the songs in the so-called White Album . . . He told me that many, many times."

Watkins and Poston also said that Manson and the Family were convinced that the Beatles were speaking to Charlie through their music. For example, in the song "I Will" are the lines: "And when at last I find you / Your song will fill the air / Sing it loud so I can hear you / Make it easy to be near you . . ." Charlie interpreted this to mean the Beatles wanted him to make an album, Poston and Watkins said. Charlie told them that the Beatles were looking for JC and he was the JC they were looking for. He also told them that the Beatles knew that Christ had returned to earth again and that he was living somewhere in Los Angeles.

"How in the world did he come up with that?" I asked him.

In the White Album is a song called "Honey Pie," a lyric of which reads: "Oh honey pie my position is tragic / Come and show me the magic / Of your Hollywood song." A later lyric goes: "Oh honey pie you are driving me frantic / Sail across the Atlantic / To be where you belong."

Charlie, of course, wanted *them* to sail across the Atlantic, to join him in Death Valley. While residing in the Gresham Street house (in January and February of 1969, just after the White Album was released), Manson and the girls sent several telegrams, wrote a number of letters, and made at least three telephone calls to England, attempting to reach the Beatles. No luck.

The line "I'm in love but I'm lazy" from "Honey Pie" meant to Charlie that the Beatles loved JC but were too lazy to go looking for him; also, they'd just gone all the way to India, following a man who they'd finally decided was a false prophet, the Maharishi. They were also calling for JC/Charlie in the first eight lines of the song "Don't Pass Me By," in "Yer Blues," and, in the earlier *Magical Mystery Tour* album, in "Blue Jay Way."

Much of this I would never use at the trial; it was simply too absurd.

The Beatles' White Album, Manson told Watkins, Poston, and others, "set up things for the revolution." *His* album, which was to follow, would, in Charlie's words, "blow the cork off the bottle. That would start it."

Much of the time at the Gresham Street house, according to Poston, Watkins, and others, was spent composing songs for Charlie's album. Each was to be a message song, directed to a particular group of people, such as the bikers, outlining the part they'd play in Helter Skelter. Charlie worked hard on these songs; they had to be very subtle, he said, like

the Beatles' own songs, their true meaning hidden beneath the awareness of all but the tuned-in people.

Manson was counting on Terry Melcher [son of the actress Doris
Day] to produce this album. According to numerous Family members
(both Melcher and Jakobson denied this), Terry had promised to come
and listen to the songs one evening. The girls cleaned the house, baked
cookies, rolled joints. Melcher didn't show. Manson, according to Poston and Watkins, never forgave Terry for this. Melcher's word was no
good, he said angrily on a number of occasions.

Though the Beatles had made many records, it was the double-disk
White Album, which Capitol issued in December 1968, that Manson
considered most important. Even the fact that the cover was white—
with no other design except the embossed name of the group—held significance for him.

It was, and remains, a startling album, containing some of the
Beatles' finest music, and some of their strangest. Its thirty songs range
from tender love ballads to pop parodies to cacophonies of noise made
by taking loops of very diverse tapes and splicing them together. To
Charles Manson, however, it was prophecy. At least this is what he convinced his followers.

That Charlie had renamed Susan Atkins "Sadie Mae Glutz" long before the White Album appeared containing the song "Sexy Sadie" was
additional proof to the Family that Manson and the Beatles were men-
tally attuned.

Almost every song in the album had a hidden meaning, which Manson interpreted for his followers. To Charlie "Rocky Raccoon" meant
"coon" or the black man. While to everyone except Manson and the
Family it was obvious that the lyrics of "Happiness Is a Warm Gun" had
sexual connotations, Charlie interpreted the song to mean that the
Beatles were telling blackie go get guns and fight whitey.

According to Poston and Watkins, the Family played five songs in the
White Album more than all the others. They were: "Blackbird," "Piggies," "Revolution 1," "Revolution 9," and "Helter Skelter."

"Blackbird singing in the dead of night / Take these broken wings and
learn to fly / All your life / You were only waiting for this moment to
arise," went the lyrics of "Blackbird." According to Jakobson, "Charlie
believed that the moment was now and that the black man was going to
arise, overthrow the white man, and take his turn." According to
Watkins, in this song Charlie "figured the Beatles were programming
the black people to get it up, get it on, start doing it."

On first hearing the song, I'd thought that the LaBianca killers had made a mistake, writing "rise" instead of "arise." However, Jakobson told me that Charlie said that the black man was going to "rise" up against the white man. "'Rise' was one of Charlie's big words," Gregg said, providing me with the origin of still another of the key words.

Both the Tate and LaBianca murders had occurred in "the dead of night." However, if the parallel had special significance to Manson, he never admitted it to anyone I interviewed, nor, if he knew it, did he admit the dictionary meaning of the phrase "helter skelter." The song "Helter Skelter" begins: "When I get to the bottom I go back to the top of the slide / Where I stop and I turn and I go for a ride . . ." According to Poston, Manson said this was a reference to the Family emerging from the bottomless pit.

There was a simpler explanation. In England, home of the Beatles, "helter skelter" is another name for a slide in an amusement park.

If you listen closely, you can hear grunts and oinks in the background of the song "Piggies."* By "piggies," Gregg and the others told me, Manson meant anyone who belonged to the establishment.

Like Manson himself, the song was openly critical of the piggies, noting that what they really needed was a damned good whacking.

"By that he meant the black man was going to give the piggies, the establishment, a damned good whacking," Jakobson explained. Charlie really loved that line, both Watkins and Poston said; he was always quoting it.

I couldn't listen to the final stanza without visualizing what had happened at 3301 Waverly Drive. It describes piggy couples dining out in all their starched finery, eating bacon with their forks and knives.

Rosemary LaBianca: forty-one knife wounds. Leno LaBianca: twelve knife wounds, punctured with a fork seven times, a *knife* in his throat, a *fork* in his stomach, and, on the wall, in his own blood, DEATH TO PIGS.

"There's a chord at the end of the song 'Piggies,'" Watkins said. "It goes down and it's a really weird chord. After the sound of piggies snorting. And in the 'Revolution 9' song, there's that same chord, and after it they have a little pause and snort, snort, snort. But in the pause, there is machine-gun fire.

* Unlike ex-Beatles John Lennon and Paul McCartney, George Harrison refused the authors permission to quote from the lyrics of any of his songs, including "Piggies."

"And it's the same thing with the 'Helter Skelter' song," Paul continued. "They had this really weird chord. And in the 'Revolution 9' song there's the same chord again, with machine guns firing and people dying and screaming stuff."

The White Album contains two songs with the word "revolution" in their titles.

The printed lyrics of "Revolution 1," as given on the jacket insert, read; "You say you want a revolution / Well you know / We all want to change the world . . . / But when you talk about destruction / Don't you know that you can count me out."

When you listen to the record itself, however, immediately after "out" you hear the word "in."

Manson took this to mean the Beatles, once undecided, now favored the revolution.

Manson made much of these "hidden lyrics," which can be found in a number of the Beatles' songs but are especially prevalent in the White Album. They were, he told his followers, direct communications to him, Charlie/JC.

Later on the lyrics go: "You say you got a real solution / Well you know / We'd all love to see the plan."

The meaning of this was obvious to Manson: Sing out, Charlie, and tell us how we can escape the holocaust.

Of all the Beatles' songs, "Revolution 9" is easily the weirdest. Reviewers couldn't decide whether it was an exciting new direction for rock or an elaborate put-on. One critic said it reminded him of "a bad acid trip."

There are no lyrics as such, nor is it music in any conventional sense; rather, it is a montage of noises—whispers, shouts, snatches of dialogue from the BBC, bits of classical music, mortars exploding, babies crying, church hymns, car horns, and football yells—which, together with the oft reiterated refrain "Number 9, Number 9, Number 9," build to a climax of machine-gun fire and screams, to be followed by the soft and obviously symbolic lullaby "Good Night."

Of all the songs in the White Album, Jakobson said, Charlie "spoke mostly of 'Revolution 9.'" He said "it was the Beatles' way of telling people what was going to happen; it was their way of making prophecy; it directly paralleled the Bible's Revelation 9."

It was also the battle of Armageddon, the coming black-white revolution portrayed in sound, Manson claimed, and after having listened to it myself, I could easily believe that if ever there were such a conflict, this was probably very much what it would sound like.

According to Poston: "When Charlie was listening to it, he heard in the background noise, in and around the machine-gun fire and the oinking of pigs, a man's voice saying 'Rise.'" Listening to the recording again, I also heard it, twice repeated: the first time almost a whisper, the second a long-drawn out scream.* This was potent evidence. Through both Jakobson and Poston, I'd now linked Manson, irrevocably, with the word "rise" printed in blood at the LaBianca residence.

In "Revolution 1" the Beatles had finally decided to commit themselves to the revolution. In "Revolution 9" they were telling the black man that *now* was the time to rise and start it all. According to Charlie.

Manson found many other messages in this song (including the words "Block that Nixon"), but as far as his philosophy of Helter Skelter was concerned, these were the most important.

Charles Manson was already talking about an imminent black-white war when Gregg Jakobson first met him, in the spring of 1968. There was an underground expression current at the time, "the shit is coming down," variously interpreted as meaning the day of judgment was at hand or all hell was breaking loose, and Charlie often used it in reference to the coming racial conflict. But he wasn't rabid about it, Gregg said; it was just one of many subjects they discussed.

"When I first met Charlie [in June 1968], he really didn't have any of this Helter Skelter stuff going," Paul Watkins told me. "He talked a little bit about the 'shit coming down,' but just barely . . . He said when the shit comes down the black man will be on one side and the white will be on the other, and that's all he said about it."

Then, that December, Capitol issued the Beatles' White Album, one of the songs of which was "Helter Skelter." The final stanza went: "Look out helter skelter helter skelter helter skelter / Look out [background scream] helter skelter / She's coming down fast / Yes she is / Yes she is."

Manson apparently first heard the White Album in Los Angeles, while on a trip there from Barker Ranch, where most of the Family remained. When Manson returned to Death Valley on December 31, 1968, he told

---

* It is first heard two minutes and thirty-four seconds into the song, just after the crowd sounds that follow "lots of stab wounds as it were" and "informed him on the third night" and just before "Number 9, Number 9."

the group, according to Poston, "Are you hep to what the Beatles are saying? Helter Skelter is coming down. The Beatles are telling it like it is."

It was the same expression, except that in place of the word for defecation Manson now substituted "Helter Skelter."

Another link had been made, this time to the bloody words on the refrigerator door at the LaBianca residence.

Though this was the first time Manson used the phrase, it was not to be the last.

Watkins: "And he started rapping about this Beatle album and Helter Skelter and all these meanings that I didn't get out of it . . . and he builds this picture up and he called it Helter Skelter, and what it meant was the Negroes were going to come down and rip the cities all apart."

After this, Watkins said, "We started listening to the Beatles' album constantly . . ."

Death Valley is very cold in the winter, so Manson found a two-story house at 20910 Gresham Street in Canoga Park, in the San Fernando Valley, not too far from Spahn Ranch. In January 1969, Watkins said, "we all moved into the Gresham Street house to get ready for Helter Skelter. So we could watch it coming down and see all of the things going on in the city. He [Charlie] called the Gresham Street house 'The Yellow Submarine' from the Beatles' movie. It was like a submarine in that when you were in it you weren't allowed to go out. You could only peek out of the windows. We started designing dune buggies and motorcycles and we were going to buy twenty-five Harley sportsters . . . and we mapped escape routes to the desert . . . supply caches . . . we had all these different things going.

"I watched him building this big picture up," Paul noted. "He would do it very slowly, very carefully. I swallowed it hook, line, and sinker.

"Before Helter Skelter came along," Watkins said with a sigh of wistful nostalgia, "all Charlie cared about was orgies."

Andru J. Reeve

■

One of the most persistent, and infamous, of rumors associated with the Beatles was the Paul-is-dead hoax that swept across the United States in 1969. Here rock myth merged with urban legend to create one of the most absurd tales in popular music history. As the story goes, McCartney was supposedly killed in an automobile accident in early November 1966, after leaving the EMI recording studios in London. The death was kept secret as the surviving Beatles hired an impostor—a Scottish look-alike named William Campbell—to pose as McCartney, and then slowly released the information in a series of cryptic clues that were included on their albums. Journalist Andru J. Reeve discusses the rumor in all its glorious detail in his book, *Turn Me On, Dead Man: The Beatles and the "Paul-Is-Dead" Hoax.* He traces the origin of the story to Ann Arbor, Michigan, and an article that ran in the October 14, 1969, issue of a campus newspaper, *The Michigan Daily,* by Fred LaBour. Even though the piece was meant to be a joke, the story was widely reported and, indeed, took on a life (pun intended) of its own. Everywhere they looked, it seems, Beatles fans—as many as one hundred—found clues to support their thesis. Finally, a reporter from *Life* magazine was assigned to uncover the real truth. Surprise. Paul and Linda were alive and well and living on their farm in Kintyre in the southwest corner of Scotland. The entire article appears in Reeve's book, which is reprinted below.

Devin McKinney also discusses the Paul-is-dead hoax in his excellent study of the Beatles, *Magic Circles: The Beatles in Dream and History.*

from *Turn Me On, Dead Man: The Beatles and the "Paul-Is-Dead" Hoax*

■ DAWN CRACKED ACROSS the cold, clear Michigan sky. As sleepy students trudged out to early morning classes, many first stopped at the news racks outside the Hatcher Library to drop in their dime for a copy of the campus newspaper. Soon it was evident that this was no ordinary issue of *The Michigan Daily.* Word began circulating that the October 14 edition was an absolute must-read and by mid-morning, the newspaper was sold out. It would eventually go through two more press runs before the day was over. The story that was getting everybody's attention carried Fred LaBour's byline and took up all of Page 2: "MCCARTNEY DEAD: NEW EVIDENCE BROUGHT TO LIGHT":

[EDITOR'S NOTE: Mr. LaBour was originally assigned to review *Abbey Road,* the Beatles' latest album, for the *Daily.* While extensively researching *Abbey Road*'s background, however, he chanced upon a startling string of coincidences which put him on the trail of something much more significant. He wishes to thank WKNR-FM, Louise Harrison Caldwell, and George Martin's illegitimate daughter Marian for their help. Mr. LaBour says it's all true. J.G.]

Paul McCartney was killed in an automobile accident in early November, 1966 after leaving EMI recording studios tired, sad and dejected. The Beatles had been preparing their forthcoming album, tentatively entitled *Smile,* when progress bogged down in intragroup hassles and bickering. Paul climbed into his Aston-Martin, sped away into the rainy, chill night, and was found four hours later pinned under his car in a culvert with the top of his head sheared off. He was deader than a doornail.

Thus began the greatest hoax of our time and the subsequent founding of a new religion based upon Paul as Messiah.

The Beatles as a whole had considered seriously what would happen to them if one should meet with death as early as 1964 when substitute drummers were utilized to fill in for an ailing Ringo Starr. However, it should be emphasized for the sake of religious records, that they had no definite premonition of the death of Paul. From all accounts, it appears to have been simply an unforeseen accident.

When word of Paul's untimely demise was flashed back to the studios, the surviving Beatles, in a hurriedly called conference with George Martin, decided to keep the information from the public for as long as possible. As John Lennon reportedly said, "Paul always liked a good joke," and it seemed that they considered the move an attempt to make the best out of a bad situation. As will be seen shortly, however, the "good joke" soon took on terrifying proportions.

George Harrison was called upon to bury Paul, Ringo conducted services, and John went into seclusion for three days. After his meditation, Lennon called another meeting of the group, again with George Martin, and laid the groundwork for the ensuing hoax. Lennon's plan was to create a false Paul McCartney, bring him into the group as if nothing had happened and then slowly release the information of the real Paul's death to the world via clues secreted in the record albums.

The plan was adopted, although Ringo expressed skepticism as to its possible success, and work began. (Brian Epstein was informed of the group's plan, threatened to expose it all, and mysteriously died, leaving five men who knew of the plot.)

First, a Paul lookalike contest was held and a living substitute was found in Scotland. He was an orphan from Edinburgh named William Campbell, and his picture can be found in the lower left-hand corner of the collage distributed with *The Beatles* album.

Minor plastic surgery was required to complete the image, and Campbell's mustache distracted everyone who knew the original McCartney from the imposter's real identity. The other Beatles subsequently grew mustaches to further integrate the "new" Paul into the group.

Voice print studies have confirmed the difference in voice timbre between the original and phoney Paul, but the difference was so slight that after studying tapes of Paul's voice and singing style, Campbell nearly erased entirely his own speech patterns and successfully adopted the late McCartney's.

Work then began upon the first post-Paul album, *Sergeant Pepper's Lonely Hearts Club Band. Smile,* incidentally, was junked and eventually picked up by Brian Wilson who attempted to salvage it but couldn't. He was allowed to work on *Smile* because the Beatles, especially Paul, had enjoyed "Good Vibrations" to a high degree and respected Wilson's ability immensely. *Smile* was finally thrown away and Capitol Records, ignorant of the whole plot, sued Wilson. Brian later paid tribute to Paul with *Smiley Smile.*

Lennon and Martin worked closely throughout the spring of 1967 on *Sgt. Pepper.* Their goal was an artistically and monetarily successful album filled with clues to Paul's death. It was decided that an appropriate cover would include a grave and so it does. At the lower part of the grave are yellow flowers shaped as Paul's bass or, if you prefer, the initial

"P". On the inside of the cover, on the fake Paul's arm, is a patch reading "O.P.D." which is a symbol used in England similar to our "D.O.A." meaning Officially Pronounced Dead. The medal upon his left breast is given by the British Army commemorating heroic death.

On the back cover, Paul's back is turned to us. The others are facing us. The songs on the album contain numerous references to Paul's accident, "A Day In The Life" being the most obvious example. "A crowd of people stood and stared. They'd seen his face before . . ." etc. When the top of a man's head is sheared off his identity is partially obscured.

The entire concept of the album, that of a different group, yet "one you've known for all these years" is significant. Another face of the plot is the emergence of Martin as an important composer, all the while masquerading as Paul. His old-time piano melodies, begun with "When I'm 64" and continuing through "Maxwell's Silver Hammer" are actually century-old barroom tunes he has extensively researched. If you recall, Martin has a scholarly background in all phases of music.

While *Sgt. Pepper* was being recorded, Lennon worked on a song called "Strawberry Fields Forever" and inserted at the end of the recording after the horn freakout, a distorted voice saying "I buried Paul." Play it at 45 rpm and check it out yourself.

"Strawberry Fields" eventually became incorporated into a larger work, *Magical Mystery Tour*, an album and film chocked full of veiled references to that rainy, tragic night.

Lennon had been doing a great deal of reading on the ritual of death in various cultures around the world (documented by Hunter Davies' authorized biography of the Beatles) and presented his knowledge graphically in *Tour*.

One instance is the constant appearance of a hand behind Paul's head in nearly every picture in the record album. The hand behind the head is a symbol to mystics of death. Another is the picture of Paul (Campbell) on page three with the poster saying "I YOU WAS" indicating change of identity. Another is the appearance of surgeons and policemen, both involved in Paul's car crash, on page five.

☼   ☼   ☼

On pages ten and thirteen Paul is shown wearing black trousers and no shoes. Dead men are buried in black trousers and without shoes. Empty shoes, as appear next to Ringo's drums on page thirteen, were a Grecian symbol of death. And finally, on page 23 where the group has just descended a long, curving staircase, Paul is wearing a black rose while the other three are wearing red roses.

The songs are again paramount. "Magical Mystery Tour" implies the hoax in its entirety and marks Lennon's developing suspicion that the plot is out of hand. They are "dying" to take us away. "The Fool On The Hill" sits "perfectly still," as though dead, and grins a dead man's "foolish grin." On "Blue Jay Way" George Harrison, wrapped up in Eastern symbolism and religious fervor, implores Paul to resurrect himself before "very long" implying for the first time a realization of the essentially religious nature of the plot.

"Walrus" is Greek for corpse. John is "crying." He is also obviously contemptuous of those unaware of the plot, not having assumed the role of God he adopts later on. Also, the end of "Walrus" contains passages from *King Lear* about death and villains recorded simultaneously with the radio broadcast that never took place announcing Paul's death to the world. Played backwards, a favorite ploy of the Beatles as early as "Rain," the words "Paul's dead" can be plainly heard.

The closing song of the album, "All You Need Is Love," lays the premises for Lennon's developing concept of his fledgling religion, with a tribute to Paul's early composing efforts at its conclusion coupled with his favorite old standard, "Greensleeves." Before going on to *The Beatles* album, it should be explained more fully how the mechanics of hiding Campbell's identity were worked out. Before his death, Paul was a homosexual (as noted in "Yellow Submarine" when it is plainly yelled "Paul's a queer," answered by "Aye, aye, Captain"), so confused girlfriends were not a major problem for the plotters.

Paul rarely saw his only surviving parent anyway, and had had few close friends. Campbell was able to cover the part perfectly. It cannot be emphasized too heavily that Campbell is the primary reason for the success of the hoax. A girlfriend was needed to keep female admirers at bay, preventing infiltration or blackmail of the five men who knew of the plan so Peter Asher's sister Jane was paid a ripe sum to keep her mouth shut and pretend she was Paul's better half.

Last summer, of course, Campbell married a New York divorcee as Jane Asher was spirited out of sight and the plotters grew more confident of their substitute. After *Magical Mystery Tour,* Campbell began playing a more prominent part in the actual realization of the plot. He was allowed to use his natural voice on "Lady Madonna" which many listeners thought was Ringo at first. This "tough guy" style of singing became integrated rapidly into the group and continued through to *Abbey Road.*

The Beatles appeared nearly a year ago with an all-white cover and hundreds of clues for the wary. The use of the white cover indicates Lennon's further adoption of a God-like image and an ever increasing sense of the value of purity of purpose to the plot.

The collage included with the album depicts Paul lying on his back in the upper left-hand corner, possibly deceased, in a pool of water, with the top of his head missing. As noted before, William Campbell's passport picture before joining the group is in the lower left-hand corner. The first song on the album, "Back In The U.S.S.R." is a thank-you note from the Beatles to Brian Wilson for his work on *Smile* and his cover-up job involving where the tapes originated.

"Dear Prudence" begs Paul to come back and "open up" his eyes. John called McCartney "Prudence" back in the old days when they were known collectively as the Nurk Twins. Nearly every tune on the album contains references to the hoax, culminating in Lennon's apocalyptic vision in "Revolution Number Nine."

This sound collage is clearly the whole story, according to a God-like Lennon. Besides the obvious chaos, the "Take this brother, may it serve you well," the religious absolution and the eventual triumph of "Good Night," the tape played backwards near the beginning has a man saying "Turn me on, dead man," etc.

Thus we come to *Abbey Road.* (Monks live in abbeys.) On the cover is John Lennon dressed in white and resembling utterly an anthropomorphic God, followed by Ringo the undertaker, followed by Paul the resurrected, barefoot with a cigarette in his right hand (the original was left-handed), followed by George the gravedigger.

And if you look closely, they have just walked out of a cemetery on the left side of the street. Thus, Paul was resurrected, given a cigarette, and led out of the tomb, thereby conquering death with a little help from his friends. The real Paul is still dead, of course, but his symbolic resurrection works fine without him. The album itself contains clues to his death and now, clues to his resurrection. "Maxwell's Silver Hammer" is a tale of religious justice, with a dashed-in head for punishment. "Octupus's Garden" is British Navy slang for the cemetery in England where naval heroes are buried. "I Want You (She's So Heavy)" is Lennon wrestling with Paul, trying to pull him out of the earth. Again John's apocalyptic vision has crystallized and after a seemingly endless amount of chaos and confusion, the music ends abruptly as Paul is extricated.

The second side announces the principles upon which the religion will be based: beauty, humor, love, realism, objectivity. It is a religion for everyday life. It analyzes interpersonal relationships in "You Never Give Me Your Money," explains Paul's part in the ritual in "Sun King" ("Here comes the Sun King . . . everybody's laughing . . ."), humorously, never cruelly, inspects money grubbers and fad followers in "Mean Mr. Mustard" and "Polythene Pam," and realistically looks at life with "Boy, you're gonna carry that weight a long time."

And at the end, Paul ascends to the right hand of John and proclaims, "the love you take is equal to the love you make."

But in the VERY end, they are joking about the Queen. The Beatles are building a mighty church, and when you emerge from it, you will be laughing, for Paul is the Sun of God.

The University of Michigan copyrighted Fred LaBour's story, but allowed it to be reprinted in at least a dozen other university publications throughout the country. According to the *Detroit Free Press* (October 23, 1969), after the pertinent issue of the *Harvard Crimson* hit the stands, a Letter to the Editor enthused, "[LaBour's article] has got us so turned on that none of the guys in the house got stoned last night."

Mark Hertsgaard

■

The Beatles officially broke up in April 1970. To most of the world, it was unexpected and, to at least one Beatle, unwanted. "As far as I was concerned," Paul McCartney said in a December 1984 *Playboy* interview, "I would have liked the Beatles *never* to have broken up. I wanted to get us back on the road doing small places, then move up to our previous form and then go and *play*." McCartney and Lennon played off each other's strengths beautifully. Without one to goad the other—or to check the other's weaknesses—the music often suffered. McCartney was crestfallen by the breakup. By his own admission, he did not handle it well. "For the first time in my life, I was on the scrap heap, in my own eyes. It was just the feeling, the terrible disappointment of not being of any use to anyone anymore." But more than that, the breakup made him question his very purpose in life. If he wasn't a Beatle, what was he? "It was," he admits, "the first time I'd had a major blow to my confidence." Hertsgaard discusses the ugly last days of the band.

"The Breakup Heard 'Round the World"

from *A Day in the Life: The Music and Artistry of the Beatles*

■ WHEN IT CAME, the breakup of the Beatles took the world by terrible surprise, like the sudden death of a beloved young uncle. The news broke on April 10, 1970, when Paul McCartney announced that he had left the group; confirming McCartney's departure, the Apple press office added that the activities of the Beatles might well remain "dormant for years." To most people, the breakup was not just shocking but baffling, for John, Paul, George, and Ringo could obviously still make great music together. Seven months earlier, in September 1969, they had released the magnificent *Abbey Road* album. In October, two of the finest songs from that album, "Something" and "Come Together," had been released as a single. And in March, a month before McCartney's stunning revelation, the "Let It Be" single had been issued. All of this material ranked among the very best the Beatles had ever produced, and it sold in very large numbers. Creatively and commercially, the Beatles were at the height of their powers. Why break up now?

That question would be analyzed and debated exhaustively in the months and years to come, and not just by heartbroken Beatles fans. For the Beatles were not simply the outstanding musical partnership of their time, they were also one of its most important cultural symbols. Thus their dissolution took on a far larger historical significance than the demise of mere pop stars; rather, like the assassination of presidents or the July 1969 moon landing, the breakup of the Beatles was regarded as one of the defining events of the 1960s. Indeed, seizing on the fact that the split came a scant four months into the new decade, media pundits invariably interpreted it as a sign that the sixties era of optimism and goodwill had conclusively ended.

Yet despite the widespread and intensive news coverage the Beatles' breakup received, the truth about it remained elusive, and not simply because of the press's usual preference for quick and easy answers. The public, for its part, often seemed to be in a state of denial, fascinated by the drama but insisting that the last act be rewritten and given a happier ending or, better yet, no ending at all. In their shock and anger, many latched on to oversimplifications—blaming Yoko Ono and Linda McCartney was a particular favorite—even as they refused to accept that the band they had loved all these years would not reunite.

The Beatles themselves were not much help. Fully human after all, they did not—with the exception of John Lennon in his famous *Rolling Stone* magazine interview, conducted nearly a year after the fact—want to speak much about what they were going through. What answers they gave tended to be opaque, one-sided, or otherwise incomplete. To the outside world, their breakup meant an end to the most widely and wisely loved music of the century. But to the Beatles themselves, the breakup was a painful, intimate matter, a personal crisis of untold proportion that tore at the heart of their identities and drove them apart from their dearest friends, their virtual blood brothers. The inevitable feelings of anger, sadness, fear, uncertainty, relief, and freedom were confusing enough on their own, but of course the Beatles had to experience them under the obsessive scrutiny of millions.

What was worse, the larger world seemed incapable of discussing the subject without demanding to know if and when the Beatles would get back together, a single-minded focus that drove the Beatles mad. "It's like asking a divorced couple: 'Are you getting back together?' . . . when you can't stand to look at each other," said McCartney. Lennon, too, likened the Beatles' breakup to a divorce, a comparison that suggested another possible reason for the foursome's reticence: They didn't explain what they were doing because they weren't entirely sure; few people are, in the middle of a divorce. In fact, there is considerable evidence to suggest that, contrary to the conventional wisdom that has taken shape in Beatles books over the years, the Beatles' breakup was not inevitable and that the four of them did not necessarily want to separate completely and forever.

As befit the Beatles' mythic stature, there was an operatic quality to their divorce. They had never intended to carry on forever, and they had promised one another that when the day came, they would go out on top, rather than fade into slow, ignominious decline. "One of the things we'd always been very conscious of with the Beatles was to have a great career and leave 'em laughing," McCartney later recalled. Yet like young adults who don't bother to draw up a will because death still seems impossibly remote, the Beatles never got around to formulating an actual exit plan. Thus their breakup was not a carefully thought out, coordinated affair, but a jumbled and sometimes nasty explosion of egos, lawyers, and bank accounts. This, too, complicated public understanding, for it meant that the story emerged in dribs and drabs and out of proper chronological order, and revolved more around volatile emotions than solid facts. In the process, appearances took on even more importance than usual and were often, though not always, deceptive.

Perhaps the best example was the event that set off the alarm bells in the first place, McCartney's statement that he had left the Beatles. This announcement coincided with the release of Paul's first solo album, *McCartney*. Tucked inside review copies of the album was a printed interview in which Paul said he had enjoyed working solo, had broken with the Beatles because of "personal differences, business differences, musical differences," and did not foresee a resumption of his songwriting partnership with Lennon. Outsiders immediately leaped to the conclusion that the Beatles had split up and that McCartney had instigated the rupture. Yet a careful reading of the interview showed that, in fact, McCartney had said nothing about the Beatles splitting up; he said only that *he* had broken with them. Moreover, he twice specifically left open the question of whether the break would be temporary or permanent, saying, "Time will tell." Nevertheless, newspaper headlines around the world reduced the story to screaming variations of PAUL BREAKS UP THE BEATLES.

What made this so misleading was that it was actually Lennon who had pulled the plug on the band a full seven months earlier, as John himself later proudly admitted. The moment of truth came during a meeting of all four Beatles, held at Apple sometime in mid-September 1969. Lennon had just returned from Toronto, where he and the Plastic Ono Band had made an impromptu appearance at a concert on September 13. It was during the flight from London to Toronto, John later said, that he made his decision to quit. He immediately shared this portentous news with Allen Klein, the Beatles' new business manager, who happened to be aboard the flight. Whatever Klein thought of the merits of John's decision, he told him to keep quiet about it for the time being, for business reasons. Precise dates are uncertain, but Klein at this time either had just finished or was still in the midst of renegotiating the Beatles' contracts with their record company, EMI. He had secured a hefty increase in royalty rates, but it would be some time before the corresponding payments actually arrived, and Klein did not want them jeopardized by the news that John Lennon had left the group. Klein did not even want John to tell Paul about his decision, but this proved impossible.

McCartney, always the Beatle most intent on keeping the group together, had suggested during the meeting at Apple that one way to overcome their internal discord was to get back to being a working live band again, perhaps by making surprise appearances at the kinds of small clubs where they had first begun. After making his pitch, McCartney later recalled, "John looked me in the eye and he said, 'I think you're daft. In fact, I wasn't going to tell you . . . but I'm leaving the group.' To my recollection, those were his exact words. And our jaws dropped. And then he went on to explain that it was rather a good feeling to get it off his chest. . . . Which was nice for him, but we didn't get much of a good feeling." Lennon recorded a similar memory in his posthumously published memoirs, writing that "when I finally had the guts to tell the other three that I, quote, wanted a divorce, unquote, they knew it was for real, unlike Ringo and George's previous threats to leave."

"I started the band. I disbanded it. It's as simple as that," Lennon continued in his memoirs. But of course it wasn't that simple. True, if there was one factor above all others that accounted for the breakup of the Beatles, it was John Lennon's decision to leave the band. But that decision seems not to have been as clear-cut as Lennon liked to claim in later years, and in any case, why did he make it? And how and why did it lead to the eventual breakup of the Beatles? For four lads whose love and talent and miraculous togetherness had indeed changed the world, as *Sgt. Pepper* had promised, how did it come to this?

There is no one answer to these questions. Although the sequence of relevant events in the Beatles' breakup can be reliably established, the whys and wherefores remain matters of opinion and perspective. The Beatles' own views, which are what matter most, have evolved over the years to where, instead of name-calling and sullenness, there are now large areas of agreement about what happened and why. But not total agreement. Paul, for example, has said that he wished the Beatles had never broken up, a view none of the others have shared. Yet, ironically, it was the other three who did work with one another quite a lot in the early 1970s. To take another example, no one much disputes that Yoko Ono was the main reason that John left the group. In his memoirs (the text of which Yoko controlled), John praised Yoko for giving him the "inner strength to look more closely at my other marriage. *My real marriage*. To the Beatles, which . . . had become a trap." In Paul's words, "John had to clear the decks of us to give space to his and Yoko's thing." Paul further observed separately, "Someone like John would want to end the Beatle period and start the Yoko period. And he wouldn't like either to interfere with the other." Fine. But Paul's additional assertion that George and Ringo took John's departure from the Beatles as a signal to leave the group themselves illustrates how tricky this story can be. Paul's interpretation is certainly consistent with *what* George and Ringo did—indeed, John later sneered that Paul's claim to have left the Beatles was laughable, given that the other three had already quit—but not necessarily with *why*, for it shortchanges the fact that George and Ringo had their own reasons for wanting out. John was guilty of the same mistake when he claimed sole credit for breaking up the Beatles. And John has less excuse, for unlike Paul, he shared many of George and Ringo's feelings.

Chief among these were the issues of personal space and freedom. As acrimonious as the Beatles' breakup turned out to be, it was not entirely their own fault. The adoring millions also played a part. Like moths to a flame, the Beatles' fans were ineluctably drawn to the four young men whose music and charisma made everyone feel so happy and alive. By overwhelming their heroes with the intensity and relentlessness of their passion, however, the fans ended up driving the Beatles into seclusion and, ultimately, retirement. As Harrison later said, in the best single explanation of why the Beatles finally decided to "burn down the factory" that was their collective identity, "It's just that it wasn't as much fun for us in the end as it was for all of you." Denying that Yoko and Linda were responsible for breaking up the Beatles, Ringo commented years later that "From 1961, 1962 to around 1969, we [the four Beatles] were just all for each other. But suddenly you're older and you don't want to devote all that time to this one object. . . . We stopped because we'd had enough. We'd gone as far as we could with each other." George, too, referred to the Beatles experience as "stifling," adding that it finally came to resemble a situation where "you've got ten brothers and sisters and you've grown up and you're all forty years old and you still haven't moved out. . . . We had to try to help break that Beatle madness in order to have space to breathe, to become sort of human."

■

SIX

Looking Back:
All Those Years Ago

Geoffrey O'Brien

■

One of the best written pieces on what made the Beatles so special is "Seven Fat Years,"a chapter from Geoffrey O'Brien's book entitled *Sonata for Jukebox: Pop Music, Memory, and the Imagined Life*. In it, O'Brien describes in quasi-religious terms seeing *A Hard Day's Night* for the first time. Indeed, he calls his emergence from the darkened movie theater out to the light of a summer afternoon a "conversion experience." For at that precise moment, O'Brien, like countless others, became a "member of a generation, sharing a common repertoire with a sea of contemporaries, strangers who seemed suddenly like family." The Beatles were characters in everyone's life. And yet they transformed before our eyes. They evolved so suddenly, changed so quickly, that people began to believe they possessed a special kind of wisdom. How else could they know what we were feeling?

And then, a little more than half a dozen years later, it was over. O'Brien refers to this remarkable spurt of creativity as "seven fat years." But the songs, of course, linger on and remain with us to this day, still speaking directly to our experiences, still saying what needs to be said. The whys and wherefores as to how they did what they did remain a mystery, as it should be.

"Seven Fat Years"

from *Sonata for Jukebox: Pop Music, Memory, and the Imagined Life*

■ ON A SUMMER afternoon in 1964 I went to a neighborhood movie theater to see the Beatles in *A Hard Day's Night*. It was less than a year since John F. Kennedy had been assassinated. Kennedy's death, and its aftermath of ceremonial grief and unscheduled violence, had if nothing else given younger observers an inkling of what it meant to be part of an immense audience. We had been brought together in horrified spectatorship, and the sense of shared public mourning seemed to go on forever, yet it was only in a matter of weeks that the phenomenally swift rise of a pop group from Liverpool became so pervasive a concern that Kennedy seemed already relegated to an archaic period in which the Beatles had not existed. The New York deejays—my father among them—who promised their listeners "all Beatles all the time" were not so much shaping as reflecting an emergence that seemed almost an eruption of collective will. The Beatles had come, as if on occult summons, to drive away darkness and embody public desire on a scale not previously imagined.

Before Christmas recess—just as "I Want to Hold Your Hand" was finally breaking through to a U.S. market that had resisted earlier releases by the Beatles—girls in my tenth-grade class began coming to school with Beatles albums and pictures of individual Beatles, discussing in tones appropriate to a secret religion the relative attractions of John or Paul or Ringo or even the underappreciated George. A month or so later the Beatles arrived in New York to appear on the Ed Sullivan show and were duly ratified as the show business wonder of the age. Everybody liked them, from the Queen of England and the *New York Times* on down. My parents and their friends, who ordinarily might have sat around listening to Edith Piaf or Charles Aznavour or Barbara Cook, were now pausing in their conversation to register enthusiasm for "And I Love Her."

Even bystanders with no emotional or generational stake in the Beatles could appreciate the adrenaline rush of computing how much this particular success story surpassed all previous ones in terms of money and media and market penetration. It was moving too fast even for the so-called professionals. The Beatles were such a fresh product that those looking for ways to exploit it—from Ed Sullivan to the aging news photographers and press agents who seemed holdovers from the Walter Winchell era—stood revealed as anachronisms as they flanked a group who moved and thought too fast for them. (Or so it seemed at the time. The anachronisms worried about it all the way to the bank, while the Beatles ultimately did their own computing to figure out just how badly they had been shortchanged by the industry pros.)

And what was their product? Four young men who seemed more alive than their handlers and more knowing than their fans; aware of their own capacity to please more or less everybody, yet apparently savoring among themselves a joke too rich for the general public; professional in so unobtrusive a fashion that it looked like inspired amateurism. The songs had no preambles or buildups: the opening phrase—"Well she was just seventeen" or "Close your eyes and I'll kiss you"—was a plunge into movement, a celebration of its own anthemic impetus. Sheer enthusiasm, yet tempered by a suggestion of knowledge held in reserve, a distancing that was cool without malice. When you looked at them they looked back; when they were interviewed, it was the interviewers who ended up on the spot.

That the Beatles excited young girls—mobs of them—made them an unavoidable subject of interest even for young boys, even if the boys might have preferred more familiar native product like Dion and the Belmonts or Freddy Cannon to a group that was foreign and long-haired and too cute not to be a little androgynous. The near-riots that accompanied the Beatles' arrival in New York, bringing about something like martial law in the vicinity of the Warwick Hotel, were an epic demonstration of nascent female desire. The spectacle was not tender but warlike. The oscillation between glassy-eyed entrancement and emotional explosion, the screams that were like chants and the bouts of weeping that were like acts of aggression, the aura of impending upheaval that promised the breaking down of doors and the shattering of glass: this was love that could tear apart its object.

Idols who needed to be protected under armed guard from their own worshippers acquired even greater fascination, especially when they carried themselves with such cool comic grace. To become involved with the Beatles, even as a fan among millions of others, carried with it the possibility of meddling with ferocious energies. Spectatorship here became participation. There were no longer to be any bystanders, only sharers. All of us were going to give in to the temptation not to gawk at the girl in Ed Sullivan's audience—the one who repeatedly bounced straight up out of her seat during "All My Loving" as if pulled by a radar-controlled anti-gravity device—but to become her.

I emerged from *A Hard Day's Night* as from a conversion experience. Having walked into the theater as a solitary observer with more or less random musical tastes—*West Side Story, The Rite of Spring, The Fred Astaire Story, Talking Dustbowl, Old Time Music at Clarence Ashley's,* the soundtracks of *Black Orpheus* and *El Cid*—I came out as a member of a generation, sharing a common repertoire with a sea of contemporaries, strangers who seemed suddenly like family. The four albums already released by the Beatles would soon be known down to every hesitation, every intake of breath; even the moments of flawed pitch and vocal exhaustion could be savored as part of what amounted to an emotional continuum, an almost embarrassingly comforting sonic environment.

Listening to Beatles records turned out to be an excellent cure for too much thinking. It was even better that the sense of refreshment was shared by so many others; the world became, with very little effort, a more companionable place. Effortlessness—the effortlessness of, say, the Beatles leaping around a meadow with goofy freedom in *A Hard Day's Night*—began to seem a fundamental value. That's what they were there for: to have fun, and allow us to watch them having it. That this was a myth—that even *A Hard Day's Night,* by portraying the impossible pressure and isolation of the Beatles' actual situation, acknowledged it as a myth—mattered, curiously, not at all. The converted choose the leap into faith over rational argument. It was enough to believe that they were taking over the world on our behalf.

A few weeks later, at dusk in a suburban park, I sat with old friends as one of our number, a girl who had learned guitar in emulation of Joan Baez, led us in song. She had never found much of an audience for her folksinging, but she won our enthusiastic admiration for having mastered the chord changes of all the songs in *A Hard Day's Night.* We sang for hours. If we had sung together in the past the songs had probably been those of Woody Guthrie or the New Lost City Ramblers, mementoes of a legendary folk past. This time there was the altogether different sensation of participating in a new venture, a world-changing enterprise that indiscriminately mingled aesthetic, social, and sexual possibilities.

An illusion of intimacy, of companionship, made the Beatles characters in everyone's private drama. We thought we knew them, or more precisely, and eerily, thought that they knew us. We imagined a give-and-take of communication between the singers in their sealed-off dome and the rest of us listening in on their every thought and musical reverie. It is hard to remember now how familiarly people came to speak of the Beatles toward the end of the '60s, as if they were close associates whose reactions and shifts of thought could be gauged intuitively. They were the invisible guests at the party, or the relatives whose temporary absence provided an occasion to dissect their temperament and proclivities.

That presumption of intimacy owed everything to a close knowledge of every record they had made, every facial variation gleaned from movies and countless photographs. The knowledge was not necessarily sought; it was merely unavoidable. The knowledge became complex when the Beatles' rapid public evolution (they were after all releasing an album every six months or so, laying down tracks in a couple of weeks in between the tours and the interviews and the press conferences) turned their cozily monolithic identity into a maze of alternate personas. Which

John were we talking about, which Paul? Each song had its own personality, further elaborated or distorted by each of its listeners. Many came to feel that the Beatles enjoyed some kind of privileged wisdom—the evidence was their capacity to extend their impossible string of successes while continuing to find new styles, new techniques, new personalities—but what exactly might it consist of? The songs were bulletins, necessarily cryptic, always surprising, from within that hermetic dome at the center of the world, the seat of cultural power.

Outside the dome, millions of internalized Johns and Pauls and Georges and Ringos stalked the globe. What had at first seemed a harmonious surface dissolved gradually into its components, to reveal a chaos of conflicting impulses. Then, too often, came the recriminations, the absurd discussions of what the Beatles ought to do with their money or how they had failed to make proper use of their potential political influence, as if they owed a debt for having been placed in a position of odd and untenable centrality. All that energy, all that authority: toward what end might it not have been harnessed?

Seven years later, when it was all over, the fragments of those songs and images would continue to intersect with the scenes of one's own life, so that the miseries of high school love were permanently imbued with the strains of "No Reply" and "I'm a Loser," and a hundred varieties of psychic fracturing acquired a common soundtrack stitched together from "She Said She Said" ("I know what it's like to be dead") or the tornado-like crescendo at the end of "A Day in the Life." Only the unnaturally close identification can account for the way in which the breakup of the Beatles functioned as a token for every frustrated wish or curdled aspiration of the era. Their seven fat years went from a point where everything was possible—haircuts, love affairs, initiatives toward world peace—to a point where only silence remained open for exploration.

All of this would eventually settle into material for biographies and made-for-TV biopics. Generations yet unborn would be rehearsing the story. In the final years of the twentieth century, the number of books on the Beatles began to approach the plateau where Jesus, Shakespeare, Lincoln, and Napoleon enjoy their bibliographic afterlife. The surviving Beatles themselves seized hold of the opportunity to control their own story with an elaborate project consisting of *The Beatles Anthology*, a six-CD compilation of outtakes, alternates, and rarities released in

1995, an accompanying video series, and finally the book version of *Anthology*, published in 2000. If *Anthology* had any claim, it was as *The Beatles' Own Story*, an oral history patched together from past and present interviews, with the ghost of John Lennon sitting in, along with an already ailing George Harrison, for an impossible reunion at which the old anecdotes were to be told one more time, and occasion provided for a last word in edgewise about everything from LSD and the Maharishi to Allen Klein and the corporate misfortunes of Apple.

Reading something like a *Rolling Stone* interview that unaccountably went on for hundreds of pages, the book could hardly compare with the authority of the previously hidden recordings included in *The Beatles Anthology*. Those recordings—from a crude tape of McCartney, Lennon, and Harrison performing Buddy Holly's "That'll be the Day" in Liverpool in 1958 to John Lennon's original 1968 recording of "Across the Universe" without Phil Spector's subsequently added orchestral excrescences—were revealing and often moving, and left no question that the Beatles were no mirage. Indeed, even the most minor differences in some of the alternate versions served the valuable function of making audible again songs whose impact had worn away through overexposure. In the print-version *Anthology*, the Beatles were limited to words, words whose frequently banality and inadequacy only increased one's admiration for the expressiveness of their art. People who can make things like *With the Beatles* or *Rubber Soul* or *The White Album* should not really be required also to comment on what they have done.

As they rehashed their career, it turned out that most of what they had to say that was interesting came early. Before "Love Me Do" and Beatlemania and the first American tour, the Beatles actually lived in the same world as the rest of us, and it was their memories of that world—from Liverpool to Hamburg to the dance clubs of northern England—that were most suggestive. The earliest memories were most often of a generalized boredom and sense of deprivation. A post-war Liverpool barely out of the rationing card era, with bombsites for parks (Paul recalled going "down the bombie" to play) and not much in the way of excitement, figured chiefly as the blank backdrop against which movies and music (almost exclusively American) could make themselves felt all the more powerfully. "We were just desperate to get anything," George remarked. "Whatever film came out, we'd try to see it. Whatever record was being played, we'd try to listen to, because there was very little of anything . . . You couldn't even get a cup of sugar, let alone a rock 'n' roll record."

Fitfully, a secret history of childhood music took form: Paul listening to his pianist father play "Lullaby of the Leaves" and "Stairway to Paradise," George discovering Hoagy Carmichael songs and Josh White's "One Meatball," and Ringo (the most unassuming and therefore often the most eloquent speaker) recalling his moment of illumination: "My first musical memory was when I was about eight. Gene Autry singing 'South of the Border.' That was the first time I really got shivers down my backbone, as they say. He had his three compadres singing 'Ai, ai, ai, ai,' and it was just a thrill to me. Gene Autry has been my hero ever since."

Only John—massively indifferent to folk ("college students with big scarfs and a pint of beer in their hands singing in la-di-da voices") and jazz ("it's always the same, and all they do is drink pints of beer")—seemed to have reserved his enthusiasm until the advent of Elvis and Jerry Lee Lewis and Little Richard: "It was Elvis who really got me out of Liverpool. Once I heard it and got into it, that was life, there was no other thing." If one could imagine an alternate future in which Paul played piano for local weddings and dances, George drove a bus like his old man, and Ringo perhaps fell into the life of crime his teenage gang exploits seemed to portend, it was inconceivable that John could have settled into any other choices he was being offered in his youth.

None of them ever did much except prepare themselves to be the Beatles. Their youths were devoid of incident (at least of incident that anyone cared to write into the record) and largely of education. John, the eldest, had a bit of art school training, but for all of them real education consisted more of repeated exposure to Carl Perkins, Chuck Berry, and Frank Tashlin's Cinemascope rock 'n' roll extravaganza *The Girl Can't Help It.* On the British side, they steeped themselves in the surreal BBC radio comedy *The Goon Show*—echoes of the non sequiturs and funny voices of Spike Milligan and Peter Sellers would be an abiding presence in their work—and in the skiffle craze of the late '50s they found a point of entry into the world of actual bands and actual gigs.

"I would often sag off school for the afternoon," wrote Paul, "and John would get off art college, and we would sit down with our two guitars and plonk away." Along with the younger George, they formed a skiffle band and played local dances, and after some changes in personnel officially became, around 1960, the Beatles, in allusion to the "beat music" that was England's term for what was left of a rock 'n' roll at that point almost moribund. Hard up for jobs, they found themselves in

Hamburg, in a series of Reeperbahn beer joints, and by their own account were pretty much forced to become adequate musicians by the
discipline of eight-hour sets and demanding, unruly audiences. Amid
the amiable chaos of whores, gangsters, and prolonged amphetamine-
fueled jamming—"it was pretty vicious," remarked Ringo, who joined
the group during this period, "but on the other hand hookers loved
us"—they transformed themselves into an anarchic rock band, "wild
men in leather suits." Back in the U.K. they blew away the local competition: "There were all these acts going 'dum de dum' and suddenly
we'd come on, jumping and stomping," in George's account. "In those
days, when we were rocking on, becoming popular in the little clubs
where there was no big deal about the Beatles, it was fun."

Once the group got back to England, the days of "sagging off" and
"plonking away" were numbered. As their ascent swiftly took shape—
within a year of a Decca executive dismissing them with the comment
that "guitar groups are on the way out" they were already awash in
Beatlemania—the life recalled in their reminiscences had less and less
to do with anything other than the day-to-day business of recording and
performing. Once within the universe of EMI, life became something
of a controlled experiment, with the Beatles subjected to unfamiliar
sorts of corporate oversight. Paul recalled: "We weren't even allowed
into the control room, then. It was Us and Them. They had white shirts
and ties in the control room, they were grown-ups. In the corridors and
back rooms there were the guys in full-length lab coats, maintenance
men and engineers, and then there was us, the tradesmen . . . We gradually became the workmen who took over the factory." If they took over,
though it was at the cost of working at a killing pace, churning out songs,
touring and making public appearances as instructed, keeping the merchandise coming. It could of course be wondered whether this forced
production didn't have a positive effect on their work, simply because
the work they were then turning out—everything from "Love Me Do"
and "Please Please Me" to *Rubber Soul* was produced virtually without
a break from performing or recording—could hardly be improved.

It is the paradox of such a life that it precludes the sort of experience on
which art usually nurtures itself. The Beatles' latter-day reminiscences
evoked the crew members on a prolonged interstellar flight, thrown back
on each other and on their increasingly abstract memories of Earth, and
livening the journey with whatever drugs or therapies promise something

like the terrestrial environment they have left behind. In this context, marijuana and LSD were not passing episodes but central events, the true subject matter of the later Beatles records. In the inner storms of the bubble world, dreams and private portents took the place of the comings and goings of a street life that had become remote.

The isolation became glaring in, say, Paul's recollections of 1967: "I've got memories of bombing around London to all the clubs and the shops . . . It always seemed to be sunny and we wore the far-out clothes and the far-out little sunglasses. The rest of it was just music." One could be sure that the "bombing around" took place within a well-protected perimeter. It was around this time that the Beatles pondered the possibility of buying a Greek island in order to build four separate residences linked by tunnels to a central dome, like something out of *Dr. No* or *Modesty Blaise,* with John commenting blithely: "I'm not worried about the political situation in Greece, as long as it doesn't affect us. I don't care if the government is all fascist, or communist . . . They're all as bad here."

Finally the Beatles were in no better position than anyone else to get a clear view of their own career. "The moral of the story," said George, "is that if you accept the high points you're going to have to go through the lows . . . So, basically, it's all good." They knew what it was to have been a Beatle, but not really—or only by inference—what it looked like to everybody else. This led to odd distortions in tone, as if after all they had not really grasped the singularity of their fate. From inside the rocket was not necessarily the best vantage point for charting its trajectory.

Paul's comments on how certain famous songs actually got to be written were amiably vague: "'Oh, you can drive my car.' What is it? What's he doing? Is he offering a job as a chauffeur, or what? And then it became much more ambiguous, which we liked." As much in the dark as the rest of us as to the ultimate significance of what they were doing, the Beatles were all the more free to follow their usually impeccable instincts. So if John Lennon chose to describe "Rain" as "a song I wrote about people moaning about the weather all the time," and Paul saw "A Day in the Life" as "a little poetic jumble that sounded nice," it confirmed that any enlightenment about deeper significance was best sought by listening to the records. (John, again: "What does it really mean, 'I am the eggman'? It could have been the pudding basin, for all I care.") The band doesn't know; they just write them.

In the end it was not the music that wore out but the drama, the personalities, the weight of expectation and identity. By the time the Beatles felt obliged to make universally acceptable exhortations like "all you need is love" and "you know it's gonna be all right," it was already time to bail out. How nice it would be to clear away the mass of history and personal association and simply hear the records for the notes and words. Sometimes it's necessary to wait twenty years to be able to hear it again, the formal beauty that begins as far back as "Ask Me Why" and "There's a Place" and is sustained for years without ever settling into formula. Nothing really explains how or why musicians who spent years jamming on "Be Bop a Lula" and "Long Tall Sally" turned to writing songs like "Not a Second Time" and "If I Fell" and "Things We Said Today," so altogether different in structure and harmony. Before the addition of the sitars and tape loops and symphony orchestras, before the lyrical turn toward eggman and floating downstream, Lennon and McCartney (and, on occasion, Harrison) were already making musical objects of such elegant simplicity, such unhectoring emotional force, that if they had quit after *Help!* (their last "conventional" album) the work would still endure.

Paul McCartney recollected that when the Beatles heard the first playbacks at EMI it was the first time they'd really heard what they sounded like: "Oh, that sounds just like a record! Let's do this again and again and again!" The workmen taking over the factory were also the children taking over the playroom, determined to find effects that no one had thought of pulling out of the drawer before. They went from being performers to being songwriters but didn't make the final leap until they became makers of records. Beyond all echoes of yesterday's mythologized excitement, the records—whether "The Night Before" or "Drive My Car" or "I'm Only Sleeping" or any of the dozens of others—lose nothing of a beauty so singular it might almost be called underrated.

Paul Du Noyer

■

The release of the *Anthology* collection in 1995 led to a whole series of articles about the Beatles and why, twenty-five years after their breakup, they continue to cast their spell over the public. The following piece by Paul Du Noyer ran in the British music magazine, *Q,* in December 1995. He also discusses two new Beatles songs, "Free as a Bird" and "Real Love."

"They Were the Most Brilliant, Powerful, Lovable Popular Pop Group on the Planet ... But Now They're Really Important"

Q Magazine
December 1995

■ THE BOOK OF The Beatles was one that we all thought was closed. But suddenly there's an amazing extra chapter. For 25 years, every McCartney press conference had some buffoon down the front asking "Paul, do you think the group will get back together?" McCartney would try to disguise his boredom. Even John Lennon's death in 1980 could not stop the speculators, who simply recruited Julian into their fantasy.

And now, incredibly, it has all come true. The Beatles plan two new singles, Free As A Bird and Real Love, using vocal tracks that John recorded in the late 1970s. Together again with George Martin at Abbey Road Studios, they're compiling three double CDs of old recordings, too. The first installment of The Beatles Anthology comes out this month (November), along with a six-part TV series which will be released on video.

How to explain this unforeseen splurge of Fabbish activity? Its origins were in a movie idea, gathering dust in Apple's offices. For years there was a vague intention to gather up film footage and make The Beatles' authorised history of their own career. Its working title was The Long and Winding Road. By the late 1980s the group were getting over the "business crap" that had divided them, and the idea re-surfaced.

Paul, George and Ringo discussed teaming up to record some instrumental music for the soundtrack.

"But we never did get around to that," McCartney reports. "It just
never felt like a good idea." What appealed more was a trawl through
EMI's vaults for the unreleased songs and alternative takes which, for
25 years, had been the bootleggers' playground or else in the domain of
the cobweb. In the same spirit, Yoko Ono offered up her tapes of John's
home demos. The old Beatles studio material (to which they've added
rarities including Decca auditions and TV slots for Morecambe & Wise
and The Ed Sullivan Show) is of bottomless interest to fans and pop his-
torians. But it is the "new" tracks using John Lennon's voice that will
arouse the biggest anticipation.

Their existence means that the unthinkable has come to pass. The
four Beatles have got back together again.

The scene for these historic sessions was Paul McCartney's recording
studio. Set in a converted windmill on a hill in Sussex, it overlooks—
beyond some gently rolling farmland—the English Channel. Around the
coastal sweep is a nuclear power station, but the location is otherwise
idyllic. It's also quite remote, which helped preserve the virtual secrecy
that surrounded this reunion. In a corner outside the control room was
propped one of Paul's treasures: the upright double bass that belonged
to Bill Black of Elvis Presley's original combo. You can see it in ancient
photographs. McCartney, in passing, would sometimes pluck it for luck.

And what of the long-separated Beatles? The crack between them,
Paul asserts, was "really good. It was better when there was three of us
than when Ringo said, 'Oh, I've done my bit" and left me and George to
do it. Me and George, as artists, we had a little bit more tension. But I
don't think that's a bad thing. It was only like a normal Beatle session;
you've got to reach a compromise . . ."

They first convened there two years ago: "And we all turned out to be
veggies. Ringo's walking around with, like, a bag of seeds, so healthy.
Ringo is fantastic for a guy who's been in intensive care, nearly dying for
most of his life. His mother was told he'd be dead when he was three.
Then when he got into really heavy drinking, in Monaco, he was once
put on a life support system with seven other very nearly dead people in
the room."

It was known that tapes existed of Lennon playing some unreleased
songs. Yoko had considered using them with modern musicians, but the
remaining Beatles believed it was a job for them. McCartney made his

approach in 1989. Yoko's initial response: "Well, maybe." Then he visited the Lennons' New York home after inducting John, posthumously, at a Rock 'n' Roll Hall of Fame ceremony.

Paul: "She was there with Sean (*John and Yoko's son, now 20*). Because of the tragedy occurring, there's only so much stuff that Yoko has of John's and she played us a couple of tracks. There were two newies, on mono cassettes which he did at home, probably demo-ing up for what became the Double Fantasy album. So I checked it out with Sean, because I didn't want him to have a problem with it. He said, 'Well, it'll be weird hearing a dead guy on a lead vocal. But give it a try.' I said to them both, If it doesn't work out, you can veto it. When I told George and Ringo I'd agreed to that they were going, 'What? What if we love it?' It didn't come to that, luckily.

"I said to Yoko, 'Don't impose too many conditions on us, it's really difficult to do this, spiritually. We don't know, we may hate each other after two hours in the studio and just walk out. So don't put any conditions, it's tough enough.'

"I said to Ringo, 'Let's pretend that we've nearly finished some recordings and John is going off to Spain on holiday and he's just rung up and said: Look, there's one more song I wouldn't mind getting on the album, it's a good song but it's not finished. If you're up for it, take it in the studio, have fun with it, and I'll trust you.' So with that scenario in place, Ringo said, 'Oh! This could even be joyous!' And it was. It actually was. We'd not met for a long time, and the press didn't bother us because nobody guessed we'd be down there.

"The good thing about Free As A Bird was that it was unfinished. The middle eight didn't have all the words. So that was like John bringing us a song and saying, 'Er, don't know how to finish it.' When he gets to the middle he goes 'Whatever happened to/The life that we once knew/Woowah wunnnnn yeurrggh!' and you can see that he's trying to push lyrics out but they're not coming. He keeps going, as if to say 'Well, I'll get them later.' Well, he never got round to getting them later, so that's probably why he didn't use the song. I think it's really strong, Free As A Bird, I love it."

As the first reports of these secret sessions reached London, there was much wonderment at The Beatles' choice of producer, namely Jeff Lynne. Why not George Martin? If there was ever a "fifth Beatle" it was Martin, who produced nearly all their records and played a key creative role in their studio achievements. In fact, McCartney believed they *should* use George Martin. He felt deep unease about Jeff Lynne, who was George Harrison's nominee for the job.

"I was worried," Paul concedes. "He's such a pal of George's. They'd done the (*Traveling*) Wilburys, and I was expecting him to lead it that way. To tell you the truth, I thought that he and George might create a wedge, saying, 'We're doing it this way' and I'd be pushed out. But he was very fair, and very thorough. He looked at things with a fine-tooth comb—if you *can* 'look' at things with a fine-tooth comb. He was very precise."

There was some irony in using Jeff Lynne. From his early make-over of The Move, through his years in ELO, Lynne was famed for turning out Beatles homages. For a while his style seemed entirely rooted in the churning string arrangement of I Am The Walrus. But as a producer of other people, Lynne enjoyed a parallel reputation for sonic expertise and—crucially, here—great tact and amiability with potentially awkward customers. Bob Dylan, Brian Wilson and the solo George Harrison had all found the bloke-ish Brummie a congenial workmate.

But Paul needed convincing. "I was saying, 'Well, George (Martin) is doing the Anthology. If his ears are good enough for that . . .' But George (Harrison) was saying, 'No, that's all stuff we know about, it's stuff that's mixed and done. He is the man for that, but if we're making a *new* record, we've got to get someone with immaculate ears.' So we chose Prince Charles . . .

"George Martin's thing—he'll tell you himself—is that his hearing's not as good as it was, and that's why he's getting out of production. So that's how it split and he didn't mind."

Free As A Bird was completed with the addition of George's closing guitar part. Again McCartney had misgivings. "I was worried because it was going to be George on slide. When Jeff suggested slide guitar I thought (*dubiously*), Oh, it's My Sweet Lord again, it's George's trademark. John might have vetoed that. But in fact he got a much more bluesy attitude, very cool, very minimal, and I think he plays a blinder."

By February of this year the three Beatles and Lynne were back at the Sussex studio, tackling the second song of John's, Real Love. But compared to recording Free As A Bird, says Paul, the new sessions were "like boiling your cabbages twice, to use an old Liverpool expression." For Jeff Lynne there were unwelcome technical problems: "There was a buzz all the way through the cassette. We just shoved that all on to Jeff. Once he'd got the buzz off, it showed up all the clicks that were on it, so he had to get them off as well."

On the other hand, Real Love is Yoko Ono's favourite—perhaps because John's voice is clearer. "I don't like it as much as Free As A Bird," Paul admits, "because I think Free As A Bird is more powerful. But it's catchier. It's a pity that there aren't more tracks like Free As A Bird, but then it's a pity that John died."

While Lynne wrestled with the audio snags, Paul and George had trouble constructing finished songs around their old partner's imperfect performances. "But because we said, 'It's only John who's left us this tape,' we could take the piss. We'd say 'It's out of time! (*Jeering*) Wouldn't you just know it.' Like if he'd been there, we would have said it. That was our attitude to each other, we were never reverent.

"Then me and George ended up doing harmonies, and Ringo's sitting in the control room. He says, 'Sounds just like The Beatles!'"

First rumours of the recordings led some commentors to wonder if The Beatles ought to have left their legacy alone.

"A lot of people were worried. 'Oh, they shouldn't attempt it.' Hopefully they're gonna eat their words. They virtually said what we've been saying for years. 'It's all over. The body of work's complete, why mess with it?' Well, why mess with it was that this opportunity came up with the Anthology to have a go at one of John's songs.

"The point is, *we were working with John.* That was the fantastic thing. We got the attitude right. We weren't worrying about what the pundits said. I was like, Fuck them. *Really* fuck them. It helped us to focus, someone saying: 'You won't be able to do this, so fuck you . . .' We fucking will now you've said that. It got our hackles up.

"I had an obnoxious customs man when I was going through New York, a very serious and pasty lad who said, 'The project you're doing with The Beatles?' I said, Yeah? 'I just wanna tell you that I don't consider it a Beatles project without John.' Now I'm in no mood after a plane flight, this guy is customs and I don't need this shit. I said, I don't *care* what you think, and it shows how much *you* know anyway 'cos John is fucking on it!

"I'm proud of the two new songs. Free As A Bird is really emotional. I've played it to a few people who've cried, because it's a good piece of music and because John's dead. The combination of that can be emotional. But I love that. I don't have a problem with something that grabs you by the balls so you've gotta cry. I rather respect that."

The CD Anthology follows the Beatles chronologically, except that it will begin with Free As A Bird. After that it's right back to the two schoolboys in Liverpool. "It's been trippy going through it all," says Paul, "sitting there in Abbey Road with George Martin and George and Ringo, trying to make some sort of story. God, it's so strange after all this time."

Of the tracks so far finalised, among his favourites is a version of the Revolver song And Your Bird Can Sing, wrecked by a fit of Lennon and McCartney giggling. "We couldn't have put it out then. It would have been, 'How fucking indulgent of them. Are they kidding?' But now it just sounds like a hoot. Then there's nice things like While My Guitar Gently Weeps, which is just George on acoustic and nothing else, no Beatles, no Clapton playing the lead. There's the first take we did of Yesterday, which hasn't got the string quartet on it. It turns out we only ever did two takes. I was 22 . . .

"The obvious questions about the Anthology stuff is, If it wasn't good enough to release then, why is it good enough to release now? But I think so much water's gone under the bridge. There's stuff that would have seemed indulgent, like a really early instrumental I'd forgotten, from when I was about 14. It's not brilliant, but when you listen you can hear a lot of stuff I'm *going* to write. So it's interesting from that point of view.

"There was a song of George's that the engineer Allan Rouse discovered (*You Know What To Do*). EMI didn't know they had it. When they called in anything anyone had in Abbey Road, or in EMI worldwide, with 'Beatles' on the box, this arrived. No one had logged it, so they thought it was lost. There's John singing Leave My Kitten Alone, a really good take that's never been released. Real keen Beatle fans who've got everything on bootleg, there's still a few things on the Anthology they won't have heard.

"But the strangest thing for me, listening to it, is that it's like drowning, it's your life flashing by in front of you. From the earliest things by me and John when we used to sag off school and the earliest demo tape we ever made, to the first little record we made which was a version of John singing That'll Be The Day, and a little song of mine on the other side, that's never been released before (*In Spite Of All The Danger*) . . . Then we're recording in EMI so you get all the alternative takes. There's a song (I'll Be Back, off the Hard Day's Night LP) that goes: 'You know/If you break my heart I'll go/But I'll be back again' and it's in 4/4. But the original take, it turns out is 3/4, and God knows why: 'You *know* chink-chink-ump, if you *break* my heart, I'll go.' But in the middle John goes, 'It's too hard to sing! I can't do it!'

"When everything broke down, we'd have mini-arguments in the studio. There's one bit where I'm playing I Saw Her Standing There on bass and I'm not doing it with a pick. I break down, and I go, 'Oh shit!' And John goes, 'What's wrong?' And I go, 'It's not my fault, soft arse!' That was the big swear word at the time. He goes, 'Why don't you use a pleck?' 'Because I haven't got one!' So it's all this."

Would John have been into this project?

"Oh yeah, I'm sure he would. He might have chosen some different takes, but we pretty much agreed on all the stuff that went out. There's a few things of mine that I didn't want in there, but George Martin said, 'Well, it's very typical.' Because at that time I was doing the cabaret-Little Richard, that was my role. I'd do the Til There Was You's and the Besame Mucho's and there's a couple of those that I wouldn't have minded removing. But as I say, it is my life. There it is. It's only me who gets really hung up about that stuff. I'll talk to someone else about it, they'll say, 'We don't mind that about you; you've always done the odd ballad.' In myself somewhere, I don't like to admit to that."

Having re-formed for this project, what might you three do together now?

"We might record. We've been offered a humungous amount of money to tour, to just do 10 dates in the States. But no way. At least with Free As A Bird and Real Love, John's on it, so it's The Beatles. The three of us touring doesn't make any sense, except for the money and you can't do it just for the money. I don't fancy touring at all, even 10 little dates and huge, huge and *really* huge money. To do that, we'd have to spoil something. I think that what we've done in the Anthology doesn't spoil anything, even for the keenest Beatle fans. If we went out on tour, what do you do? Do you get another singer? It's all that shit. I can't see it happening at all."

When the Anthology CDs are complete, McCartney says, that will be the end of all Beatle music: "Me and George Harrison are talking about the next album being called Scraping The Bottom Of The Barrel. And George Martin reckons if we put anything out after this, it'll have to be issued with a government health warning.

"I sat through the project as we were going through the tapes, praying that I wouldn't make a mistake. It's like I was still doing it live, hoping the bass doesn't make a mistake. There's another person in your head saying, 'It's all over, mate. No need to worry. You've done it, you've passed the audition.' But I think we all sat there terrified.

"But it's been nice to work with the guys because you realise, after all the bullshit, we love each other. We put up with each other's bullshit. There was one real nice moment when we were doing Real Love and I was trying to learn the piano bit, and Ringo sat down on the drums, jamming along. It was like none of us had ever been away. And the best thing was, it was hysterical, Ringo with his little plastic bag of grains . . .

"For the Anthology film we did an interview, and we couldn't remember anything in common. That's how life really is. You live this dream that there's a definitive version, and there isn't. There's this story we tell about being in Paris when one of us had a sore throat. Ringo was telling this story and he said, 'And George had a sore throat.' The camera pans to George to get his reaction and George goes, 'No, I thought it was Paul who had the sore throat.' It pans over to me. I go, 'I'm telling you, it was John who had the sore throat.' But I've worked it out since: if Ringo thought it was George, it couldn't be Ringo. If George thought it was me, it couldn't be George. If I thought it was John it couldn't be me, and it *was* John.

"The director said that's how we should end this whole series. The three of us going, 'But it wasn't him!' We've got completely different memories. And that's one reason why the timing's good. Give it another couple of years, when a couple more brain cells have gone *blink!* . . . and there's no bloody story left."

Ken Womack

■

Why were the Beatles so great? Ken Womack, a Beatles aficionado and professor at Penn State University's Altoona College, offers his own reasons in this piece that originally ran in *The Morning News,* an online magazine (the morningnews.org). (See also musician Steve Earle's "The Ten Most Important Beatles Songs" in this volume.)

"Ten Great Beatles Moments"

The Morning News
May 17, 2002

1. "I SAW HER STANDING THERE" (1963)

The first track on the Beatles' inaugural album [released only in Britain], *Please Please Me* (1963), "I Saw Her Standing There" explodes with a sense of urgency and abandon equaled only by the opening strains of "I Want to Hold Your Hand," the song that would prefigure the group's triumphant first visit to North America in February 1964. Composed by McCartney and Lennon in McCartneys' living room while playing hooky, "I Saw Her Standing There" bespeaks the same teenage amalgam of hopeful romance and ready acceptance that marks the band's other works of the era: "Well, she was just 17 / You know what I mean." Lennon later observed, "We were just writing songs à la the Everly Brothers, à la Buddy Holly, pop songs with no more thought to them than that—to create a sound. And the words were almost irrelevant." Indeed, the song's lyrics merely revolve around a kind of innocuous optimism—but, as an *audibly* excited McCartney counts off the beginning of "I Saw Her Standing There," it signals the ushering in of a new sound that would forever change the face of popular music.

2. THE "MIDDLE EIGHT" ON "AND I LOVE HER" (1964)

With a knack for crafting "middle-eights"—the eight-bar refrains that characterize their songwriting in the early 1960s—the Beatles were already searching for new musical vistas as early as *A Hard Day's Night*

(1964). With "And I Love Her," the band easily assumes a stirring Latin beat. Ornamented with Harrison and McCartney's flamenco-like guitar arpeggios, "And I Love Her" swells with the rhythmic intensity of Ringo Starr's bongos and Harrison's intermittent claves.

For McCartney, this song is nothing short of a watershed moment. His enormous catalogue of romantic melodies and ballads finds its origins in "And I Love Her," and a line can be drawn from its composition to the emergence of such classics as "Yesterday," "Michelle," "Let It Be," and "The Long and Winding Road."

3. GEORGE HARRISON'S SITAR ACCOMPANIMENT ON "NORWEGIAN WOOD (THIS BIRD HAS FLOWN)" (1965)

On *Rubber Soul* (1965), the Beatles effectively signaled the expansion of their musical horizons via Harrison's well-known experimentation with sitar music—the exotic, microtonal flavor of which would adorn such Beatles tunes as "Norwegian Wood (This Bird Has Flown)" and *Sgt. Pepper's Lonely Hearts Club Band*'s (1967) "Within You Without You."

In "Norwegian Wood" Harrison's sitar lines accent the flourishes of Lennon's haunting acoustic guitar. But they also provide a curious palette for Lennon's confessional lyrics about an extramarital affair. As with "Baby's in Black" and "I Don't Want to Spoil the Party" from *Beatles for Sale* (1964), "Norwegian Wood" represents a significant departure from the watery love songs that accounted for the band's initial parcel of hits. The lyrics themselves—far from underscoring love's everlasting possibilities—hint at something far more fleeting, even unromantic: "She asked me to stay and she told me to sit anywhere / So I looked around and I noticed there wasn't a chair."

4. "A DAY IN THE LIFE" (1967)

Fans and critics alike often refer to *Sgt. Pepper's Lonely Hearts Club Band* as popular music's first "concept" album. In truth, though, the Beatles' notion of a fictitious ensemble peters out after "With a Little Help from My Friends," the album's second track. The concept "doesn't go anywhere," Lennon later remarked. "But it works 'cause we *said* it works." Most significantly, *Sgt. Pepper* saw the Beatles erasing the boundaries that they had been challenging since *Rubber Soul* and *Revolver.* "Until this album, we'd never thought of taking the freedom to do something like *Sgt. Pepper,*" McCartney observed. "We started to realize there weren't as many barriers as we'd thought, we could break through with things like album covers, or invent another persona for the band." And with "A Day in the Life"—the album's dramatic climax—the Beatles virtually re-imagined themselves as recording artists. Filled with variegated sonic hues and other assorted sound effects, the song contrasts Lennon's impassive stories of disillusion and regret with McCartney's deceptively buoyant interlude about the numbing effects of the workaday world. The song's luminous, open-ended refrain—"I'd love to turn you on"—promises a sense of interpersonal salvation on a universal scale. Yet Lennon and McCartney's detached lyrics seem to suggest, via their nuances of resignation and unacknowledged guilt, that such a form of emotional release will always remain an unrealized dream. As the music of the Beatles and a studio orchestra spirals out of control and into oblivion, that thundering, massive piano chord punctuates and reverberates within the song's unflinching melancholic ambiance.

5. "I AM THE WALRUS" (1967)

Inspired by Lewis Carroll's nonsensical poem "The Walrus and the Carpenter," "I Am the Walrus" opens with Lennon's Mellotron-intoned phrasings, meant to replicate the monotonous cry of a police siren. As the song's spectacular lyrics unfold—"I am he as you are he and you are me and we are altogether"—Ringo's wayward snare interrupts the proceedings and sets Lennon's intentionally absurdist catalogue of images into motion. While an assortment of cryptic voices and diabolical laughter weave in and out of the mix, Lennon's pungent lyrics encounter an array of ridiculous characters—from a "crab locker fishwife" and a "pornographic priestess" to the "expert texpert choking smokers" and Edgar Allan Poe himself. When "I Am the Walrus" finally recedes amongst its ubiquitous mantra of "Goo Goo Goo Joob," the song dissolves into a scene from a BBC radio production of Shakespeare's *King Lear.* Described by Ian MacDonald as "the most idiosyncratic protest song ever written," "I Am the Walrus" features Lennon's most inspired verbal textures, as well as the Beatles' greatest moment of musical diaphora: in one sense, "I Am the Walrus" seems utterly devoid of meaning, yet at the same time its songwriter's rants about prevailing social strictures absolutely demand attention.

6. SIDE TWO OF THE *WHITE ALBUM* (1968)

These nine tracks, from "Martha My Dear" through "Julia," illustrate the *White Album*'s stunning eclecticism—the true measure of the album's resilience. McCartney's baroque-sounding "Martha My Dear," with its crisp brass accompaniment, meanders, rather lazily, into Lennon's bluesy "I'm So Tired." Lennon later recalled the song as "one of my favorite tracks. I just like the sound of it, and I sing it well." Written during the Beatles' famous visit to the Maharishi Mahesh Yogi's retreat at Rishikesh during the spring of 1968, McCartney's folksy "Blackbird" imagines a contemplative metaphor for the civil rights struggles in the United States during the 1960s. The sound of a chirping blackbird lightly segues into Harrison's uncomfortable but unforgettable political satire, "Piggies." The song cycle continues with McCartney's countrified "Rocky Raccoon," a track that shifts, rather astonishingly, from the disquieting universe of cowboys, gunplay, and saloons into a gentle paean about nostalgia and loss. Ringo's "Don't Pass Me By," with its barrelhouse piano chorus, abruptly steers the sequence into the sudsy world of the beer hall. Originally entitled "Some Kind of Friendly," the song became a number-one hit—why not?—in Scandinavia. One of McCartney's finest blues effusions, "Why Don't We Do It in the Road?" explodes from the embers of "Don't Pass Me By" and brilliantly sets the stage for the side's final two numbers, "I Will" and "Julia." A soothing melody about the tenuous argument between romance and commitment, "I Will" remains one of McCartney's most memorable experiments in brash sentimentality. Arguably his most powerful ballad, Lennon's "Julia" memorializes the songwriter's late mother while simultaneously addressing his spiritual deliverance at the hands of "ocean child" Yoko Ono, his newfound soul mate.

7. THE GUITAR LICK AT THE END OF "EVERYBODY'S GOT SOMETHING TO HIDE EXCEPT FOR ME AND MY MONKEY" AND THE PIANO MELODY ON "SEXY SADIE" (1968)

A moment of pure excitement and adrenaline, the guitar riff at the conclusion of "Everybody's Got Something to Hide Except For Me and My Monkey" accentuates an otherwise peculiar song about social politics with the bruising panache of rock-and-roll. A rhythmic burst of high-octane modulation, the guitar phrasings exemplify the breadth of the band's now-extraordinary musical prowess. As Lennon's acidic lullaby to the Beatles' experiences under the Maharishi's dubious tutelage, "Sexy Sadie" bears mention for its salacious lyrical contents alone: "We gave you everything we owned just to sit at your table / Just a smile would lighten everything." In terms of sheer artistry though, the song reveals the band in full aesthetic throttle. As McCartney's tinkling piano phrases spar with Harrison's bristling guitar, "Sexy Sadie" maneuvers effortlessly through chord changes and one harmonic shift after another. When the song finally ascends to its closing musical interchange, the Beatles' instrumentation and Lennon's spellbinding vocal coalesce in a breathtaking instance of blissful resolution.

8. GEORGE HARRISON'S GUITAR SOLO ON "SOMETHING" (1969)

Harrison comes into his own on *Abbey Road,* the Beatles' magnificent swan song: the unbridled optimism of Harrison's "Here Comes the Sun" is matched—indeed, surpassed—only by "Something," his crowning achievement that none other than Frank Sinatra would call "the greatest love song of the past 50 years." For much of the song, Harrison's soaring guitar—his musical trademark—dances in counterpoint with McCartney's jazzy, melodic bass, weaving an exquisite musical tapestry as "Something" meanders toward the most unforgettable of Harrison's guitar solos, the song's greatest lyrical feature—even more lyrical, interestingly enough, than the lyrics themselves. A masterpiece in simplicity, Harrison's solo reaches toward the sublime, wrestles with it in a bouquet of downward syncopation, and hoists it yet again in a moment of supreme grace.

9. THE *ABBEY ROAD* MEDLEY (1969)

The medley that concludes *Abbey Road* and, with that, the band itself, essentially consists of an assortment of unfinished songs. Beginning with "You Never Give Me Your Money," McCartney's plaintive piano strains give way to Lennon and Harrison's dueling rhythm guitars. As Harrison later observed, the song "does two verses of one tune, and then the bridge is almost like a different song altogether, so it's quite melodic." The lyrics bespeak the tragedies of misspent youth and runaway fame: "Out of college, money spent / See no future, pay no rent / All the money's gone, nowhere to go." The song's bluesy guitar riffs segue into the chorus of a children's nursery rhyme: "One, two, three, four, five, six, seven / All good children go to heaven." Later, in "Golden Slumbers," McCartney resumes the medley's earlier themes with a deft reworking of Thomas Dekker's four-hundred-year-old poem of the same name. As the medley progresses toward its symphonic conclusion, the song's bitter nostalgia—"Once there was a way to get back homeward / Once there was a way to get back home"—yields itself to a larger realization, in "Carry that Weight," that we inevitably shoulder the past's frequent irredeemable burden for the balance of our lives. In "Carry that Weight," McCartney acknowledges his own culpability in the Beatles' dissolution, yet his rather humbling, self-conscious lyrics extend an olive branch to his increasingly distant mates: "I never give you my pillow / I only send you my invitations." From "You Never Give Me Your Money" through "The End," his lyrics impinge upon the inherent difficulties that come with growing up and growing older. Only the power of memory, it seems, can placate our inevitable feelings of nostalgia and regret—not only for our youthful days, but for how we lived them. Appropriately, McCartney concludes the medley with, in Lennon's words, "a cosmic, philosophical line": "And in the end the love you take / Is equal to the love you make."

10. "YOU KNOW MY NAME (LOOK UP THE NUMBER)" (1970)

Recorded by the band in 1967, completed by Lennon, McCartney, and the Beatles' faithful roadie Mal Evans in 1969, and released as the B-side of "Let It Be" in 1970, "You Know My Name (Look Up the Number)" is a uniquely comic moment in the group's discography. "We had these endless, crazy fun sessions," McCartney fondly recalls in Mark Lewisohn's *The Beatles Recording Sessions* (1988). A pastiche of lounge-style vocal stylings and Monty Pythonesque humor, the song features the late Rolling Stones guitarist Brian Jones on saxophone, Lennon playing the maracas, and Harrison on the xylophone. From its soul-pounding blues introduction to the song's swanky samba refrain, "You Know My Name" is propelled—in unforgettably comic fashion—by Lennon's hilarious falsetto vocals and the dappled chorus of grunts and mumbles that mark the tune's sizzling conclusion. In its own peculiar way, "You Know My Name" brilliantly captures the spirit of the Beatles' remarkable pop-musical career: their personality, their willingness to experiment—to whatever results—and their irrepressible humanity.

Part Two

■

APART

■

ONE

John Lennon:
Above Us Only Sky

—"I'm shy. If somebody attacks, I shrink."

Ray Coleman

■

In 1956, sixteen-year-old John Lennon's life changed forever when he first heard Elvis Presley on Radio Luxembourg. "After that," he told biographer Ray Coleman, "nothing was the same for me." To Lennon, music, and rock and roll in particular, became nothing less than a religion. Like fellow rocker and roller, Bruce Springsteen, rock saved John Lennon as well. Coleman recalls that time in this excerpt from *Lennon: The Definitive Biography*.

from *Lennon: The Definitive Biography*

■ IT CANNOT HAVE BEEN a coincidence: John's hell-raising final two years at Quarry Bank coincided with the arrival in his life of a force that was to be his *cause célèbre*, his saviour, his lifeline. To John Lennon at fifteen, the arrival of two films was virtually a mirror-image of his own outlook on life.

Rebel Without a Cause, starring the mumbling, sharp, resentful hero James Dean, was youth's first stab at the establishment, its first statement against such cozy pictures as *Oklahoma* and *A Star Is Born*. And *Blackboard Jungle* was even more important, for it reflected schoolboy aggression and catapulted a new music into the world. The music was electrifyingly urgent; the message of the film might have been written for Lennon and his cronies at Quarry Bank. But the star, Bill Haley, wouldn't do. He had no real charisma, and his personality totally lacked the tough directness of his driving songs like "Rock Around The Clock." Still, the die was cast; the old guard of what was then called the hit parade, including ballad singers Jimmy Young, Tony Bennett, Dickie Valentine, and Tennessee Ernie Ford, now had a deadly rival. The infant was called rock 'n' roll.

In 1956, when John Lennon was sixteen, the film that was dramatically to re-route pop music was shown in Britain. *Rock Around The Clock*, starring Bill Haley and the Comets, disc jockey Alan Freed, the Platters, and Freddie Bell and the Bellboys, was not a strong movie, even by those days' standards. It had no story line and was merely a vehicle for the bands to play this new music called rock 'n' roll. In

196 READ THE BEATLES

America, the film went unnoticed. In Britain, it began what is still called the generation gap.

This new music, loud, irreverent rock 'n' roll, thundered through the cinema halls of Britain. Parents looked on in horror as their sons and daughters—but mostly sons—identified with this clarion call to confrontation. The best news of all, for young people, was that adults thought it wasn't 'music.' It wasn't, indeed, mere music: it signalled a new approach to growing up. Rock 'n' roll was the new international anthem of youth.

American teenagers emulated their big heroes of the screen, the mumbling Marlon Brando and the gaunt, haunted James Dean, by adopting jeans and T-shirts. In Britain, a much more definite uniform was adopted. It was called the teddy boy outfit, so described because of its vague similarity to Edwardian fashions.

Greasy hair was one of the major requirements of a ted. It had to be shaped like an elephant's trunk at the front, coming down on the forehead and—crucially—a DA (duck's arse) at the back, with side whiskers extending well down the face. Very tight trousers, called drainpipes, bright socks, perhaps luminous, thick crepe-soled shoes (called 'brothel creepers'), and a long drape jacket were *de rigueur.*

Pop music may have been fey until this point, but it was at least a little escape from the drudgery of school work. And in a house with no television, the nightly listen to Radio Luxembourg, broadcast at the time on the difficult-to-tune 208 metres from deep inside Europe, was mandatory for schoolchildren. The B.B.C. broadcast light music. Luxembourg was well ahead of the game, playing non-stop pop. Its poor reception somehow added to its clandestine magic.

Lennon did not have to wait long for his Pied Piper. It was from this station one night that he heard Elvis Presley's earthshaking new anthem for rock 'n' roll, "Heartbreak Hotel." "After that," John told me in 1962, "nothing was the same for me. He did it for me, him and Lonnie Donegan."

Elvis's weapon was a triple ace. His robust voice was powerful, virtually beyond plagiarism; his songs, with the worldwide chart topper "Heartbreak Hotel" quickly followed by "Don't Be Cruel" and "Hound Dog," were revolutionary. They grabbed every listener by the ears as well as the hips. And then there was the way he looked.

Elvis was an Americanized version of the teddy boy. For him, the uniform was not necessary, but he was quickly christened King of Rock 'n' Roll because of his look, his leer, his loudness, and his rudeness: his hip swivelling was the talk of the critics who branded him as a danger to morality. Sexuality oozed from him. For anyone remotely concerned with teenagers at that time, Presley was the partisan demarcation line: make up your mind, whose side are you on? It was them and us, the kids and the adults. The more adults bemoaned Presley's arrival, the more the newspapers screeched about the new music of youth, the more Lennon and thousands of sixteen-year-olds like him loved it.

Aunt Mimi remembered the period well. "It was Elvis Presley all day long. I got very tired of him talking about this new singer. I was particularly upset because suddenly he wouldn't let me into his bedroom. If I opened the door, he'd say: 'Leave it, I'll tidy it up.' He became a mess, almost overnight, and all because of Elvis Presley, I say. He had a poster of him in his bedroom. There was a pyjama top in the bathroom, the trousers in the bedroom, socks somewhere else, shirts flung on the floor."

Mimi's voice would boom up the stairs: "There's going to be a change in this house. We're going to have law and order." Throughout his life John would use the same sentence to tease Mimi about the "Elvis period" as he reflected on it.[1] "And of course," said Mimi, "when John said it, later on, we would just both burst out laughing about the past. He was lucky to get away with what he did. It was because I'm a book lover and a bit of an artist myself, so I understood his attitude. What he wouldn't come to terms with was that I had a house to run. Oh, he *was* a mess and a problem in those years. Elvis Presley! If John's Uncle George had been alive even he certainly wouldn't have understood the bohemian bit."

The anchor of Elvis, his music and what he represented, marked John's life as significantly as Lennon was to mark millions of young lives only ten years later. There was to be one vast difference between Presley and Lennon: the American rock giant was a physical phenomenon who rarely spoke, and when he did it was an unimportant mumble. Elvis called nearly all strangers "sir" as a mark of polite nervousness. John was to combine an intuitive grasp of fundamental rock 'n' roll ethics with highly cerebral leadership. He probably never called anyone "sir" in his life.

But in the mid-1950s the personal pull of Presley, quickly followed by Little Richard, Jerry Lee Lewis, Buddy Holly, the Coasters, Carl Perkins, and the Everly Brothers, meant liberation for the academic flop that John Lennon had become. It also perfectly fuelled his inherent resentment of authority.

If Presley was John's clarion call to stand up and stand out, Lonnie Donegan was, in 1956 when John was sixteen, just as great a catalyst for his life. This time the hero was not just a distant, masculine figure propelling rock 'n' roll into millions of teenagers' brains. Donegan, clean-cut and formal, in suit and tie as befitted his jazzy background, was no-body's idea of high fashion. He was nasal-voiced, played guitar and banjo, but mesmerized a nation with a curiously British interpretation of the songs of the great American folk singers Woody Guthrie and Huddie "Leadbelly" Ledbetter. Donegan, who emerged from the tradi-tional jazz ranks of the Chris Barber band, galvanized British youth into his music, named skiffle, with a record called "Rock Island Line."

Donegan's influence on British pop music has been incalculable. He had a basic three-chord style, easy to copy, and the line-up of his group at the time (one other guitarist, upright double bass, and washboard player) inspired hundreds of thousands of young people to make do-it-yourself music. The sound was unimportant. What was crucial was that it wasn't difficult; the guitars were props, allowing the singers to be actors. Here was do-it-yourself rock 'n' roll for thousands of young people. Donegan's cute little songs, like "Putting On The Style," "Does Your Chewing Gum Lose Its Flavour (On The Bedpost Overnight)," and "Cumberland Gap," became the anthems of sixteen-year-olds every-where. Skiffle groups, formed in schools and clubs, played as much for fun as for money.

Lennon, then a bellicose schoolboy, went for skiffle like a homing pi-geon. Jazz audiences already knew of skiffle, because splinter groups formed from the bands led by Chris Barber and Ken Colyer played mostly in London clubs and a few knowledgeable provincial clubs like Liverpool's Cavern and Iron Door. All Lennon knew initially was "Rock Island Line," which even the B.B.C. was playing. He thought its accep-tance by *that* bastion of respectability, which even Aunt Mimi acknowl-edged as tolerable listening, was the key to his breakthrough. "All the boys of my age are getting guitars," he told Mimi. "Could you lend me the money to get one?"

John was seeing more of his mother and asked both Julia and Mimi to buy him a guitar. Every afternoon, on her daily visits to Mendips, Julia would be asked, but she did not want to override Mimi's authority by installing John with a guitar under her roof. John alone was enough of a responsibility for her sister. Julia could see, anyway, from his inter-est in her banjo playing, that with a guitar in his hand his studies at school, already a cause for concern, would plunge into irretrievable disaster.

John, faced with the two women in his life not helping him get a gui-tar, decided to send away for his first model himself. From a mail order advertisement in the *Daily Mail* he ordered a £5 10s ($9) model, "guar-anteed not to split," and was canny enough, at this stage, to have the guitar posted to Julia's address where he would run less risk of a scolding. His musically minded mother was less of a risk than Mimi. He took it to Mendips eventually, telling Mimi that Julia had got it for him.

Armed with the cheap guitar, which he would occasionally leave at Julia's in order not to push his luck with Mimi, John concentrated heavily on all the pop music sounds he could hear on Radio Luxembourg. Buying records was generally out of the question: they cost six shillings. But he did invest in a 78 r.p.m. record of Donegan's "Rock Island Line."

The person to whom Lennon quickly sold that record, for two shillings and sixpence, once he had played it to death on Julia's old record player, was to be one of the players in the group that John formed at school. Rod Davis, a studious, successful, A-stream student at Quarry Bank, met Lennon only because he too lived in Woolton. At the forty-five-minute prep sessions after each day's classes, students got together in classrooms according to the house they were in. As Davis and Lennon and his inseparable partner Pete Shotton were in Woolton, they met on most days. The record Lennon persuaded Rod Davis to buy had a damaged centre hole: Davis felt conned when he realized why John wanted to sell it.

Inspired by the Donegan craze, Rod Davis had bought a Windsor banjo for £5 from his uncle. Excited about his purchase, he said to a classmate, Eric Griffiths, "I went and bought a banjo yesterday." Davis was surprised to be told that Lennon and Griffiths already had guitars, and that Shotton was learning to play the washboard, an integral part of any skiffle band's line-up. "Why don't we have a practice on Thursday?" said Griffiths. "We're going to start a skiffle group."

Davis had known Lennon and Shotton since they were all about six. He remembered Lennon as the scourge of St. Peter's Sunday School classes. "He arrived looking resentful at having to come on Sunday mornings," says Davis, "and he chewed gum throughout the lessons. It just wasn't done to chew gum at the Sunday School." Eventually John and Shotton were invited to leave, although Mimi said that he was confirmed, at his own request, at the same church. "Religion was never rammed down his throat, but he certainly believed in God, all through his childhood, and he asked to be confirmed," she said.

But the only religion that seriously grabbed Lennon at the age of sixteen was music. Even William Pobjoy, headmaster of Quarry Bank, noticed the passion with which young Lennon, the terror of the school, was interesting himself in skiffle. It was, he reflects, good to see him feeling positive about *something*.

Mr. Pobjoy was also surprised, and pleased, that making music seemed to be encouraging a generous side to John's nature; some schoolboy entertainers, however amateur, would ask for money to play at school dances and other functions. "But John would always be most polite, and certainly not ask for money, when he offered the services of his group," says the ex-headmaster, who retired in 1982. "Some boys asked outrageous fees but John was really grateful for the chance to play free." Pobjoy pointed out this attribute to those teachers who were despairing of him.

Inevitably Lennon and Shotton were the pilots of the skiffle group. After a few weeks of practice, with John hammering out "Rock Island Line" and "Cumberland Gap" as his *tour de force* songs and Shotton playing the washboard with thimbles—the accepted percussion for all skiffle groups of that period—Lennon felt in full swing.

Now that this "new music" of Lonnie Donegan and Elvis Presley was the talk of the school, particularly in the C-stream into which Lennon had plunged, the official formation of a school skiffle group was the next move. When John told his mother of his group, she suggested holding practices at her house after school. The first line-up was John (guitar), Rod Davis (banjo), Eric Griffiths (guitar), and Colin Hanton (drums). The first rehearsal was in Griffiths's house in Woolton. Later they would play in Julia's bathroom, one player standing in the bath to get the tinny echoey sound of amplification. "John's mother really enjoyed us playing and encouraged us a lot," says Davis. "She obviously preferred the banjo to the guitar so I got on well with her. I was always impressed with the fact that she played banjo with the back of her nails.

"John was the undisputed leader for two reasons. First, he knew one more chord than the rest of us. His mother's banjo playing had given him the edge—she used to teach John some banjo chords, and they used to tune the top four strings of his guitar to banjo intervals, forget about the bottom two strings, and play banjo chords on the guitars! It was all right for me—Julia would help me tune my banjo properly. So I'd probably be the only one in tune. I think everything was in C—I remember having terrible trouble playing F chords on the banjo.

"Secondly John was keen on singing and the rest of us were never particularly good at vocals. We joined in choruses but he sang lead." The earliest songs were "Don't You Rock Me, Daddy-O," "Love Is Strange," "Rock Island Line," "Cumberland Gap," "Freight Train," the big hit made famous by Chas McDevitt and Nancy Whiskey, Johnny Duncan's "Last Train To San Fernando," and "Maggie May."

"John used to belt the daylights out of his guitar and was forever breaking strings," says Davis. "When this happened, he'd hand me his guitar and I'd have to change the string for him because I was better at it than him. While I was changing it, he'd borrow my banjo, so he's actually played my banjo quite a few times." Today he guards the instrument as a priceless memento.

The first name for the group was the Blackjacks. They hit upon the uniform for their much-hoped-for public performances: black jeans, with green stitching, and plain white shirts. Two new recruits to the band alternated on playing tea-chest bass; Ivan Vaughan, who had gone to Dovedale Primary School with John but went on to the posh Liverpool institute when John joined Quarry Bank; and Nigel Whalley, who went to Bluecoat Grammar School, but who knew John from his Sunday School days. In a rare show of allegiance to his school, John quickly changed the name to the Quarry Men, the line-up of which was erratic, and at one time included a bass player, Bill Smith, who was in John's class. But he did not arrive regularly for rehearsals and soon left. Eventually, the bass-playing role fell to Len Garry.

The fact that Nigel Whalley and Ivan Vaughan were not at Quarry Bank made their regular inclusion in the line-up difficult to arrange, anyway; but Nigel, highly organized and ambitious for the group, said he would try to get them some bookings. He persuaded shopkeepers in Woolton to put notices, free, in their windows: "Country, Western, Rock 'n' Roll, Skiffle, The Quarry Men, Open for Engagements."

John named the group the Quarry Men partly as a tongue-in-cheek dig at the school in which they had been born, and partly because the name had a ring of skiffle about it, anyway. "Quarry Men Strong Before Our Birth" was the school song, sung lustily by most boys at the end of term. Lennon and Shotton, when they were not smiling or making up rude words to the school song under their breath, quietly admired its sentiments. John saw the adoption of the school song within the name of the group as a means to an end; it gave them a stamp of credibility. And he was to foster the "means to an end" rule throughout his life. It was Lennon who thought of the name, and he told the others. That was that.

Slowly but encouragingly, occasional engagements were secured for the Quarry Men by Nigel Whalley. Childwall Golf Club, St. Barnabas Church Hall at Penny Lane, and St. Peter's Youth Club were among the earliest. The group had made its public debut playing on the back of a lorry at a carnival in Rosebery Street, Liverpool 8.

202 READ THE BEATLES

John's beer drinking had its beginnings during these days. Payments for Quarry Men concerts at Conservative dances and youth club parties were only a few pounds, but of equal attraction to John was the liberation of an evening out, the chance to chat up girls outside his normal Woolton beat, and drink, often "on the house" as he was a performer.

The teddy boy movement was gaining ground by the time the Quarry Men secured some bookings. At dances, teds would ask the group to play some rock 'n' roll instead of the comparatively mild skiffle. The request hit a chord inside the ever-restless Lennon, who had adopted a bit of a teddy boy look with the beginnings of "sidies" down his face and tight jeans which were as near as he could get to the obligatory drainpipe trousers. The Quarry Men entered several skiffle contests, failed to win or get a position at any one, and John was particularly taken aback by a group from Rhyl which won the Carroll Levis Discoveries night at the Liverpool Empire. "They were really putting their act over, the guitarist was all over the stage and really full of a show," recalls Rod Davis. "We were really purist by comparison. John learned a lesson from that night. He said: 'You've got to put it over a bit to do rock 'n' roll.'" In his mind, if not in the minds of the others, that was going to be the route to success. If Lonnie Donegan had provided the *will* to play, Elvis Presley was still the foundation upon which his musical attitude was based.

"None of us thought of it going any further than a good school lark that earned a few bob," says Rod Davis. But Lennon thought differently and swung the songs towards rock 'n' roll. "Jailhouse Rock" and "Blue Suede Shoes," Lennon favourites, took him way beyond the purism of the early skiffle sounds and gave full rein to his increasing stage personality. His mother taught him, in one week of solid tuition after school, the chords to a hot Lennon favourite, Buddy Holly's "That'll Be The Day." It was the first song John learned to play and sing accurately. There was growing dissent in the group about the increasing rock element from John. Nigel Whalley secured the Quarry Men a coveted booking at a jazz stronghold in Liverpool city centre, the Cavern in Mathew Street. Lennon disliked jazz fans because they were, he thought, elitist. Here, in a club which tolerated skiffle because it was a jazz offshoot but which banished rock 'n' roll as the trashy sound of youth, Lennon bit off more than he could chew.

Davis argued on stage with him that the idea of doing rock songs would be unacceptable to the audience, and anyway that wasn't the original idea behind the Quarry Men. John maintained that as he was the only singer in the group, he had a right to decide what would be sung; anyway, the skiffle repertoire was restricting and boring. It was time to move on. And so the jazz crowd, dressed, as Lennon later sneeringly described them, in their G.C.E. sweaters', jeered and booed as Lennon went through his rockers. Davis said to him: "We shouldn't be playing rock 'n' roll on stage at the Cavern of all places, John. It's a jazz place." He was also concerned that John didn't know the words to many other rockers he was putting forward. He was making up any words as he sang along. But Lennon totally ignored Davis's opinions and announced the songs as he wanted them: Presley's "Jailhouse Rock," "Don't Be Cruel," and "Heartbreak Hotel" were more exciting than the restricting skiffle repeats.

The £5 guitar was not standing up to the strain of all these public performances. "He kept bothering me for what he called a real one," said Mimi. "I wasn't too ready to provide it because I thought he should be getting on with his school work a little more seriously. But he kept on and on: 'Let me get it out of my system, Mimi.'

"I said: 'All right, get it out of your system.'"

And so, one Saturday morning she took him along to the famous musical instrument shop, Hessy's, off Whitechapel in Liverpool. "There were guitars hanging all around the room and John didn't know which one to choose for the best. Finally, he pointed to one and the man took it down and he played it and said, 'I'll have that one.' What I do remember is John nodding his head to me and me paying the £17 there and then for it. He was as happy as could be on the bus home." The Spanish-styled guitar had steel strings which quickly made John's fingers sore from his many hours of strumming, in his bedroom, to the exclusion of homework and to the continuing irritation of Mimi.

Finally, when she could no longer stand his foot tappings on the ceiling, Mimi ordered him into the porch at Mendips. It was to become his refuge, and coincidentally, he preferred the acoustics, with the echo. On one occasion when he was banished there by an impatient Mimi, she boomed the words: "The guitar's all very well, John, but you'll never make a *living* out of it."

Note

1. The King and the Fab Four couldn't quite bridge the cultural gap. The Beatles' absurdist brand of humor was lost on Presley. It seems that, based on accounts of their disastrous first meeting in Los Angeles, Presley didn't know what to make of the four lads who (especially Lennon), out of sheer nervousness and perhaps disbelief at finally meeting their idol, stared at him as if he were a mannequin in a department store window.

Jon Wiener

■

Jon Wiener, a university professor, has spent a considerable amount of time studying the files that the FBI kept on John Lennon. To Wiener, they constitute "an abuse of power, a kind of rock 'n' roll Watergate." The ultimate goal of the investigation was to find enough evidence to deport Lennon (at the time of the deportation proceedings, Lennon was spending most of his time in New York). Many prominent people supported his efforts to stay in the United States. Among the luminaries coming to Lennon's defense were New York mayor John Lindsay, Henry Miller, Kurt Vonnegut, Edmund Wilson, Saul Bellow, Lawrence Ferlinghetti, Leonard Bernstein, Virgil Thomson, Bob Dylan, Jack Lemmon, and Allen Ginsberg. What's more, *The New York Times* urged the government to renew Lennon's visa. Columnist Jack Anderson of *The Washington Post* was also a staunch advocate of Lennon. In the following excerpt Wiener discusses Lennon's legal problems with the American government.

from *Gimme Some Truth: The John Lennon FBI Files*

■ WHEN FBI DIRECTOR J. Edgar Hoover reported to the Nixon White House in 1972 about the bureau's surveillance of John Lennon, he began by explaining that Lennon was a "former member of the Beatles singing group." Apparently Hoover wanted to show that although he was no rock fan, at least he knew who Lennon was. When a copy of this letter arrived in response to my 1981 Freedom of Information Act (FOIA) request, the entire text was withheld, as were almost 200 other pages, on the grounds that releasing it would endanger the national security. That seemed unlikely. So, with the help of the American Civil Liberties Union (ACLU) of Southern California, I filed a lawsuit under the FOIA in 1983, asking the court to order the release of the withheld pages. Fourteen years later, after the case went to the Supreme Court, the FBI finally agreed to settle almost all the outstanding issues of the case, to release all but ten of the documents, and to pay $204,000 to the ACLU for court costs and attorney fees. The most significant 100 pages of the Lennon file are reproduced in this volume.

The Lennon FBI files document an era when rock music seemed to have real political force, when youth culture, for perhaps the first time in American history, was mounting a serious challenge to the status quo in Washington, when President Nixon responded by mobilizing the FBI and the Immigration and Naturalization Service (INS) to silence the man from England who was singing "Give Peace a Chance" at his first live concert in the United States since 1966. Lennon's file dates from 1971, a year when the war in Vietnam was killing hundreds of thousands, when Nixon was facing reelection, and when the "clever Beatle" was living in New York and joining up with the antiwar movement. The Nixon administration learned that he and some radical friends were talking about organizing a national concert tour to coincide with the 1972 election campaign, a tour that would combine rock music and radical politics, during which Lennon would urge young people to register to vote, and vote against the war, which meant, of course, against Nixon.

The administration learned about Lennon's idea from an unlikely source: Senator Strom Thurmond. Early in 1972 he sent a secret memo to Attorney General John Mitchell and the White House reporting on Lennon's plans and suggesting that deportation "would be a strategy-counter-measure."

That was exactly the sort of thing John Dean, the counsel to the president, had suggested in his famous 1971 memo: "We can use the available political machinery to screw our political enemies." The word was passed to the INS, which began deportation proceedings a month later. The Nixon administration's efforts to "neutralize" Lennon—their term—to silence him as a spokesman for the peace movement, are the central subject of Lennon's FBI file.

Throughout fourteen years of FOIA litigation over the files, which began in 1983, the FBI maintained that its surveillance of Lennon was not an abuse of power but rather a legitimate law enforcement activity. It's true that in 1972 Lennon associated with antiwar activists who had been convicted of conspiring to disrupt the Democratic National Convention four years earlier. It's true that he spoke out against the war at rallies and demonstrations. But the files contain no evidence that Lennon committed any criminal acts: no bombings, no terrorism, no conspiracies. His activities were precisely the kind protected by the First Amendment, which is not limited to U.S. citizens.

The story of the Lennon files is also the story of the fourteen-year legal battle to win release of the withheld pages, a story about the ways the Reagan, Bush, and Clinton administrations resisted the requirements of the FOIA. The basic issue here was not simply John Lennon. The basic issue was that government officials everywhere like secrecy. By keeping the public from learning what they have done, they hope to avoid criticism, hinder the opposition, and maintain power over citizens and their elected representatives. Classified files and official secrets lie at the heart of the modern governmental bureaucracy and permit the undemocratic use of power to go unrecognized and unchallenged by citizens.

Democracy, however, is not powerless before this practice. In the fight against government secrecy, America has led the world. In 1966 Congress passed the FOIA, which requires that officials make public the information in their files to "any person" who requests it, unless it falls into a small number of exempted categories, including "national security." The Act was substantially expanded in 1974 in the wake of revelations of White House abuse of power during the Watergate scandal. The FOIA, in effect, created a notable challenge to the history of government secrecy; it provided a set of rules and procedures, officials and offices dedicated not to the collection and maintenance of secrets but rather to their release to the public. Journalists, scholars, and activists have used the FOIA to scrutinize the operations of government agencies and expose official misconduct and lying, including the FBI's illegal efforts to harass, intimidate, disrupt, and otherwise interfere with lawful political actions. The John Lennon FBI files provide an example.

Before considering that history, it's important to acknowledge that the FOIA in many respects has been a spectacular success, as Americans have demonstrated an impressive appetite for government information. In 1990, for example, federal agencies received 491,000 FOIA requests and spent $83 million responding to them. The Defense Department received the most, 118,000 requests, while the FBI received 11,000, and the CIA, 4,000. The FOIA further requires that agencies report the extent of their denials of such requests: the agency with the highest denial rate in 1990, strangely enough, was the Office of Ethics, which refused to release 75 percent of requested documents. In contrast, the Department of Health and Human Services denied only 2 percent of the requests it received. The staff at the FBI's Freedom of Information Section processing FOIA requests consists of eight agents and 245 support employees, 65 of whom work on national security declassification. In 1990, 421,000 previously classified pages were released; requesters filed 993 administrative appeals of decisions to withhold documents; 263 requests that had been denied were in litigation.

The most fundamental justification for governmental secrecy is "national security." Thus the FOIA exempts from disclosure any material "which reasonably could be expected to cause damage to the national security." What constitutes a "reasonable expectation" is obviously the issue. Because of the long-standing belief in the legitimacy of keeping secret diplomatic and military information, the claim that releasing any particular document could reasonably be expected to damage "national security" has been difficult to refute, which opens the FOIA to abuse by officials with something to hide. How federal officials have interpreted the national security exemption to the FOIA provides the most important test of government practice, and lies at the heart of the John Lennon FBI files litigation.

The original FOIA of 1966 had no provision for judicial review of "national security" information. The Act exempted material "specifically required by Executive Order to be kept secret in the interest of national defense or foreign policy." The law, however, contained no provisions authorizing courts to consider government decisions to withhold documents under the "national security" claim. In a 1973 Supreme Court ruling, Justice Potter Stewart pointed out this flaw: the FOIA provided "no means to question any Executive decision to stamp a document 'secret,' however cynical, myopic, or even corrupt that decision might have been." The Court went on to note that Congress could establish procedures to permit courts to review such decisions.

This use of the "national security" exemption to conceal government misconduct came to the fore in 1974, in the wake of the Watergate revelations of White House abuses of power. At that time the issue was framed in an apolitical way as a problem of "overclassification of national security information." Congress held extensive hearings documenting the problem and accepted the Supreme Court's suggestion, passing a series of amendments that significantly strengthened the FOIA, especially in relation to "national security" claims. The 1974 amendments instructed courts to determine *de novo* whether the national security exemption was being properly applied in particular cases. Courts were authorized to conduct *in camera* reviews of documents for which the government claimed the national security exemption. Most important, courts were empowered to overrule executive officials' decisions classifying documents under the "national security" claim. For the first time, courts could order the release of improperly classified documents. President Ford vetoed the legislation, objecting specifically to the provision empowering the courts to overrule executive branch classification decisions. This provision, he declared, was an unconstitutional infringement on executive power. Congress overrode Ford's veto, and the amendments became part of the FOIA. Nine years later, the ACLU of California asked the court to overrule the Reagan administration's claims that parts of the Lennon FBI file had to be withheld to protect "national security."

Secret government files like Lennon's have a history. The Cold War provided a great impetus to government secrecy, which was justified as a necessary response to Soviet efforts to "destroy our free and democratic system" at a time when their "preferred technique is to subvert by infiltration and intimidation," as the government explained in 1950 in the policy statement "NSC 68." Cold War presidents secretly authorized the FBI to monitor radical activists, who included not just potential spies or saboteurs but "writers, lecturers, newsmen, entertainers, and others in the mass media field" who "might influence others against the national interest," as the Senate's Church Committee explained after Watergate.

But the federal government began spying on Americans long before the Cold War, as Daniel Patrick Moynihan observes in his book *Secrecy*. Most of the structure of secrecy now in place, he argues, has its origin in the World War I Espionage Act, passed into law in 1917 at the urging of President Woodrow Wilson. The former Princeton history professor declared in his 1915 State of the Union message that recent immigrants had "poured the poison of disloyalty into the very arteries of our national life," and he urged Congress to "save the honor and self respect of the nation. Such creatures of passion, disloyalty, and anarchy must be crushed out." Congress responded with the Espionage Act and, in 1918, the Sedition Act, which made it a crime to "utter, print, write, or publish any disloyal, profane, scurrilous, or abusive language about the form of government of the United States." It also made it a crime to "advocate any curtailment of production in this country of any thing . . . necessary or essential to the prosecution of the war."

In fact the first FBI files on people suspected of disloyalty date from before World War I. The bureau was created in 1908; it opened a file on Ezra Pound in 1911, after he published in the first issue of *The Masses*, a socialist magazine. It opened a file on Max Eastman in 1912 on the grounds that he was editor of *The Masses* and "a true believer in free love." It opened a file on Walter Lippmann the same year, noting that the recent Harvard graduate was secretary to the socialist mayor of Schenectady. Herbert Mitgang and Natalie Robins have shown that the

FBI kept files on at least 150 of the country's leading writers, from Sinclair Lewis to William Faulkner to Ernest Hemingway to Norman Mailer and James Baldwin. Thus the insatiable appetite of Hoover's FBI for derogatory gossip and malicious trivia, evident in the Lennon file, was nothing new. But unlike other writers and artists the FBI watched, Lennon wasn't persecuted simply because of what he thought or wrote. The Nixon administration was after him because of what he did—and what he planned to do.

The Lennon files constitute a small but significant chapter in the history of the sixties, and of the Watergate era, and also in the history of bureaucratic secrecy and government abuse of power. They confirm Richard Nixon's place in the annals of rock 'n' roll as the man who tried to deport John Lennon, and thus they support the claim that rock in the sixties had some kind of political significance. Of course some have seen Nixon's pursuit of Lennon as a simple case of paranoia, in which the president and the New Left shared the same delusion. But the record shows there was a rationale behind Nixon's campaign to silence Lennon that was not simply nutty. Lennon's plan to mobilize young voters against the war may not have affected the outcome of the 1972 election, but it had a clear and reasonable logic behind it.

The Lennon FBI files include some comic and hilarious moments. The FBI at points looks more like the Keystone Cops than the Gestapo. But the campaign to "neutralize" Lennon wasn't a joke; it was a crime.

The experiences of exaltation and anger that rock music provided in the late sixties were not in themselves political experiences. Lennon knew that. He also knew that rock could become a potent political force when it was linked to real political organizing, when, for example, it brought young people together to protest the Vietnam War. The Lennon FBI files chronicle Lennon's commitment to test the political potential of rock music. They also document the government's commitment to stop him. The investigation of Lennon was an abuse of power, a kind of rock 'n' roll Watergate.

David Sheff

■

On the eve of the release of *Double Fantasy*, John Lennon and Yoko Ono agreed to a sit-down interview with *Playboy* magazine. The subject matter was wide-ranging, from the Beatles, of course, to Lennon's solo career to his decision to be a househusband following the birth of son Sean in 1975. The following is just a portion of the lengthy interview that appeared in the January 1981 issue of *Playboy*, a month after Lennon was assassinated outside the entrance of his home, the Dakota, in New York City on December 8, 1980. The interview was also published in book form as *All We Are Saying: The Last Major Interview with John Lennon and Yoko Ono* (St. Martin's Griffin, 1981).

Playboy Interview:
John Lennon and Yoko Ono
January 1981

To describe the turbulent history of the Beatles, or the musical and cultural mileposts charted by John Lennon, would be an exercise in the obvious. Much of the world knows that Lennon was the guiding spirit of the Beatles, who were themselves among the most popular and profound influences of the Sixties, before breaking up bitterly in 1970. Some fans blamed the breakup on Yoko Ono, Lennon's Japanese-born second wife, who was said to have wielded a disproportionate influence over Lennon, and with whom he has collaborated throughout the Seventies. In 1975, the Lennons became unavailable to the press, and though much speculation has been printed, they emerged to dispel rumors—and to cut a new album—only a couple of months ago. The Lennons decided to speak with Playboy *in the longest interview they have ever granted. Free-lance writer* **David Sheff** *was tapped for the assignment, and when he and a* Playboy *editor met with Ono to discuss ground rules, she came on strong: Responding to a reference to other notables who had been interviewed in* Playboy, *Ono said, "People like Carter represent only their country. John and I represent the world." But by the time the interview was concluded several weeks later, Ono had joined the project with enthusiasm. Here is Sheff's report:*

"*There was an excellent chance this interview would never take place. When my contacts with the Lennon-Ono organization began, one of*

Ono's assistants called me, asking, seriously, 'What's your sign?' The interview apparently depended on Yoko's interpretation of my horoscope, just as many of the Lennons' business decisions are reportedly guided by the stars. [Anthony DeCurtis said much the same thing. See his essay in this volume.] I could imagine explaining to my Playboy editor, 'Sorry, but my moon is in Scorpio—the interview's off.' It was clearly out of my hands. I supplied the info: December 23, three P.M., Boston.

"Thank my lucky stars. The call came in and the interview was tentatively on. And I soon found myself in New York, passing through the ominous gates and numerous security checkpoints at the Lennons' headquarters, the famed Dakota apartment building on Central Park West, where the couple dwells and where Yoko Ono holds court beginning at eight o'clock every morning.

"Ono is one of the most misunderstood women in the public eye.[1] Her mysterious image is based on some accurate and some warped accounts of her philosophies and her art statements, and on the fact that she never smiles. It is also based—perhaps unfairly—on resentment of her as the sorceress Svengali who controls the very existence of John Lennon. That image has remained through the years since she and John met, primarily because she hasn't chosen to correct it—nor has she chosen to smile. So as I removed my shoes before treading on her fragile carpet—those were the instructions—I wondered what the next test might be.

"Between interruptions from her two male assistants busy screening the constant flow of phone calls, Yoko gave me the once-over. She finally explained that the stars had, indeed, said it was right—very right, in fact. Who was I to argue? So the next day, I found myself sitting across a couple of cups of cappuccino from John Lennon.

"Lennon, still bleary-eyed from lack of sleep and scruffy from lack of shave, waited for the coffee to take hold of a system otherwise used to operating on sushi and sashimi—'dead fish,' as he calls them—French cigarettes and Hershey bars with almonds.

"Within the first hour of the interview, Lennon put every one of my preconceived ideas about him to rest. He was far more open and candid and witty than I had any right to expect. He was prepared, once Yoko had given the initial go-ahead, to frankly talk about everything. Explode was more like it. If his sessions in primal-scream therapy were his emotional and intellectual release ten years ago, this interview was his more recent vent. After a week of conversations with Lennon and Ono separately as well as together, we had apparently established some sort of rapport, which was confirmed early one morning.

212 READ THE BEATLES

"As the interview progressed, the complicated and misunderstood re-lationship between Lennon and Ono emerged as the primary factor in both of their lives. 'Why don't people believe us when we say we're sim-ply in love?' John pleaded. The enigma called Yoko Ono became accessi-ble as the hard exterior broke down—such as the morning when she let out a hiccup right in the middle of a heavy discourse on capitalism. Non-plused by her hiccup, Ono giggled. With that giggle, she became vulner-able and cute and shy—not at all the creature that came from the Orient to brainwash John Lennon."

PLAYBOY: Why did you become a househusband?

LENNON: There were many reasons. I had been under obligation or con-tract from the time I was 22 until well into my 30s. After all those years, it was all I knew. I wasn't free. I was boxed in. My contract was the physical manifestation of being in prison. It was more important to face myself and face that reality than to continue a life of rock 'n' roll—and to go up and down with the whims of either your own performance or the public's opinion of you. Rock 'n' roll was not fun anymore. I chose not to take the standard options in my business—going to Vegas and singing your great hits, if you're lucky, or going to hell, which is where Elvis went.

ONO: John was like an artist who is very good at drawing circles. He sticks to that and it becomes his label. He has a gallery to promote that. And the next year, he will do triangles or something. It doesn't reflect his life at all. When you continue doing the same thing for ten years, you get a prize for having done it.

LENNON: You get the big prize when you get cancer and you have been drawing circles and triangles for ten years. I had become a craftsman and I could have continued being a craftsman. I respect craftsmen, but I am not interested in becoming one.

ONO: Just to prove that you can go on dishing out things.

PLAYBOY: You're talking about records, of course.

LENNON: Yeah, to churn them out because I was expected to, like so many people who put out an album every six months because they're supposed to.

PLAYBOY: Would you be referring to Paul McCartney?

LENNON: Not only Paul. But I had lost the initial freedom of the artist by becoming enslaved to the image of what the artist is *supposed* to do. A lot of artists kill themselves because of it, whether it is through drink, like Dylan Thomas, or through insanity, like van Gogh, or through V.D., like Gauguin.

PLAYBOY: Most people would have continued to churn out the product. How were you able to see a way out?
LENNON: Most people don't live with Yoko Ono.
PLAYBOY: Which means?
LENNON: Most people don't have a companion who will tell the truth and refuse to live with a bullshit artist, which I am pretty good at. I can bullshit myself and everybody around. Yoko: That's my answer.
PLAYBOY: What did she do for you?
LENNON: She showed me the *possibility* of the alternative. "You don't *have* to do this." "I don't? Really? But—but—but—but—but. . . ." Of course, it wasn't that simple and it didn't sink in overnight. It took constant reinforcement. Walking away is much harder than carrying on. I've done both.

PLAYBOY: Why are you returning to the studio and public life?
LENNON: You breathe in and you breathe out. We feel like doing it and we have something to say. Also, Yoko and I attempted a few times to make music together, but that was a long time ago and people still had the idea that the Beatles were some kind of sacred thing that shouldn't step outside its circle. It was hard for us to work together then. We think either people have forgotten or they have grown up by now, so we can make a second foray into that place where she and I are together, making music—simply that. It's not like I'm some wondrous, mystic prince from the rock 'n' roll world dabbling in some strange music with this exotic, Oriental dragon lady, which was the picture projected by the press before.

PLAYBOY: John, you've been asked this a thousand times, but why is it so unthinkable that the Beatles might get back together to make some music?
LENNON: Do you want to go back to high school? Why should I go back ten years to provide an illusion for you that I know does not exist? It cannot exist.
PLAYBOY: Then forget the illusion. What about just to make some great music again? Do you acknowledge that the Beatles made great music?
LENNON: Why should the Beatles give more? Didn't they give everything on God's earth for ten years? You're like the typical sort of love-hate fan who says, "Thank you for everything you did for us in the Sixties—would you just give me another shot? Just one more miracle?"

PLAYBOY: We're not talking about miracles—just good music.

LENNON: When Rodgers worked with Hart and then worked with Hammerstein, do you think he should have stayed with one instead of working with the other? Should Dean Martin and Jerry Lewis have stayed together because *I* used to like them together? What is this game of doing things because other people want it? The whole Beatle idea was to do what *you* want, right? To take your own responsibility.

PLAYBOY: All right, but get back to the music itself: You don't agree that the Beatles created the best rock 'n' roll that's been produced?

LENNON: I don't. The Beatles, you see—I'm too involved in them artistically. I cannot see them objectively. I cannot listen to them objectively. I'm dissatisfied with every record the Beatles ever fucking made. There ain't *one* of them I wouldn't remake—including all the Beatles records and all my individual ones. So I cannot possibly give you an assessment of what the Beatles are.

When I was a Beatle, I thought we were the best fucking group in the goddamned world. And believing that is what made us what we were—whether we call it the best rock 'n' roll group or the best pop group or whatever.

But you play me those tracks today and I want to remake every damn one of them. There's not a single one. . . .

PLAYBOY: You keep saying you don't want to go back ten years, that too much has changed. Don't you ever feel it would be interesting—never mind cosmic, just *interesting*—to get together, with all your new experiences, and cross your talents?

LENNON: Wouldn't it be *interesting* to take Elvis back to his Sun Records period? I don't know. But I'm content to listen to his Sun Records. I don't want to dig him up out of the grave. The Beatles don't exist and can never exist again. John Lennon, Paul McCartney, George Harrison and Richard Starkey could put on a concert—but it can never be the Beatles singing *Strawberry Fields* or *I Am the Walrus* again, because we are not in our 20s. We cannot be that again, nor can the people who are listening.

PLAYBOY: But aren't you the one who is making it too important? What if it were just nostalgic fun? A high school reunion?

LENNON: I never went to high school reunions. My thing is, Out of sight, out of mind. That's my attitude toward life. So I don't have any romanticism about any part of my past. I think of it only inasmuch as it gave me pleasure or helped me grow psychologically. That is the only thing that interests me about yesterday. I don't believe in yesterday, by the way. You know *I don't believe in yesterday.* I am only interested in what I am doing now.

PLAYBOY: What about the people of your generation, the ones who feel a certain kind of music—and spirit—died when the Beatles broke up?

LENNON: If they didn't understand the Beatles and the Sixties then, what the fuck could we do for them now? Do we have to divide the fish and the loaves for the multitudes again? Do we have to get crucified again? Do we have to do the walking on water again because a whole pile of dummies didn't see it the first time, or didn't believe it when they saw it? You know, that's what they're asking: "Get off the cross. I didn't understand the first bit yet. Can you do that again?" No way. You can never go home. It doesn't exist.

PLAYBOY: How does it feel to have influenced so many people?

LENNON: It wasn't really me or us. It was the times. It happened to me when I heard rock 'n' roll in the Fifties. I had no idea about doing music as a way of life until rock 'n' roll hit me.

PLAYBOY: Do you recall what specifically hit you?

LENNON: It was *Rock Around the Clock,* I think. I enjoyed Bill Haley, but I wasn't overwhelmed by him. It wasn't until *Heartbreak Hotel* that I really got into it.

ONO: I am sure there are people whose lives were affected because they heard Indian music or Mozart or Bach. More than anything, it was the time and the place when the Beatles came up. Something did happen there. It was kind of chemical. It was as if several people gathered around a table and a ghost appeared. It was that kind of communication. So they were like mediums, in a way. It's not something you can force. It was the people, the time, their youth and enthusiasm.

PLAYBOY: For the sake of argument, we'll maintain that no other contemporary artist or group of artists moved as many people in such a profound way as the Beatles.

LENNON: But what moved the Beatles?

PLAYBOY: You tell us.

LENNON: All right. Whatever wind was blowing at the time moved the Beatles, too. I'm not saying we weren't flags on the top of a ship; but the whole boat was moving. Maybe the Beatles were in the crow's-nest, shouting, "Land ho," or something like that, but we were all in the same damn boat.

ONO: As I said, they were like mediums. They weren't conscious of all they were saying, but it was coming through them.

PLAYBOY: Why?

LENNON: We tuned in to the message. That's all. I don't mean to belittle the Beatles when I say they weren't this, they weren't that. I'm just trying not to overblow their importance as separate from society. And I don't think they were more important than Glenn Miller or Woody Herman or Bessie Smith. It was our generation. It was Sixties music.

PLAYBOY: What do you say to those who insist that all rock since the Beatles has been the Beatles redone?

LENNON: *All* music is rehash. There are only a few notes. Just variations on a theme.

PLAYBOY: Wasn't a lot of the Beatles' music at least more intelligent?

LENNON: The Beatles were more intellectual, so they appealed on that level, too. But the basic appeal of the Beatles was not their intelligence. It was their music. It was only after some guy in the London *Times* [William Mann, whose essay is reprinted in this volume] said there were Aeolian cadences in *It Won't Be Long* that the middle classes started listening to it—because somebody put a tag on it.

PLAYBOY: Did you put Aeolian cadences in *It Won't Be Long*?

LENNON: To this day, I don't have any idea what they are. They sound like exotic birds.

PLAYBOY: How about *Strawberry Fields Forever*?

LENNON: Strawberry Fields is a real place. After I stopped living at Penny Lane, I moved in with my auntie who lived in the suburbs in a nice semidetached place with a small garden and doctors and lawyers and that ilk living around—not the poor slummy kind of image that was projected in all the Beatles stories. In the class system, it was about half a class higher than Paul, George and Ringo, who lived in government-subsidized housing. We owned our house and had a garden. They didn't have anything like that. Near that home was Strawberry Fields, a house near a boy's reformatory where I used to go to garden parties as a kid with my friends Nigel and Pete. We would go there and hang out and sell lemonade bottles for a penny. We always had fun at Strawberry Fields. So that's where I got the name. But I used it as an image. Strawberry Fields forever.

PLAYBOY: And the lyrics, for instance: "Living is easy—"

LENNON: [*Singing*] "With eyes closed. Misunderstanding all you see." It still goes, doesn't it? Aren't I saying exactly the same thing now? The awareness apparently trying to be expressed is—let's say in one way I was always hip. I was hip in kindergarten. I was different from the others. I was different all my life. The second verse goes, "No one I think is in my tree." Well, I was too shy and self-doubting. Nobody seems to be as hip as me is what I was saying. Therefore, I must be crazy or a genius—"I mean it must be high or low," the next line. There was something wrong with me, I thought, because I seemed to see things other people didn't see. I thought I was crazy or an egomaniac for claiming to see things other people didn't see. As a child, I would say, *"But this is going on!"* and everybody would look at me as if I was crazy. I always was so psychic or intuitive or poetic or whatever you want to call it, that I was always seeing things in a hallucinatory way.

It was scary as a child, because there was nobody to relate to. Neither my auntie nor my friends nor anybody could ever see what I did. It was very scary and the only contact I had was reading about an Oscar Wilde or a Dylan Thomas or a Vincent van Gogh—all those books that my auntie had that talked about their suffering because of their visions. Because of what they saw, they were tortured by society for trying to express what they were. I *saw* loneliness.

PLAYBOY: Were you able to find others to share your visions with?

LENNON: Only dead people in books. Lewis Carroll, certain paintings. Surrealism had a great effect on me, because then I realized that my imagery and my mind wasn't insanity; that if it was insane, I belong in an exclusive club that sees the world in those terms. Surrealism to me is reality. Even as a child. When I looked at myself in the mirror or when I was 12, 13, I used to literally trance out into alpha. I didn't know what it was called then. I found out years later there is a name for those conditions. But I would find myself seeing hallucinatory images of my face changing and becoming cosmic and complete. It caused me to always be a rebel. This thing gave me a chip on the shoulder; but, on the other hand, I wanted to be loved and accepted. Part of me would like to be accepted by all facets of society and not be this loudmouthed lunatic musician. But I cannot be what I am not.

Note

1. In an article that appeared in *The New Yorker* about the relationship between C. S. Lewis and Joy Davidman, writer and critic Adam Gopnik, using Yoko as a reference point, invented a new word, "Yokoishly," to describe when a person insinuates him- or herself into the life of another. See Adam Gopnik, "Prisoner of Narnia," *The New Yorker*, November 21, 2005.

Andy Peebles

■

A mere forty-eight hours before John Lennon was gunned down outside his home at the Dakota, he and Yoko Ono were interviewed by Andy Peebles of the BBC. In this last public conversation before his death, Lennon talked about many things: the early years of the Beatles, their breakup, the release of *Double Fantasy*. During the three-hour interview, Lennon appears very hopeful and excited about his future and "all sorts of plans and ideas we have in our heads." Ironically, he mentions the sense of freedom he feels in New York, the joy of being able to walk around the streets without fear. "You want to know how great that is?" To Lennon, the eighties were destined to be a glorious time, full of exciting projects and new music. And then, in an instant, it was over.

from *The Last Lennon Tapes*

ANDY PEEBLES: Let's talk about the single *Just Like Starting Over*. Was that an obvious choice for the both of you, as a single? Were you happy with that?

JOHN LENNON: Yeah, because it was . . .

YOKO ONO: It's the message.

JOHN LENNON: It was really called *Starting Over* but, while we're making it, people kept putting things out with the same title. You know, there was a country and western hit called *Starting Over*, so I added "Just Like" at the last minute. The thing was, it was obvious because it was the one where the musicians got very loose because it was so simple rock 'n' roll, there was no problem. They really relaxed and they'd all be like that after it. And it just, even though I don't think it's the strongest track perhaps but it was in . . . some of the other tracks are stronger, I mean like *Losing You* might be a stronger piece of material, but *Starting Over* was the best way to start over. And to me it was like going back to fifteen and singing à la Presley. All the time I was referring to John [Smith], the engineer, here in the room I was referring to Elvis Orbison. It's kinda *I Want You, I need . . . Only The Lonely*, you know . . . (*Sings*) . . . a kind of parody but not really parody.

ANDY PEEBLES: A little tongue in cheek?

YOKO ONO: Oh very.

JOHN LENNON: A little! . . . Oh when I was doing it, I was cracking up . . . (*Sings*) . . .

ANDY PEEBLES: You relieve me greatly, because we still do *Round Table,* the review show on Radio One, and I was one of the guests the night that the Lennon single arrived in the studio, and there was absolute panic and pandemonium and it was on the turntable and the man who hosts the show, Adrian Love, said to me, what do you think? And I said, terrific but a little tongue in cheek.

JOHN LENNON: Right exactly . . . some people took it seriously, you know, saying what's he trying to do and all but, you know, they forget . . .

YOKO ONO: They, he was winking, you know, that one.

JOHN LENNON: I've had tongue in cheek all along. *I'm the Walrus,* all of them had tongue in cheek, you know, I don't, just because other people see depths of whatever in it, you know, what does it really mean "I Am the Eggman"? You know, it could have been the pudding basin for all I cared. I was just tongue in cheek, it's not that serious.

ANDY PEEBLES: Do you and did you, get fed up with people ostracising your lyrics and trying to read marvellously intellectual interpretations into them? Both of you, this must apply to?

JOHN LENNON: It was fun, sometimes it's fun but then it gets to be stupid, you know, that's why I started from the *Mother* album onwards trying to shave off all imagery, pretensions of poetry, illusions of grandeur, I call à la Dylan Dylanesque, you know. I didn't write any of that. Just say what it is, simple English, make it rhyme and put a backbeat on it and express yourself as simply as possible, straightforwardly as possible. As they say, Northern people are blunt, right, so I was trying to write like I am and I enjoy the poetic side and I'll probably do a little dabble later because Yoko's lyrics are so poetic. I get, well maybe I should do some of that, you know, and the track you were talking about *Walking on Thin Ice* was one of the extra tracks. We cut twenty-two tracks in ten days, I mean we were just like had diarrhoea of rock here, you know, and we just zapped out these twenty-two tracks and got it down to fourteen; and one I played you before was *Walking on Thin Ice* which was one of Yoko's tracks that we didn't put on for many, many reasons. Some were selected, some not. . . .

ANDY PEEBLES: Do you feel now at this stage, here we are in December 1980, that the theme and the ease of writing is now back with you?

JOHN LENNON: Yes.

ANDY PEEBLES: And that you're going to be extremely prolific in the months and years to come?

JOHN LENNON: Yes, I think it's going to be the one period they say, Those two will do anything for publicity, for Christ's sake get them off the front pages, oh get them off. You know, people are bitching at us, because we were always doing something; and then they were bitching at us because we weren't doing anything. And I have a funny feeling that it's going to be the other way round again, because we're talking and talking and talking and all sorts of plans and ideas we have in our heads, it's just a matter of getting it done, you know? We already got half the next album, and we'll probably go in just after Christmas and do that. And we're already talking about what the idea for the third album is, already laid out and I can't wait, you know. So it's a matter of just getting it done, and I'm sorry about you people that get fed up of hearing about us, but you know, we like to do it, so it's too bad. . . .

ANDY PEEBLES: One final question to you. What about your private life and your own sense of security these days? David Bowie has recently said that the great thing about New York is that he can walk down the street and people, instead of rushing up and ripping his clothes off, will come up, or rather will just walk past him and say, Hi, David, how are you? And he'd say, I'm very well. Is it the same for John and Yoko?

JOHN LENNON: Yeah, that's what made me finally stay here. It wasn't a conscious decision. I just found that I was going to movies, going to restaurants, and I had—the five years, you think, you know, it was just baking bread and the baby—no—because I went to Hong Kong and walked round. And people cannot appreciate what it was—when I left England and I still couldn't go on the street. It was still Carnaby Street and all that stuff was going on. We couldn't walk around the block, couldn't go to a restaurant, unless you wanted to go "with the business of the star going to the restaurant" garbage. I've even been walking the streets for the last seven years. When we first moved here, we actually lived in the village, in Greenwich Village, which is the sort of artsy-fartsy section of town, for those who know, where all the students and the would-bes live, you know? A few old poets and that. You know, people that have lived there for years, still live there. We got into this before—we didn't finish it—she told me that, Yes, you can walk on the street. You know. She says, You will be able to walk here; but I would be walking around tense like, waiting for somebody to say something, or jump on me, and it took me two years to unwind. I can go right out this door now and go in a restaurant. You want to know how great that is? Or go to the movies? I mean, people come and ask for autographs or say, Hi, but they don't bug you, you know. They just—Oh, hey, how you doin'? Like your record. Because we've got a record out now, but before they'd shout, How you doing? You know. How's the baby? Oh, great, thanks.

YOKO ONO: Talking about restaurants, I'm getting hungry.

JOHN LENNON: I'm starving too. What happened to the chicken soup?

ANDY PEEBLES: John, Yoko, on behalf of us, thank you very very much.

JOHN LENNON: A pleasure. It's a great pleasure to talk to you and the BBC and all the English, and Scots and Welsh and Irish listening.

ANDY PEEBLES: Cheers.

JOHN LENNON: Pip, pip, toot, toot.

Simon Frith

■

Many people commented on the circumstances of John Lennon's death. "To hear that John Lennon had been murdered by a fan," wrote music critic Greil Marcus, "that he had been killed for who and what he was, was like watching someone you love being hit by a car." Marcus also noted that Lennon's murder was unprecedented in another way: It was the first time that a fan— someone who ostensibly is an admirer—killed a public figure. Novelist Scott Spencer felt his death "everywhere. Like his life and his art, it is a unifying force. The astonishing—and, for me, unduplicated—characteristic of his art was it brought people together who may have had no other single thing in common. . . . Part of the grief we feel about his murder is our longing to once more belong to something larger than ourselves, to feel our hearts beat in absolute synchrony with hearts everywhere." Legendary New York journalist Pete Hamill wrote a long and anguished piece in *New York Magazine.* Like Marcus, he too acknowledged that this time it was different: "This was something new. . . . This time the ruined body belonged to someone who had made us laugh, who had taught young people how to feel, who had helped change and shape an entire generation. This time someone murdered a song." And where did it happen? In a city where Lennon had come, writes Hamill, "in order to be private, in order to be safe. *¿Que pasa,* New York?"

Simon Frith continues to be one of the most astute music critics in the world today. In this moving piece, he examines the media frenzy that surrounded the murder of John Lennon in New York City on December 8, 1980—the genuine sadness at his sudden and shocking death—but also explores what it means to be a "hero" in the popular imagination. Lennon was a complex and often polarizing figure and both his life and his untimely death affected people in profoundly different ways. Frith looks at the special genius that was John Lennon.

"Something to Be—John Lennon"

from *Music for Pleasure:*
Essays in the Sociology of Pop

"I read the news today, oh boy . . ."

■ "DEATH OF A HERO" it said in big black letters across the front of the *Daily Mirror,* and if I hadn't known already I'd have expected a story

about a policeman or soldier in Northern Ireland. The media respon
John Lennon's death was overwhelming as what began as a series of
vate griefs was orchestrated by disc jockeys and sub-editors into a national
event, but it was difficult to decide what all this mourning meant. The media themselves seemed less slick than usual, more ragged in their attempts to respond to a genuinely popular shock. What came through
was not just Beatle-nostalgia but a specific sadness at the loss of John
Lennon's Beatle qualities—qualities that never did fit easily into Fleet
Street ideology. "The idea," as Lennon once told *Red Mole*, "is not to comfort people, not to make them feel better but to make them feel worse."

The *Mirror*, its populist instincts currently sharpened by Thatch-
erism, got the mood most right. John Lennon was certainly the nearest
thing to a hero I've ever had, but though I knew what this meant in fan
terms (buying Beatle records at the moment of release, dreaming about
my own Lennon friendship—"I'll never meet him now," said one friend
when she heard the news), I'd never really stopped to think what the
pleasure I got from Lennon's music had to do with heroism. "What does
it mean?" called another friend from long ago, who knew I'd share his
sense of loss. He rang off without an answer and I watched the television tributes and tried to make sense of a sadness that was real enough,
but that seemed somehow shameful and self-indulgent, according to
the politics of culture which I usually pursue. Why should I feel this way
about a *pop* star?

The answer began to push through the obituaries. John Lennon was
a hero because he fought the usual meanings of pop stardom, because
he resisted the usual easy manipulations, and in the newspaper editori-
als, the radio interviews, the specially illustrated supplements with full
colour souvenir portrait, the struggle continued—everyone was still
claiming John Lennon as their friend, their cultural symbol. As Bryan
McAllister put it in his *Guardian* cartoon, "One has only to look at the
people who claim to have known John Lennon to understand perfectly
why he went to live in America." As John Lennon put it himself in 1971,
"One had to completely humiliate oneself to be what the Beatles were,
and that's what I resent. I didn't know, I didn't foresee. It happened bit
by bit, gradually, until this complete craziness is surrounding you, and
you're doing exactly what you don't want to do with people you can't
stand—the people you hated when you were ten."

The most repulsive of the Lennon friends ("I knew him quite well")
was Harold Wilson, who explained on "The World At One" that he gave
John an MBE "because he got the kids off the streets." "But wasn't he a

bad example," snapped Robin Day. "Didn't he encourage youngsters to take drugs?" "Ah yes," agreed Wilson, "he did go wrong, later."

Lennon went wrong and it seemed then, and it still seems to me now, that a Beatle going wrong was an important political event—John Lennon knew just what sort of (working-class) hero Harold Wilson wanted him to be.

"You know it ain't easy . . ."

John Lennon was a 1950s not a 1960s teenager. He started playing rock-'n'roll in 1956, the year of Suez, but the music fed his sense of adult rottenness in a more personal way—rock'n'roll was a sound made to accompany struggles at home and school, struggles against the insinuating pull to a career, to good marks and respectability. John Lennon became a teddy boy and a musician as part of his erratic opposition to the expected grateful conformities of a working-class grammar school boy.

So did hundreds of other 1950s school boys—Lennon was five days older than Cliff Richard—but they mostly lost their edge, softened by showbiz's own notions of steadiness and respectability. "Teddy boys," as Ray Gosling puts it, were "tidied up into teenagers. The youngsters sang one good rock song and the next moment they were in pantomime and all-round entertainment on the pier." Cliff Richard called his 1960 autobiography *It's Great To Be Young* and by then his way of being young seemed the "natural" teenage way to be.

John Lennon didn't have such a great youth. For a start he lived in Liverpool. It was a cosmopolitan port with musical advantages (American R&B records could be heard in Liverpool whatever the metropolitan pop industry's successes in cleaning up white rock'n'roll) and unique material opportunities—Liverpool had clubs where groups were employed to play grown-up *gutsy* music. There was a public nightlife, an aggressive way of leisure that had survived TV and the rise of family consumption. The Beatles' first manager, Allan Williams, explains the Liverpool Sound in terms of gangs and fights and territorial claims— the Beatles always had to *stand* for something, and they learnt to "entertain" in circumstances far removed from the London Palladium. Whether in Liverpool or Hamburg, the music had to be loud and hard—there was no space for subtlety or self-pity. Equipment was poor, songs were built around the combined beat of drums, bass and rhythm guitar (Lennon's own pivotal role), around the combined voices of

Lennon and McCartney. The Liverpool noise was hoarse and harsh, an effect of night after night of long, unrelieved sets.

While Tommy Steele and Cliff Richard were becoming family entertainers, the Beatles were learning street-survival tactics, and when they hit showbiz their defences were intact. As Liverpool's now veteran musicians remembered after Lennon's death, what was inspiring about the Beatles in their Cavern days was the *certainty* with which they claimed American music for themselves, and the most striking sign of this confidence was John Lennon's voice. The Beatles sang American music in a Liverpool accent—nasal rather than throaty, detached, passion expressed with a conversational cynicism.

Lennon's genius

Lennon's genius is usually described by reference to his song-writing ability, but it was his voice that always cut through. He conveyed a controlled, forthright intimacy that enabled him to rock out in early days with a barely suppressed fury, and in later, post-Beatle days to express remorse and optimism equally grippingly. Beatle fans "knew" Lennon above all through this singing voice, and perhaps all his obituarists needed to say was that he was the only rock singer who ever sang "we" convincingly. Certainly, when the Beatles finally had their extraordinary success story, they were different from other pop stars. Their qualities were not those of showbiz—they came across as arrogant and restless. Beatle trappings came to represent an attitude as well as the usual fan fervour, and the Beatles appealed to a mass audience that had previously been uneasy in its relationship to pop—sixth-form, student youth. The Beatles were the first English pop group that didn't insult the intelligence. They made an "underdog" sound (to use Hobsbawm's description), pilfered from black American sources, and retained a grittiness, an awkwardness that couldn't quite be swallowed up in commercialism.

John Lennon was, in this context, the most obviously gritty, intelligent Beatle—the one with edge. He was street-sharp as much by choice as necessity. He was a grammar-school boy who, for all his rebelliousness, drew on a grammar-school boy's intellectual pride; he was an art school student who retained an art school student's radical cultural ambitions; he was a bohemian who had learned to scoff at "nowhere" people in Hamburg's Reeperbahn. It was Lennon who leapt more

quickly (more desperately?) than the other Beatles at the unfolding possibilities of 1960s rock and youth culture, and the importance of the
Beatles in 1966–8 was not that they led any movement, but that they
joined in. They became (John Lennon in particular), for all their established star status, comrades in the mid-sixties "liberation" of leisure.
What's more, Lennon confirmed what I believed then and believe
still—that it is not possible to separate the hippy aspects of 1960s youth
culture, the drugs and mind-games and reconsiderations of sexuality,
from the political process which fed the student movement, the antiwar movement, May 1968, the women's movement, gay liberation. It
was thanks to his hippy commitments, to his open response to Yoko
Ono's anti-pop ideas, that John Lennon survived the Beatles experience
to make his most political music as the sixties came to an end.

"All I want is the truth . . ."

The week John Lennon was shot, the Clash released a three-record album called *Sandinista!* Infuriating, indulgent, exciting, touching, packed
with slogans and simplicities, guns and liberation, images of struggle
and doubt, it is a wonderful tribute to Lennon's influence—a record
that would have been impossible to imagine without him.

Lennon believed more intensely than any other rock performer that
rock and roll was a form of expression in which *anything* could be said,
but more importantly (in this sense he was a "proto-punk") he believed
too that rock and roll was the *only* form of expression in which many
things—to do with growing up working-class—could be said. His music
(like the Clash's) involves an urgent eagerness *to be heard* (an eagerness
which often obscured what was actually meant). As a 16-year-old, John
Lennon heard in rock'n'roll an anti-authoritarian voice that everywhere
else was silenced. This voice—essentially youthful—is still heard publicly only in rock music. Where else, for example, is the young's own experience of youth unemployment expressed or dealt with, except in the
music of local bands, on the occasional independent record on John
Peel's show?

Much of Lennon's musical life was about keeping this voice heard,
keeping its edge cutting through the ideological trappings of pop,
the commercial packaging of the Beatles, the ceaseless labels of the
exploiters. In coping with the trivializing tricks of the pop medium,

John Lennon faced many of the issues addressed later by the punks. Yoko Ono's position was particularly important in making the problems of Lennon's star position explicit. She confronted him with the taken-for-granted masculinity of the rock and roll voice, she asked questions about musical meaning itself (particularly about the rock conventions of spontaneity and realism, about the "truth" of the singing voice), she focused the problem of the rock relationship between the public and the private.

The energy of Lennon's music had always come from this tension—between the private use of song (as a way of handling emotion, a celebration of personal powers) and a sense of public duty. Lennon was committed to public music, accepted his "responsibility" to his audience (in a way that Bob Dylan, for example, did not). This was apparent not just in collective songs like "All You Need Is Love" and "Give Peace A Chance," but also in Lennon's continuing attempts in the early 1970s to use his song-writing skills to illuminate *everything* that was happening around him.

Public music depends on a material community as well as an abstract commitment, and by the mid-seventies, Lennon, like most of the original rock stars (especially those isolated in international stardom), had lost this sense of audience (it took the punks to revive it). *Double Fantasy,* his comeback LP, reflected his withdrawal—comfortable and happy in its commitment to his wife and child and friends, it lacked the political tension that had always come from Lennon's nervous need to account for his feelings publicly as well. This was just a record to be sold. There was nothing, apparently, to be said about marriage and fatherhood that mattered enough to make Lennon challenge his audience again.

"You say you want a revolution . . ."

John Lennon understood the contradictions of capitalist music-making, but he didn't solve them, and he rarely pretended that he wasn't involved in a money-making process. "Imagine no possessions," he sang, but I never thought he could. There was a sloppiness to John and Yoko's concept of peace and love and changing things by thinking them so, that concealed what mattered more—the Lennons had an astute sense of the mass market and how it worked. Their happenings at the end of the

1960s drew not only on Yoko Ono's experience as a performance artist but also on John Lennon's own cynical appreciation of the peculiarities of the British popular press (Malcolm McLaren applied a similar combination of cynicism and artiness to his manipulation of the media with the Sex Pistols in 1977). "Thank you very much for talking to us," murmured Andy Peebles humbly at the end of Radio 1's final Lennon interview. [An excerpt from the interview appears in this volume.] "Well," said John, "we've got a new record out and I needed to talk to people in Britain."

The central contradiction of John Lennon's artistic life (of any attempt to make mass music in a capitalist society) lay in the uneasy enthusiasm with which he packaged and sold his dreams. The problem for the working-class, he told *Red Mole* in 1971, is that "they are dreaming someone else's dream, it is not even their own." The problem for a working-class hero is that he too is defined in other people's dreams. John Lennon was murdered by a fan, by someone who pushed the fantasies that pop stardom is *designed* to evoke into the appalling stupidity of a madness.[1] The problem is that the grief that the rest of us Beatle fans then felt drew on similar fantasies, and the bitter irony is that John Lennon, whose heroism lay in his struggle against being a commodity, whose achievement was to express the *human* origins of pop ideas, should be trapped, finally, by a desperate, inhuman, nightmarish version of the pop fan's need to be a star.

Note

1. Daniel Schwartz, the court-appointed psychiatrist, concluded that Chapman suffered from chronic paranoid schizophrenia and a narcissistic personality disorder. Said Schwartz, "[Chapman] killed [Lennon] physically, and he killed himself psychologically." See Murray Kempton, "Mark David Chapman," *Rolling Stone*, October 15, 1981.

Adrian Henri

■

One of the so-called Liverpool poets, along with Brian Patten and Roger McGough, Adrian Henri was also a painter and frontman in the 1960s for the rock/poetry band, the Liverpool Scene. Much of his poetry was influenced by pop songs and, in turn, his popularity helped make poetry fashionable, bringing it off the bookshelves to the street. He was also one of the founders of a popular Liverpool band, Scaffold, whose members included Mike McCartney, brother of Paul. Henri died in December 2000 in Liverpool. He was 68. "New York City Blues" is a tribute from one Liverpudlian to another.

"New York City Blues" (for John Lennon)

You do not cross the road
To step into immortality
An empty street is only the beginning

The words will still flow through you
Even on this cold pavement,
Are heard in some far place
Remote from flowers or flash-bulbs.

In that city, on Gothic railings
Dark against the snowy park
Still a dead flower, a faded letter,
Already one month old.

'Life is what happens to you
When you're busy making other plans,'
This empty street
Is only the beginning.

Here, in your other city,
Riot vans prowl the December dark,
Remember angry embers of summer,
Familiar ghost guitars echo from stucco terraces.

Meanwhile, in the Valley of Indecision,
We rehearse stale words, store up expected songs,
Celebrate sad anniversaries.
Flowers and flash-bulbs. Cold pavements.

You do not cross the road
To step into immortality
At the dark end of the street
Waits the inevitable stranger.

John Lennon

∎

In Beatle lore, John Lennon was the Literary Beatle. During the height of Beatlemania, he published two works, *In His Own Write* (1964) and *A Spaniard in the Works* (1965), both influenced by his love of surrealism and word play. *In His Own Write* recalled the work of Lewis Carroll, but Spike Milligan's absurd humor (on the British radio program *The Goon Show*), as well as the droll satire of Peter Sellers and Stanley Unwin, also made a considerable impact on Lennon. Of *In His Own Write, The Times Literary Supplement* wrote, "Worth the attention of anyone who fears for the impoverishment of the English language and the British imagination." *Skywriting by Word of Mouth,* an endearing and occasionally scathing collection of short pieces, was published posthumously in 1986. In the following selection, he discusses in typically disjointed Lennonesque fashion his persecution by American authorities (for more on the subject, see Jon Wiener's *Gimme Some Truth: The John Lennon FBI Files,* in this volume), and his decision to withdraw from public life, among other topics. Two years after he wrote this piece, Lennon and Yoko released *Double Fantasy*.

"The Mysterious Smell of Roses"

from *Skywriting by Word of Mouth*

∎ THE BIGGEST MISTAKE Yoko and I made in that period was allowing ourselves to become influenced by the male-macho "serious revolutionaries," and their insane ideas about killing people to save them from capitalism and/or communism (depending on your point of view). We should have stuck to our own way of working for peace: bed-ins, billboards, etc. And now here we were, fighting the U.S. government with a lawyer who at first didn't believe that it was a politically-motivated court case (he thought we weren't "that important"), or that the F.B.I. was harassing us with phone taps and the like.

He believed later when his own phone was tapped.

We stopped them when we announced on *The Dick Cavett Show* that they were following us and bugging us. (This was the same show where the liberals got a little upset when I said that I didn't believe in this "overpopulation bullshit." But they weren't as upset as an English audience on a similar show back home where they actually booed and hissed us in a most unpleasant manner for being pacifists, backed up by that famous darling of the "serious" music world, none other than Yehudi "Zometimes You Haft to Kill" Menuhin. He, that rumor has it, records one note at a time!)

In the car the first morning on the way to court, we were both very nervous. We had followed the psychic's instructions carefully: read the right passages in the King James Bible, had put the right verses in our boots, and dowsed our ritually folded handkerchiefs with the magic oil.

From pilgrimages to India with magic Alex Mardas, to what turned out to be a phony miracle worker called Babaji (?), who performed conjuring tricks such as pulling cheap watches with his picture on them "out of nowhere" to a packed house of mainly middle-aged American women (whilst outside the camp, thousands of crippled Indians were selling the same cheap stuff to make a living), we found ourselves living outside of San Francisco in San Mateo in the home of an alcoholic Kung Fu master and acupuncturist and his family. It was he who was responsible for helping us survive methadone withdrawal, which had almost killed Yoko. He also convinced me that my English doctor was wrong (the guy had told me that we could never have babies because I'd blown my sperm with years of misuse of drugs, etc., causing me to have a terrible depression, especially after immigration authorities had revoked my visa in the middle of Art Janov's primal therapy and we had immediately got hooked on smack). Withdrawing cold turkey by taking a boat to Japan from L.A. (similar to a boat trip that Dr. Hong told us he had taken in his youth to get off opium), we arrived in Yokohama, drug-free and happy. It was then that I met Yoko's parents for the first time.

When we recovered from the methadone trip with the good doctor, his good-cooking wife, and helpful daughter, he said, "You want baby? Stop taking drugs, eat good food, in one year you will have it. I promise you." God bless him, he was right. He died without seeing Sean in the flesh, but we did manage to send him a Polaroid I'd taken of the baby when we were still in New York hospital. We are still in touch with the Hongs.

I was talking to Helen (well, at Helen, really), and as usual I found myself on the defensive about "mystics." I didn't get too frantic for a change. Anyway, I found myself saying something like the following— that many, if not all, great men and women were "mystics" in a sense: Einstein, who at the end of his life remarked that if he had to do it over, he would have spent more time on the spiritual; Pythagoras and Newton were mystics. But the main point I was getting at was the fact that in order to receive the "wholly spirit," i.e., creative inspiration (whether you are labelled an artist, scientist, mystic, psychic, etc.), the main "problem" was emptying the mind.

You can't paint a picture on dirty paper; you need a clean sheet.

Van Gogh's "going crazy," Dylan Thomas's "drinking himself to death," etc., were just efforts on their behalf to break out of the straightjacket of their own minds. I include myself and my generation's so-called "drug abuse." Self-abuse would be a more apt expression.

Anyway, I saw the life of Gauguin on TV, and it struck me that he'd died in such a pitiful way (V.D., for which the "cure" was mercury), with a foot broken and twisted from a drunken brawl after returning home for his first "successful" opening in Paris. He had gone to Tahiti to escape his own straightjacket: Working at a bank. A wife and children, one whom he was particularly fond of, a daughter to whom he had been dedicating a personal journal he kept whilst living in the South Pacific, explaining why he had left his family. When he returned to Tahiti, he received a letter from home telling him his daughter had died! What a price to pay to "go down in history." He finally finished his large "master-work," and died, the point being that, O.K., he was a good painter, but the world could manage quite well without one scrap of his "genius." I believe the "master-work" was destroyed by fire after his death. The other point being, had he had access to so-called mysticism . . . fasting . . . meditation . . . and other disciplines (as in disciple), he could have reached the "same space." Hard work, I grant you, but easier than killing yourself and those around you.

It's the same with the Christians (so called). They're so busy condemning themselves and others, or preaching at people, or worse, still killing for Christ. None of them understanding, or trying in the least, to *behave* like a Christ. It seems to me that the only true Christians were (are?) the Gnostics, who believe in self-knowledge, i.e., becoming Christ themselves, reaching the Christ within. Christ, after all, is Greek for *light.** The Light is the Truth. All any of us are trying to do is precisely that: Turn on the light. All the better to see you with, my dear.

*We all recognize that the accepted translation of Christ is "the anointed one." We, however, were told that in the original Dead Sea Scrolls it is revealed that the true translation of Christ is "light," which to us made more sense.—Y.O.L.

Christ, Buddha, Mohammed, Moses, Milarepa, and other great ones spent their time in fasting, praying, meditation, and left "maps" of the territory of "God" for all to see and follow in our own way.

The lesson for me is clear. I've already "lost" one family to produce what? Sgt. Pepper? I am blessed with a second chance. Being a Beatle nearly cost me my life, and certainly cost me a great deal of my health— the drinking and drugs having started before we were professional musicians—all in an effort to reach "out there."

I will not make the same mistake twice in one lifetime. This time around, inspiration will be called down by the ancient methods laid down for all to see.

If I never "produce" anything more for public consumption than "silence," so be it.

Amen.

—1978

TWO

■

Paul McCartney: Take a Sad Song and Make It Better

—"I don't think I'm a very hard boss, but I kick ass when things go wrong."

Jim Miller

∎

On the verge of turning forty in 1982, Paul McCartney agreed to an interview with Jim Miller of *Newsweek* magazine. In it, he discussed his new album, *Tug of War,* John Lennon's murder a scant two years earlier, and being a member of the most famous band in the history of the world.

"Paul McCartney Looks Back"

Newsweek

May 3, 1982

Paul McCartney, his hair flecked with the first few hints of gray, sits staring out a window. The once-upon-a-time Beatle has come to New York to plug his new album, "Tug of War" (Columbia), and to face again the awkward, inevitable questions about John Lennon's death, their stormy love-hate relationship, the mythic past McCartney can never quite escape. In a talk with Newsweek *critic Jim Miller, he refers haltingly to "the event," to "John's thing." He more easily loses himself in small talk about his extraordinary new album, recalling the awe he felt working with Stevie Wonder, fondly recounting the days spent recording with Carl Perkins, an early idol of his and the man who wrote "Blue Suede Shoes." "I've been feeling, personally, a lot better the last couple of years," he says—and McCartney does have an air of serenity whenever he speaks of music and family. Still, he admits that "I'm only at ease with people I know." When his wife, Linda, walks in, his face lights up, and he greets her with a heartfelt hug. Otherwise, he is always "on," summoning at will his own outsize aura—that buoyant image of youth, the sweetest face in the world's best-loved band.*

MILLER: What does this new album mean to you?
MCCARTNEY: Before we'd even started anything, I had the title, "Tug of War." I wanted to do the whole album around that theme. The idea was conflict—that everything is a tug of war.
Q. Were you responding to criticism of your previous solo work as too shallow?

A. Once or twice people did hit home with things. They'd ask whether I ever got fed up with writing a bit flippantly. And I said yeah, sure. You know, I could sit down there and literally come back in three hours' time with about a hundred of those songs—and the terrifying thing is that ten of them might be big hits. I had reached a point where I thought, if there is some danger of being shallow, let's not—let's get more passion in it. "Tug of War" appealed to me.

Q. Did you have John Lennon in mind?

A. No. But halfway through it, John was killed. I can't believe it to this day, I can't even say those words . . . But "Here Today" [reprinted in this volume] is the only song specifically about that. Obviously, "Tug of War" ties in . . . And so does "Somebody Who Cares." I remember being aware of John's death while writing it.

Q. Did you see much of him before he died?

A. I saw him quite a bit. Always, the problem was talking business. Whenever we got into business, we got into an argument. It wasn't a pleasant framework for a relationship. When Sean [John and Yoko's son] was first born, I visited him a few times at the Dakota [Lennon's apartment house in New York]. And then it had gone snotty. I used to turn up without calling him. One time, he got annoyed with me. He said, "Well, look, man, why do you just keep turning up here and surprise us? Why don't you just call first?" And I took that the wrong way. After that, I don't think I did see him. I phoned a few times. And as long as we were talking about family, about life, it was good. The last time I spoke to him, I got off the phone, and it felt like old friends again. I've talked to Yoko since, and she's said to me, "You know, he was really quite fond of you." I think we were pretty close. But sometimes, with brothers, you argue. They can be the most intense arguments, too.

Q. Looking over some old interviews, I was struck by all the harsh things John said about you. It must be very hard to live with that kind of legacy.

A. It's tough. Because I know he said all that. But with something as final as an event like that, it's funny what comes to mind. You'd expect your memories to be the big things. Of course, it isn't. It's just the silly little things. Like this furious argument we were having about Apple [the Beatles' record label], really going tooth and nail. And I can remember him looking at me, pulling down his glasses and saying softly, "It's only me." That's how I prefer to remember it. See, I think the big problem is that when he and Yoko were madly in love, the rest of us

Beatles didn't handle it very well. We got very uptight about stuff that wasn't offensive. If they want to go pose in the nude, who cares? But at the time, it was, "Oh bloody hell, look at 'em, they've gone off their rockers, these two." It wasn't easy to cope with all that. We knew good old Johnny. But he'd changed. Our friend was suddenly on an album cover nude, and it was just weird. I think a lot of people felt that way: "Hey, why didn't he just stay like he was in the Beatles, why'd he go freaky?" I feel sorry for John and Yoko that we weren't able to be cool about the whole bloody thing. But in retrospect, I can understand it. Hey, "Give Peace a Chance"—great stuff, man! Nude on "Two Virgins"—why not? I'm not a prude, really. It's just the shock.

Q. What parts of the Beatle experience do you remember most fondly?

A. All of it. Mostly it's pretty fond memories. Because, you know, you go on a holiday, you have a real bad time, you come back, and a year later you can only remember the good bits. For me, it tends to be the moments where John dropped his guard. Like one night we were in a hotel listening to a cassette, I think it was "Rubber Soul." There were my songs and there were his songs on this side, basically. We listened through it all, and I remember him saying to me, "I think I probably like your stuff; if the truth was known, I probably really like your stuff." I'm not saying he liked my stuff better than his. It's just that for one little second there—it was not very typical of him. He always fought for himself. He was very selfish, but in a good way. You know, looking after No. 1. Not to the detriment of others. He was very un-that. Actually, he could be a very warm guy.

Q. You recently told an interviewer, "I'd always thought that, in order to be liked, you had to be unwarty . . . I've only just realized, after all this time, that people like to see warts." Thinking of John Lennon's candor about himself, I wonder: what are some of Paul McCartney's warts?

A. Some of my warts? Oh boy . . . I don't particularly want to reveal them. I've got plenty. What I meant was that John could show how human he was by vocalizing all of that. It's just my character not to vocalize that kind of stuff.

Q. After John's death, Yoko said that people mistook your real feelings because you couldn't express them very easily.

A. That's one of the things I often don't like about the way I come off. Like when John died, a reporter stuck a mike in my face and said, "What do you think?" And I said, "It's a drag." Which of course seemed a really flippant thing to say. But later that night, I was weepin' and a-wailin' and it all came out. I wasn't at all the little composed figure who had said, "It's a drag." But I've given up excusing myself, saying, "I'm awfully sorry, I'm not very good at this." Sod it. It's me. I'm not going to thrash myself with a soggy noodle because of who I am. You've got to think positive.

Q. What matters to you these days?

A. My family, first. Music second. There isn't an awful lot else. Money doesn't really matter to me. People say, "Aw, it's easy when you've got it." But Linda and I have always felt that if everything we owned disappeared, we could head on down to Jamaica. They've got these little huts on the beach. I'd be a gardener or a carpenter.

Q. Do you consider looking after your business affairs a hassle or a pleasure?

A. It's not a priority, but I do take pleasure in it. Because, you know, I set off from the sticks to make it—and making it as a songwriter is one thing, and making it financially is another thing, and they're both things I set out to do.

Q. You're about to turn 40. How do you feel about growing older?

A. It's nothing that really worries me. If it was just down to me, I think I would hardly notice it. Plus, with the kids, I don't particularly want to be youthful. I want to be a father. Being youthful, rock 'n' roll—I've done that for so long. I'm *ready* to move over to a bit of maturity. I like my attitudes better. I don't sneer at stuff quite so much; I try to give it a chance. Which is the thing my dad was always trying to teach me. He would say, "Try to understand the other person's point of view, son." And I would say, "Yes, dad." "Tolerance, son!" "Yes, dad." "Moderation!" "Yes, dad." It wasn't as bad as that; I'm summarizing a few years there— but now those are all big things for me. Moderation? Terrific! Half of the people who are dead today wouldn't be if they had known that one. Tolerance? Great. I hope people show it toward me. I'm ready to show it toward them.

Paul McCartney

■

In the introduction to Paul McCartney's *Blackbird Singing: Poems and Lyrics 1965–1999* (2001), poet and playwright Adrian Mitchell calls the ex-Beatle a popular poet whose best lyrics rank up there with the work of a William Blake or a Robert Burns. At the same time, Mitchell acknowledges that old prejudices die hard and that the debate between what is and what isn't poetry still exists, especially within academic circles or among the literary elite. "Whenever critics say there is something inferior about poetry that is sung," writes Mitchell, "my advice is to sing Blake's 'Tyger' or Robert Burns's 'My Luve is Like a Red, Red Rose' at them." "Here Today," McCartney's poignant homage to John Lennon, appears in *Blackbird Singing* and in recorded form on his 1982 album *Tug of War*.

"Here Today"

(Song for John)

from *Blackbird Singing*

And if I said
I really knew you well
What would your answer be?
If you were here today.

Well, knowing you
You'd probably laugh and say
That we were worlds apart
If you were here today.

But as for me
I still remember how it was before
And I am holding back the tears no more
I love you.

What about the time we met?
Well I suppose that you could say that
We were playing hard to get,

Didn't understand a thing
But we could always sing.

What about the night we cried?
Because there wasn't any reason left
To keep it all inside,
Never understood a word
But you were always there with a smile.

And if I say I really loved you
And was glad you came along,
Then you were here today
For you were in my song
Here today.

Jon Wilde

∎

In this very long and candid interview in 2004 from *Uncut* magazine, of which only a portion is excerpted, Paul McCartney talks about growing up in Liverpool, the price of fame, his former band and its cultural impact on the world, his relationship with John Lennon, and his subsequent life as a solo Beatle. Interviewer Jon Wilde asks probing questions, challenging McCartney and constantly searching for more thorough answers (McCartney has been known for supplying only the information that is necessary to get his point across, revealing almost nothing of substance about himself). At times, McCartney's responses appear almost self-consciously literary, a bit arch perhaps, as if he is jotting down words in a memoir instead of speaking to someone in conversation. Certainly though, he remains affable and polite throughout the interview, and yet, thanks to Wilde's assertiveness, a more complex portrait emerges: that of a thoughtful, intelligent, complex, and defiant man, immensely proud of his accomplishments and optimistic about the future.

"McCartney: My Life in the Shadow of the Beatles"

Uncut

July 2004

UNCUT: Paul, do you ever have days when you think to yourself, "The Beatles . . . we weren't really that good"?

MCCARTNEY: Everyone has those moments, don't they? "Am I as good as people say I am? Were we as good as people say we were?" As soon as I start thinking it, I tell myself I'm just being bloody daft. I could sit here and try convincing you that The Beatles weren't really that good. And you'd be sitting there, telling me that we were really fabulous. It would be a bullshit conversation. The jury's in, and I don't think there's any argument. Basically, The Beatles were a shit hot band. We were very, very good. We were . . .

The best ever?

OK, stack us up against James Brown, record for record, he's definitely hotter because he's James Brown. But he didn't do the stuff we did. He's

James Brown and he's sodding fantastic. We can all agree on that. But there's something else to The Beatles. Look, we did a lot of good music. You look at *Revolver* or *Rubber Soul,* they are decent efforts by any standards. If they're not good, then has anyone ever been any good? Because, if they're not good, then no one has ever really been that good. It's when you get to the question of whether The Beatles were about more than music. When you get to what The Beatles came to . . .

Symbolise?

That's exactly it. We were a strangely different kind of animal that mutated in England somewhere after the Second World War. There'd never been this four-headed monster, this cultural phenomenon. There'd never been anything like The Beatles, who were about music but also about something more far-reaching. See, we've never properly taken credit for it. We've always taken the line that what happened in the '60s was about an astonishing movement that came in the wake of the Second World War, the end of all that repressive Victorian thought and it all came together at a certain time. We just happened to become leaders of whatever cosmic thing was going on. We came to symbolise the start of a whole new way of thinking.

PHILIP LARKIN FAMOUSLY WROTE: *"Sexual intercourse began /* *In Nineteen Sixty-Three / Between the end of the Chatterley ban / And the Beatles' first LP."* **What do you make of that?**

I know the poem. I guess Larkin was saying that, between those two things, *Chatterley* and The Beatles, something crucial happened. For The Beatles and for anyone who was around at that time, life had been very much in black and white. For myself, I'd been to a particularly Dickensian school. When I look back on that school, I do see it all in monochrome. I remember winter in short trousers with the harsh wind whipping around my poor young frazzled knees. Looking back now, especially sitting here in the cool warmth of LA, it feels so deprived, like it was 6000 years ago. I just remember it being dark all the time back then. It was a post-war thing. Our parents had all had to join the army, as National Service had been compulsory. Growing up, we were all looking at that as a grim possibility. . . .

What was the turning point for you?

The end of National Service. Not just for me. For anyone of a certain age. Without that, there could have been no Beatles. . . .

You have to remember that we'd watched all that happen to Elvis. Because, y'know, the army had kind of ruined Elvis. He'd been this ultimate rebel figure who we'd all worshipped. Then they made him cut his hair and he had to call everyone "sir," and he was never really the same again. You can imagine that going into the army would have done it for us, too. Before we knew what was happening, we were like errant schoolkids off the leash.

As The Beatles, we went off to Hamburg, which was still a bit black and white. But it was getting a little brighter. Then we came back to England and we were a proper working band. So we'd avoided this dreadful thing of having to get a job. Now we'd had a little practice and we were getting, well, quite good. And the colour began to fill into the whole thing. By that time, we were beginning to make a bit of a splash. We knew that we had a chance of making it.

In terms of being in a band, were you thinking much further than avoiding jobs and getting girls?

Those were the main reasons. Being in a band meant you had a chance of avoiding a boring job and, as a nice bonus, you'd get the occasional knee-trembler after a gig. It went beyond that pretty quickly. Almost as soon as me and John started writing together, we thought we could be the next great songwriting team. The next Rodgers and Hammerstein. When we wrote songs, I'd jot down ideas in a school notebook. At the top of every page I'd write, "A Lennon-McCartney Original," which was some indication of how committed we were. Looking back, it was always about the craft, the art of it. From early on, we always wanted to go in an artistic direction.

Did you see The Beatles differently from John Lennon?

Hmm. I don't think so. We all had a common vision, at least in the early days. Then everyone seemed to think that we wanted to go in different directions. But I'm not even sure that's true. The thing about me and John is that we were different, but we weren't that different. I think Linda put her finger on it when she said me and John were like mirror images of each other. Even down to how we started writing together, facing each other, eyeball to eyeball, exactly like looking in the mirror. That's how songs like "I Want to Hold Your Hand" were written.

You were like two sides of the same person?

Well said. But the sides would switch. On the surface, I was very easygoing, always accommodating. That came easy to me. That's how I was brought up. But, at certain times, I would very much be the hard man of the duo. At certain moments, I could bite. But that would be when no one outside the group was watching. John would allow me to take that role because it enabled him to drop his guard and be vulnerable. On the surface, he was this hard, witty guy, always on hand with a cutting witticism. He appeared caustic, even cruel at times. But really he was very soft. John was very insecure. He carried a lot of that from his upbringing, what with his father leaving when he was five. Then, of course, we'd both lost our mothers so we had that in common. Ultimately, we were equals. All The Beatles were equals. If things got too deep, Ringo would crack a one-liner and that kept us on a level. If things were getting too sentimental, John would harden it up. If John was getting too hostile, I'd soften it down. Then George was always on hand with his own kind of unique wisdom.

How competitive were you and John?

There was amazing competition between us and we both thrived on it. In terms of music, you cannot beat a bit of competition. Of course, there's times when it hurts, and it's inevitably going to reach a stage where it's hard to live with. Sooner or later, it's going to burn itself out. I think that's what happened at the end of The Beatles. But, for those early years, the competition was great. It was a great way for us to keep each other on our toes. I'd write "Yesterday" and John would go away and write "Norwegian Wood." I'd come up with "Paperback Writer" and John would come back with "I'm Only Sleeping." If he wrote "Strawberry Fields," it was like he'd upped the ante, so I had to come up with something as good as "Penny Lane."

When did it first occur to you that The Beatles were set to be something rather more significant than just another Merseybeat band?

There were a number of little and not-so-little flashpoints. At the start, we were just one of a large number of bands. There were the Stones. The Yardbirds, all the other Liverpool bands. We were just one of a million bands looking to have a good time and make a little money. We felt we were just a part of this huge throng of similarly minded people. Only later did we emerge from the pack. But there were those flashpoints. Our first Top 20 hit ["Love Me Do"]. Our first Top 5 hit ["Please Please Me"]. Our first No. 1 ["From Me to You"]. I remember hearing the milkman whistle "From Me to You" and thinking, "Wow! We've really made it." Then, of course, it just got bigger and bigger. America was probably the definitive big flash, the real clincher. We'd gone to No. 1 there with "I Want to Hold Your Hand." But we had no idea how big we were out there. So we stepped off the plane and the crowd was enormous. The noise was deafening. On a scale of one to 10, that was about a hundred in terms of the shock of it.

Was there an actual point when you realised the kind of cultural impact The Beatles were having?

Not at the time, no. Everything happened so fast. There was no time to think, "What does all this mean?" But, looking back, there was a time in the mid-'60s when everything was about The Beatles. We were simply everywhere you looked. There was no other frame of reference. When we started, we just thought about playing rock 'n' roll, being involved with . . . showbiz. We didn't consider the wider possibilities. They were thrust upon us. Suddenly we were the chosen ones that had lit this incredible touchpaper. We were the symbol for everything that was happening—free love, free sex, free thinking. I still think that it was the events of the '60s that lit the touchpaper, and we were just a part of it. But, to so many people, it's still all about The Beatles.

Was there a point around the mid-'60s when it felt like The Beatles vs The World?

To some extent. Even physically, we were apart from everyone else. We were The Boys, y'know. We spent most of our time in this self-enclosed world. No one really knew what we were thinking. Then we'd do these press conferences or whatever and we were just four Liverpool lads taking the piss. It was very funny at first. They'd ask the most ridiculous questions and we'd come straight back at them.

During the making of *Rubber Soul*, were you all aware that the music was taking such a dramatic shift?

Not as such. People say now, "Oh, The Beatles were breaking all the rules." But we didn't know what the rules were. We had no knowledge whatsoever of musical theory. We just did what felt right. The Beatles were always looking forward. Our new album was never nostalgic for the ones we'd last made. I think the Stones were different. At certain points, they seemed to be paying too much attention to what we were doing. Like *Satanic Majesties*, that was like their direct answer to *Pepper*. In that way, they took their lead from us. But we were just doing our own thing. It wasn't that we set out to make ground-breaking albums. The reason those records were so musically diverse was that we all had very diverse tastes. Also, we'd served our apprenticeship in Hamburg where businessmen would come into the club and say, "Can you play a mambo? Can you do a rhumba?" And we couldn't just keep saying no, so we had to learn these different styles.

**There's a wonderfully evocative story about how The Beatles finished
Pepper and took the just-completed tapes over to Mama Cass' flat in
Chelsea, playing the album at top volume just as dawn was breaking
so that the entire neighbourhood woke up to it.**

It's a dim recollection but I think that's true, yeah. The weekend we finished the album is a bit of a blur. I just remember that we all felt so ex-
hilarated. *Pepper* had taken six months to make—longer than any other
album. When we first heard it back, we knew we'd pulled it off. We'd
made something a little bit special, something that would blow people's
minds. It was mind-blowing for us. To us, it wasn't so much that it was a
great album musically. It was more that it was an anthem for our generation. It was an album that marked the times and summed up the times.
As it turned out, *Pepper* led the times as much as it marked the times.
To get to grips with it, you had to spend time with it. It was influential
in lots of ways, and not just musically. Suddenly, music writers had to
find new ways to respond because, suddenly, they weren't dealing with
Perry Como or whatever.

**How do you respond to the argument that *Pepper* has dated less well
than most other Beatles albums, that it stands as something of a
period piece?**

I don't know about that. It's not how I see it. I can't look at it in those
terms. To me, there was an absolute inevitability to something like *Pepper*. It just had to happen. When it finally happened, it was apocalyptic.
It wasn't like Gandhi or something. Whatever *Pepper* amounted to, call
it wisdom, call it a vision, call it what you like, it didn't come out of a
great struggle. It came out of a great party we were having. But it was a
party that had to happen because of all the Victorian thinking we'd
grown up with. To be at the centre of that felt just amazing.

***The White Album* has been described as "the sound of a band
disintegrating beautifully." Is that a fair comment?**

I'd go along with that. There was a lot of stress around by that point,
stress between all four of us. In a way, that helped make for a good
record. Sometimes that tension can be pretty good for the creative flow.
Maybe some of my later records would have benefited from a bit more
stress in the studio. With *The White Album*, it was a strange old time.
Y'know, Brian [Epstein] had died. We were all a bit exhausted. John was
dabbling in heroin. Allen Klein had started to get involved at the business end. That's the time when we started to separate.

**You once said that the only regret in life was that The Beatles'
break-up was so bitter.**

Mmm. There might have been a few regrets after that. But, yeah, the way we broke up was very regrettable. I've always said that The Beatles should have finished with a puff of smoke and magic robes and envelopes stuffed with cash. Sadly, it didn't. John always talked about it in terms of marriage and divorce and it was very much like that. Without a shadow of a doubt, that period was the weirdest time in my life.

Would it be fair to say that you experienced something of a nervous breakdown in the early '70s?

Something like that. In The Beatles, we'd always had this running joke: "What are we going to do when the bubble bursts?" Then it did burst and I went up to my farm in Scotland, wondering what the hell I was going to do next. I seriously thought about giving up music altogether. I was thinking, "Maybe I should become a nuclear physicist or something." It was a bloody hard time. It was difficult to get up in the morning. I was drinking quite a lot. Probably having a bit of a nervous breakdown, like you say. Looking back, I was in a state of grief. I realise that now. Grief for the end of The Beatles.[1] The only way I could get out of that was get back to recording, then going out on the road. And all that led eventually to the formation of Wings.

How quickly did you come to realise that everything you did would be completely overshadowed by The Beatles?

It didn't take long. Mainly because we took such a slagging. Some of it was justified, I'll admit. Early Wings were pretty rough, not terribly good. There was a time when The Beatles weren't very good but we were able to be not very good in private. Wings had to do it in public and there was always the shadow of The Beatles, which didn't help. . . . The whole period with The Beatles was so richly iconic that it was always going to be very difficult to follow. As it proved.

Wasn't part of the problem that, however good your post-Beatles music was, it was never going to have anything like the cultural impact of The Beatles' work? Your solo work and your work with Wings was never going to be the soundtrack to people's lives in the way that *Revolver* or *Pepper* had been.

That's it, yeah. In terms of its significance, you can't go on making *Pepper* all your life. It just can't be done. *Pepper* was a peak in terms of that kind of thing. It hit the right notes, the right moment in time. It was strange. It was weird. It was hugely popular. It embraced all the things you want to embrace as an artist. In terms of impact, it hit the whole world across the back of the head with a plank of wood. At the same time, it was smart and soothing and it resonated. A very clever trick, that. But it was always going to be impossible to top. Not just for me and The Beatles, but for everyone. Even now, you still get great things like Radiohead. But, as to whether those things are going to alter the world . . . One of the difficult things is that so many things have now been done. Some would argue that it's all been done. Some would even say that it was The Beatles that did all those things. We set those standards. That makes it difficult to do the same things again. But I do enjoy trying even though it doesn't mean I'm going to pull it off.

A common criticism of your post-Beatle work is that much of it lacked real invention; that you'd lost the courage to gamble. How would you respond to that charge?

One thing you have to say is that I've put out an awful lot of records. Some of them I shouldn't have put out, sure. I'd gladly accept that. There's many different reasons for putting a record out. Sometimes I might just put one out because I'm bored and I've got nothing better to do. That happens. Also, people might want everything I do to be loaded with significance. You have to understand that, for 10 years, my sounding boards had been The Beatles, mainly John. Beyond The Beatles, I had different sounding boards. I had a family. I saw nothing wrong in doing songs for my kids. Wings' "Mary Had a Little Lamb" was like that. I saw nothing wrong in writing songs for Linda. Some people quite liked that. Other people hated it and probably never forgave me for it.

For many, "Mull of Kintyre" was the final straw.

I realised at some point that I do certain things because they're a bit of an exercise for me. . . . I'm not concerned with the genre or the style of the thing. I've got very wide tastes. In 1977, I fancied doing a Scottish bagpipe song, so I wrote "Mull of Kintyre." The people who hated it were pissed off with me. And even some of the people who bought it were pissed off with me because they'd bought it. Of course, it didn't help that it came out at the height of punk rock. But what should I have done at that time? Stuck a safety pin through my nose and done some bonkers punk song? I'll admit that something like "Mull of Kintyre" contributes to my patchwork quilt reputation. What that probably means is that I'm never one-dimensional enough for some people. I've developed a hard skin for that sort of attitude. I do get annoyed at having to justify myself. Since school, I've never liked having to do that. I never liked anyone telling me what to do. I never liked that bullying tendency. I have a "fuck you" feeling about all of that.

Getting back to The Beatles . . . the revisionism [see Anthony DeCurtis's take on Beatles' revisionism in this volume] that came in the wake of John's death seemed to irk you. Was that essentially a concern for how posterity would view you?

There was a time when the idea of posterity was important for all of us. I remember being shocked one day when John started worrying how people would remember him when he was gone. It was an incredibly vulnerable thing for him to come out with. I said to him then, "They'll remember you as a fucking genius because that's what you are. But you won't give a shit because you'll be up there flying across the universe." Then I got to a point where I could see what John meant and maybe I started worrying too much about how my part in it was going to be remembered. There was that time after John's death where it really got out of hand. It was like, "John was the only real talent in the band and Paul booked the studios and stuff." I started to think I ought to speak up because, well, this was my own history that was being written up. . . .

Maybe it was starting to look like I was dancing on John's grave. A lot of people felt I was trying to take more credit than was due, like I was trying to put John down. But John would have been happy to have acknowledged my part in it all. He was never one to grab credit that wasn't due to him.

So is posterity less important to you now than it used to be?

Now I feel I've got enough credit for what I did in The Beatles. Even so, there's no getting away from them. They still exert this astonishing power. They're like a magnetic force. The more all four of us tried to pull away from them, the harder they pulled us back. And they still do. It continues to amaze me. There's days when I wake up and have to remind myself that I wrote songs with John Lennon. I know John must have had moments when he thought, "I wrote with Paul McCartney." It's fantastic that he was a part of my life in that way. Imagine the luxury of being stuck on a song and being able to hand it over to John Lennon to finish off. Do I miss that? Of course I do. Hugely.

Back in 1967, you were talking about hitting your thirties and wondering whether you'd branch out from pop music, maybe do a little painting, maybe write some poetry, maybe try some classical music. Yet it wasn't until the '90s that you properly launched into those creative areas. Why wait so long?

Good question. It's like I've had four lives in a way. There were my schooldays, there was the whole Beatles period, then my life with Linda and the kids, which included Wings and so on. Maybe that third life ended when Linda passed away and, now, with Heather[2] and everything else, this is like a fourth instalment which, creatively speaking, has already involved things like painting and poetry and classical music. The truth is that, over the last few years, I've put out what I've really wanted to put out. I do tend to go where my fancies take me these days. . . . The truth is that I wouldn't still be doing all this stuff if I didn't want to do it and I wouldn't be able to carry on doing it if I didn't have some "screw-you" attitude about it. Because it is my life and I do these things for my own enjoyment. Y'know, I'm not doing all this so people think, "Hey, he's cool."

Is it not important to you to be considered "cool"?

To be honest, it's not that important. Like anyone, I'm not going to complain if someone perceives me or something I've done to be cool. But it's not that being considered cool is some grand ambition of mine. I'm just trying to write a good song and sing well on stage or do a good painting, whatever. As corny as it sounds, I'm also trying to be a good human being. Not a Goody Two-Shoes. I'm simply trying to get it right. Because I'm alive, for Christ's sake. I'm not out to screw anyone. Neither am I a pushover. If anyone screws me, then I'll say, "Fair enough, let's go to it." That's how I've always been. We people from Liverpool, we do stick up for ourselves.

There must be days when you look in the mirror and think, "Fuck me, I'm Paul McCartney!"

Sure. I look in the mirror and think, "Nice one! You wrote songs with John Lennon on his porch, then you went to his bedroom and listened to Fats Domino and Elvis! How brilliant is that?" Or I find myself thinking, "That bloke playing with The Beatles in Hamburg, that was you." It's not daunting; it's magical.

For most of your adult life, you've been absurdly famous. One of the most famous men in the world. How mad is that?

George [Harrison] once said that fame cost him his nervous system. I can understand that. Fame happened to us all when we were just kids, really. Being recognised wherever we went, that came really quick. . . . Until the whole world knew who we were. So there was nowhere, absolutely nowhere, we could go where we weren't instantly recognisable. And, whatever we did, even if we never made another record, we could never be *un*famous again. So it's sink or swim.

My way through it is being normal. That was always my way and it comes easy because I like living a normal life or at least being normal inside my own head.

A fairly blunt question. Do you fear death?

Let's face it, no one gets out of this one alive. When my number's up, that will be that. I don't fancy it particularly. But I don't fear it, either. It obviously makes a difference that I've led this pretty fulfilled life.

You must feel so fucking blessed to have had the life you've had.

I'd be mad not to feel blessed, wouldn't I? I've been a lucky bugger and so many things that happened to me were pure chance. So much of it was an amazing accident. If I'd never gone to that fete behind the church and met John in 1957. If I hadn't known the chords to "Twenty Flight Rock" and "Be-Bop-A-Lula" which got me into the band, I might have got the elbow and ended up playing in some little pub band. And so might John, George and Ringo.

That's the miracle of it right there. The chances of those four people coming together as they did. I'm lucky, very fucking lucky, just to still be vibing and loving life and holding onto my enthusiasm for things.

Notes

1. "For the first time in my life," McCartney told *Playboy* magazine in 1984, "I was on the scrap heap, in my own eyes. . . It was just the feeling, the terrible disappointment of not being of any use to anyone anymore . . . I'd never experienced it before. In this case, the end of the Beatles, I really was done in for the first time in my life. Until then, I really was kind of a cocky sod. It was the first time I'd had a major blow to my confidence." See Joan Goodman, "*Playboy* Interview: Paul and Linda McCartney," *Playboy*, December 1984.

2. The couple announced they would be seeking a divorce in May 2006.

■

THREE

George Harrison: Beware of Darkness

—*"I'm not really a career person. I'm a gardener, basically."*

Jim Kirkpatrick

■

In September 1963, before the Beatles "conquered" America, George Harrison spent a fortnight with his sister, Louise, and her family, at 113 McCann Street, in Benton, Illinois, a small coal-mining town about one hundred miles southeast of St. Louis, Missouri, and some three hundred miles south of Chicago. Within weeks of moving there in March 1963, she received a promotional copy of "Please Please Me." She promptly began contacting the local radio stations, encouraging them to play her brother's music. But very few people at the time were aware of the exotic band from England with the funny name and odd haircuts. Nevertheless, a little bit of Beatle history took place in southern Illinois. According to Jim Kirkpatrick, WFRX in West Frankfort, Illinois, became the first radio station to play Beatles records in the United States on a regular basis, as well as the first radio station to interview a Beatle.

While visiting, George spent most of his time camping in the Shawnee Forest area and, occasionally, sitting in with a local band, the Four Vests. One of the musicians, Gabe McCarty, remembers Harrison as "real polite and very skinny." And then there was the hair: "I wasn't used to seeing something like that. I'd never seen a man with so much hair. Everywhere we went, people stared at him and probably wondered what I was doing with him." In fact, Harrison sat in with the band on September 28, 1963, at a VFW hall in Eldorado, Illinois, before some seventy-five to one hundred people, where he sang songs recorded by Hank Williams, Chuck Berry, and Carl Perkins. It was the first time that Louise heard her brother perform in public. "The whole place was electrified," she said.

Harrison also visited the Barton and Collins Furniture Store, where he bought some twenty to thirty records; experienced a local drive-in in Marion (one of the films he saw was *Wonderful to Be Young*, which featured the popular English rocker—and rival—Cliff Richard); and bought, at the Fenton Music Store in nearby Mt. Vernon, Illinois, a new Rickenbacker guitar for $400.

In January 1995, efforts were made to save "The Beatle House," as it came to be called. Bought by the Illinois Department of Mines and Minerals, it was scheduled to be demolished to make way for—what else?—a parking lot. Sometimes there are happy endings, though. A group of investors purchased the house. Today, it has been renamed the Hard Day's Nite Bed and Breakfast. In Benton, Illinois, you can indeed sleep where George once slept.

"The WFRX Interview"

from *Before He Was Fab:*
George Harrison's First American Visit

■ IT WAS NOT one of the large radio stations in New York, Chicago or Los Angeles that first introduced the Beatles to the United States. It was WFRX, a small station in West Frankfort, Illinois. WFRX, unofficially, can take the credit for playing the first Beatle records in the United States on a regular basis. WFRX also was the first radio station over here to interview a Beatle. "To my knowledge, this station was the first to play Beatle records on a regular basis," said Lou Harrison.° The disc jockey who was playing those "wild and uninhibited" songs was Marcia Schafer, now Marcia Raubach, who also became the first person in the United States to "talk over the air" with one of the Fab Four.

It all happened in late summer 1963 when Raubach, who was just 17, was getting ready to enter her senior year of high school. At the time, she had a teen radio program called *Saturday Session* on the station, where her father was one of the owners. "I started doing it because there really wasn't a teen program out there," said Raubach.

Every weekend, the attractive young deejay would go to Van-Wood Electric in downtown West Frankfort to pick up the top 20 teen hits on 45s to play on her show. They included songs by the Chiffons, Elvis, Roy Orbison, Bobby Vinton and others. However, on occasion she would add a song or two—"From Me to You" and "Love Me Do"—by the then unknown British group, the Beatles, after Lou Harrison came by the station trying to promote their records. "I remember her coming in several times," Raubach said of George Harrison's sister. "And because of the type of music that she had, my father turned her over to me."

Marcia Raubach said although she realized the Beatles were big in England at the time, she never gave it any thought that they would

° When the Beatles first came to the United States in February 1964, Carroll James, a disc jockey at WWDC-AM in Washington, D. C., was publicly recognized as the first American deejay to play Beatles music over the airways. James reportedly played "I Want to Hold Your Hand" on the station on December 17, 1963. However, although WFRX-AM in West Frankfort, Illinois, was a much smaller station, its deejay Marcia Schafer was several months ahead of James. George Harrison's sister Louise, of course, was giving Schafer Beatle records to play by mid-summer 1963. (Harry, Bill. *The Ultimate Beatles Encyclopedia*, page 337. New York: Hyperion, 1992.)

eventually become big here. "It really didn't dawn on me that this group would really become as big as Elvis or bigger than Elvis," Raubach said. "I played their records because it was a unique situation and the music was different."

But Lou Harrison said that when her brother George first came to this country to visit her, one of the things he wanted to do was to stop by and see Marcia and personally thank her for playing the Beatle tunes. Lou remembers that her husband drove her, George, and their brother Peter to the Freeman Coal Company office north of West Frankfort. From that point, because Gordon Caldwell had to use the car that day, the Harrison siblings walked the two miles south on Route 37 to get to the station.

Unfortunately, when the trio arrived, they were informed that Marcia had already gone home for the day. At the station were Art Smith, an advertising salesman, and Joe Browning, the weekend announcer. Smith remembers George Harrison as being "a very nice fellow," and Browning agreed. But Browning added, "I thought he needed to get a haircut."

Marcia was called back to the station, but said she wasn't really all that surprised about the young Englishman's visit. "I knew that he was coming and that Louise wanted him to meet me and, of course, I wanted to meet him," she said. "But I didn't know exactly what his schedule would be."

When she arrived at the station, Raubach recalls, George Harrison was very excited about the car she was driving. It was her father's black 1959 Oldsmobile Delta 88 with tail fins. "He really looked it over; he asked me if it was my car," she said. "I told him no, but he was really impressed with it. He was impressed with a lot of things."

Marcia recalls George Harrison as being "very, very clean cut," wearing a white shirt, jeans and brown sandals. "But I thought that was a little unusual," she said. "The guys here, they didn't wear brown sandals. So, he was dressed a little differently." And she couldn't help but notice his hair. "Of course, the hair was the thing; it wasn't really long hair because the boys here wore DAs," she said. "But he had so much in his face with those bangs." Another immediate observation was that he was "so thin."

Raubach said she found the young British musician to be "really soft-spoken and almost hesitant to ask me questions." She said, "It was almost like he waited for you to make the first move in the conversation and give the input." Her interview with George Harrison, Raubach estimated, lasted only about 15 to 20 minutes, after she gave him a tour of the station and its studio. But no tape of the interview was made, although Peter filmed it all on a home movie camera. "So, somewhere out there, a film of that interview exists," she said. "But who knows where?"

George told the teen-aged deejay that all of the Beatles were "do-it-yourselfers"; they did all of the musical arrangements and background. "Really, this was their music; nobody did it for them," she said. George also told her about the group's personal appearances in England, "where they were getting mobbed all the time over there." She said, "I could believe it as far as England went, but I never thought it was going to happen over here."

Later that year, as editor of the West Frankfort high school newspaper, *Redbird Notes*, Marcia Raubach wrote an account of her interview with the young Beatle. "Their music is wild and uninhibited and outsells the world's greatest recording artists, although not one of the Beatles can read music," she wrote. Later, she said, "I'm not quite sure what I meant by that. But maybe it was compared to what was out at the time."

George also gave her an autographed photo of his group and a copy of their new single, "She Loves You," before he left the station. Lou Harrison recalls that when George gave Marcia the photo of the Beatles, the young deejay's immediate thought was, do you have one of just you? But George responded by saying, "No, no; we all stay in the picture together. That way there is a better chance of someone liking at least one of us," Lou said.

Marcia Raubach said that George Harrison's visit to the station lasted less than an hour, and then he was gone. The next time she saw him was less than five months later, on *The Ed Sullivan Show* on national television. "It was almost unbelievable; I just could not believe it," she said. "Everybody was screaming and Ed Sullivan was beaming. I just didn't have any idea that this group was going to be what they became." Over the years, Marcia Raubach has thought about the day she met George Harrison and often says to herself, "Why we didn't tape that interview, I'll never know."

Elliot J. Huntley

■

George Harrison was often known as the most private Beatle, the one who was the most uncomfortable with fame. He hated living his life in a fishbowl. After Lennon's assassination, he was particularly security conscious, and understandably so.

The following excerpt from Elliot J. Huntley's biography of Harrison discusses a stalking incident at George's Hawaiian residence and, even more chilling, the almost-fatal attack on Harrison's life at his home in Friar Park, just outside of London, on the eve of the millennium.

from *Mystical One: George Harrison*

I could feel blood entering my lungs. I could feel my chest deflate. I felt blood in my mouth and air exhale from my chest. I believed I had been fatally stabbed.

George Harrison, 2000

■ CHRISTMAS 1999 saw Harrison receive the ultimate flattery any celebrity can ever wish for, when he got his first official stalker. Two days before Christmas Day 1999, a twenty-seven-year-old girl by the name of Cristin Keleher was discovered in the main house of the Harrison estate on Lower Nahiku Road in Maui.

Unfortunately Cristin wasn't the only fruitcake on the loose and by the end of the week George would have another unwelcome visitor, although this time he wouldn't be so lucky as to be on a different continent.

Keleher, who believed she had a "psychic connection" to George, allegedly entered the former Beatle's home through an open sliding glass door. Once inside, she did her laundry, telephoned her mother in New Jersey, and helped herself to a can of root beer and a DiGiorno frozen pizza—showing that stalkers want the same guarantee of quality as the rest of us when it comes to their frozen foods of choice. The brand of root beer, however, was not established at the pre-trial hearing.

Luckily George was not in Hawaii to share the smorgasbord. Keleher was found by his sister-in-law, Linda Tuckfield, who alerted the caretaker, who called the police who then arrested the confused, unemployed twenty-seven year old.

When Keleher appeared in a Maui courtroom in the new year she pleaded not guilty to first-degree burglary and fourth-degree theft, which is bizarre logic when you consider she was caught red-handed with her fingers covered in melted cheese.

"She was there without permission," a police spokesperson told *The Honolulu Star-Bulletin* newspaper. It came to light that Keleher was born in New Jersey and had been a Maui resident for the previous three years.

Judge Shackley Raffetto ordered Keleher's bail to be set at $10,000 and set a pre-trial conference for April 6. The Associated Press reported that if convicted, Keleher faced up to ten years in prison and a $10,000 fine. Her bail was later reduced to $1,500 when her legal representative explained that though she was homeless, she did have a place to stay if released. For the meanwhile Keleher was remanded to custody.

Proving that stalkers are a lot like busses (you wait around for ages and then two come at once), further tragedy was to strike a mere seven days later. As the rest of the world prepared for their millennium celebrations, horror of the most awful kind almost befell another Beatle. It's almost too much to bear the thought of two Beatles killed by insane fans, just for being in a pop group.

George's worst nightmare happened at about 3:00 a.m. Thursday, December 30, 1999, when a thirty-three-year-old man named Michael Abram from Liverpool broke into Friar Park, using a statue of George and the Dragon he'd ripped up from the garden to smash a window.

Asleep in their upstairs bedroom, George and Olivia were awakened by the sound of the breaking glass. Olivia woke up first, thinking a chandelier had crashed to the floor before realising that there was an intruder downstairs. While Olivia alerted staff on an intercom, George fearlessly went to investigate.

From the top of the stairs, Harrison spotted a man's figure illuminated in the kitchen area. George would recount, "He stopped and looked towards me. He started shouting and screaming. He was hysterical and frightening. He said words to the effect of, 'You get down here, you know what it is.' I could see a knife in one hand and the spear from part of the statue in the other."

Harrison called out and was lunged at by the man. Due to the accent, George was immediately able to identify that the man was a scouser [from Liverpool], and George made the split second decision to tackle the man, aware that he was the last line of defence between the madman and his family.

"Armed only with the element of surprise, I ran at him," George detailed. "My first thought was to grab the knife and knock him off balance. He thrust the knife at me. I was fending off the blows with my hands and arms. He was stabbing down towards my upper body."

Upon hearing her husband's screams for help, Olivia ran downstairs. Seeing Olivia on the landing, Abram stepped over George's body and moved towards her.

In a desperate attempt to subdue her assailant, Olivia struck Abram first with a poker, and then with a table lamp with a heavy brass base, smashing Abram across the side of his head, stunning him. Abram then staggered up to the landing where he collapsed.

After the attack, Tom Petty sent George a fax joking, "Aren't you glad you married a Mexican girl?"—a reference to how, in Petty's words, Olivia "really kicked ass."

"I had to," Olivia would later tell Katie Couric in 2002. "George was coaching me, I have to say. And George was very brave and people don't know that. Because he had already been injured and he had to jump up and bring him down to stop him from attacking me. You know, he saved my life too."

"I was aware of my wife approaching and striking him about the head with a brass poker," Harrison stated in his court deposition. "It appeared to have little effect. He stood up and chased my wife. I feared greatly for her safety and hauled myself up to tackle him. I placed my hands around the blade. He again got the better of me and got on top of me. I felt exhausted and could feel the strength draining from me. My arms dropped to my sides and I vividly remember a deliberate thrust of the knife down into my chest. I could feel blood entering my lungs. I could feel my chest deflate. I felt blood in my mouth and air exhale from my chest. I believed I had been fatally stabbed. My wife struck the man with the vase and he slumped down. I encouraged my wife to keep on hitting him."

During the ten-minute altercation Olivia sustained minor cuts to her forehead and wrists. George was not so lucky. During the scuffle, George was stabbed at least ten times as he bravely tried to protect his family. The struggle would leave him with a punctured right lung, and a trail of blood through three rooms.

After overpowering Abram, George and Olivia somewhere found the strength to hold him down until police arrived at 3:30 a.m., after being called by a member of the staff. When the police did arrive at the scene they found George lying on the floor, holding a towel to his chest, and Olivia kneeling beside him trying to comfort him.

Abram was treated for injuries at John Radcliffe Hospital before being taken into police custody where the Thames Valley Police booked him for breaking and entering and attempted murder charges.

Initially, Abram's motives appeared unclear. Was he merely a chancer trying to nick a few baubles or an obsessed fan intent on killing a Beatle? Police spokesman Guy Bailey told Reuters, "Taste in music is pretty far down the questions police initially ask a suspected murderer . . . The intruder has head injuries so there was a serious struggle put up by Harrison and his wife."

Paramedics initially rushed George and Olivia to the Royal Berkshire Hospital in nearby Reading to be treated for their injuries. Since no major organs had been injured, George was then transferred to Harefield Hospital in northwest London, where he was listed in stable condition. A statement issued by the hospital said the transfer was precautionary, since Harefield had a chest surgeon on duty and Royal Berkshire did not. Olivia was treated for a laceration to the skull, scrapes and bruises, but thankfully her injuries were not serious enough to warrant admission to Harefield, though she remained at her husband's side. Dhani [George's son] had also been at Friar Park, but was sleeping in another wing at the time of the attack and therefore remained unharmed by Abram's bloodlust.

Detective Chief Inspector Euan Read, the officer leading the investigation, described the attack as "vicious," and relayed the fact that Harrison had credited his wife with saving his life. The knife blade, deflected by a rib, had actually missed his heart by less than an inch, which of course meant that George had only narrowly escaped death. Chest surgeon William Fountain at Harefield Hospital told reporters George's injuries were "not life-threatening but that is mainly by chance."

George did not need to undergo surgery, though the main stab wound required six stitches to close and a chest drain was fitted to remove excess fluid and air from his partially collapsed lung.

George had also suffered cuts to his left hand from trying to take the knife away from Abram during the attack. Although stitches were also needed on his thumb and fingers, George was thankfully reassured that he would regain full use of his hand. The hospital would also say that George was "in excellent spirits and he certainly hasn't lost his sense of humour."

George was certainly well enough to make the short statement from his hospital bed saying that the man "wasn't a burglar and he certainly wasn't auditioning for the Traveling Wilburys." Thankfully this gave hope that Harrison's condition was not similar to Lennon's.

Within hours, many fans sent flowers, cards and gifts to the Apple Offices and Friar Park. No doubt breathing a communal sigh of relief that Harrison's injuries were not fatal as at first feared.

After a night's sleep the next day tests and X-rays showed that a full recovery was expected within three weeks, with a small scar being the only physical reminder of this nightmare. "I can see the headlines already," Harrison joked, "George has had a hard day's night."

Paul and Ringo (who were warned to be on the alert for copycat attacks by Thames Valley Police) each made public statements. Paul would say, "Thank God that both George and Olivia are all right. I send them all my love." Ringo added, "Both Barbara and I are deeply shocked that this incident has occurred. We send George and Olivia all our love and wish George a speedy recovery."

Yoko was also notified, and an "insider" would later say that Yoko was understandably "spooked" by the attack on George. Yoko sent her sympathies stating, "My heart goes out to George, Olivia and Dhani, and I hope he will recover quickly."

More touchingly, Bangladesh's State Minister for Foreign Affairs, Abul Hasan Chowdhury, expressed his deep regret at the attack and wished him an early recovery. In a statement Chowdhury recalled George's support during the Liberation War "that drew the attention of the world community to the sufferings of our people." "The people of Bangladesh are indebted to him," Chowdhury would say on behalf of his country, showing that they had never forgotten George's efforts nearly thirty years previously.

Early in the morning of New Year's Eve, Abram appeared before Oxford magistrates' court where he was formally charged with breaking and entering, aggravated assault and attempted murder. Harrison would spend his New Year's Eve drowsy from painkillers in his hospital suite at Harefield Hospital, instead of enjoying the Millennium Eve party he and Olivia had planned, at Friar Park.

David Simons

■

In this insightful piece, music critic David Simons praises the often under-rated contributions that George Harrison, whom he calls "the man in the mid-dle," made to the Beatles.

"The Unsung Beatle:
George Harrison's Behind-the-Scenes
Contributions to the
World's Greatest Band"

Acoustic Guitar
February 2003

■ To the casual Beatles fan, George Harrison was the unassuming sideman, the sitar-playing spiritualist and competent composer whose occasional song contributions ("Something," "Here Comes the Sun") made a ripple or two in the stream of Lennon-McCartney classics. Peel back another layer—as Beatles archaeologists are wont to do—and there exists a far more intriguing portrait of the man and his music, one that is significantly more complex and not nearly as well documented.

In the years since the Beatles' 1970 breakup, an array of bootlegged recordings—as well as one officially sanctioned collection, *Anthology*—has provided fans with a glimpse inside the world of EMI's No. 2 Studio during the years 1962 through 1969. Early demo takes of John Lennon fumbling his way through "Happiness Is a Warm Gun" and "Polythene Pam" may not be everyone's idea of a good time, but to Beatles devotees, they're artifacts, pieces of a puzzle, connectable dots, all helping to add substance to the theory that George Harrison had more to do with the making of the Beatles' legacy than we've been led to believe.

Harrison's 1970 solo outing *All Things Must Pass* provided the first real indication of the extent of his musical talent. Meticulously orchestrated and containing over a dozen songs remaindered from the last few Beatles albums, *All Things Must Pass* demonstrated that not only could Harrison play choice lead guitar, he could also write, arrange, overdub, produce, mix, and edit—and reach No. 1 with a hook about a religious cult ("My Sweet Lord"). Any lingering doubts were laid to rest with Ringo Starr's Harrison-produced Top Five hit "It Don't Come Easy," a brilliantly produced pop effort brimming with familiar touches like Leslie lead, soulful horns, and spirited backing harmonies.

Like all great mythological moments, a good portion of the Beatles' studio activity remains shrouded in secrecy, making it nearly impossible to say with absolute certainty in what instances Harrison went beyond the standard fills-and-riffs sideman stuff and instead helped transform some promising Lennon-McCartney ideas into outstanding finished works. But like great paintings, the music of the Beatles continues to reveal new insights and subtle nuances, giving Beatles archaeologists reason to pursue plausible new theories and shedding new light on the man in the middle.

Identifying Riffs

The Beatles packed an enormous amount of musical dexterity into their seven-year recording career, and a good deal of those finer moments belong to Harrison, a guitarist who was neither fast nor flashy yet ultimately defined the role of lead guitarist during the mid-'60s. As a rhythm guitarist, Harrison was no less innovative; his use of a capoed acoustic guitar, in particular, became a prominent songwriting vehicle, resulting in standouts "Here Comes the Sun," "I Me Mine," and "For You Blue" and adding a new dimension to the Beatles' sound.

Right from the start, Harrison dug deep into the Lennon-McCartney song structures, adding a simple guitar counterpoint ("I Saw Her Standing There"), echoing melody lines ("Every Little Thing"), and crafting guitar hooks from scratch ("Help"). His Gretsch electric guitar work incorporated elements of country, rockabilly, and even jazz chord voicings. Such versatility meant that the Beatles could slay the teenies with "All My Loving" and then placate their parents moments later with "Till There Was You."

"George always felt comfortable working in a multitude of styles," observes *Rolling Stone* contributing editor Anthony DeCurtis. "In a lot of ways, he was the most R&B-oriented guy in the band. At the same time, he had this beautiful sort of folk-rock style of playing—'If I Needed Someone,' for instance—and then he had that amazing slide guitar style that was not only bluesy but also had a real lyrical quality about it."

Time and time again, Harrison crafted intros, fills, and lead lines that were nearly as hooky as the songs themselves. Putting his newly minted Rickenbacker 360/12 electric 12-string to the test, Harrison opened John Lennon's rocker "A Hard Day's Night" with a single ringing G7sus4 chord, in the process creating one of the most celebrated intros in rock. Throughout 1964 and '65, Harrison uncorked one Rickenbacker riff after another, from the descending fills of "Help" to the ear-grabbing opening in "Ticket to Ride." "That was his gift," says Andy Babiuk, author of *Beatles Gear: All the Fab Four's Instruments, from Stage to Studio* (Backbeat Books). "It's hard to imagine those songs without the bits George came up with. Divorce any one of them from the track, and the song just doesn't sound right."

But Harrison was not content to remain the creative sidekick. By 1965, entries like "Think for Yourself," I Need You," and "If I Needed Someone" showed signs of the emerging songsmith in Harrison. "Though I think George's playing was more devoted to finding particular kinds of sounds than hooks," remarks *New York Times* music critic Allan Kozinn, "one little device that he used several times is the D-major chord with the third replaced by a major second and a suspended fourth, which was the driving force behind 'If I Needed Someone' and an important part of 'Here Comes the Sun' four years later."

Any discussion of the Beatles archive typically revolves around two major themes: that the Beatles wrote great songs and that they turned them into great-sounding records. It's a point that becomes especially relevant during the band's post-1966 efforts, the period of Harrison's greatest achievements in the studio. As any guitarist with a keen ear knows, it's not just the parts Harrison played—it's the way he made them sound. "George's style of playing—his tone, his phrasing, his ability to articulate the very small parts—is very difficult to replicate," says DeCurtis. "And because that's so much a part of the fabric of the song, if you don't get it right, you don't get it at all."

When rock took a more aggressive turn in 1966, Harrison once again switched instruments, acquiring a Gibson SG and announcing his presence with authority on McCartney's "Paperback Writer," the toughest-sounding A side in the Beatles' collection. On *Revolver,* Harrison's experimental nature led to yet another new wrinkle: backwards guitar. "He would play the solos normal, then we'd flip the tapes and he'd listen to them backwards, just to see how they sounded," recalls former Beatles engineer Richard Lush. But creating a solo that would sound musical when played backwards was a long and tedious process. "This would go on for maybe 70 takes," says Lush, "turning the tape over, listening, turning it back again—it would take literally hours to accomplish."

After spending the better part of 1967 mastering the sitar and writing songs primarily on organ ("Only a Northern Song") and harmonium ("Within You Without You"), Harrison returned to the guitar in peak form, saving some of his best work for last during the marathon medley that closes *Abbey Road,* the band's swan song. Even as the distance between Lennon and McCartney increased in later years, Harrison's guitar work continued to create the impression of a unified group.

"From *Sgt. Pepper's* forward, it was really Lennon songs or McCartney songs," says Babiuk, "but George helped keep the cohesion because he'd put his signature parts on all of them. If you want proof, all you have to do is listen to any of McCartney's first few solo albums right after the break. Harrison wasn't on them, and consequently they just didn't sound the same."

Acoustic Output

The Beatles were the first act to make the acoustic guitar a prominent part of a pop rhythm section, and a good portion of the credit belongs to Harrison, whose acoustic guitar parts were central to the development of the band's sound and approach to songwriting. Like Lennon, Harrison played a Gibson J-160E (with electric pickup) early on, using it on such tracks as "Love Me Do" and "I'll Be Back." He soon expanded his collection to include a José Ramírez Guitarra de Estudio nylon-string guitar, the featured instrument on "Till There Was You" and the 1964 McCartney standard "And I Love Her." A year later, Harrison provided the extra texture on Lennon's Dylanesque "You've Got to Hide Your Love Away" using a 12-string in dropped-D tuning.

Coincidentally or not, Harrison's most remarkable stretch of songwriting—from 1968 through 1970—began with the purchase of a Gibson J-200, the big-bodied acoustic heard on White Album cuts "Long, Long, Long," "Piggies," and the tour de force "While My Guitar Gently Weeps."

Harrison's acoustic direction was, in part, fostered by his friendship with Bob Dylan. Though Lennon briefly reflected Dylan's folk influence, Harrison remained a steadfast admirer and by 1968 was making regular trips to the bard's home in upstate New York. One visit resulted in the co-write "I'd Have You Anytime," which matched Dylan's simple poetry with a sophisticated Harrison chord progression.

"I was saying to him, 'You write incredible lyrics,' and he was saying, 'How do you write those tunes?'" Harrison later told *Crawdaddy*. "So I began showing him chords like crazy, because he tended to just play a lot of basic chords and move a capo up and down."

With his premiere solo single "My Sweet Lord," Harrison elevated the sound and scope of recorded acoustic guitar to even greater heights. Over a basic Fm–B progression, he created a lush bedrock of rhythm, enlisting the guitar services of Peter Frampton as well as Badfinger's Pete Ham, Tom Evans, and Joey Molland. "They put us inside this huge blue wooden box made out of plywood, with doors in the front of it," says Molland of the *All Things Must Pass* sessions. "We'd go in there and get on these tall stools, they'd mic us up, and we'd begin recording. I remember hearing the rough-mix playback of 'My Sweet Lord.' The balance was all there, it was so incredibly full—an enormous acoustic guitar sound without any double tracking or anything. Just all of us going at once, straight on."

Anonymous Arrangements

Those paying tribute to Harrison following his untimely death from cancer in November 2001 made note of his skill as a sideman, his un-flagging devotion to humanitarian causes, even his wry sense of humor. And yet Harrison's greatest attribute—his ability to shape the sounds that would result in some of the Beatles' most notable works—was some-how given short shrift.

"Everybody talks about Lennon and McCartney and what a great songwriting team they were," says Babiuk, "but when you listen to some of the original rough demos, they're just OK. Had they left them like that, would they still have become these great songs that we've come to know and love? That's where George played such an important part."

In a conversation included in 1999's *Anthology* book, Harrison gave an example of how much impact he had on one Lennon song in particular. "I was at John's house one day, and he was struggling with some tunes," recalled Harrison, "loads of bits, maybe three songs that were unfinished. I made some suggestions and helped him to work them together so that they became one finished song. 'She Said, She Said.' The middle part was a different song—'I said no, no, no, you're wrong'—then it goes into the other one, 'When I was a boy.' That was a real weld! So I did things like that."

Other titles—including "Happiness Is a Warm Gun," another three-piece "weld"—suggest that Lennon regularly sought Harrison's input during the gestation of a song, both before and after arriving for an EMI session. As the *Anthology* demos reveal, McCartney's skill as an arranger clearly outdistanced that of his mate's, who would frequently present the group with little more than a good idea and a set of words, particularly as his interest in the Beatles began to wane. Not that this made Lennon a lesser talent; to his credit, Lennon understood the value of giving Harrison the leeway to contribute spontaneous ideas.

"With 'Come Together,' I just said, 'Look, I've got no arrangement for you, but you know how I want it,'" Lennon remarked shortly after the completion of *Abbey Road* in 1969. "I think that's partly because [George and I have] played together for such a long time."

"I think it's consistent with the way John's state of mind was during that time," says DeCurtis. "He was depressed, he was having problems with drugs—he really wasn't at the top of his game by any stretch of the imagination. And the result was this very stripped-down approach to songwriting and demo-making. I don't think Paul would ever come right out and say it—'My songs were all there, but we'd have to break our asses on John's'—but I think it's very likely that that was the case."

"Unlike Paul, John couldn't really hear all the different parts," Babiuk speculates. "He was artistic in a different sense. As a result, in many instances it was up to George to make those songs come to life the way they did on the record."

With little more than a rough sketch to work with, Harrison frequently embellished and augmented in the studio as he saw fit. The results were often revelatory.

"You listen to a song like 'Dear Prudence,'" says Ian Hammond, who runs www.beathoven.com, "and you realize that they did it all without the aid of an orchestra—even though the closing climactic section is a natural candidate for brass and/or strings. How? They relied heavily on Harrison—who came up with these great moving inner lines in the last verse and chorus."

From Harrison's standpoint, the blank page that Lennon sometimes presented was considerably more enticing than merely following McCartney's strict guidelines. "In the later years of the Beatles, McCartney actually became increasingly specific, autocratic, and even precious about what he wanted from the rest of the band," says Elliot J. Huntley, author of *Behind That Locked Door: George Harrison after the Breakup of the Beatles*. "This became a source of rancor for Harrison." The situation came to a head during the filmed recording sessions for *Let It Be*, when a frustrated Harrison suddenly tells McCartney, "I'll play whatever you want me to play or I won't play at all if you don't want me to—whatever it is that will please you."

Keeping a Low Profile

Despite his obvious ability as an arranger, guitarist, and songwriter, Harrison wasn't always completely confident in his own skills. "There was often a desire on his part to hide," notes DeCurtis. "When he went out on his own, he made a point of surrounding himself with a huge crowd of players, looking to these big figures like Eric Clapton or Bob Dylan to handle some of the guitar work. He was a very self-effacing character—his aesthetic as a player was to blend, not to inject anything that would seem too obvious."

Never one to trumpet his own accomplishments, Harrison gave very few interviews during the last portion of his life and spoke of the Beatles' years only when he saw fit. The other band members were also evasive and provided only sketchy details about who did what and when. "And a lot of the people whom you'd expect to remember the great details really don't," says Babiuk.

Without any "official" record to go on—and with both Harrison and Lennon no longer with us—it's likely that Harrison's best behind-the-scenes moments, like those of any other session great, will continue to remain unknown and underappreciated. "It would be difficult to reconstruct who contributed the ideas that ended up on the finished product," says Kozinn.

Yet, as DeCurtis points out, any substantive discussion of Harrison's musical legacy—official or otherwise—is enough to entice listeners to revisit the music with fresh ears and an open mind. "Put on anything the Beatles did, and you'll hear in George a willingness to work within the possibilities of the song—to really find a way to make a fresh statement," says DeCurtis. "In a sense, much of what George did was so good that you can easily miss it. But the second you start paying attention, you become aware of what he was doing in each song. To me, that's been the most powerful aspect of George's role in the band."

Philip Glass

■

In this heartfelt obituary, American composer Philip Glass discusses George Harrison's love of Indian music and culture, an interest that he shared with the ex-Beatle. Harrison, of course, was among the first Western musicians to integrate Eastern music into rock and roll and, as a result, played a major role in the development of what was later called world music.

"George Harrison, World-Music Catalyst and Great-Souled Man: Open to the Influence of Unfamiliar Cultures"

The New York Times
December 9, 2001

■ WE ALL NATURALLY remember George Harrison as one of the cornerstones (but weren't they all?) of the late-20th-century phenomenon known as the Beatles. But for some, George, who died on Nov. 29 at the age of 58, was an icon of another phenomenon, equally influential in shaping the music of today. I'm referring to the world-music culture, which, starting in the 60's, has become an inescapable aspect of our music life. George was among the first Western musicians to recognize the importance of music traditions millenniums old, which themselves had roots in indigenous music, both popular and classical. Using his considerable influence and popularity, he was one of those few who pushed open the door that, until then, had separated the music of much of the world from the West.

His close, lifelong friendship with Ravi Shankar was the opening of this new world for George. They met in London in 1966, and shortly after he went to India for a six-week visit. He bought a sitar in Delhi, and not long after it was heard in new Beatles recordings, beginning with "Norwegian Wood" from "Rubber Soul," then "Within You Without You" from "Sgt. Pepper" and going on from there.

I never met George. But what we shared was our encounters with Indian classical music through Ravi Shankar. My first meeting with Ravi was in 1965 in Paris and, for me, the experience was as powerful, and as important for my musical development, as it was for George. I, likewise, was drawn to India and, in fact, was in Bombay in 1966 when George was there. He was staying at the prestigious Taj Mahal Hotel where he had begun studying the sitar with Ravi. (I, unknown to Ravi, was staying only a few blocks away in the distinctly unprestigious, but quite comfortable, Salvation Army lodgings.) In Ravi's autobiography, "Raga Mala," (with a foreword by George Harrison and many additional contributions by him), he writes generously and quite touchingly of the early years of their friendship.

The role that Ravi played in George's life was so important I think a few words must be included about him as well. By the time they met, Ravi was 46—an acclaimed master musician who had been playing and traveling in the West for decades. It's impossible to overstate the importance and influence his long-term presence has had for Western music as a whole.

He was first involved in the tradition of Western concert music through Yehudi Menuhin, whom he met in London in 1956, and later with many other musicians in the classical field. Besides composing a series of concertos for sitar and orchestra, he performed frequently in chamber music ensembles with his friends. In fact, I met Ravi, Menuhin and Jean-Pierre Rampal in New Delhi in January 1998 when they were wrapping up what was to be their last tour together.

I can speak personally for Ravi's influence on the "experimental" music of the 60's. He was as great a mentor for me as he was for George. He set the musical direction for the first few years of my amplified ensemble, and he has remained a close friend, sometime collaborator and music confidant up until the present.

Ravi's contact with pop culture began in the 60's with Rory McEwan, whom he met in 1963. However, it was George, no doubt, who brought Ravi to a larger public. Ravi writes about the effect of George on his career in the following way: "I was planning to leave India again in February 1967, for a long, long tour. I had already become well known by then through my classical career and the recitals I had given at some folk clubs, even before my contact with George. But from the Bombay incident onwards"—George was recognized by a bellhop at the Taj Mahal, which created a huge uproar—"there was such a big flash all around the world in the newspapers connecting him and me, about how I had become George's guru. It was like wildfire, creating such a big explosion of fascination with the sitar that there was a tremendous demand for my concerts. I had become a superstar!"

After that Ravi appeared at the Monterey Pop Festival in June 1967 (which he seems to have enjoyed). Later he was at Woodstock in August 1969 (which he did not enjoy at all). Still later came the concert for Bangladesh in August 1971—surely the most important of these events. Ravi had asked George to help him organize the concert. George, besides writing his song "Bangladesh," arrived with Bob Dylan, Eric Clapton, Billy Preston, Leon Russell and others. Eventually there would be a Grammy Award–winning album.

Beyond being involved with the music of India, George was sincerely and deeply touched by its culture and religion. Anyone seriously involved with India eventually (sooner than later) will have to take on the whole culture. In my own case it led to an opera about Gandhi ("Satyagraha"), and a lifelong interest in the philosophy, history, art, people, food, et al. of India. My empathy with George comes about through this broader encounter with Indian culture, which we equally shared, enjoyed and were inspired by.

This rediscovered interest in ancient, spiritual traditions (mainly Eastern) seems to have swept through a host of artists, writers and musicians at this time. The likes of John Cage, Allen Ginsberg, George Harrison and many others were all deeply distressed and affected by the ethos of postmodern American-European life. It seemed that the materialism of the society as a whole had extended well past the simple consumerism of our capitalist environment and invaded the world of culture itself, producing a plethora of inhibited and cold works of art in the fields of dance, theater and music—from trashy "pop" to intellectual exercises in modernism.

My view of mid- to late-20th-century music is born from this experience. For me the great event of the 20th century was not the continuation of the central European avant-garde to its last final gasp. I see the great musical adventure of our time as the emergence of a world-music culture, which crosses lines of geography, race and gender. From this perspective, the impact of George Harrison's life and times has been enormous. He played a major role in bringing several generations of young musicians out of the parched and dying desert of Eurocentric music into a new world. I have no doubt that this part of his legacy will be his most enduring. And not only that. He opened the doors to this new world of music with deep conviction, great energy and his own remarkable clarity and simplicity.

And then, of course, there was the Beatles.

■

FOUR

Ringo Starr:
Acting Naturally

—"I thought I was the best drummer there was."

Robert Deardorff

■

In the following article, *Redbook* writer Robert Deardorff captures the Ringo
Starr (aka the "Miserable Beatle") on the movie set of *Help!* Ringo comes
across as polite, affable, and willing to please. But there is also an under-
current of sadness ("He is resigned to the fact that he has lost his freedom")
as he, and the rest of his band mates, try their best to retain their sanity
amid the unprecedented fame.

"Ringo Starr: Domesticated Beatle"

Redbook
September 1965

■ RINGO STARR IS THE drummer of the Beatles, that quartet of fab-
ulously successful young Englishmen whose various activities will gross
over $100 million this year. Along with the other Beatles, he was re-
cently named a Member of the Most Excellent Order of the British
Empire by the Queen. In addition, he has become an outstanding actor
with an unusual ability to create much the same wistful humor that
Charlie Chaplin did. In the Beatles' first movie, *A Hard Day's Night,*
Ringo was so successful that their second picture, a comedy called *Help!,*
has been built around him and his talent for being both sad and funny.

His marriage early this year and the news that he will become a father in November have, surprisingly, increased his popularity still more.
Today he is a world-famous family man, a teen-age idol and a movie star
with enormous appeal for adult audiences.

Long before his appearance in *A Hard Day's Night* he had been nick-
named the "Miserable Beatle." He doesn't agree with that. "The thing
is, I've got one of those faces that doesn't smile very much. I'm feeling
good inside, having a great time, but it just never shows."

People who know all four men well sometimes give him another
name. "He's the 'Apart Beatle,'" Walter Shenson, the producer of their
pictures, explained. "He sits apart from the other three on stage and he
doesn't sing. But there's more to it than that. He is the most introspective and the gentlest, too."

He is also the last one who joined the Beatles, he has had the least schooling and he is the only one who comes from a poor family. He is completely without pretentions. In the entertainment world, when people become famous they often begin retouching their past. Not Ringo. He makes no effort to cover up the fact that his family was poor, and he is equally matter-of-fact about the hardships of former years and the enormous success that has come to him now. Although he makes mistakes in grammar, he has an unusual flair for language; he thought of the title *A Hard Day's Night* for the Beatles' first film.

A number of reporters have discovered recently that it is not always an easy matter to talk to the Beatles. One national magazine, promised an interview last year, ended with an article describing the troubles of the reporter and explaining why it was impossible to get much information. Another magazine sent a woman on one of the Beatles' tours. In a month of traveling she did not get a single chance to talk to them. According to people who know all four men well, they are beginning to feel the tremendous pressure of having their every move scrutinized. Sometimes they react by retreating behind a wall of silence.

On the movie set of *Help!* the morning I first met Ringo, he was under great tension. He shook hands politely, then disappeared in front of the camera. From then until midafternoon he was busy playing the same scene, one in which his coat was wired so that his sleeve would fly off and sail through the air at a given moment in the action. But the wires didn't work properly, and Ringo had to do the scene over and over.

Between takes he alternated horseplay with brooding, at times boxing with the director, Richard Lester, a young Philadelphian who also directed *A Hard Day's Night,* and at other times standing off by himself, chewing his lower lip. By the time the wires worked correctly on cue and the scene was completed, it was three o'clock. He came over immediately, apologizing for having wasted so much of my time. That evening instead of rushing home as he had intended, he changed his mind, and after phoning his wife said we could begin.

A slight man, about five feet six, he sat in an overstuffed chair in his dressing room as we talked. He told me that he was born on July 7, 1940, in Dingle, a section of Liverpool near the docks of that smoky port city. Like dock areas everywhere, "it's not pretty, but I liked it. I was happy there."

He is an only child; his real name is Richard Starkey. "It's *still* Starkey," he pointed out earnestly, in spite of the fact that his parents were divorced when he was a baby and his mother later remarried. He doesn't remember his father's ever living with him and his mother.

One of his earliest recollections is of being sick when he was six and a half. "I had appendicitis. I remember being carried downstairs to the ambulance. I saw all my aunties and uncles sitting around in the kitchen as I passed. At the hospital there was this doctor. He may not have done it—this is just how it *felt*—but he was sort of bashing me in the stomach, or so I thought. And I remember"—he exploded into laughter—"I remember thinking, He shouldn't do that! I'm not *well!*"

In the operating room his appendix burst, and later he developed peritonitis. "I was kept in a cot with sides to keep me from falling out of bed. After six months in that cot the doctor was going to discharge me. Then somebody brought me a toy bus. I was leaning over the side, showing it to the kid in the next cot, when I fell out and wrecked everything. It was the biggest disappointment I ever had. They had to start all over, and I had to stay in that hospital another six months—a year in all.

"I was eight and a half or nine when I went back to school, and I was put in a class with big boys my own age. There's a big difference between the work of six-and-a-half-year-olds and nine-year-olds, and I don't think I ever made up the schooling I missed. I wouldn't say I was thick, but I'm not very good at spelling. And arithmetic isn't my greatest subject either." With this he sat up abruptly in his chair and, face beaming, cried in a triumphant voice, "But I can work a *few* things out, folks!"

In those days the family never had much money. "We're working-class people," he pointed out. "My mother worked all her life—as long as I can remember. She was a barmaid first. Then she worked in a shop, selling fruit. Besides that, she had to keep an eye on me, you know, and take care of herself and the house. But we had a nice home—for what we had, you know. We didn't ever live in squalor."[1]

He remembered too that he had always had "the best my mother could give me. She'd go without herself just so I could have a good suit and a good pair of shoes. Not only that," he went on. "She did other things for me—lots of things. She never let me down. If I wanted something expensive, she'd say, 'Well, I'll *try*, but don't build your hopes up.' And I knew if she could possibly manage, I'd get it. When she *did* promise something, she never failed me. Never! So now when I think of my own baby . . . Never lie to a child!" he exclaimed. "That's the worst thing!"

His mother also had been deeply understanding. "When I first learned a very bad word—I was a little boy and I heard some big boys say it, so I came in and said it too—like, you know, 'There's no *la-la* sugar' or 'Can I have another *boop-boop* cup of tea?' my mother just looked at me and said"—his voice dropped gently as he imitated her tone—"'You mustn't say that word. It's a bad word. Now, I'm not going to hit you for saying it, but you're *not* to say it again.' Many a parent would have slapped me right away," he pointed out, "but, you see, she knew that I didn't know what it meant.

"She gave me a lot of freedom, too. If the lads were going out, I used to say, 'Can I go out with the lads? We're going somewhere.' I was about ten then. And she'd say, 'Okay, but look after yourself, and don't do anything silly.' She was just great, you know."

In those days he "went out with the lads" a lot. "I was only lonely when it rained and I had to stay in alone. That's why I always say I'll never have just one kid. It's all right when you can go out and play with your mates, but when it's bad weather you have to fetch kids in. Sometimes I think my mother got fed up a bit. Sometimes when it rained I'd bring two hundred people in to play. I think that's the only drag about being an only child."

Ringo was 13 when his mother married again. "What is funny," he went on, his voice filled with incredulity, "is that she *asked* me, you know: 'Do you mind if we get married?' No! No! Because I loved him anyway. He'd been coming around for four or five years, and he was like a dad to me. You know, there was none of that 'Look here, we're getting married!' It was nice to know that you counted, even at that age.

"So now my mother is Mrs. Graves—which the papers will never print. They still call her Mrs. Starkey. I'm sure she's not ashamed that she was a divorcee. I'm sure I'm not."

After the wedding, Ringo continued, he began calling his mother Elsie and his stepfather Harry. "I didn't call her 'Mum' any more because, the thing is, I didn't like saying 'Mother' to her and then 'Harry' to my stepfather. I changed that to make him feel better, and my mother understood.

"Harry," he said softly, "is a gentle man. You know, *gentle*. Not as in *gentleman*, though he's that, too. He's patient and kind. He loves kids and animals. You know, people say that kids and animals can always tell if someone's good or if he's dirt, and they always like Harry. I know I always did. Even before the marriage he used to take me out. He'd play with me. I had some building things, and he'd show me how to do them. He was just like a dad to me. He has a good sense of humor, too, and he's musical as well. When I was eighteen or nineteen we used to go to a couple of clubs—workingmen's clubs, you know—and they used to ask him to sing. We had a little double act, both of us singing. Just for laughs."

From the time he was a small boy, Ringo had been interested in music. Friends of his say that he knows most of the major songs of the last 40 years; he can also analyze fine points in the styles and interpretations of the singers and orchestras that made the songs famous. His first interest, however, was drums, and he never got over that.

"When I was about thirteen I used to walk to school down this main street where there was a secondhand music shop," he told me. "In the window there was just one drum. The price was six pounds ten shillings [about $18], which was a lot of money in those days. I used to think, I'd love that! But because I knew I couldn't have it I made drums out of little tin cans, and put bits of metal on them to make them sizzle. I made my own sticks, too."

About the time his mother remarried, Ringo went back to the hospital for another year, this time with fluid in his lungs. He was almost 15 before he was discharged—the age when the children of working-class parents in Britain begin looking for jobs. He didn't return to school. He found a job as a messenger boy for a railroad, but was fired within five weeks. "I can't remember why. I think I was cheeky. I went for my uniform," he explained, "and all they gave me was a hat."

Next Ringo joined the merchant navy. That too lasted only a few weeks. "Then," he continued, "my stepfather, who knew a man with a firm, who knew a man with a bigger firm, helped me get a job. I don't know whether you have this in America: 'Learn a trade, son, and you'll be all right.' Well, my family wanted me to learn a trade, so I went there. I was still running around as a messenger, but I was going to be trained as a wood joiner. After six months, when no one offered me work with a joiner, I went to the boss and said, 'I came here to be a joiner, you know.' And he said, 'Well, there are no vacancies. Would you like to become an engineer?'" Ringo burst into laughter. "So I became an apprentice engineer. I went to night school, too."

Now that he was a workingman, Ringo felt he could afford to buy a drum at last. He bought a 30-shilling bass drum. "That is about—" He paused, frowning. "I'm trying to work it out in American for you—about four dollars and twenty cents," he said. "I used to bang it with a couple of sticks and annoy everybody. It made just one big *boom* sound. Then my parents bought me a drum kit. I used to carry my drums on my back down to my mates because they had a guitar, and we could play together."

Soon Ringo was playing with a group in local clubs, each boy getting about $14 for each show. A little later he began to play with another group, which was doing even better. "So I was playing with two groups at the same time and earning about fourteen dollars a week. That was tops in those days!"

Ringo managed to work at both his music and his job as apprentice engineer, which paid about $18.20 weekly. Then he received an offer to play in a summer camp at $45 a week. "That was amazing," he declared. "No one got that much in those days. I couldn't believe it. So I gave up my apprenticeship, and the boss said, 'You'll be back here in three months!'"

At home his family also protested. "My mum and stepfather and my aunties—everybody said, 'You'll want your trade, son. Stay another year and learn. Then you can go and do what you like.' But I'd decided. I didn't like working there."

Although his family was concerned, they dropped their objections when they were sure Ringo had made up his mind. "They'd had their try, you see. The thing is, as long as I'm happy, they're happy."

From the time Ringo began working at 15, he always gave his mother money to help out at home, "and after I quit my apprenticeship to play, I'd give her the odd extra pounds I earned as well. I'd give her three pounds or so a week no matter what I made. When I had an especially good week, I'd give her more. I never kept the difference."

His group, Rory Storm and the Hurricanes, played in the summer camp, then played American military bases in France and went on to tour Germany. In Germany they made friends with the Beatles, already in business and also on tour. Back in Liverpool, Ringo was still playing with the Hurricanes when the Beatles' drummer, Pete Best, became ill, and Ringo was asked to fill in for one appearance. Although not yet famous elsewhere, the Beatles were already earning "the biggest money in Liverpool—I think I got fourteen dollars for that one day. This was in 1962. Then the drummer went sick again and I played with them again. I played—oh, eight or nine times like that, filling in a day at a time."

When it became evident that Pete would not be able to return, the Beatles asked Ringo to join the group on a permanent basis. The first time he played with them as a full-fledged Beatle, there was a demonstration in the club. Part of the crowd was shouting, "Pete Best forever! Ringo never!" Part of it was shouting, "Ringo forever! Pete Best never!" Both boys had loyal followings, Ringo from his appearances with Rory Storm.

At that time nobody, least of all the Beatles, foresaw the fantastic success that they were going to have. Liverpool was the whole world for them. They didn't even think about going to London. On October 5, 1962, after Ringo had joined them, their first record, "Love Me, Do," was released. It came in around 47th or 48th on the top-50 list in Britain, and they couldn't believe it. "This knocked us out," Ringo said. In 1963 they made another record, which rose to the Number One spot. Then a third one came in at Number One, and they were on their way. Their phenomenal success in Britain dates from 1963. That summer Ed Sullivan saw their mob of fans at London Airport and signed them for their first United States appearance. They made their U.S. debut in the winter of '63–'64.

When Ringo joined the Beatles, he already had taken the name Ringo Starr for professional purposes. He also had been experimenting with different haircuts. "I used to change it every couple of months— up, down, sideways. When I was asked to join the Beatles I had it swept right back, with a beard. But the Beatles told me, 'Get your hair flattened down. Shave off the beard and keep your sideburns.' So I did. We didn't originate these haircuts, you know. It's been done this way for thousands of years."

He also had bought a car, and one night in the Liverpool club where the Beatles were playing he spotted a young girl in the audience and later approached her and asked, "Do you want a lift home?" The young lady told him, "I've got a girl friend with me."

"Well, I couldn't back out then," Ringo explained, "so I said, 'Okay,' and I took her friend home and then I took her home. Her name was Maureen Cox."

After that he didn't see her for a week or so, Ringo recalled. "But whenever I did, I'd say, 'Take you home?' and she'd say, 'I've got a *friend* with me.' This went on for a month or so, and then I said, 'Look, I'll take you out, but I'm not taking two of you out. That's a bit much.'" He grinned. "See, she *always* had this friend. It used to drive me mad!

"We just sort of started going steady. More or less. How can you go steady in my job? I kept leaving and going on tour. Then when I came back last December from the U.S. tour and went into the hospital here in London to have my tonsils out, she came to see me. In fact, she stayed with my mother in my London flat. It was then I said, 'Do you want to get married?' and she said, 'Yes. . . .'"

When Ringo left the hospital, he and Maureen drove to Liverpool one night to ask her parents' consent. "They said yes." Ringo's parents had already approved, "so we got married. I don't remember the date! February or March." He paused, frowning, then burst out, "That's grand! Dates I'll never remember! I hope my wife doesn't read this!" (A phone call later to his manager revealed that the date was February 11th.)

Like everything else in his life these days, getting married had to be clothed in secrecy to protect Ringo and his bride from the hysterical 14- and 15-year-old girls who haunt his days and nights. Although his address is supposed to be secret, they always find out where he lives and loiter in droves in the street. "When they get a bit fed up sitting around, they play games," he told me. "You know the way girls scream? It's annoying." He grinned. "Can't hear the TV."

"They're not fans really," he pointed out. "Real fans don't behave that way. These are lunatics, screaming and stamping, knocking on the bell and pounding on the door. I've gone downstairs time and again and signed all their autograph books, but that doesn't satisfy them. They come back night after night. The same ones."

As a result of the disturbance they cause, neighbors have signed petitions against Ringo, and in a period of 18 months three different landlords demanded that he move.

He has trouble with adults as well as adolescents. When he is appearing in a theater, they play all sorts of tricks in their efforts to see him and talk to him. Ringo has several aunts and uncles in Liverpool, but scores of strangers have come to the stage door claiming to be aunts, uncles— even brothers, though he has no brothers—as they ask to be admitted.

One of the reasons all the Beatles like to make movies is that they are protected from crowds in the studio. Even so, every afternoon just before they are due to stop work, the street outside the studio fills up with teen-aged girls. Although the gate is guarded by two or three policemen, in addition to studio personnel, now and then one of the girls manages to climb over the fence or rush through the gate when it is opened to admit a car. And whenever the girls glimpse a Beatle, or any person connected with a Beatle, they begin their shrill, high, unearthly "*E-e-e-e-e-e*" scream that has become their theme song.

Partly because he can never escape from such crowds or from news-papermen who want to know why he is doing whatever he is doing. Ringo does not go away for vacations. When he has time off he stays at home, never venturing out during the day unless accompanied by people who can protect him if crowds build up. So far nothing serious has ever happened to any Beatle or Beatle fan because of mob hysteria, but once in New York somebody did get close enough to tear Ringo's shirt and rip off a St. Christopher medal he wore on a chain around his neck.

As a result of this potential danger to themselves and others, when the Beatles play in Britain the police often will not allow them to stay overnight in the city where they perform. They arrive around four P.M., give two performances, and are whisked away to some secret destination in the country for the night. The situation has grown so bad that many of the comfortable hotels where they would like to stay when they go on tour refuse to give them rooms.

To escape reporters and fans, Ringo's double-ring marriage ceremony took place at eight A.M. in Caxton Hall, the registry office in London. For his own ring he used the wedding ring that had belonged to his paternal grandfather. Holding out his hand, he showed me the wide, heavy gold band. "You can see the join," he said, pointing to a dim line in the gold. "I loved my grandfather, and this is the only keepsake of his I have. It's fifty or sixty years old."

After the ceremony he and Maureen drove to the seaside resort of Brighton. They hadn't been there two hours when reporters, having discovered them, were knocking on their door. Ringo telephoned his agent in London and he in turn got in touch with the reporters. They struck a bargain. Ringo and Maureen would hold a press conference the following day if the reporters would agree to leave them alone.

They stayed in Brighton for several days. A local shop wrote to ask if Ringo and his wife would accept a poodle as a wedding present. There were no strings attached, not even publicity for the shop, and Ringo and Maureen accepted gladly. They are devoted to the dog.

"It's the smallest poodle you can get, just a tiny ball of fluff—peach fluff," he told me. "We call him Tiger, only it's a she. Well, you see, when she came she was so small we couldn't tell; we thought she was a boy. She's house-trained, though—anywhere in the house," he quipped. "But you can't hit a dog that's as small as that. You look at it and you think, You *can't touch* the little thing. It's about this big." He leaned out of his chair and held his hand a few inches above the floor. "So you yell, 'STOP IT!'" His voice, loud and sharp, faded to a croon. "'You naughty dog.'"

When the Starrs returned from Brighton they moved into a new duplex apartment in London. This time Ringo bought the apartment so that no landlord could force them out. Maureen looks after it with the help of the wife of Ringo's chauffeur. According to people who know Ringo well, he rushes home impatiently every evening after work. He is devoted to Maureen, and his friends say he is more relaxed with her than at any other time. Ringo phrased it another way. "She's my anchor. It's back to reality. Everything's normal once I get home.

"I'll say, 'I did *this* today. What did *you* do?' Or, 'That's great meat!' And she'll say, 'I bought this today,' and, "Do you like it?' When we make a new record I fetch it home and say, 'Well, what do you think of it?' Things are, you know, *normal*," he repeated.

Like Ringo, Maureen, who worked in a beauty shop before her marriage, has a quick sense of humor. And like her husband, she is shy and quiet. When the press calls to inquire about the coming baby, Ringo said, "She always says, 'You'll have to speak to Richie.' She calls me 'Richie,'" he explained. "I'm glad she's a quiet girl. I wouldn't want her to be in all the hullabaloo of show business. If I'd wanted someone like that, I'd have married somebody else."

Ringo believes a new husband needs a lot of patience, "especially at the beginning. Because you may go with a girl for years, but as soon as you're married—well, married life is different. Everything changes. You have more responsibility. And having a baby is an even bigger responsibility, because it can't defend itself.

"The thing is, you have to be adaptable," he continued. "If Maureen wants something for the flat and I don't like it—well, things can look nice, but you don't *have* to have them—still I say, 'Get it.' Because she's in the house more than I am, you see, and it would make her happy. A woman has to be adaptable too. If I'm buying a suit, Maureen never says, 'Get *this* one or *that* one.' She lets me make my own choices. But she *can* say, 'I saw this great shirt or tie,' and if she's bought it and I don't like it, I can say: 'Will you change it for something different?'

"When we're going out she'll say, you know, the usual: 'I've got nothing to wear!' You open the closet and fifty thousand dresses fly out! Then she'll say, 'Well, *you* tell me what to wear,' and I'll say, 'Oh, I like this one, or that.'"

When Ringo is not working, as a rule he and Maureen get up late. Sometimes they visit a friend or take a drive in the country, but usually they spend the day indoors and friends come to them for conversation or a game of cards. He likes to play records and tapes, which he makes himself, and recently—since he cannot go to the movies without being mobbed—he bought a projector and now shows films at home.

When he and his wife go out at night it is usually to visit friends or to drop into a London nightclub that is popular with show people. Most of the other customers there leave him alone; when they don't, the management makes them move to another part of the room. In the average restaurant or club it is impossible for him to have a quiet meal because both writers and customers crowd around for autographs.

When he is home, he said, "I just sort of lie around and give orders. Only on some days, though. One day I'll be jumping up, getting a drink or making the tea, and the next couple of days Maureen will do it. I don't mind helping out, but when I'm very tired Maureen just doesn't ask me, because she knows and understands. When I'm working, she gives me everything."

Asked what he thought was the most important requirement for a happy marriage, Ringo replied, "Understanding. Trying to see both points of view. It doesn't matter who your wife is, she's a different person, with different likes and dislikes. You can't always agree on everything. There's no point in saying just like that, 'Well, I won't do it!' Or, 'I'm boss,' just because it's me! If you disagree, you have to say, 'Okay, we won't do it until we've figured it out right.' There's no big boss," he said earnestly. "You just have to sort things out for the two of you. Because, you know, you're joined together in holy matrimony, and the two of you are like one."

Asked to describe Maureen, Ringo smiled shyly. "She's pretty," he said. "She has brown hair and brown eyes. Small features. She's smaller than I am—though she's not so small now. Now she's—*flaring* a bit. These days when I look at her, I keep thinking, She's going to turn into two people! It's a funny feeling. It's marvelous!"

At this point Ringo said, "We both fancy a boy. He and I would be able to wrestle together. But if it's a girl—well, I'll just teach *her* to wrestle. I hope in time to have one or two of each." He shifted in his chair. "You know," he said, "I'd like to be a bit of a pretender—live more like an ordinary workingman. When you're having a kid, you'd like to have it grow up in *that* atmosphere. Then when he's older, maybe twenty-one, I could let him know I'm not working for ten pounds a week. The trouble is, you can't do it. . . ."

Ringo's most fervent hope is that he'll never fail his child. "I just may do something wrong, like not teaching him something I should. But love is the most important thing—that and understanding. You've got to try to get close to a child by fetching your intelligence down to his level. Then you can talk to him."

At this moment Ringo and Maureen are trying to decide how to handle the first few months of the baby's life. "Where we both come from, you just have the baby in your bedroom and *you* look after it. But I was thinking, Well, I can afford it, so we might as well get a nurse for the first couple of months. It will be easier on Maureen, though she doesn't like the idea, really."

One thing he won't do, however—"send my child to boarding school. And I'll never push him. If he passes tests and gets diplomas and everything, all well and good, but I'll never say, 'You won't get this bike unless you go to college!' And I'll let him decide, as he grows up, what he wants to be."

Ringo and Maureen both have considered the possibility that the Beatles may "go out of style." Whether they do or not, Ringo would like to stop going on tour after the age of 30 "because my family will need me." As for future income, he cited a friend's example. "A few years ago this man was selling potatoes door to door. Then he borrowed money and built one house. With the profit from that he built a couple more, and sold those at a profit as well. I respected him because he worked himself up from selling potatoes. And I liked what he was doing, so we formed a firm. Now we're building twelve houses together."

Unlike many people who have experienced extraordinary overnight fame, Ringo remains essentially unchanged. Movie critics were just about unanimous in praising his performance in *A Hard Day's Night*. He is pleased by that, of course, but he does not think of himself as a brilliant actor. Nor does he have a blown-up sense of himself as a musician or as a person. "I know it sounds corny to say it, but I feel just about the same inside as I did before I had all this success. Maybe I have a little more self-confidence, though I've never felt *full* of authority. I'm still a softie." He grinned. "Ask Maureen."

However, fame has made some differences in his life. He finds it harder to make friends "because people look at you differently," and he has to determine whether they like him for himself or for his success.

He has kept some of his Liverpool friends and made others in London among young musicians there. He is resigned to the fact that he has lost his freedom. Every move outside his home has to be made at night, or he must be accompanied by guards who will protect him from crowds. As a home-loving man he is also tired of touring, and like the rest of the Beatles he would like to make more movies and reduce the time he now spends away from his family. But in the end, Ringo declares, "I wouldn't change anything. I'd do it all again!"

The only immediate change that Ringo plans is to buy a house in the country "with land and a fence around it. With a baby," he said, "you have to have some *quiet*. Then, when I'm not working, I'm just going to sit in the garden and watch my kid grow up."

Note

1. In a February 1965 *Playboy* interview, the Beatles downplayed their allegedly poverty-stricken upbringings. The following wit-laced exchange is typical:

    PAUL: Contrary to rumor, you see, none of us was brought up in any slums or in great degrees of poverty. We've always had enough; we've never been starving.

    JOHN: Yeah, we saw these articles in the American fan mags that "Those boys struggled up from the slums. . . ."

    GEORGE: We never starved. Even Ringo hasn't.

    RINGO: Even I.

    See Jean Shepherd, *"Playboy* Interview: The Beatles," *Playboy*, February 1965.

Walter Everett

■

Despite his fame, Ringo has not always received the proper respect he deserves. Ringo always seemed to make everything look easy. In the following analysis, though, Walter Everett, associate professor of music in music theory at the University of Michigan, does an admirable job of describing Ringo's unique qualities as a drummer and the specific techniques that set him apart from other rock drummers, then or now. First, he sets the scene: In August 1962, Starr replaced the Beatles' original drummer Pete Best, who was unceremoniously sacked by manager Brian Epstein. Best made his final appearance with the Beatles at the Cavern Club on August 15; three nights later, Starr made his debut at an annual dance at Hulme Hall in Port Sunlight, across the Mersey from Liverpool on the Wirral peninsula.

"The First EMI Recordings (September 1962–February 1963): New Drummer Ringo Starr"

from *The Beatles as Musicians: The Quarry Men through* Rubber Soul

■ FACED WITH THE NEED for a new drummer, the Beatles turned first to Johnny Hutchinson of the Big Three, who had played with them once in 1960. Hutchinson rejected the offer, so Lennon and McCartney drove to Skegness to invite Ringo Starr (whose band was booked at the North Sea resort through the summer of 1962) to join, which he happily did. Best was fired on the morning of August 16, and Hutchinson filled in for two days before Ringo could join on the 18th, finally solidifying the Lennon-McCartney-Harrison-Starr lineup.

The Beatles' new drummer was born Richard Starkey on July 7, 1940. His earliest musical memories are of Gene Autry, Hank Snow, Buck Owens, Merle Haggard, Ernest Tubb, and other yodeling cowboys. When the teenager showed a strong interest in the drums around 1954, his stepfather bought him "a huge one-sided bass drum" for 30 shillings. For Christmas 1956, Ritchie was given a patchwork kit including bass drum with pedal, snare, hi-hat [a pair of cymbals operated by a foot pedal], tom, and cymbal, and he joined the Eddie Clayton Skiffle Group in February 1957. That kit was replaced in the summer of 1958 by a single-headed British-made Ajax set, purchased with a borrowed £46. This set gave way in late 1959—when Starkey's earnings as a member of Al Caldwell's Texans, later the Raving Texans, later Rory Storm & the Hurricanes, had grown enough to justify it—by a standard mahogany Premier kit, with bass drum and pedal, a very shallow white snare, mounted tom, floor tom, two suspended cymbals (a thin crash and a thicker ride), and hi-hat. The Hurricanes were one of Liverpool's most popular bands early in Ringo's tenure, playing a supporting role in Gene Vincent's Liverpool Stadium concert on May 3, 1960, but after having been overtaken in popularity by the Beatles, they were slipping fast by late 1961. Ritchie adopted the western-sounding stage name "Ringo Starr" in the summer of 1959 ("Ringo Kid" was John Wayne's character in John Ford's 1939 blockbuster *Stagecoach*). He proudly, if amateurishly, embossed the name onto his bass drum head with black tape. Ringo sat for one short set called "Ringo Starr-time" in each performance, covering such tunes as "Alley Oop," "You're Sixteen," "Boys," "Hit the Road Jack," and "What'd I Say?"

The Hurricanes' 1962 gig at Skegness was at Butlin's, a chain of British holiday camps, another of which was located at Pwllheli (on Cardigan Bay), home for the group through the summers of 1960–61. The Hurricanes also got work in Hamburg, meeting the Beatles there in autumn 1960. Ringo had played well with John, Paul, and George in Hamburg on several dates in October 1960 and April 1962, so his great experience in the clubs, his easy friendship with the other Beatles, and the Hurricanes' unpromising future all made Starr the natural replacement for Best. A two-hour rehearsal on the afternoon of August 18 prepared Ringo for his performance that night as a Beatle.

Largely due to a distant microphone placement, the bass drum is often difficult to hear in many of the Beatles' early recordings, except in rare solo and near-solo appearances, as with the measure of bass drum eighths married to McCartney's repeated bass eighths that "whisper" in the refrain of "Do You Want to Know a Secret" and that "chug" in the refrain of "The One after 909" of 1963. Not that Ringo relied on "dropping the bomb" for effect. That factor necessarily aside, Starr's drum technique is much more varied than his predecessor's. Occasionally, Best's ♪♫♪ pattern is heard in his replacement's playing, as in the original single version of "Love Me Do" and in "Twist and Shout," "Please Mr.

Postman," and "Little Child." Along with this or other backbeat patterns on the snare, Ringo's right stick would tap all eighths on the closed hi-hat or ride cymbal, as in "Misery," "Thank You Girl," "I'll Get You," "It Won't Be Long," "Roll Over Beethoven," the verse of "Hold Me Tight," and many others. The ride pattern was heard in $\frac{12}{8}$ for "To Know Her Is to Love Her" and "You Really Got a Hold on Me" and in a shuffle beat for "Chains" and "All My Loving." In selected verses of other numbers, principally the "ravers"—numbers played particularly loudly so as to excite the crowd—the crash cymbal would be used extensively, sometimes hit on all eighths. This is heard in "Little Queenie," "Shimmy Like Kate," "Roll Over Beethoven" (in the final chorus of the December 31, 1962, recording and others), and "I'm Gonna Sit Right Down and Cry (Over You)." In some subdued numbers, as in "A Taste of Honey," Ringo would use his brushes to sweep the snare or—in the bridge—brush a shuffle rhythm. In others, as in "The Honeymoon Song (Bound by Love)" and "Till There Was You," the tom-tom or bongos would replace the snare. The toms are also featured in rowdier songs, including "Sheila" (rolled throughout, reminiscent of Jerry Allison's accompaniment to [Buddy] Holly's "Peggy Sue") and many performances of "Memphis"; rolls on the tom-tom introduce "I'm Gonna Sit Right Down and Cry (Over You)." Both "Lend Me Your Comb" and "Lonesome Tears in My Eyes" feature many dotted and subdivided figures on both toms.

Ringo's cymbals usually help define a song's structure. For instance, in "Twist and Shout," eighths are tapped on the open ride cymbal for the verse but on the closed hi-hat for the solo. The hi-hat is also used for a different color in both "Anna (Go to Him)" and "All I've Got to Do," in which it is closed right after the top cymbal is tapped, for a damping effect in a regularly recurring place (the second half of the third beat in $\frac{4}{4}$) in each measure. Steven Baur has spoken of Ringo's "subtle manipulation of the drum kit's timbral properties," including a later adoption of loose head tunings.

These simple patterns form only the basis of Ringo's technique. What sets him apart from Best, and truly from all rock drummers, are the expressive and idiosyncratic "fills" that often appear at structural points, defining endings of phrases and sections, or providing transitional impetus when necessary. Ringo has said (1964) that his fills are "like a giant walking. My breaks are always slow; usually half the speed of the [other drumming on the] track." He has elaborated in his inimitable prose:

I used to get put down in the press a lot for my silly fills, as we liked to call them, and that mainly came about because I'm a left-handed right-handed drummer; that means I'm left-handed but the kit's set up for a right-handed drummer, so if I come off the hi-hat and the snare . . . any ordinary drummer would come off with the right hand . . . so if I wanna come off, I have to come off with the left hand, which means I have to miss a . . . minuscule of a beat . . . I can go around the kit from the floor tom to the top toms which are on the bass drum easy, but I can't go the other way because the left hand has to keep coming in underneath the right one.

Ringo's joining the group in mid-1962 was good timing for covering the interesting fills in "Chains" and "You Really Got a Hold on Me," both added to the repertoire in early 1963. Among early recordings, Ringo's fills are evident following every verse of "Twist and Shout," in the refrain and the entries to the bridge of "Please Please Me," "Anna (Go to Him)," "There's a Place," "I'm Gonna Sit Right Down and Cry (Over You)," and "Don't Ever Change," in the retransitional hooks of "From Me to You" (using both toms and snare), and in his coda solos in "Thank You Girl." Ringo's fills become interesting—to the point of being essential to a song's artistry—in the middle of the Beatles' recording career, notably in "Day Tripper," "Rain," "Strawberry Fields Forever," and "A Day in the Life." Norman Smith, balance engineer for every Beatle audio recording and mixing session through 1965, said, "He'll start off with one sort of rhythm, then be enlightened by John and Paul as to the particular way they 'hear' it in their original song. Usually, they make the point of referring to some American disc that I probably have never heard of. Ringo then comes up with it." In 1980, McCartney added, "We *always* gave Ringo direction—on every single number. It was usually very controlled. Whoever had written the song, John for instance, would say, 'I want this.' Obviously a lot of the stuff came out of what Ringo was playing; but we would always control it." It has frequently been said that unlike many rock drummers, Starr would play songs rather than simply beats.

■

FIVE

A Way of Remembering: Why the Beatles Still Matter

Wyn Cooper

■

Wyn Cooper has published three books of poems: *The Country of Here Below* (Ahsahta Press, 1987), *The Way Back* (White Pine Press, 2000), and *Postcards from the Interior* (BOA Editions, 2005), as well as a chapbook, *Secret Address* (Chapiteau Press, 2002). His poems, stories, essays, and reviews have appeared in *Poetry, Ploughshares, Crazyhorse, AGNI, Verse, Fence,* and more than sixty other magazines. His poems are included in twenty anthologies of contemporary poetry, including *The Mercury Reader, Outsiders,* and *Ecstatic Occasions, Expedient Forms.*

In 1993, "Fun," a poem from his first book, was turned into Sheryl Crow's Grammy-winning song "All I Wanna Do." He has also cowritten songs with David Broza, David Baerwald, and Bill Bottrell. In 2003, Gaff Music released *Forty Words for Fear,* a CD of songs based on poems and lyrics by Cooper, set to music and sung by the novelist Madison Smartt Bell.

"Girls, Screaming"

■ THE BEATLES SET ME FREE. The first time I saw them on TV, at age seven, I started thinking of going places, of doing something as exciting as what they were doing.

Every Sunday night in our home in Michigan we had grilled cheese sandwiches and Campbell's tomato soup, and watched *The Ed Sullivan Show.* Things were pretty normal, maybe too normal. Maybe we needed to be stirred up by these four young men, so sure of themselves, and having so much fun I could barely believe it.

Why wasn't I having that much fun, even at age seven? And what if I didn't have as much fun as the Beatles seemed to be having when I reached their age? My two sisters are eight and ten years older than me, so they were naturally pretty enamored of the Fab Four. They went on dates, and were driven away from our ranch house in fast cars, laughing as they peeled away from the driveway, happy to get away not because it was bad at home but because it was so much more exciting Out There. My main worry was that I wouldn't have that much fun when I was their age, that all the fun would have been taken away by then, that the world might change that much in a decade. It did change that much, just not in the way we expected it.

The brightness of the early Beatles songs captured me at just the right age, and my state of mind from then on was influenced by their songs, their hair, their clothes, their ironic way in front of the cameras, their fame. More recognized than Jesus, as John Lennon said, thus lighting a fire in the American South.

I began to really listen to them when I had my own stereo, when I was thirteen, which was also the year they broke up. So my early troubled years followed their arc after the fact, from bright and cheery to psychedelic, then down to *Abbey Road*.

When I was twelve or so, my family went to visit friends of my parents in Michigan's Upper Peninsula. One night the adults took my sisters out to dinner, and I was left with a fourteen-year-old, a sixteen-year-old, and an eighteen-year-old, all brothers, the older two ready to mess with me a little. The fireplace was lit, which I loved to see, but all of a sudden the two older brothers were swinging me around in circles, holding on to my feet, my head coming a little too close for comfort to the burning hearth. They were smoking something I had never smelled before, the same thing Bob Dylan is said to have given the Beatles when they first came to the United States to appear on *Ed Sullivan*. No wonder they looked so happy . . .

The soundtrack to this memorable night was "Norwegian Wood," which was played over and over on what passed for a stereo in that old farmhouse. They wanted to make sure I understood what the song really meant, and by the tenth time I was pretty sure it wasn't about wood, or Norway, or bathtubs. I still get a little dizzy when I hear it today, and still I feel free.

The songs the Beatles wrote and sang influenced me greatly as a writer. They showed me what could be done in single songs but also on entire albums, which were put together more like operas or collections of short stories than rock records. I think of the White Album as a book of poems and stories, assembled in an order that makes a kind of sense, which isn't always graspable at first, and that for me is what makes it so enduring. *Magical Mystery Tour, Sgt. Pepper,* and *Abbey Road* are written like operas, too, the order of songs as tied to keys, and the emotions they represent, as much to content, which gives them their power.

Most important, the Beatles also influenced me as a person, made me feel part of a larger community of people whose lives had Beatle soundtracks, haircuts, and even a particular way of walking down the street. The Beatles were living large when I was small, and it struck me that I might do better by going out into the world, which it seemed to me they were doing in a very big way.

All you had to do was listen to the girls screaming.

Anthony DeCurtis

■

In this warmly written piece, Anthony DeCurtis reflects on how the Beatles influenced his own life and career. He also humanizes Yoko Ono, Paul McCartney, and George Harrison in ways that make them appear as flawed and vulnerable human beings.

A contributing editor at *Rolling Stone* magazine, DeCurtis is the author of *In Other Words: Artists Talk about Life and Work,* which includes interviews with Paul McCartney and George Harrison, and *Rocking My Life Away: Writing about Music and Other Matters.* He is a guest editor of *The Best in Rock Fiction,* and he took the Beatles' "Norwegian Wood (This Bird Has Flown)" as inspiration for his short story, "She Once Had Me," published in *Lit Riffs.* He holds a Ph.D. in American literature and teaches at the University of Pennsylvania.

"Crossing the Line: The Beatles in My Life"

■ SOME BANDS CHANGE YOUR LIFE, but deeper still are the bands that shape your life and make you the person you are. The Beatles were that band for me. Of course, that was true for many people of my generation. I was twelve when the band arrived in New York, my hometown, in February of 1964, and looking back, I can see the ongoing impact of so many emotions I felt at the time, glimmerings I sensed but was far too young to understand.

So much of the cultural aspect of what we refer to generally as "the sixties" began at that moment. Yes, the rock and roll explosion of the fifties had filled young people with the energy of rebellion. And the racial components of the music—white kids hearing the call of the cultural wild in black rhythms—were completely in line with the bias-shattering battles of the burgeoning civil rights movement.

Socially conscious folk music and African-American spirituals were the official soundtracks of the civil rights struggle, to be sure. But even though the Beatles were overly nonpolitical, their every gesture was rife with foreshadowing of the generational battles to come. Their hair, most obviously, suggested a gender blurring and sexual provocation that would ultimately liberate both men and women. Though often wrongly dismissed as a fad, those haircuts drew an extraordinary amount of attention in the band's earliest days. Once I saw the Beatles, the days of my pre-adolescent pompadour were fatally numbered.

But what impressed me most about them, beyond their great songs and the originality of their look, was their intelligence. The jaded beat reporters sent to cover the Beatles' arrival at John F. Kennedy Airport— recently renamed to honor the president slain just weeks earlier—were no match for the band's disarming wit. Casual though it seemed, the band's verbal acuity—tellingly reminiscent of John Kennedy's own sly humor—was a weapon in an as-yet undeclared war on adult cynicism and complacency. The Beatles' smarts suggested that young people could have their own way of seeing the world and could articulate their views as well, if not better, than the grown-ups who were supposedly running things. While I never thought this consciously or explicitly, I absolutely felt it, and its implications seemed enormous.

From the start, the Beatles didn't seem merely entertaining or exciting. They felt important. My engagement with them would lead me into a much larger world than I had experienced before, and it's a world that I have lived in since that time. Their being English, to cite just one example, mapped neatly onto my growing literary interests and forced me to grapple with the language (or at least the accents), styles, and customs of another country.

Not that I was unfamiliar with other languages and people from other countries. Quite the contrary. And as far as I was concerned, that was the problem. I grew up in a working-class, immigrant enclave of New York's Greenwich Village and heard Italian spoken nearly as often as English in the streets of my neighborhood. Rock and roll and literature had already launched what I would come to think of as my discovery of America, a product of my frustration with the European outpost I had been born into.

After the Beatles, my relationship to the bohemian elements of the Greenwich Village community that surrounded me began to shift. The world I knew had already started to feel far too cloistered, Catholic, and outmoded. I might as well have been living in a tiny Neapolitan hamlet rather than in the heart of the most dynamic city in the world during one of the century's most cataclysmic decades. The Beatles brought that awareness to me, and made a new life possible.

In addition to their own peerless musical virtues, the Beatles opened the door for harder, more provocative bands like the Rolling Stones, the Who, and the Animals, and began the process of questioning that made the counterculture possible. Being a Beatles fan for me meant facing down friends who held onto their love of more traditional vocal groups like the Four Seasons, and the practice of those arguments was a trial run for turning against the Vietnam War and embracing values that challenged the narrow world of my upbringing.

Two decades after those battles for my soul were pitched and won—and much to my amazement—I began encountering firsthand some of the people who were the agents of those dramatic transformations in my life. The first came early in 1987; it was an interview with Yoko Ono that took place at the Café La Fortuna, the intimate coffee shop near the Dakota that she and John Lennon used to frequent. The place had become something of a shrine to John and Yoko, with many framed photographs of them adorning the walls, which only increased my disorientation as I sat opposite Yoko at our small table. It was the first, though hardly the last, time I felt a dizzying psychic dislocation at meeting someone from the Beatles' universe.

I was there to interview Yoko about a recent trip she had made to the Soviet Union for a news story in *Rolling Stone.* As we spoke I kept flashing on images of her and Lennon that I had seen while growing up—particularly the one of Lennon cradling her in his arms as they left a London courthouse after a 1968 drug arrest. John and Yoko always looked vulnerable in that photo, which may be why it came to mind. It's eerily similar, now that I think of it, to the photograph of Yoko leaving the hospital with David Geffen the night Lennon was murdered. Perhaps those reminders of the pain she had experienced in her life made being in Yoko's presence less daunting.

Before the actual interview started, Yoko asked me dozens of questions about myself. Though she didn't say so, some of them had to do with her astrological interests—where and when I was born, that sort of thing. The one time she seemed taken aback was when I told her about how intensely I had come to love the Rolling Stones, which she clearly regarded as an adolescent interest. I would go on to interview Yoko many times after that, often in her office or in the apartment she had shared with John at the Dakota. When I was working on the liner notes for *The John Lennon Anthology,* we met weekly at her apartment, and she would play me tracks she had selected or was considering for the set, and we would talk about what we wanted the written material accompanying the collection to accomplish.

One day was particularly emotional. As we sat in her kitchen doing an interview, Yoko began to cry as she spoke about John. There was the vulnerability I had remembered in those photos. I left the Dakota with Yoko shortly after that and as we walked down the stairs we were talking about the deadlines for the project and how busy we were. Yoko casually remarked that it was good to be busy, that work could serve as a necessary antidote to excessive self-involvement and a preoccupation with the sadness in our lives. Just as she finished saying those things, we walked through a door into the courtyard where she had seen her husband shot to death.

I have come to think of experiences like that as "crossing the line," somehow moving from being a rapt observer of the Beatles' world to encountering it directly. It's one thing to interview Yoko and intellectually understand that she was married to John Lennon and played a major role in his life. It's quite another to walk with her across the courtyard of the Dakota.

Sometimes the crossing-the-line experience is far more internal. Once after interviewing Yoko at the Dakota I had an erotic dream about her. I'd always been as professional as possible in my dealings with her, but the subconscious knows no boundaries and never lies. She was—and continues to be—slender, youthful, and intellectually playful, with a powerful physical presence. Watching her move gracefully in bare feet amid the perfect whiteness of her living room, or sitting casually on her couch smoking with her as the light flooded through the windows overlooking Central Park, obviously had its effect. You can live with and study someone's work for decades, but nothing has brought me closer to the spirit of Lennon's "I Want You (She's So Heavy)" or his sexual drawings of Yoko than that dream. I didn't just hear it or see it. I got it.

My opportunities to interview Paul McCartney and George Harrison (twice each) provided many more experiences of crossing the line. Probably the most resonant instance occurred when Harrison asked me in 1987, "I understand you spoke with Paul yesterday. How is he doing?" That simple question—and the idea that I could be the conduit of information between those two men—said so much about how the relationships among the band's four members had disintegrated. Harrison and McCartney, of course, would later cooperate during the recording of new tracks for the Beatles' *Anthology*, though Harrison's discomfort at being in McCartney's presence was palpable throughout the interviews filmed for that project. More meaningfully, the two men would reconcile before Harrison's death in 2001.

My two interviews with McCartney involved riveting conversations with him about his relationship with Lennon, and it was intriguing to see how his emotions had shifted between 1987 and 2001. Though it seemed far in the past at the time, Lennon's death had occurred only seven years before the first interview, and McCartney still seemed to be struggling to understand how their friendship had gone so wrong. "Anyway, looking back on it with John," he said at one point, "you know, he was a really great guy. I always idolized him. . . . He was like our own little Elvis in the group."

Fourteen years later, McCartney seemed much more concerned about his stature in relation to Lennon's. To a degree, that's understandable. After Lennon's death, many writers seemed to feel that the best way to praise his achievements was to disparage McCartney's. It's an attitude that is both stupid and unfair. But McCartney's fear that history will somehow forget him drives insecurity to the brink of unseemly desperation. "People would say, 'Paul, people know,'" he told me. "I said, 'Yeah, but what about fifty years in the future?' If this revisionism gets around, a lot of kids will be like, 'Did he have a group before Wings?' There may come a time when people won't know." And his desire to tamper with the legendary "Lennon-McCartney" songwriting credit—putting his name first in certain instances—is petty, completely unworthy of an artist of his importance.

But what I remember most from that second McCartney interview is that it took place just weeks after September 11, 2001. My wife and I had gotten married on September 8, and we were set to fly to Greece for our honeymoon on the day the planes hit the buildings. We never even made it to the airport.

New York was emotionally devastated in the wake of the attacks, and McCartney was doing everything he could to help restore the city. He was raising America's spirits, just as the Beatles had done after John Kennedy's assassination. He organized "The Concert for New York City," but more than that, he was a constant, visible presence at a time when many people were avoiding New York out of fear. When we met to do our interview, he suggested that we walk the three or four blocks from his midtown office to the restaurant where we were to have lunch. I'm certain he was motivated by a desire to show that he wasn't afraid to be in New York. Walking along Sixth Avenue with him and watching the stunned reactions of passers-by turn to elation was sheer joy.

Those actions reflect the best parts of both McCartney's art and personality: Take a sad song and make it better, indeed. It's ironic then that

I was the person to inform him that an anthrax attack had been reported at the NBC studio in New York earlier that day, the first of a series that would set the entire nation on edge. His face went pale and he seemed genuinely fearful, as everyone was, that the attacks would never end.

The story of the Beatles, finally, is a kind of cultural fairy tale. Something that begins with great promise bitterly shatters, and everyone who cared about it has to somehow find a way to preserve its best elements for themselves—and go on. Every few years we find another reason to relive the Beatles' story, to take their sad song and make it better for all of us. Their ultimate gift is the music, needless to say—and, for me, my experiences crossing the line.

Steve Earle

∎

One of the best singers and songwriters working today, roots rocker Steve Earle is well known for his leftist politics and biting lyrics. He has no problem expressing an opinion. Less known, perhaps, is that Earle is a huge Beatles fan. In the Spring 2004 issue of *Tracks* magazine, he wrote about growing up in Schertz, Texas, and seeing the Beatles for the first time on *The Ed Sullivan Show.* "In the beginning, the whole Beatles thing, even for me," he writes, "was as much about fashion—the suits, the haircuts—as music." Their influence on him remains constant to this day. "[Y]ou can hear the Beatles mostly in the way I record and I'm absolutely unapologetic about that," he continues. "I truly believe that no one has done anything to make records sound better than the ones that were made in the early to mid-'60s in England. They are the yardstick. They still sound incredible."

His many records include *Guitar Town, Exit O, Copperhead Road, Train a Comin', I Feel Alright, El Corazón, The Mountain, Transcendental Blues, Jerusalem,* and, most recently, *The Revolution Starts Now.* He has written some of the most gorgeous songs of the rock era, from heartbreakingly beautiful love songs ("My Old Friend the Blues," "Fearless Heart") to poignant pleas for peace ("Jerusalem"), antideath penalty songs ("Over Yonder [Jonathan's Song]") as well as spiritual paeans ("Pilgrim"). Earle is also the author of a collection of short stories, *Doghouse Roses,* and a play, *Karla,* about Karla Faye Tucker, the first woman executed in Texas since the Civil War era. He has even done a bit of acting, on HBO's *The Wire.*

"The Ten Most Important Beatles Songs"

▪ THE BEATLES WERE the most influential artists of their generation . . . that's "artists," not "pop artists."

While the degree that four working-class kids from the wrong part of England affected pop culture can never be underestimated, no performer before, or since, has managed to make such a lasting impression on the world in which they lived. Academics in the forties and fifties didn't publish papers on the sociological implications of Frank Sinatra or Elvis Presley. Hard news journalists don't turn out in force when Coldplay touches down at JFK. By the time they delivered their last record in 1969, the Beatles had elevated pop music to an art form, once and for all.

In retrospect, some have attributed the boys' preeminence to a simple twist of fate, the right band coming along at the right moment in history. As a songwriter who grew up on the Beatles, I subscribe to an alternate theory.

It was the songs.

John Lennon, Paul McCartney, and George Harrison's track record as songwriters is astounding: twenty-one number-one records, hundreds of covers by other artists, including versions by Duke Ellington, Bob Marley, Ray Charles, Otis Redding, Ella Fitzgerald, Chet Atkins, David Bowie, Michael Jackson . . . the complete list would exhaust my allotted space on these pages.

When asked to make a list of the ten most important Beatles songs, I began by defining "important," and I found that I wasn't comfortable with expounding on the social significance of another writer's body of work. I'll leave that to music critic Robert Christgau and Charles Manson. Nor are these my favorite Beatles songs. This list, instead, attempts to trace the Beatles' development as songwriters and to single out a few of the songs that I believe we'll still be singing in a hundred years. In more or less chronological order, they are:

1. "Ticket to Ride." The culmination of four years of writing all day and gigging all night. I chose this song to represent the entire body of work through late 1964. There are *many* other candidates. This is a formulaic pop song created by a craftsman (in this case, John Lennon) at the peak of his form. This was as far as two electric guitars, bass, drums, and a hook line could take them. From here on out the boys were in uncharted territory.

2. "You've Got to Hide Your Love Away." Lennon making the kind of deeply personal statement previously reserved for his prose-poetry meanderings (*In His Own Write* and *A Spaniard in the Works*) for the first time on a Beatles record.

3. "Yesterday." Paul McCartney sticks to the formula but takes it to another level and beyond a teenage audience.

4. "Nowhere Man." Lennon applies his newfound lyrical voice to a melodic rocker.

5. "Norwegian Wood." Lennon penned blues for the sexual revolution in which he wakes up and finds that the *girl* is gone.

6. "Michelle." McCartney tries out his high school French over a stunning café-inspired melody.

7. "Eleanor Rigby." The darkest, and therefore my favorite, Paul McCartney song.

8. "Strawberry Fields Forever." Groundbreaking, impressionistic Lennon lyrics that inspired what producer George Martin referred to as the "song picture" recording process of the *Sgt. Pepper* sessions and set the course for the album-oriented music industry of the next thirty years.

9. "Hey Jude." McCartney keeps us singing along for seven minutes and eleven seconds.

10. "Something." Sadly, none of us will ever know what this list would look like had George Harrison been a few years older. Working in the shadow of Lennon and McCartney had to be a somewhat less-than-nurturing environment for a fledgling songwriter, if not downright intimidating. Years of fighting for his place on Beatles albums vindicated him in the end, however. "Something" has been covered more than any other Beatles song with the exception of "Yesterday."

Well, that's my list, and I'm sticking to it. Compiling it was challenging. Defending it is futile, as glaring omissions are unavoidable when one is asked to choose only ten songs from the greatest catalog in pop music history. Criticism of art in any form is a thankless task at best, especially for an artist, and here, at the end of my labors I find myself wondering if my agreed fee will be adequate compensation for the anguish of the past twenty-four hours. If not, then perhaps you, the reader, may afford me one compensation:

The next time you find yourself tempted to equate Oasis with the Beatles, refer to this list.

Colin Hall

■

"Mendips," 251 Menlove Avenue, John Lennon's childhood home in Liverpool, has been open to the public since March 2003. He lived there for eighteen years with his Aunt Mimi, his Uncle George (who died in 1955), Mimi's three cats, his pet dog, Sally, and a succession of student lodgers for whom his Aunt Mimi cared from 1949 until 1963. John first began living in Mendips in 1945 when he was just five years old. He finally moved out in 1963, aged twenty-three, just as the Beatles' star rocketed into the ascendant. It was the longest he was to live anywhere. Mimi sold the house in 1965 and moved to Poole in Dorset where John had bought her a bungalow overlooking the harbor. When Mendips came up for sale in 2002, John's widow, Yoko Ono Lennon, bought it and generously donated it to the National Trust so that "it would be well looked after as a place for people to visit and see." Restored to how it was in the late fifties, Mendips now stands as a celebration of John's life where, as Yoko explains, "everyone who loves John's music and his message of peace can see for themselves where it all began." In keeping with Yoko's wishes the National Trust employs a custodian who lives at Mendips to care for it and to act as a guide for visitors to the property. Since 2004 Colin Hall, who is also a music journalist, has held that post, and here he provides an insight into what his job involves.

"Inside Mendips"

■ "How DID YOU get this job?"

"Living in John Lennon's house—how good is that?"

As custodian of Mendips, John Lennon's childhood home in Liverpool, these are questions I am asked on a daily basis. The answer to the first is simple—I applied for it! As for the second, the answer is that as jobs go, it is pretty damn good. True, I do have to clean, wash, and garden, but once visitors start to arrive it becomes exhilarating and constantly rewarding. Faced with the positive energy these guests bring into the house, it could never be anything else.

Such is John's continued, universal appeal that the guest book at Mendips reads like the index to an atlas. There seems to be no part of the world his songs, his message of peace, and the music of the Beatles have not touched. I never know who is going to appear when the bus that brings visitors to the house arrives. It never fails to amaze me.

In recent years it has brought a Quarry Man, Rod Davis, to the house, several ex-student lodgers, and, memorably, Peter Tork of the Monkees. But the guests don't have to be celebrities to spring surprises.

In August 2004, during the busiest week in the season, two Japanese ladies appeared at the doorstep, dressed in full national attire. This was their way of honouring John. They looked sensational. All eyes were on them, yet they maintained a quiet dignity all through the brief talk I give at the beginning of each tour. Immediately after I finished, they left the lounge and went upstairs. As I talked to other visitors in the hall, we heard sobbing coming from overhead. I went to investigate. The weeping was coming from inside John's tiny bedroom where I found one of the Japanese ladies lying on John's bed, racked in tears. The other stood close by, also crying. Gently I coaxed them into Aunt Mimi's room where they sat on the bed and recovered their composure. It took a while. In halting English the lady who had thrown herself on John's bed explained that she had had a tough childhood and that John's music had helped and comforted her through that very difficult time. She had been so devastated by his death that once inside his room she had been unable to hold back her emotions.

Remarkably, this is not unusual. Tears are often shed when guests visit John's bedroom or look at the family photograph album and see pictures of him taken as a small boy at the house. An American visitor, who had lived close to the Dakota in New York, became instantly tearful when she saw a photograph from 1963 of John standing in the garden at Mendips holding his baby son, Julian. She told me she had seen John and Yoko many times outside the Dakota and would always say hello. They were neighbors and always friendly.

The emotions stirred by visiting Mendips are not always expressed in tears, or solemnity. People can get very demonstrative, particularly during the last week in August when Liverpool hosts a fantastic Beatles festival. Thousands of visitors from around the globe descend on the city for a week-long party. Guests turn up at Mendips, often dressed as the Beatles. *Sgt. Pepper* outfits are particularly popular. On several occasions I have been spontaneously embraced by visitors in need of "a hug," as a means of giving vent to their feelings.

A greater insight into just what John means to visitors to Mendips can be gained from dipping into the comments they write in the guest books:

"Every night I talked to John—I think I actually prayed to John whose face was everywhere in my bedroom. Thank you for the peace you brought into my life, xxx."

"Everyday since 1963, there has not been a day that goes by that in some way I don't pay tribute to the brilliance of John, Paul, George and Ringo. You are the lifeblood that flows through me. Thank you for the greatest music and memories of my entire life."

"Thank you Yoko for keeping John's memory alive."

"I don't really have any memories of John Lennon because I am only 11 but my Mum enjoys listening to The Beatles and that's why I am here today. I really like the house and The Beatles look cool."

"Your spirit brought me here. Thank you John."

"'Imagine' was my most memorable song as a child and my introduction to world issues. Thank you."

"This has been such a moving experience—to be in Liverpool and especially in this house. John's music has helped me celebrate the good times and got me through the difficult times."

"Time does not diminish your magic and passion. Thanks for the music and the memories."

Most visitors are keen to establish that I am a bona fide John Lennon "fan." It really matters to them. I think they know the answer, but like the reassurance of hearing me confirm it. Indeed, it would not be possible to be custodian if I did not really like John Lennon, love his music and the Beatles. Truthfully, the Beatles have been a passion since I was a teenager. Born and brought up in Liverpool and on the Wirral peninsula across the Mersey, I was a teenager in the sixties, which makes it nigh impossible *not* to have fallen under the spell of what Klaus Voormann, an early Beatles cohort from their Hamburg days, once described to me as "the band of bands."

What seals it with the fans is that on Saturday, July 6, 1957, at St. Peter's Church in Woolton, I attended the garden fête where the

Quarry Men played and where, famously, John met Paul for the first time. As a young boy I lived for nearly nine years in Woolton, the same area in which Mendips is located. Every year my Mum and Auntie Elsie took me to the village fête. It was an annual treat. That year I remember they took me specifically to see the City of Liverpool Police Dogs perform. It was a beautiful sunny day, and I remember those dogs very well. But, sadly, my memories of the Quarry Men are not so vivid.

My Beatles memories pale into insignificance, however, when compared to visitors to Mendips. Their encounters with John and the Beatles are always interesting and reveal just how accessible the group was in the early days. One of my favourites is this one from a man in his late fifties who, some forty-three years on, was still clearly miffed:

> John Lennon got me into trouble with my girlfriend. I was at the Cavern in early 1963 to hear The Beatles. They had just released "Please Please Me." At the end of their set they stood behind a booth, signing copies of the single. I was there with my new girlfriend who was mad about them, especially John. I really fancied her and so, being eager to impress, I volunteered to get their autographs for her. It was stiflingly hot and packed solid with fans desperate to get their records signed. It took ages. Eventually my turn came and I got all four Beatles' signatures . . . or so I thought. Pleased as punch I returned to my girlfriend and handed over the prized possession. She was thrilled but, as she eagerly studied the names written on the record label, her expression changed from glee to abject disappointment. "Who's this 'Bonaparte'?" she inquired angrily, pointing at the disc. Seizing it from her hands I looked closely at the names written on the label . . . Paul McCartney, George Harrison, Ringo Starr and 'Bonaparte'! Clearly this was John's little joke but it had not gone down at all well with my girl—I mean—I had failed to get the proper signature of the Beatle she adored the most! What kind of boyfriend was I? She was in tears, I was desperate to please, so back I went. I was well pissed off, I'll tell you—the queue was as big as ever. I remember John giving me a cheeky grin as he signed again . . . this time as himself. What peed me off even more was that a few weeks later my girlfriend chucked me—and she kept the bloomin' single! How much would that be worth now I often ask myself—a signed copy of "Please Please Me" on the original red Parlophone label? I could retire on that.

Another fascinating memory of encountering the Beatles up close is this one from a visitor from Birmingham that shows the more combative side of John's nature—or his leadership qualities—depending on your point of view:

> I saw The Silver Beatles in 1960. They played the British Road Services Club in Bromford, Irdington. They played in between the bingo. Nobody seemed very impressed. Three years later I saw them play as the Beatles in Birmingham itself—at The Plaza I think it was—and it was a different story. The place was packed and the girls were going crazy. I was right at the front and remember John got into a fight with some Teds [Teddy Boys] who were leaning on the stage, taking the mickey out of The Beatles' stage suits. He jumped off stage to confront them and immediately a scuffle broke out. Fortunately Security split them up before anyone got really hurt.

Another visitor to Mendips who had also been at this show explained why the Teds had put in an appearance at The Plaza. Jerry Lee Lewis was set to play Birmingham the same evening but had cancelled at the very last moment. So, in town with nothing to do, feeling disgruntled and looking to vent their frustration, some of them turned up at The Plaza instead!

One anecdote I enjoyed came from an American visitor. A giant of a man, I was not surprised to learn he had once served in the U.S. Navy. His encounter with John occurred during the Beatles' tumultuous first visit to the States in 1964. Like many before and since he learned that we may speak the same language but it doesn't mean we understand each other any better:

> I was on shore leave in Miami during the Beatles first visit to the USA. By pure coincidence I was in the bar at the same hotel where the Beatles were staying. I was ordering some beers when I became aware of John standing next to me. I was fascinated—not only was this the first time I'd met a Brit but here was John Lennon whose face—along with the rest of the Beatles—was all over the TV and newspapers in the U.S. at that time. They were the big story of the moment and here I was standing right next to one of them. He was smoking and I was intrigued by the way he was holding his cigarette— between his third and fourth fingers. That's not how we held our

cigarettes in the USA. I must have been staring a bit too hard because John asked me if I'd like a "fag." Being an all-American boy and unaware that "fag" was English slang for a cigarette I countered immediately by saying, "No thanks, man, I'm here for the girls." I remember emphasizing the word "girls"! I wanted him to be in no doubt I was not remotely interested in what I thought was on offer! The other alternative was to start a fight! John just smiled and continued with his order. When his drinks arrived and he turned to go he said, "Nice to meet you—and good luck with the chicks!" Only later when someone explained to me the English meaning of the word "fag" did I realize the absolute innocence of John's remark!

I am honoured when people choose to share memories that are clearly very precious. One of the most touching stories I heard was from Anthony Bowman, a generous, unassuming man. He came to the house one evening to inquire if the National Trust would be interested in an old fifties black-and-white television that he owned and which was, remarkably, still in working condition. He wished to donate it to either Mendips or 20 Forthlin Road (Paul McCartney's former Liverpool home, also owned by the National Trust). I found his story moving because it was told without boast, just as simple, honest fact:

> In 1960 Paul and John invited me to join their band as lead singer. I was already the singer with a band called the Bootleggers (later, the Blackjacks). We all played the Casbah. That's how all the Liverpool groups got to know each other—by playing the same venues. Also my girlfriend (later to become my wife), Valerie Danher, was a distant relation of Paul's. It was fashionable at the time to have a lead singer who did not play an instrument. Here in Liverpool Rory Storm and the Hurricanes had popularised that sort of line-up. I thought about it but declined because I was an apprentice TV engineer and the Blackjacks were all mates of mine from work so it would have been a bit awkward. Also with the boom in television my job was too secure for me to leave it on the off chance of "making it." A year or so later I moved to the Wirral [peninsula] and heard that Paul and the Beatles were going to make a record. My band had called it a day three months earlier.

One of the most frequent inquiries I receive is whether I am ever aware of a "presence" or "spirit" inside Mendips. At these times I would desperately like to say I have encountered John on the stairs or, in the early hours of the morning, have been awoken to hear the sound of his guitar being strummed in his bedroom. I know it's what many fans would love to hear. The truth is that I have experienced no such psychic moments. Mendips is an extremely comfortable and easy house to live in. For me that is how the "spirit of the house" expresses itself. It has felt like "home" ever since I came here. However, one particular morning something unusual did occur that made me stop and think.

In the Morning Room (John's favourite downstairs room where he would spend hours drawing) there hangs a splendid clock, Uncle George's clock. Presented to him by Woolton Tavern, the original hangs in the Dakota but for years its home was here in the Morning Room. It was of great sentimental value to John. When Sean was born he had Aunt Mimi ship it out to him in New York so that he could share it and other childhood memories of growing up in Liverpool with his new son. When Yoko donated the house to the National Trust she knew that the Morning Room would not be the same without Uncle George's clock, so she had an exact replica made for the house.

When Mendips opened for its third season in 2005, for some reason, Uncle George's clock stopped ticking. Whatever I did, however much I wound it, I could not get it to work. On the morning of June 5, 2005, I especially wanted it to be working because it was the fiftieth anniversary of George's death. As I set the pendulum swinging once more—fully expecting it to stop within five minutes as it had done for the past three months—I shouted at the clock in a loud voice to "honor George" by working again. To my amazement it kept going all day. A week later it was still ticking!

One of the great honours of being custodian is that occasionally I do get to meet people who were very close to John and the Beatles. Their insights into John or of life inside Mendips in the fifties are invaluable. Such information helps me to fill in the small everyday details that fans love to hear—it makes their being inside Mendips all the more real.

Julia Baird (John's half-sister) mentioned that one of her abiding memories of the house was the smell of apples and fish in the kitchen. Mimi and George grew apples in the gardens and Mimi was well known in the family for her apple pies. She was also a great cat lover and would often cook fish for them (and no doubt for John, George, and the student lodgers to eat as well).

Alan Bannister and Jim Dawker were student lodgers at Mendips in 1961 and remember John returning from Hamburg with a white label

promo copy of "My Bonnie," the record he and the Beatles had cut as
the backing group for Tony Sheridan. He was very excited and played it
to everyone who would listen, eager to learn their opinion. Alan and Jim
were very polite to John to his face but in private admitted they didn't
think much of the record and, in fact, were convinced John would need
to find something better to do for a career than play music. As Alan says
now—how wrong can a person be?

The more I live and work at Mendips the more I realise how appropriate is the job title of "custodian." As custodian, I am definitely the
"guardian" or "keeper" of the physical space that was once John's much
cherished childhood home, but on another level I feel my role is as
"keeper" of the memories his fans share with me. When they visit
Mendips it is not just to say they've sat on John's bed; it is much more
than that. It is a journey of discovery, a modern-day pilgrimage. John
would undoubtedly feel very uncomfortable with that concept but
he would also realize the reality of what Mendips has come to symbolise for his fans. The tour provides fans with a great sense of community.
They come to discover what made John who he was. Here, their love of
John and the Beatles is brought into focus and, hopefully, made sense
of. For younger fans it is an opportunity to connect with the man whose
music and message inspire them. Older fans come for that as well, and
also to reconnect with their own youth when having fun seemed easier
and hope for a better world was, fleetingly, within our grasp. Mendips is
a physical affirmation of their relationship with John and the ideals they
shared. It unites them in a way they have not been able to do since gathering to mourn his passing. As I have become more familiar with my
role as custodian, so I have come to understand that it is also my role to
help preserve these memories. For me that is an honour and what being custodian is all about. Such lofty ideals come resoundingly down to
earth, however, when Americans inquire, "So you're the janitor?"

John would have liked that one.

Note: Visits to Mendips are by prior arrangement only—to book a place on a
scheduled tour visitors are requested to contact the National Trust in Liverpool at
0151 427 7231.

Ashley Kahn

■

Thirty-five years after the Beatles broke up, or year 35 *Anno Beatli* as journalist Ashley Kahn explains in this essay, the world has changed irrevocably,
and yet, on a more profound level, it remains essentially the same. As it was
during the sixties, war clouds darken our fragile planet (indeed, the day this
piece was filed, bombing attacks terrorized London). Do we still need the
Beatles? Kahn answers with a resounding *yes*.

Kahn, who has written often on the Beatles, is the author of *A Love
Supreme: The Story of John Coltrane's Signature Album, Kind of Blue: The
Making of the Miles Davis Masterpiece,* and *The House That Trane Built: The
Story of Impulse Records,* and is the cultural reporter for National Public Radio's "Morning Edition." He was the primary editor of *Rolling Stone: The Seventies,* and has also served as a music editor at VH1 and as a tour manager
with Paul Simon, Peter Gabriel, Ladysmith Black Mambazo, Debbie Harry,
and the Jazz Passengers, among other groups.

"All You Need"

■ MY GENERATION WAS the one that just missed their arrival. We
didn't know of a time when the world was more black-and-white. We
couldn't yet measure how much color they brought into the world.

We grew up thinking the Beatles had always been with us. Songs like
"Help!" and "Ticket to Ride" were already oldies. We reached cultural
consciousness at the time of *Sgt. Pepper* and the White Album. We approached them carefully, studiously—like darkened doorways promising entry to a hip and mature world we couldn't wait to explore.

My family was living in suburban New York in the summer of '67, my
folks in the first years of marriage and parenthood. My father was struggling through medical residency, my mother with paralyzing depression. The Fogliettas were downstairs, and their teenage daughter would
come up to baby-sit, bringing her well-played copy of *Sgt. Pepper.*

We listened to the LP over and over. I would spread out the hinged
cover and read the black lyrics printed on bright red background, learning more of life than any grade school lesson could teach. I was seven, but
old enough to feel the deep, aching sadness of "She's Leaving Home."
Two years later, after the lawyers and therapists and a divorce that was
rough on everyone, we moved to Cincinnati. Mom stayed behind.

My generation reached puberty around 1970, just when the Beatles split up. We shared in the common disbelief and disappointment. Teenage years followed, then adulthood. The Beatles still cast a long and enduringly refreshing shadow. Reissues of their music topped the charts every ten years. Radio continued to play their songs, even as styles moved on. The message in their music never flagged in relevance.

As adulthood melted into middle age, MTV happened. The cable channel and cable itself—and later the Internet—sparked an information revolution and an obsession with music and popular culture, our traditions, and recurring look-backs like never before. It seemed all paths of inquiry and influence led back to the Beatles. They were the source.

They were the pioneers, the hyphen between singer and songwriter. They were the true inheritors of the promise of Porter and Gershwin: intelligent song craft based on folk forms, raised to the heights of art *and* popularity. They forged the pattern of the modern day pop career, defining each rung on the ladder to lasting pop stardom. Write the song. Record the hit. Make the green. Live the life. Grow the beard. Get the guru. Find the way. Sail the ship. Chop the tree.

In 2001, two jetliners smashed into two towers a few miles south of my New Jersey apartment. As I read through the collective obituaries in *The New York Times* I noticed that among the thousands who perished, a significant number were from my generation. Within days, John Lennon's ode to innocence and dreaming became their dirge and a musical symbol of the country's grief.

I'm happy to argue that "Imagine" is a Beatles tune, spiritually and musically consistent with other words of wisdom in the songs. "The Word." "Come Together." "Let It Be." "All You Need Is Love." (I'm happier still that the choice of a 9/11 anthem was not left to the likes of any flag-waving spin doctor, or "Born in the U.S.A." may well have been nominated, to the annoyance of Bruce Springsteen. Again.)

When the Beatles were flying high, it was an easy time to lie back and imagine. The sixties helped make it so: Tolerance and free-thinking bloomed all around. Notions of peace seemed as probable and easy to reach as the music that four musicians delivered to us with easy, melodic charm and uncanny regularity. With each album, the Beatles pulled back the huge curtain of conformity a little more, revealing how the future would sound—and how things could be.

Then 1970 came. "Nothing's really changed," Lennon complained that year, looking around at what the sixties had wrought, at what had come of the possibilities the Beatles had sung about. "The dream is over, it's just the same only I'm thirty and a lot of people have got long hair, that's all!" In America, an administration was in power promising a turn to the right like never before (Attorney General John Mitchell's promise). In Vietnam, U.S. troops were still fighting, the conflict escalating despite all the marches and moratoriums.

It was only a year later that Lennon sat down at a white piano and wrote "Imagine": a Beatles sound carrying an enduring message conceived in a time filled with lost hope and darkness and dying. Little could he have known how timeless and healing his song would prove to be thirty years later.

It's now year 35 *Anno Beatli:* thirty-five years since the Beatles disbanded. Perspectives have changed, memories have melted away, and U.S. troops are overseas. Again.

I can't help being the curmudgeon, like Lennon in 1970. The spirit of the sixties seems to have been little more than a quaint, fleeting dalliance and idyllic daydreaming. Who wears their hair long anymore? Casual Fridays and artfully hidden tattoos might be the quiet remnants of all the free-living and free-thinking of forty years past.

In today's I-Me-Mine, bling-bling world, I find that the lasting significance of the Beatles is all about their track record (all those number ones that can still reach number one) and is too often measured by the value of their song catalog (owned in part, and ill-used, by Michael Jackson). Call me an innocent ("you may say I'm a dreamer . . .") but with all the youthful dreams and planet-changing visions the Beatles wove into their work, it seems that their musical revenues should help keep those visions alive, that it should somehow feed public need, not private greed.

But let me step down from my soapbox. After all, the true and enduring worth of the Beatles was not their commercial achievements but the life lessons in the songs that have yet to diminish in value. Lessons in acceptance and tolerance and compassion and positive belief in the future that even a wide-eyed seven-year-old could grasp. I still marvel at the mature wisdom and musical genius shared between those four twenty-somethings, which they shared with all of us.

I am forty-five now, older than my father was when he remarried. I'm part of a generation that still listens to the Beatles and smiles, holding on to a hope that generations to come will be able to hear the lessons in their music that mine did. In 2006, Paul McCartney *turned* sixty-four. As the lyric asks, will we still need them?

The answer? It's easy . . .

Greg Kot

■

In this thoughtful essay, Greg Kot looks at the remarkable achievements of the Beatles and concludes that we will never see their likes again. We might as well finally get used to it.

Greg Kot has been the *Chicago Tribune*'s pop music critic since 1990. He also cohosts *Sound Opinions,* the world's only rock and roll talk show, on radio, TV, and the Internet. His biography of Wilco and the state of the music industry, *Wilco: Learning How to Die,* was published in 2004.

"Toppermost of the Poppermost"

■ THE BEATLES screwed it up for everyone—including themselves.

They joked about being the biggest band in the world—the "toppermost of the poppermost"—and then pulled it off with such self-deprecating humor, such sustained musical brilliance, such casually savvy self-marketing, such off-the-cuff charm, that no rock band since has even come close to achieving that level of fame and influence. Not even John, Paul, George, and Ringo could pull it off twice.

Those who had the best shot of achieving Beatles-like fame in recent decades—whether U2, R.E.M., Pearl Jam, Oasis, Nirvana, or a half dozen others—fell short, for various reasons. We live in the era of the niche band, the subgenre, the cult following. It is a world defined by rapidly reproducing Internet fanzines and audio blogs, countless cable TV channels, home recording studios, and direct-to-consumer music distribution. There's something out there for everyone, and everyone has their own pet band.

Sure, it's still possible for Coldplay or U2 to sell millions of albums by enlisting a multinational corporation to distribute, advertise, and market their music. But the mainstream is a much more complex and multilayered beast today than it was forty years ago when three television networks dominated the dissemination of information and entertainment. When the Beatles first appeared on *The Ed Sullivan Show* in February 1964, they were seen by 73 million people. The impact was instant, the domination total. At one point that year, the Beatles held the top five spots in the *Billboard* singles chart, a still unmatched achievement. By year's end, they had released six top-ten albums and starred in a movie, *A Hard Day's Night*.

The Beatles had it all, the bastards. They made leading a revolution look easy. Yes, they had huge sales and worldwide celebrity, but not at the expense of artistic excellence. It's dangerous to simply speculate why that was, but here's my best guess. They were at the leading edge of a still relatively new art form and they essentially got the opportunity to invent what it meant to be a rock 'n' roll band. They didn't screw it up, even though they didn't really know what they were doing. Nor did they have the ability to calculate their impact or choreograph their rise, even if they did joke about it. On the contrary, John Lennon, Paul McCartney, George Harrison, and Ringo Starr were startled when America embraced them so voraciously from the start. All they were doing, Lennon explained, was crossing the ocean to sell America's homegrown music—Chuck Berry's rock 'n' roll, Little Richard's twist and shout—back to it.

Of course, the Beatles did much more than that. Like all geniuses, they put their own imprint on all that had preceded them, and reshaped it in a way that made it impossible to hear pop music the same way after "I Want to Hold Your Hand," "Norwegian Wood," or "Strawberry Fields" was carved in our collective heads.

Their example still resonates, and they made it seem effortless. After they split up, all that changed. Not even the Beatles, it turns out, could be as big as the Beatles were in their moment.

In the band's authorized account of their rise and fall, the eight-volume home video *The Beatles Anthology* (Turner), the band members do not sugarcoat the days leading to their April 1970 divorce.

Harrison recounts a "dreadful and unhappy" demise. Starr looks back on "months and years of misery." McCartney blames it all on the beleaguered Yoko Ono: "I always thought [Lennon] would have to clear the decks of us to give her enough attention." And Lennon, mincing no words, as usual, likens the quartet's many splintered decline to "a slow death."

But the Beatles didn't die. Instead, their story has been more like a never-ending series of resurrections and reincarnations. "Phony Beatlemania has bitten the dust," the Clash's Joe Strummer spat in 1979, but Beatlemania, phony or otherwise, has outlived Strummer and his band.

The Beatles aren't the only pop deities to enjoy new life after death, of course. From Elvis Presley to Tupac Shakur, few icons ever die, at least in the figurative sense. Jimi Hendrix released only three studio albums in his lifetime, but more than four hundred "new" Hendrix albums have surfaced since his death. The Grateful Dead called it quits in 1995 when Jerry Garcia died, but each year since has brought a fresh bounty of material from the Dead's bottomless trove of concert recordings.

This practice, now commonplace for any act with an archive to pillage, was all but unheard of when the Beatles broke up. But the Beatles raised the stakes for everybody—not just the artistic standards, but the possibility that their work would continue to have value decades down the line.

During their lifetime as a working group, Lennon, McCartney, Harrison, and Starr created a template for how to be a rock band, defining the classic two-guitar, bass, and drums lineup and then expanding the possibilities of that configuration in seemingly infinite ways. Without one another, the parts never measured up to the whole. With few exceptions—Lennon's *Plastic Ono Band,* Harrison's *All Things Must Pass,* McCartney's *Band on the Run*—the ex-Beatles ceased to become a creative force. But they entered a new phase, and helped define the notion of a rock 'n' roll band as a corporation, a money machine that took the art of repackaging, reselling, and perpetuating itself to new levels in the mid-nineties.

In the twelve months that followed November 1995, the first year of the campaign to sell a series of *Anthology* CDs containing outtakes and rarities, the Beatles were the biggest-selling act in America—even though they had essentially been "dead" for twenty-five years. During that year, *The Beatles Anthology* sold 3.3 million double CDs and *Anthology 2* 1.3 million, according to Soundscan. Meanwhile, the band's back catalog sold more than 6 million records.

This from a band that had barely been on speaking terms since its demise. They had traded lawsuits, written nasty songs about one another, and said repeatedly that all the worthwhile music they ever made had already been released—that is, until there was money to be made from the *Anthology* campaigns.

But it didn't matter. Mediocre Beatles, erratic Beatles were better than no Beatles at all, the public resoundingly reminded those who dared criticize the band for scavenging its archives and then selling the scrapings as top-dollar "new" CDs.

As one teary-eyed fan blubbers in the Beatles video documentary, "Please, let them come back to us, at least once, just to be the same that they used to be, with no changes at all . . ." It would be easy to distill never-ending Beatlemania to this one quote, a case of incurable baby boomer nostalgia, the collective yearning of the original Beatles fans to relive their youth, over and over again.

But an analysis of the *Anthology* sales figures suggests that wasn't the case. In that twelve-month boom for all things Beatles in 1995–96, more than half the buyers were either teenagers or twenty-somethings. Boomers in their forties made up only about one-quarter of the sales, perhaps because they already had the best of the Beatles catalog in their collection and were therefore relatively immune to a multimillion-dollar marketing campaign aimed at persuading them to pay top-shelf prices for second-tier Beatles songs.

Though younger generations of listeners bought into the Beatles second coming, they have not responded to the Beatles in the same way the band's generational peers did. Once, there was little doubt that the Beatles were the most influential band of their time; the British Invasion, which they spearheaded, led to the emergence of a rock-band culture in America. Thousands of kids took to their garages, guitars in hand, after seeing one of the Beatles performances on *The Ed Sullivan Show* in 1964, and bands like the Byrds and Creedence Clearwater Revival were born.

But the Beatles no longer are ground zero for contemporary rock. The Velvet Underground, with their darker leanings and a sound at once more primitive and more experimental than the Beatles, have had a far greater impact on the sounds and attitudes that have shaped rock in the last twenty years. And today's rising bands—the Killers, the Strokes, Franz Ferdinand—are taking their cues from seventies post-punk and New Wave bands such as Joy Division, New Order, and Gang of Four, rather than the Beatles or even the Rolling Stones.

The most celebrated Beatles acolytes of the last decade, Brit pop stars Oasis, flirted with massive success in America during the mid-nineties, but haven't been able to sustain the momentum. Their charm, their humor, and above all their songs simply weren't good enough to maintain more than a sizable cult following outside their native United Kingdom. The notion of rock royalty—of a band so thoroughly dominating its time the way the Beatles did during the period between 1964 and 1970—becomes more remote with each year, as pop culture continues to divide atomlike into ever-smaller pockets of creativity. U2's Bono, for one, is horrified by this development. He insists that rock needs to be big to be relevant. But he's wrong. Rock, reinvented countless times and now fifty years old, must content itself with smaller brands of innovation that can still be immensely satisfying (albeit on a much smaller scale). There will be no "new Beatles," so let's get over it, shall we?

This void testifies to how singular the Beatles' original achievement actually was. It was fame and celebrity built on a foundation of music.

Today, music's role in the fame game—even in the megasuccess of such best-selling pop stars as Eminem, Jennifer Lopez, Madonna, or Justin Timberlake—is that of just another revenue stream in a menagerie of product lines: movies, TV commercials, clothing lines, etc.

The Beatles put music at the center of popular culture; specifically, rock music. The group's fluency across that spectrum, from protometal ("Helter Skelter") to progressive rock (side 2 of *Abbey Road*), psychedelia ("I Am the Walrus") to folk ("I've Just Seen a Face"), remains staggering. No music seemed out of their reach. George Martin, their longtime producer, once explained why: "Their curiosity was their strength," he said. "They always wanted to peer over the edge of the horizon, and ask, 'What other sounds can we make?' They never did anything twice."

But the same could be said of a dozen bands from that era, not to mention P. J. Harvey, Radiohead, the Flaming Lips, or Nirvana from more recent times. What put the Beatles a cut above everyone was their humor, their self-confident ease as performers and human beings. They projected a clean-cut, boyish magnetism that charmed their elders while maintaining a dry, subversive humor that spoke to their peers. They managed the nearly impossible feat of winning acceptance within the mainstream while continuing to function as independent spokesmen for a generation determined to forge a new path.

Even their self-marketing, their commercial ambition—while appearing on *The Ed Sullivan Show* or rolling out a cartoon such as *Yellow Submarine*—seemed utterly effortless and in keeping with their collective personality. They always seemed a step ahead. The *Anthology* campaigns, in contrast, rang hollow, perhaps because they were so earnest, solemn, and sentimental—everything the Beatles were not. More to the point, the music wasn't up to Beatles standards. Two wretched "new" songs built on scratchy Lennon discards, "Free as a Bird" and "Real Love," were dredged up and patched together in the studio to help sell the project. No one remembers them now.

For the first time, the Beatles let us down. In their prime, the Beatles never broke a sweat. *Beatles for Sale*? The boys were always in on the joke. Now, Beatlemania just sounded forced, like the boys of '64 were trying too hard to recapture what had long been lost.

If nothing else, it was a reminder that the biggest band in the world did die, for good, in 1970, and we'll never see the likes of them again— no matter how many bands, including the Beatles themselves, try to reach the summit of Mount Poppermost.

Paul Mariani

■

Paul Mariani is a poet and biographer of books on William Carlos Williams, John Berrymen, Robert Lowell, and Hart Crane. In this wistful piece, he recalls the reasons why the Beatles touched him and continue to resonate with him decades after they ceased to exist as a group.

"Remembering the Beatles"

■ OF COURSE, they impacted on me, as they did millions of others, but in odd ways. Song lyrics—what Ezra Pound once called melopoeia—were always difficult for me to figure out. But for someone raised on Elvis Presley and Bo Diddley, I was as struck as anyone of my generation by these new and surprising arbiters of taste, these larger-than-life figures, four kids from working-class Liverpool who appeared one night on *The Ed Sullivan Show* on my black-and-white screen—as Elvis had earlier—amid the screams of teenage girls that refused to abate—it seemed—during their entire time on stage.

I remember them coming down the steps off the plane that had brought them to JFK amidst a fury of reporters and wondered what the hype was about. But of course they were about to retake America where George III's grenadiers had failed two centuries before.

Images: I remember taking my oldest son—perhaps six at the time—to see the cartoon version of *Yellow Submarine* in Amherst, in a movie theater filled with University of Massachusetts and Amherst College students, and realizing that the air was laced with the scents of marijuana. "What is that smell, Daddy?" he asked me. "Oh, that's called Puff the magic dragon," I told him, and settled back into my seat.

Lines stay with me to this day—"Won't you please please help me." Or the powerful, ironic refrain of "Let it be, let it be, let it be/Whisper words of wisdom, let it be." Or the opening lines of "Yesterday":

> *Yesterday all my troubles seemed so far away,*
> *Now it looks as though they're here to stay*
> *Oh, I believe in yesterday.*

Somehow I used to think of Shakespeare and Elizabethan love lyrics, and William Blake, mixed with Philip Larkin's post–World War II England and the streets of Liverpool.

And, then, with the years, the American assassination of John Lennon on the streets of New York, my native city . . . I remember the lit candles along the sidewalk, and the mementoes left on the windy streets. He was eight months younger than me, and he died at the age of forty. The sharp cold salt wind of death blew past me, and I hurried on, not wanting to look again. But of course it was an end of an era, the end of any possibility that the group, which had shaped us and shaped our culture as no poet in our time had, might regroup and come together again. Ghost music and new edits of old tapes were now all that was left to hear.

And then, like that, another death. Twenty-one years passed, and we heard of the death of George Harrison at fifty-eight of cancer: the Eastern guru, the deep one, who had grown more reclusive with time. And the loss of Paul McCartney's wife . . .

Another image: the Super Bowl in February 2005 with the larger-than-life image of Sir Paul McCartney on my spiffy, new high-definition widescreen television. Shades of Dorian Gray. I am staring at a still-youthful face that reminds me in its agelessness of Dick Clark, and it is singing before a packed stadium of thousands at the half-time intermission, itself a paean to the new gods of football. This is and is not the McCartney of the Beatles of forty years ago, but still: a whiff, a kind of momentary throwback, a guy in his sixties singing (with chaffed grace) the old songs. But what was then, you realize, is irretrievably gone. Beowulf in old age before the dragon.

Still, the Beatles gave us permission to do what Bob Dylan also did—to understand the classics (Eastern as well as Western) in vitally new ways—hearing their music against the images of Vietnam and sensing a spiritual reality deeper than the fighting going on there. And the humor and sophistication, unlike so much of the throwaway music I'd grown up with. In my family, I was always the serious one, and I had a lot of ground to cover in the world of academia and did not stop long enough to listen and take in the gift these four young men gave us, as they went about changing the very world we came to inhabit.

But the music echoes down the long corridors of time, and comforts me now, when I switch off the learning tapes I listen to as I make my long drive to work—still at work at sixty-five—tapes discoursing on the ontologies and epistemologies of the Age of Enlightenment—Locke and Hobbes and Bacon and Pascal—and switch instead to the comic strains of "Money can't buy me love/Can't buy me love/Everybody tells me so" and smile, that knowing smile, as I prepare for yet another week of teaching classes.

Tom Piazza

∎

The Beatles were the epitome of the new. For writer Tom Piazza, they also represented hope, a fresh beginning for both rock and roll and the country. They offered, too, the promise of transformation. But most of all, they were just plain cool.

Piazza's eight books include the Faulkner Society Award–winning novel *My Cold War* and the highly praised short story collection *Blues and Trouble*, as well as several books on jazz and the post–Hurricane Katrina book-length essay *Why New Orleans Matters*. He won a 2004 Grammy Award for his album notes to *Martin Scorsese Presents the Blues: A Musical Journey*.

"Where You Once Belonged"

∎ IT FELT AS IF they'd come out of nowhere. The guitar phrase that announces the beginning of "I Want to Hold Your Hand" could stand with the opening of *Also Sprach Zarathustra,* or the first, declamatory phrases of Beethoven's Fifth Symphony—a declaration of presence, Fate kicking open the door.

They stepped in at just the right moment, grabbed the tiller during a period of weird national drift after the assassination of President Kennedy. For three years, being American had sounded and looked like JFK—sleek, young, serious but fun-loving, handsome, articulate. Now, suddenly, being American ratcheted back to an older template—LBJ, heavy-jowled, dour, shifty-eyed, embarrassingly regional. Somebody had stolen an intensely invigorating icon in the middle of the night and substituted a profoundly depressing one. Being American suddenly felt like being stuck in a house with an unpleasant stepfather after the death of one's beloved father. One retreats into fantasy. *Let's be something else for a while!*

James Bond had already made being English kind of cool. But the Beatles were a group being cool together. They were the Rat Pack without the booze, the Mob without the nastiness. The Beatles showed you how to take control of the room. Even Sinatra—he needed a band. Elvis needed a band. The Beatles *were* the band. They were Guys Together,

Having Fun. Best of all was that they were aware of the essential silliness of it all—the screaming girls, the radio promo announcements on behalf of Murray the K (*"It's what's happening, baby!"*) and God knows how many other deejays, the merchandising. As time went by, the initial charm of that awareness turned into a deeper awareness of the strangeness of it all.

They took everyone with them on that particular trip, straight up the Amazon of the Sixties' jungle of media images of Vietnam brought into American living rooms for dinnertime, assassinations, unfamiliar modes of dress and hygiene and protest and drugs, all of that, and they always seemed to regard their audience as being complicit, with them— complicity is the essence of charm—with a wink or a nod, like the nod two stoned people might give each other across a room full of oblivious conventioneers. From "She Loves You" to "Get Back" was a long and winding road indeed, and it disappeared eventually into the desert somewhere just beyond the Spahn Movie Ranch.

But their arrival. . . . The shape of space and of reality seemed to change. Elvis did it for people who were ten or twelve years older, who came of age in the Fifties—opened up fun and playfulness and the body and sex and music and dance. Some would claim that the Beatles did this exclusively for white kids, but I'm not so sure of that. I have a black friend my age from a working-class family in Fort Worth, Texas, who swears that his brother owned, and wore, a Beatles wig.

And anyway, what would white American youth have known about American music without the British Invasion? The jazz singer Abbey Lincoln has an unfortunate moment in documentarian Ken Burns's PBS series *Jazz,* in which she portentously insinuates that the Beatles— the whole British Invasion—were part of a deliberately, craftily engineered, and sinister plot to kill jazz music. Yet bland teenage American heartthrobs like Frankie Avalon had already smothered black music on the airwaves. The Beatles and the other Invaders whetted our appetite for it again. I heard of Chuck Berry and Little Richard (and Carl Perkins and Buddy Holly, for that matter) because the Beatles performed their songs. When the Rolling Stones appeared on the mid-sixties rock-and-roll TV show *Shindig* they insisted that the producers also hire Howlin' Wolf for a segment on the show. I was hardly the only one who followed the trail back, through the early rock and rollers, through Muddy Waters and company, to Robert Johnson and Blind Lemon Jefferson and Leadbelly and Bessie Smith and eventually into the wide valley of jazz. Thank the Beatles for that. It wasn't a *duty,* it wasn't something forced on you. It was the natural outgrowth of living in a world of vigor and mystery and possibility.

"It is possible to have fun," the Beatles said. "Watch us."

"Is that so?" said the Sixties. "Watch *this.*"

And this. And this.

Still having fun?

As the Sixties wore on, it was hard to escape the context in which your fun was happening. The context was all too obvious—burning cities, burning jungle, dying brothers and cousins covered with blood and flies being rushed through the jungle on stretchers by rag-tag teams of medics, their thick-framed glasses repaired with adhesive tape, on the five o'clock news. Eventually fun wasn't about fun anymore. The Weathermen had orgies as a political statement—to smash bourgeois monogamy. Everything got political. He not busy being born was busy dying. If you weren't part of the solution you were part of the problem, and who wanted to be part of the problem? So even your simpler pleasures had to be conscripted into a rationalizing template. The Beatles didn't escape. As soon as *Rubber Soul* hit the racks the writing was on the wall.

Still, the Beatles' early presence has stayed fresh. I wonder if it is because I was there and saw it. I don't know. I saw Freddie and the Dreamers, too (on television). And Gerry and the Pacemakers. They aren't fresh. I don't think it's just nostalgia. The Beatles were smart and had an awareness. Ezra Pound said that literature was news that stayed news. The early Beatles were fun that stayed fun. They were, at least partly, *about* themselves, the way literature has been at least since *Don Quixote.* And partly because of that self-awareness, that irony, they represented a kind of Indian Summer, maybe the last moment when pop culture could be purely fun without being insultingly oblivious to reality. After that, the fun had to burn going down.

Touré

■

Fiction writer and critic Touré was born a year after the Beatles separated and yet their music formed the soundtrack to his growing-up years. In this piece, he offers a unique perspective on the post-Beatles musical world as filtered through an African-American point of view.

Touré is the author of *Soul City,* a novel, and a contributing editor at *Rolling Stone.* He is also the author of *Never Drank the Kool-Aid,* a collection of essays and profiles on music, sports, and politics, and the *Portable Promised Land,* a collection of short stories. He was CNN's pop culture correspondent and his writing has appeared in *The New Yorker* and *The New York Times,* among other publications, and in several collections, including *Best American Essays of 1999, Best American Music Writing of 2004,* and *Martin Scorsese Presents The Blues.* He studied at Columbia University's graduate school of creative writing and lives in Fort Greene, Brooklyn. His website is www.Toure.com.

"Too Late for the Show"

■ AFTER I GREW TOO OLD to watch *Sesame Street* and *The Electric Company,* one of the first television shows I regularly watched was *The Monkees.* I was four and didn't realize they were a parody. I figured that out when I was five. Not because someone pointed it out to me, but because as soon as I became aware of broad popular culture I became aware of the Beatles. I didn't become an active fan until college, but I was born in 1971 and throughout that decade the Beatles were in the air. As an American, they came into your life automatically without you lifting a finger. There were Beatles references in Bugs Bunny cartoons and commercials and movies. At summer camp we sang "With a Little Help from My Friends." The light pop radio station my mother listened to in the car played lots of the sweeter Beatles songs as well as songs by Wings and Lennon's solo work. The Beatles were such a big part of my young life that I recall learning from them. When "(Just Like) Starting Over" appeared on my mother's favorite radio station many months after Lennon's death, I learned that music on the radio is sometimes made months in advance of us hearing it. I learned the phrase "double entendre" when my father explained that "Lucy in the Sky with Diamonds" was a song about LSD (which is why we shouldn't go around singing it, according to him). And, of course, I learned the word "parody" when I realized that's what the Monkees were doing. Back when there was no MTV, before I was old enough to think about buying music, I knew more songs by the Beatles than by any other group. I'm not sure how old I was when I realized this band that had been a presence in my life for as long as I could remember had broken up before I was born.

In my teens, when MTV arrived and I could drive to the mall and buy the music I wanted to listen to, I stayed away from the Beatles. Largely because I was infatuated with this new thing called rap and partly because I felt the Beatles were for white people, but also because I heard two Beatles songs that scared me. "Eleanor Rigby" and "Yesterday" sometimes showed up on Mom's favorite radio station and they were songs that took me to a place of intense sadness and loneliness, a place I didn't want to go. I was scared of how those songs made me feel and scared they had other songs that would make me feel that way. So I stayed away from exploring their catalog.

Then one day my favorite aunt, a tough and brilliant former Black Panther, mentioned that she liked the Beatles and had great respect for them. That unblocked me, gave me the courage to not care if they were too white. At college, one day in the middle of freshman year, someone on my hall was playing a Beatles album, and as I walked by his room I heard "Eleanor Rigby" again. This time it hit me in a different way, and I actually liked the sadness it conveyed. I borrowed my hallmate's *The Beatles Anthology* and began to burrow into the catalog. I soon realized that, for the most part, it had been Paul's sweet, hopeful, inviting, catchy songs that had come through the zeitgeist to make me feel happy and make me feel good about the Beatles ("With a Little Help from My Friends," "Penny Lane," "When I'm Sixty-Four.") But it was John's songs that I'd once found haunting and now found so compelling because of their introspection, their depth, their wordplay, their song structure ("A Day in the Life," "Across the Universe," "Norwegian Wood," "Strawberry Fields Forever"). Smart songs that gave me a lot to think about and unpack, dark melodies with puzzling elements. Paul made me like the Beatles, John took me places I didn't necessarily want to go and he made me curious to see how he'd come to be so deep. At the library I pored through old *Rolling Stone* articles, learning the long, crazy story of the Beatles. When I should have been studying, I can admit now, I watched some Beatles movies and documentaries and read some books about them and began to understand the magnitude and brilliance of this band. But, the more I discovered, the more I felt I'd shown up late to some great circus.

I was born the year after the Beatles broke up, meaning I discovered the band as a completed entity. The final chapter had already been written, and I knew how it would turn out. I heard about Ed Sullivan and Yoko Ono at the same time. The first time I saw the mop-headed so-called leader of the Fab Four proclaim they were more popular than Jesus I already knew they'd grow up to become musical philosophers who would study with the Maharishi. The first time I heard the White Album I knew Paul wasn't dead because he was making records with Stevie Wonder and Michael Jackson.

In the eighties we lived for the musical unpredictability of Prince and U2, waiting breathlessly for each new album with no idea what it would sound like. We also lived with the life unpredictability of Michael Jackson and Madonna, never sure where their soap operas would go next. The Beatles gave musical unpredictability and soap opera lives to the sixties, and even though the love of the Beatles was still in the air in the seventies, it's not quite the same when you don't feel a band going through their megazenith moment, when they're ruling the zeitgeist.

There's a connection that forms with a band when you're living through their time. My connection to Michael Jackson is wrapped up in going to my friend Eddie's house because he had cable, and sitting in front of the television set for two hours on a sunny day because we wanted to see the video for *Thriller*, or in watching with my mom Michael go up on his toes like a funky Baryshnikov on *Motown 25*. I felt Michael Jackson at his zenith, and if you weren't there you'll never truly understand Michaelmania.

Part of loving any musical entity is about establishing a connection with the community of people who are also fans of the band and enjoying your inclusion in that group. I mean both the actual community— people you see at concerts and people at school or work who agree with you about the group's greatness—and the perceived community—the sort of people you imagine also like the group. This is the true value of street cred in hip hop—if white kids in the suburbs think that tough black kids from the street respect a certain artist, then that makes them feel better about being a fan. But the relationship between an individual fan, a band, and a community of fans is no longer a dynamic once the band is dead. The Beatles gave fans unpredictability in both music and life, as well as high theater, but you can't feel that through a history book. There'll always be something special between me and Michael Jackson because I saw *Thriller* when it was the hottest video on MTV, between me and Run-DMC because I snuck off school grounds to buy *Tougher than Leather* the day it came out, between me and Prince because I saw *Purple Rain* when it was all people could talk about. The music of the Beatles still matters in America and still matters to me because the songs are timeless and the band is fascinating, but for me, a child of the seventies, there's a little something missing. I was born a touch too late to catch the Beatles at their height and being told about the roller coaster is no comparison to riding it.

Discography

For several years, Beatles record releases in the United Kingdom differed from American Beatles releases. The former, though, represented the way the Beatles wished to showcase their music. It wasn't until Sgt. Pepper that both U.K. and U.S. original releases matched.

U.K. Releases

Please Please Me (Parlophone 1963)
As music critic Richard Williams has pointed out in Mojo, *the Beatles first U.K. album was hardly revolutionary but rather it announced "the arrival of the age of the self-contained group whose members created their own material."*
I Saw Her Standing There/Misery/Anna (Go to Him)/Chains/Boys/Ask Me Why/Please Please Me/Love Me Do/P.S. I Love You/Baby It's You/Do You Want to Know a Secret/A Taste of Honey/There's a Place/Twist and Shout

With the Beatles (Parlophone 1963)
The album that made the rest of the world take notice. The famous black-and-white portrait of the foursome deep in shadow (or as Paul Du Noyer so eloquently put it, "Their four faces hung like brand new planets, half-lit in the inky blackness of space, full of a wonderful promise") appears on the American release, Meet the Beatles.
It Won't Be Long/All I've Got to Do/All My Loving/Don't Bother Me/Little Child/Till There Was You/Please Mister Postman/Roll Over Beethoven/Hold Me Tight/You Really Got a Hold on Me/I Wanna Be Your Man/(There's a) Devil in Her Heart/Not a Second Time/Money (That's What I Want)

A Hard Day's Night (Parlophone 1964)
A Hard Day's Night/I Should Have Known Better/If I Fell/I'm Happy Just to Dance with You/And I Love Her/Tell Me Why/Can't Buy Me Love/Any Time at All/I'll Cry Instead/Things We Said Today/When I Get Home/You Can't Do That/I'll Be Back

Beatles for Sale (Parlophone 1964)
No Reply/I'm a Loser/Baby's in Black/Rock 'n Roll Music/I'll Follow the Sun/Mr. Moonlight/Kansas City/Hey-Hey-Hey-Hey!/Eight Days a Week/Words of Love/Honey Don't/Every Little Thing/I Don't Want to Spoil the Party/What You're Doing/Everybody's Trying to Be My Baby

Help! (Parlophone 1965)
Help!/The Night Before/You've Got to Hide Your Love Away/I Need You/Another Girl/You're Going to Lose That Girl/Ticket to Ride/Act Naturally/It's Only Love/You Like Me Too Much/Tell Me What You See/I've Just Seen a Face/Yesterday/Dizzy Miss Lizzy

Rubber Soul (Parlophone 1965)
Drive My Car/Norwegian Wood (This Bird Has Flown)/You Won't See Me/Nowhere Man/Think for Yourself/The Word/Michelle/What Goes On/Girl/I'm Looking Through You/In My Life/Wait/If I Needed Someone/Run for Your Life

Revolver (Parlophone 1966)
Taxman/Eleanor Rigby/I'm Only Sleeping/Love You To/Here, There and Everywhere/Yellow Submarine/She Said She Said/Good Day Sunshine/And Your Bird Can Sing/For No One/Doctor Robert/I Want to Tell You/Got to Get You into My Life/Tomorrow Never Knows

U.S. Releases

THE BEATLES

Introducing the Beatles (Vee Jay, 1963)
The sound that changed the musical landscape.
I Saw Her Standing There/Misery/Anna (Go to Him)/Chains/Boys/Love Me Do/P.S. I Love You/Baby It's You/Do You Want to Know a Secret/A Taste of Honey/There's a Place/Twist and Shout

Meet the Beatles (Capitol, 1964)
For most Americans, this was their introduction to the Fab Four.
I Want to Hold Your Hand/I Saw Her Standing There/This Boy/It Won't Be Long/All I've Got to Do/All My Loving/Don't Bother Me/Little Child/Till There Was You/Hold Me Tight/I Wanna Be Your Man/Not a Second Time

The Beatles Second Album (Capitol, 1964)
Roll Over Beethoven/Thank You Girl/You Really Got a Hold on Me/(There's a) Devil in Her Heart/Money (That's What I Want)/You Can't Do That/Long Tall Sally/I Call Your Name/Please Mr. Postman/I'll Get You/She Loves You

A Hard Day's Night (United Artists, 1964)
Recorded in just one day, the soundtrack to their first—and hugely successful—movie contains one classic after another.
A Hard Day's Night/Tell Me Why/I'll Cry Instead/I Should Have Known Better [George Martin and orchestra instrumental]/I'm Happy Just to Dance with You/And I Love Her [George Martin and orchestra instrumental]/I Should Have Known Better/If I Fell/And I Love Her/Ringo's Theme (This Boy) [George Martin and orchestra instrumental]/Can't Buy Me Love/A Hard Day's Night [George Martin and orchestra instrumental]

Something New (Capitol, 1964)
I'll Cry Instead/Things We Said Today/Any Time at All/When I Get Home/Slow Down/Matchbox/Tell Me Why/And I Love Her/I'm Happy Just to Dance with You/If I Fell/Komm, Gib Mir Deine Hand (I Want to Hold Your Hand)

Beatles '65 (Capitol, 1964)
No Reply/I'm a Loser/Baby's in Black/Rock 'n Roll Music/I'll Follow the Sun/Mr. Moonlight/Honey Don't/I'll Be Back/She's a Woman/I Feel Fine/Everybody's Trying to Be My Baby

The Early Beatles (Capitol, 1965)
Love Me Do/Twist and Shout/Anna (Go to Him)/Chains/Boys/Ask Me Why/Please Please Me/P.S. I Love You/Baby It's You/A Taste of Honey/Do You Want to Know a Secret

Beatles VI (Capitol, 1965)
Kansas City/Hey-Hey-Hey-Hey!/Eight Days a Week/You Like Me Too Much/Bad Boy/I Don't Want to Spoil the Party/Words of Love/What You're Doing/Yes It Is/Dizzy Miss Lizzy/Tell Me What You See/Every Little Thing

Help! (Capitol, 1965)
A transitional album—introspective, a bit melancholy, and heavily influenced by the burgeoning folk-rock movement, especially the music of Bob Dylan as well as the Byrds.
James Bond Theme [instrumental]/Help!/The Night Before/From Me to You Fantasy [instrumental]/You've Got to Hide Your Love Away/I Need You/In the Tyrol [instrumental]/Another Girl/Another Hard Day's Night [instrumental]/Ticket to Ride/The Bitter End [instrumental]/You Can't Do That [instrumental]/You're Gonna Lose That Girl/The Chase [instrumental]

Rubber Soul (Capitol, 1965)
The Beatles truly begin their experimental stage with this album, which consisted of innovative songs (especially the unconventional "Norwegian Wood," about an illicit love affair that features George Harrison on the sitar), songs of breathtaking beauty ("In My Life"), and the use of groundbreaking techniques in the studios. What's even more remarkable, Lennon and McCartney wrote the entire album in just four weeks. It ranked No. 5 on Rolling Stone's *500 Greatest Albums of All Time list.*
I've Just Seen a Face/Norwegian Wood (This Bird Has Flown)/You Won't See Me/Think for Yourself/The Word/Michelle/It's Only Love/Girl/I'm Looking Through You/In My Life/Wait/Run for Your Life

Yesterday and Today (Capitol, 1966)
Drive My Car/I'm Only Sleeping/Nowhere Man/ Doctor Robert/Yesterday/Act Naturally/And Your Bird Can Sing/If I Needed Someone/We Can Work It Out/What Goes On/Day Tripper

Revolver (Capitol, 1966)
The Beatles' artistic growth is manifested here in the sophistication of the lyrics and in the continued use of studio techniques, including tape loops ("Tomorrow Never Knows"), a guitar recorded backward ("I'm Only Sleeping"), unusual instruments (French horn, sitar, and tabla), and various sound effects. "It seems now," wrote music critic Richard Goldstein in the Village Voice, *"that we will view this album in retrospect as a key work in the development of rock 'n' roll into an artistic pursuit." It landed at the No. 3 spot on* Rolling Stone's *500 Greatest Albums of All Time list.*

Taxman/Eleanor Rigby/Love You To/Here, There and Everywhere/Yellow Submarine/She Said, She Said/Good Day Sunshine/For No One/I Want to Tell You/Got to Get You into My Life/Tomorrow Never Knows

Sgt. Pepper's Lonely Hearts Club Band (Capitol, 1967)
Probably the most famous album of the rock era, Sgt. Pepper is known for its many firsts, including the first time song lyrics were printed in a major-release album. Critical commentary went over the top, including "a decisive moment in the history of Western civilization" by Kenneth Tynan in the Times. *It has also been called the best rock album of all time by numerous critics and broadcasters and, most recently, by Rolling Stone: "An unsurpassed adventure in concept, sound, songwriting, cover art and studio technology by the greatest rock & roll group of all time." As the magazine also noted, "No other pop record of that era, or since, has had such an immediate, titanic impact." Noted Jon Pareles in* The New York Times, *"for better or worse," Sgt. Pepper made rock "respectable."*
Sgt. Pepper's Lonely Hearts Club Band/With a Little Help from My Friends/Lucy in the Sky with Diamonds/Getting Better/Fixing a Hole/She's Leaving Home/Being for the Benefit of Mr. Kite/Within You Without You/When I'm Sixty-Four/Lovely Rita/Good Morning, Good Morning/Sgt. Pepper's Lonely Hearts Club Band (Reprise)/A Day in the Life

Magical Mystery Tour (Capitol, 1967)
Glorious soundtrack to a rare Beatles failure, the film release of Magical Mystery Tour.
Magical Mystery Tour/The Fool on the Hill/Flying/Blue Jay Way/Your Mother Should Know/I Am the Walrus/Hello Goodbye/Strawberry Fields Forever/Penny Lane/Baby You're a Rich Man/All You Need Is Love

The Beatles (Apple, 1968)
The White Album, as it is called, is notable for its length (a two-disc set consisting of more than ninety minutes of music) and its remarkable diversity (hard rock, pop, blues, country, avant-garde). Ranked No. 10 on Rolling Stone's *500 Greatest Albums of All Time list, the magazine called it "an exhilarating sprawl—some of the Beatles' most daring and delicate work."*
Back in the U.S.S.R./Dear Prudence/Glass Onion/Ob-La-Di, Ob-La-Da/Wild Honey Pie/The Continuing Story of Bungalow Bill/While My Guitar Gently Weeps/Happiness Is a Warm Gun/Martha My Dear/I'm So Tired/Blackbird/Piggies/Rocky Raccoon/Don't Pass Me By/Why Don't We Do It in the Road/I Will/Julia/Birthday/Yer Blues/Mother Nature's Son/Everybody's Got Something to Hide Except Me and My Monkey/Sexy Sadie/Helter Skelter/Long Long Long/Revolution/Honey Pie/Savoy Truffle/Cry Baby Cry/Revolution 9/Good Night

Yellow Submarine (Apple, 1969)
Also available as a 1999 remixed reissue.
Yellow Submarine/Only a Northern Song/All Together Now/Hey Bulldog/It's All Too Much/All You Need Is Love

Abbey Road (Apple, 1969)
The Beatles' last recording session (Let It Be, recorded earlier, was released after Abbey Road). A carefully crafted album of terrific individual efforts as well as the sublime pleasures of the suitelike side 2.

Come Together/Something/Maxwell's Silver Hammer/Oh! Darling/Octopus's Garden/I Want You (She's So Heavy)/Here Comes the Sun/Because/You Never Give Me Your Money/Sun King/Mean Mr. Mustard/Polythene Pam/She Came In Through the Bathroom Window/Golden Slumbers/Carry That Weight/The End/Her Majesty

Hey Jude (Apple, 1970)
Can't Buy Me Love/I Should Have Known Better/Paperback Writer/Rain/Lady Madonna/Revolution/Hey Jude/Old Brown Shoe/Don't Let Me Down/The Ballad of John and Yoko

Let It Be (Apple, 1970) (soundtrack)
The Beatles final studio release, this time around produced by sixties wunderkind Phil Spector, who, much to McCartney's chagrin, added strings, brass, and choirs. Created under fractious circumstances, it is surprising that it still contains a few Beatles classics, including the ineffable "Across the Universe," the hymnlike title track, the infectious "For You Blue," and the irresistible "Get Back."
Two of Us/Dig a Pony/Across the Universe/I Me Mine/Dig It/Let It Be/Maggie Mae/I've Got a Feeling/The One After 909/The Long and Winding Road/For You Blue/Get Back

The Beatles 1962–1966 (Apple, 1973)
Love Me Do/Please Please Me/From Me to You/She Loves You/I Want to Hold Your Hand/All My Loving/Can't Buy Me Love/A Hard Day's Night/And I Love Her/Eight Days a Week/I Feel Fine/Ticket to Ride/Yesterday/Help!/You've Got to Hide Your Love Away/We Can Work It Out/Day Tripper/Drive My Car/Norwegian Wood (This Bird Has Flown)/Nowhere Man/Michelle/In My Life/Girl/Paperback Writer/Eleanor Rigby/Yellow Submarine

The Beatles 1967–1970 (Apple, 1973)
Strawberry Fields Forever/Penny Lane/Sgt. Pepper's Lonely Hearts Club Band/With a Little Help from My Friends/Lucy in the Sky with Diamonds/A Day in the Life/All You Need Is Love/I Am the Walrus/Hello Goodbye/The Fool on the Hill/Magical Mystery Tour/Lady Madonna/Hey Jude/Revolution/Back in the U.S.S.R./While My Guitar Gently Weeps/Ob-La-Di, Ob-La-Da/Get Back/Don't Let Me Down/The Ballad of John and Yoko/Old Brown Shoe/Here Comes the Sun/Come Together/Something/Octopus's Garden/Let It Be/Across the Universe/The Long and Winding Road

Rock and Roll Music (Capitol, 1976)
Twist and Shout/I Saw Her Standing There/You Can't Do That/I Wanna Be Your Man/I Call Your Name/Boys/Long Tall Sally/Rock 'n Roll Music/Kansas City/Hey-Hey-Hey-Hey!/Money (That's What I Want)/Bad Boy/Roll Over Beethoven/Dizzy Miss Lizzy/Any Time at All/Drive My Car/Everybody's Trying to Be My Baby/The Night Before/I'm Down/Revolution/Back in the U.S.S.R./Helter Skelter/Taxman/Got to Get You into My Life/Hey Bulldog/Birthday/Get Back

The Beatles Live! At the Star Club in Hamburg, Germany, 1962
(Lingasong, 1977)
I Saw Her Standing There/Roll Over Beethoven/Hippy Hippy Shake/Sweet Little Sixteen/Lend Me Your Combo/Your Feet's Too Big/Twist and Shout/Mr. Moon-

light/A Taste of Honey/Besame Mucho/Reminiscing/Kansas City/Hey-Hey-Hey-Hey!/ Nothin' Shakin' (but the Leaves on the Trees)/To Know Her Is to Love Her/Falling in Love Again/Ask Me Why/Be-Bop-a-Lula/Hallelujah, I Love Her So/Red Sails in the Sunset/Everybody's Trying to Be My Baby/Matchbox/I'm Talking About You/ Shimmy Shake/Long Tall Sally/I Remember You

The Beatles at the Hollywood Bowl (Capitol, 1977)
Twist and Shout/She's a Woman/Dizzy Miss Lizzy/Ticket to Ride/Can't Buy Me Love/Things We Said Today/Roll Over Beethoven/Boys/A Hard Day's Night/Help!/ All My Loving/She Loves You/Long Tall Sally

Love Songs (Capitol, 1977)
Yesterday/I'll Follow the Sun/I Need You/Girl/In My Life/Words of Love/Here, There and Everywhere/Something/And I Love Her/If I Fell/I'll Be Back/Tell Me What You See/Yes It Is/Michelle/It's Only Love/You're Gonna Lose That Girl/Every Little Thing/For No One/She's Leaving Home/The Long and Winding Road/This Boy/Norwegian Wood (This Bird Has Flown)/You've Got to Hide Your Love Away/I Will/P.S. I Love You

Rarities (Capitol, 1980)
Across the Universe/Yes It Is/This Boy/The Inner Light/I'll Get You/Thank You Girl/ Komm, Gib Mir Deine Hand (I Want to Hold Your Hand)/You Know My Name (Look Up the Number)/Sie Liebt Dich (She Loves You)/Rain/She's a Woman/Matchbox/I Call Your Name/Bad Boy/Slow Down/Long Tall Sally

Reel Music (Capitol, 1982)
A Hard Day's Night/I Should Have Known Better/Can't Buy Me Love/And I Love Her/Help!/You've Got to Hide Your Love Away/Ticket to Ride/Magical Mystery Tour/I Am the Walrus/Yellow Submarine/All You Need Is Love/Let It Be/Get Back/The Long and Winding Road

20 Greatest Hits (Capitol, 1982)
She Loves You/Love Me Do/I Want to Hold Your Hand/Can't Buy Me Love/A Hard Day's Night/I Feel Fine/Eight Days a Week/Ticket to Ride/Help!/Yesterday/We Can Work It Out/Paperback Writer/Penny Lane/All You Need Is Love/Hello Goodbye/Hey Jude/Get Back/Come Together/Let It Be/The Long and Winding Road

Past Masters Volume 1 & Volume 2 (EMI/Capitol, 1988)

Live at the BBC (Apple, 1994)
From Me to You/I Got a Woman/Too Much Monkey Business/Keep Your Hands Off My Baby/I'll Be on My Way/Young Blood/A Shot of Rhythm and Blues/Sure to Fall (in Love with You)/Some Other Guy/Thank You Girl/Baby It's You/That's All Right (Mama)/Carol/Soldier of Love/Clarabella/I'm Gonna Sit Right Down and Cry (Over You)/Crying, Waiting, Hoping/You Really Got a Hold on Me/To Know Her Is to Love Her/A Taste of Honey/Long Tall Sally/I Saw Her Standing There/The Honeymoon Song/Johnny B. Goode/Memphis, Tennessee/Lucille/Can't Buy Me Love/ Till There Was You/A Hard Day's Night/I Wanna Be Your Man/Roll Over Beethoven/Things We Said Today/She's a Woman/Sweet Little Sixteen/Lonesome Tears in My Eyes/Nothin' Shakin'/The Hippy Hippy Shake/Glad All Over/I Just

Don't Understand/So How Come (No One Loves Me)/I Feel Fine/I'm a Loser/ Everybody's Trying to Be My Baby/Rock 'n Roll Music/Ticket to Ride/Dizzy Miss Lizzy/Kansas City/Hey-Hey-Hey-Hey!/Matchbox/I Forgot to Remember to For- get/I Got to Find My Baby/Ohh! My Soul/Don't Ever Change/Slow Down/ Honey Don't/Love Me Do (single version with Ringo)/From Me to You/Thank You Girl/She Loves You/I'll Get You/I Want to Hold Your Hand/This Boy/Komm, Gib Mir Deine Hand (I Want to Hold Your Hand)/Sie Liebt Dich (She Loves You/Long Tall Sally/I Call Your Name/Slow Down/Matchbox/I Feel Fine/She's a Woman/Bad Boy/Yes It Is/I'm Down/Day Tripper/We Can Work It Out/Paperback Writer/ Rain/Lady Madonna/The Inner Light/Hey Jude/Revolution/Get Back/Don't Let Me Down/The Ballad of John and Yoko/Old Brown Shoe/Across the Universe/Let It Be/You Know My Name (Look Up the Number)

The Beatles Anthology 1 (Apple/EMI, 1995)
Disc 1:
Free as a Bird/That'll Be the Day/In Spite of All the Danger/Hallelujah, I Love Her So/You'll Be Mine/She Loves You/Till There Was You/Twist and Shout/This Boy/I Want to Hold Your Hand/Cayenne/My Bonnie/Ain't She Sweet/Cry for a Shadow/ Searchin'/Three Cool Cats/The Sheik of Araby/Like Dreamers Do/Hello Little Girl/Besame Mucho/Love Me Do/How Do You Do It/Please Please Me/The One After 909/Lend Me Your Comb/I'll Get You/I Saw Her Standing There/From Me to You/Money (That's What I Want)/You Really Got a Hold on Me/Roll Over Beethoven
Disc 2:
She Loves You/Till There Was You/Twist and Shout/This Boy/I Want to Hold Your Hand/Moonlight Bay/Can't Buy Me Love/All My Loving/And I Love Her/A Hard Day's Night/I Wanna Be Your Man/Long Tall Sally/Boys/Shout/I'll Be Back/You Know What to Do/No Reply/Eight Days a Week/Kansas City/Hey-Hey-Hey-Hey!

The Beatles Anthology 2 (1996)
Disc 1:
Real Love/Yes It Is/I'm Down/You've Got to Hide Your Love Away/If You've Got Trouble/That Means a Lot/Yesterday/It's Only Love/I Feel Fine/Ticket to Ride/Yes- terday/Help!/Everybody's Trying to Be My Baby/Norwegian Wood (This Bird Has Flown)/I'm Looking Through You/12-Bar Original/Tomorrow Never Knows/Got to Get You into My Life/And Your Bird Can Sing/Taxman/Eleanor Rigby/I'm Only Sleeping/Rock 'n Roll Music/She's a Woman
Disc 2:
Strawberry Fields Forever/Penny Lane/A Day in the Life/Good Morning, Good Morning/Only a Northern Song/Being for the Benefit of Mr. Kite/Lucy in the Sky with Diamonds/Within You Without You/Sgt. Pepper's Lonely Hearts Club Band (Reprise)/You Know My Name (Look Up the Number)/I Am the Walrus/Fool on the Hill/Your Mother Should Know/Hello Goodbye/Lady Madonna/Across the Universe

The Beatles Anthology 3 (1996)
Disc 1:
A Beginning/Happiness Is a Warm Gun/Helter Skelter/Mean Mr. Mustard/Poly- thene Pam/Glass Onion/Junk/Piggies/Honey Pie/Don't Pass Me By/Ob-La-Di, Ob- La-Da/Good Night/Cry Baby Cry/Blackbird/Sexy Sadie/While My Guitar Gently Weeps/Hey Jude/Not Guilty/Mother Nature's Son/Rocky Raccoon/What's the New

Discography

Mary Jane/Step Inside Love–Los Paranoias/I'm So Tired/I Will/Why Don't We Do It in the Road?/Julia
Disc 2:
I've Got a Feeling/She Came In Through the Bathroom Window/Dig a Pony/Two of Us/For You Blue/Teddy Boy/Rip It Up/Shake, Rattle, and Roll/Blue Suede Shoes/The Long and Winding Road/Oh! Darling/All Things Must Pass/Mailman, Bring Me No More Blues/Get Back/Old Brown Shoe/Octopus's Garden/Maxwell's Silver Hammer/Something/Come Together/Come and Get It/Ain't She Sweet/Because/Let It Be/I Me Mine/The End

1 (2000)
Love Me Do/From Me to You/She Loves You/I Want to Hold Your Hand/Can't Buy Me Love/A Hard Day's Night/I Feel Fine/Eight Days a Week/Ticket to Ride/Help!/Yesterday/Day Tripper/We Can Work It Out/Paperback Writer/Yellow Submarine/Eleanor Rigby/Penny Lane/All You Need Is Love/Hello Goodbye/Lady Madonna/Hey Jude/Get Back/The Ballad of John and Yoko/Something/Come Together/Let It Be/The Long and Winding Road

Let It Be . . . Naked (Capitol, 2003)
The way the Beatles intended it. See original release above.

JOHN LENNON

Unfinished Music No. 1: Two Virgins (Apple, 1968)
Two Virgins Side One/Two Virgins Side Two/Remember Love

Unfinished Music No. 2: Life with the Lions (Apple, 1969)
Cambridge 1969/No Bed for Beatle John/Baby's Heartbeat/Two Minutes Silence/Radio Play/Song for John/Mulberry

Wedding Album (Apple, 1969)
John & Yoko/Amsterdam/Who Has Seen the Wind?/Listen, the Snow Is Falling/Don't Worry, Kyoko (Mummy's Only Looking for Her Hand in the Snow)

The Plastic Ono Band: Live Peace in Toronto (Apple, 1969)
Blue Suede Shoes/Money/Dizzy Miss Lizzy/Yer Blues/Cold Turkey/Give Peace a Chance/Don't Worry, Kyoko (Mummy's Only Looking for Her Hand in the Snow)/John John (Let's Hope for Peace)

John Lennon/Plastic Ono Band (Apple, 1970)
Lennon's first real solo album, this highly confessional work spews with self-loathing amid its punk-style anger. It features the sublime anguish of "God" and the brutal "Working Class Hero," but also "Love," Lennon at his most delicate.
Mother/Hold On John/I Found Out/Working Class Hero/Isolation/Remember/Love/Look at Me/Well, Well, Well/God/My Mummy's Dead

Imagine (Apple, 1971)
Lennon's most successful solo effort features the gorgeous "Jealous Guy" and, of course, the title track, his universal call for peace.

Imagine/Crippled Inside/Jealous Guy/It's So Hard/I Don't Want to Be a Soldier Mama/Gimme Some Truth/Oh My Love/How Do You Sleep?/How?/Oh Yoko!

Some Time in New York City (Apple, 1972)
Woman Is the Nigger of the World/Sisters O Sisters/Attica State/Born in a Prison/ New York City/Sunday Bloody Sunday/The Luck of the Irish/John Sinclair/Angela/ We're All Water/Cold Turkey/Don't Worry, Kyoko (Mummy's Only Looking for Her Hand in the Snow)/Well (Baby Please Don't Go)/Jamrag/Scumbag/Au

Mind Games (Apple, 1973)
Mind Games/Tight As/Aisumasen (I'm Sorry)/One Day (At a Time)/Bring on the Lucie (Freeda People)/Nutopian National Anthem/Intuition/Out of the Blue/Only People/I Know (I Know)/You Are Here/Meat City

Walls and Bridges (Apple, 1974)
Going Down on Love/Whatever Gets You Thru the Night/Old Dirt Road/What You Got/Bless You/Scared/# 9 Dream/Surprise Surprise (Sweet Bird of Paradise)/Steel and Glass/Beef Jerky/Nobody Loves You (When You're Down and Out)

Rock 'n' Roll (Apple, 1975)
Be Bop a Lula/Stand By Me/Ready Teddy/Rip It Up/You Can't Catch Me/Ain't That a Shame/Do You Want to Dance/Sweet Little Sixteen/Slippin' and Slidin'/ Peggy Sue/Bring It On Home to Me–Send Me Some Lovin'/Bony Moronie/Ya Ya/Just Because

Shaved Fish (Apple, 1975)
Give Peace a Chance/Cold Turkey/Instant Karma/Power to the People/Mother/ Woman Is the Nigger of the World/Imagine/Whatever Gets You Through the Night/ Mind Games/# 9 Dream/Happy Xmas (War Is Over)/Give Peace a Chance

Double Fantasy (Geffen, 1980)
(Just Like) Starting Over/Kiss Kiss Kiss/Cleanup Time/Give Me Something/I'm Losing You/I'm Moving On/Beautiful Boy (Darling Boy)/Watching the Wheels/Yes I'm Your Woman/Beautiful Boys/Dear Yoko

The John Lennon Collection (Geffen, 1982)
Give Peace a Chance/Instant Karma/Power to the People/Whatever Gets You Through the Night/# 9 Dream/Mind Games/Love/Imagine/Jealous Guy/Stand by Me/(Just Like) Starting Over/Woman/I'm Losing You/Beautiful Boy (Darling Boy)/Dear Yoko/Watching the Wheels

Milk and Honey (Polygram, 1984)
I'm Stepping Out/Sleepless Night/I Don't Wanna Face It/Don't Be Scared/Nobody Told Me/O' Sanity/Borrowed Time/Your Hands/(Forgive Me) My Little Flower Princess/Let Me Count the Ways/Grow Old with Me/You're the One

Live in New York City (EMI, 1986)
New York City/It's So Hard/Woman Is the Nigger of the World/Well, Well, Well/ Instant Karma (We All Shine On)/Mother/Come Together/Imagine/Cold Turkey/ Hound Dog/Give Peace a Chance

Menlove Avenue (EMI, 1986)
Here We Go Again/Rock & Roll People/Angel Baby/Since My Baby Left Me/To Know Her Is to Love Her/Steel and Glass/Scared/Old Dirt Road/Nobody Loves You (When You're Down and Out)/Bless You

Lennon Legend (Parlophone, 1997)
Imagine/Instant Karma/Mother/Jealous Guy/Power to the People/Cold Turkey/Love/Mind Games/Whatever Gets You Thru the Night/#9 Dream/Stand by Me/(Just Like) Starting Over/Woman/Beautiful Boy (Darling Boy)/Watching the Wheels/Nobody Told Me/Borrowed Time/Working Class Hero/Happy Xmas (War Is Over)/Give Peace a Chance

Lennon Anthology (Capitol/EMI, 1998)

Acoustic (Capitol, 2004)
Working Class Hero/Love/Well, Well, Well/Look at Me/God/My Mummy's Dead/Cold Turkey/The Luck of the Irish/John Sinclair/Woman Is the Nigger of the World/What You Got/Watching the Wheels/Dear Yoko/Real Love/Imagine/ It's Real

PAUL MCCARTNEY

The Family Way (London, 1967)
Instrumental film soundtrack.

McCartney (Apple, 1970)
McCartney's first solo album.
The Lovely Linda/That Would Be Something/Valentine Day/Every Night/Hot as Sun/Glasses/Junk/Man We Was Lonely/Oo You/Momma Miss America/Teddy Boy/Singalong Junk/Maybe I'm Amazed/Kreen-Akrore

Ram (Apple, 1971)
Too Many People/3 Legs/Ram On/Dear Boy/Uncle Albert–Admiral Halsey/Smile Away/Heart of the Country/Monkberry Moon Delight/Eat at Home/Long Haired Lady/Ram On (version 2)/The Back Seat of My Car

Wild Life (Apple, 1971)
Mumbo/Bip Bop/Love Is Strange/Wild Life/Some People Never Know/I Am Your Singer/Tomorrow/Dear Friend

Red Rose Speedway (Apple, 1973)
Big Barn Bed/My Love/Get on the Right Thing/One More Kiss/Little Lamb Dragonfly/Single Pigeon/When the Night/Loup (1st Indian on the Moon)/Hold Me Tight/Lazy Dynamite/Hands of Love/Power Cut

Band on the Run (Apple, 1974)
Considered McCartney's finest post-Beatles moment and a classic of its own.
Band on the Run/Jet/Bluebird/Mrs. Vandebilt/Let Me Roll It/Mamunia/No Words/Helen Wheels/Picasso's Last Words (Drink to Me)/1984

Venus and Mars (Capitol, 1975)
Venus and Mars/Rock Show/Love in Song/You Gave Me the Answer/Magneto and Titanium Man/Letting Go/Venus and Mars (Reprise)/Spirits of Ancient Egypt/Medicine Jar/Call Me Back Again/Listen to What the Man Said/Treat Her Gently/Lonely Old People/Crossroads Theme

Wings at the Speed of Sound I (Capitol, 1976)
Let 'Em In/The Note You Never Wrote/She's My Baby/Beware My Love/Wino Junko/Silly Love Songs/Cook of the House/Time to Hide/Must Do Something About It/San Ferry Anne/Warm and Beautiful

Wings over America (Capitol, 1976)
Venus and Mars/Rock Show/Jet/Let Me Roll It/Spirits of Ancient Egypt/Medicine Jar/Maybe I'm Amazed/Call Me Back Again/Lady Madonna/The Long and Winding Road/Live and Let Die/Picasso's Last Words (Drink to Me)/Richard Cory/Bluebird/I've Just Seen a Face/Blackbird/Yesterday/You Gave Me the Answer/Magneto and Titanium Man/Go Now/My Love/Listen to What the Man Said/Let 'Em In/Time to Hide/Silly Love Songs/Beware My Love/Letting Go/Band on the Run/ Hi, Hi, Hi/Soily

London Town (Capitol, 1978)
London Town/Café on the Left Bank/I'm Carrying Backwards Traveller/Cuff Link/Children Children/Girlfriend/I've Had Enough/With a Little Luck/Famous Groupies/Deliver Your Children/Name and Address/Don't Let It Bring You Down/ Morse Moose and the Grey Goose

Wings Greatest (Capitol, 1978)
Another Day/Silly Love Songs/Live and Let Die/Junior's Farm/With a Little Luck/ Band on the Run/Uncle Albert Admiral Halsey/Hi, Hi, Hi/Let 'Em In/My Love/Mull of Kintyre

Back to the Egg (Columbia, 1979)
Reception/Getting Closer/We're Open Tonight/Spin It On/Again and Again and Again/Old Siam, Sir/Arrow Through Me/Rockestra Theme/To You/After the Ball–Million Miles/Winter Rose–Love Awake/The Broadcast/So Glad to See You Here/ Baby's Request

McCartney II (Columbia, 1980)
Coming Up/Temporary Secretary/On the Way/Waterfalls/Nobody Knows/Front Parlour/Summer's Day Song/Frozen Jap/Bogey Music/Darkroom/One of Those Days

Tug of War (Columbia, 1982)
Tug of War/Take It Away/Somebody Who Cares/What's That You're Doing/Here Today/Ballroom Dancing/The Pound Is Sinking/Wanderlust/Get It/Be What You See/Dress Me Up as a Robber/Ebony and Ivory

Pipes of Peace (Columbia, 1983)
Pipes of Peace/Say Say Say/The Other Me/Keep Under Cover/So Bad/The Man/ Sweetest Little Show/Average Person/Hey Hey/Tug of Peace/Through Our Love

Give My Regards to Broad Street (Columbia, 1984)
No More Lonely Nights/Good Day Sunshine/Corridor Music/Yesterday/Here, There and Everywhere/Wanderlust/Ballroom Dancing/Silly Love Songs/Silly Love Songs (Reprise)/Not Such a Bad Boy/No Values/No More Lonely Nights (Reprise)/ For No One/Eleanor Rigby–Rigby's Dream/The Long and Winding Road/No More Lonely Nights (Reprise Two)

Press to Play (Capitol, 1986)
Stranglehold/Good Times Coming–Feel the Sun/Talk More Talk/Footprints/Only Love Remains/Press/Pretty Little Head/Move Over Busker/Angry/However Absurd/ Write Away/It's Not True/Tough on a Tightrope/Spies Like Us/Once Upon a Long Ago (Long Version)

Flowers in the Dirt (Capitol, 1989)
My Brave Face/Rough Ride/You Want Her Too/Distractions/We Got Married/Put It There/Figure of Eight/This One/Don't Be Careless Love/That Day Is Done/How Many People/Motor of Love/Où Est le Soleil

Liverpool Oratorio (EMI, 1991)
McCartney and Carl Davis pooled resources to create this heartfelt paean to Liverpool featuring the vocals of Kiri Te Kanawa, the Royal Liverpool Philharmonic Orchestra and Choir, and the Choristers of Liverpool Cathedral.

Off the Ground (Parlophone, 1993)
Off the Ground/Looking for Changes/Hope of Deliverance/Mistress and Maid/I Owe It All to You/Biker Like an Icon/Peace in the Neighbourhood/Golden Earth Girl/ The Lovers That Never Were/Get Out of My Way/Winedark Open Sea/C'mon People

Flaming Pie (Parlophone, 1997)
The Song We Were Singing/The World Tonight/If You Wanna/Somedays/Young Boy/Calico Skies/Flaming Pie/Heaven on a Sunday/Used to Be Bad/Souvenir/Little Willow/Really Love You/Beautiful Night/Great Day

Standing Stone: A Symphonic Poem (EMI, 1997)
McCartney's collaboration with the London Symphonic Orchestra conducted by Lawrence Foster.

Run Devil Run (Parlophone, 1999)
Blue Jean Bop/She Said Yeah/All Shook Up/Run Devil Run/No Other Baby/Lonesome Town/Try Not to Cry/Movie Magg/Brown Eyed Handsome Man/What It Is/Coquette/I Got Stung/Honey Hush/Shake a Hand/Party

Working Classical (EMI, 1999)
Orchestral and chamber music by McCartney as conducted by the London Symphony Orchestra.
Junk/A Leaf/Haymakers/Midwife/Spiral/Warm and Beautiful/My Love/Maybe I'm Amazed/Calico Skies/Golden Earth Girl/Somedays/Tuesday/She's My Baby/The Lovely Linda

Driving Rain (Parlophone, 2001)
Lonely Road/From a Lover to a Friend/She's Given Up Talking/Driving Rain/I Do/Tiny Bubble/Magic/Your Way/Spinning on an Axis/About You/Heather/Back in the Sunshine Again/Your Loving Flame/Riding into Jaipur/Rinse the Raindrops/ Freedom

Chaos and Creation in the Backyard (Capitol, 2005)
McCartney's best reviewed release since 1974's Band on the Run.
Fine Line/How Kind of You/Jenny Wren/At the Mercy/Friends to Go/English Tea/Too Much Rain/A Certain Softness/Riding to Vanity Fair/Follow Me/Promise to You Girl/This Never Happened Before/Anyway

GEORGE HARRISON

Wonderwall Music (Apple, 1968)
First Beatles solo album on Apple and one of the first world music releases.
Microbes/Red Lady Too/Tabla and Pakavaj/In the Park/Drilling a Home/Guru Vandana/Greasy Legs/Ski-ing and Gat Kirwani/Dream Scene/Party Seacombe/Love Scenes/Crying/Cowboy Museum/Fantasy Sequins/Glass Box/On the Bed/Wonderwall/To Be Here/Singing Om

Electronic Sound (Apple, 1969)
Under the Mersey Wall/No Time or Space

All Things Must Pass (Apple, 1970)
A mammoth triple LP that is one of rock's defining works; considered Harrison's best.
I'd Have You Anytime/My Sweet Lord/Wah Wah/Isn't It a Pity (version one)/What Is Life/If Not for You/Behind That Locked Door/Let It Down/Run of the Mill/Beware of Darkness/Apple Scruffs/Ballad of Sir Frankie Crisp (Let It Roll)/Awaiting on You All/All Things Must Pass/I Dig Love/Art of Dying/Isn't It a Pity (version two)/Hear Me, Lord/Out of the Blue/It's Johnny's Birthday/Plug Me In/I Remember Jeep/Thanks for the Pepperoni

The Concert for Bangladesh (Capitol, 1971)
Bangla Dun/Wah Wah/My Sweet Lord/Awaiting on You All/That's the Way God Planned It/It Don't Come Easy/Beware of Darkness/While My Guitar Gently Weeps/Jumpin' Jack Flash/Here Comes the Sun/A Hard Rain's Gonna Fall/It Takes a Lot to Laugh/It Takes a Train to Cry/Blowin' in the Wind/Mr. Tambourine Man/Just Like a Woman/Something/Bangla Desh

Living in the Material World (Apple, 1973)
Give Me Love (Give Me Peace on Earth)/Sue Me Sue You Blues/The Light That Has Lighted the World/Don't Let Me Wait Too Long/Who Can See It/Living in the Material World/The Lord Loves the One (That Loves the Lord)/Be Here Now/Try Some Buy Some/The Day the World Gets Round/That Is All

Dark Horse (Apple, 1974)
Hari's on Tour/Simply Shady/So Sad/Bye Bye Love/Maya Love/Ding Dong/Dark Horse/Far East Man/It Is He (Jai Sri Krishna)

Extra Texture (Read All About It) (Apple, 1975)
You/The Answer's at the End/This Guitar (Can't Keep You from Crying)/Ooh Baby (You Know That I Love You)/World of Stone/A Bit More of You/Can't Stop Thinking About You/Tired of Midnight Blue/Grey Cloudy Skies/His Name Is Legs (Ladies and Gentlemen)

33 and 1/3 (Dark Horse, 1976)
Woman Don't Cry for Me/Dear One/Beautiful Girl/This Song/See Yourself/It's What You Value/True Love/Pure Smokey/Crackerbox Palace/Learning How to Love You

The Best of George Harrison (EMI, 1976)
Something/If I Needed Someone/Here Comes the Sun/Taxman/Think for Yourself/For You Blue/While My Guitar Gently Weeps/My Sweet Lord/Give Me Love (Give Me Peace on Earth)/You/Bangla Desh/Dark Horse/What Is Life

George Harrison (Dark Horse, 1979)
Love Comes to Everyone/Not Guilty/Here Comes the Moon/Soft Hearted Hana/Blow Away/Faster/Dark Sweet Lady/Your Love Is Forever/Soft Touch/If You Believe Me

Somewhere in England (Dark Horse, 1981)
Blood from a Clone/Unconscious Rules/Life Itself/All Those Years Ago/Baltimore Oriole/Teardrops/That Which I Have Lost/Writing's on the Wall/Hong Kong Blues/Save the World

Gone Troppo (Dark Horse, 1982)
Wake Up My Love/That's the Way It Goes/I Really Love You/Greece/Gone Troppo/Mystical One/Unknown Delight/Baby Don't Run Away/Dream Away/Circles

Cloud Nine (Dark Horse, 1987)
Cloud Nine/That's What It Takes/Fish on the Sand/Just for Today/This Is Love/When We Was Fab/Devil's Radio/Someplace Else, Wreck of the Hesperus/Breath Away from Heaven/Got My Mind Set on You

Best of Dark Horse (1976–1989) (Dark Horse, 1989)
Poor Little Girl/Blow Away/That's the Way It Goes/Cockamamie Business/Wake Up My Love/Life Itself/Got My Mind Set on You/Crackerbox Palace/Cloud Nine/Here Comes the Moon/Gone Troppo/When We Was Fab/Love Comes to Everyone/All Those Years Ago/Cheer Down

George Harrison Live in Japan (Dark Horse, 1992)
I Want to Tell You/Old Brown Shoe/Taxman/Give Me Love (Give Me Peace on Earth)/If I Needed Someone/Something/What Is Life/Dark Horse/Piggies/Got My Mind Set on You/Cloud Nine/Here Comes the Sun/My Sweet Lord/All Those Years Ago/Cheer Down/Devil's Radio/Isn't It a Pity/While My Guitar Gently Weeps/Roll Over Beethoven

All Things Must Pass (2001; Capitol, rerelease)
See above.

Brainwashed (Capitol, 2002)
Any Road/P2 Vatican Blues (Last Saturday Night)/Pisces Fish/Looking for My Life/Rising Sun/Marwa Blues/Stuck Inside a Cloud/Run So Far/Never Get Over You/Between the Devil and the Deep Blue Sea/Rocking Chair in Hawaii/Brainwashed

The Traveling Wilburys

The Traveling Wilburys (Volume One) (Warner, 1988)
Handle with Care/Dirty World/Rattled/Last Night/Not Alone Any More/Congratulations/Heading for the Light/Margarita/Tweeter and the Monkey Man/End of the Line

The Traveling Wilburys (Volume Three) (Warner, 1990)
She's My Baby/Inside Out/If You Belonged to Me/The Devil's Been Busy/7 Deadly Sins/Poor House/Where Were You Last Night?/Cool Dry Place/New Blue Moon/You Took My Breath Away/Wilbury Twist

RINGO STARR

Sentimental Journey (Apple, 1970)
The first solo vocal album from a Beatle, it features Ringo's idiosyncratic take on the standards.
Sentimental Journey/Night and Day/Whispering Grass (Don't Tell the Trees)/Bye Bye Blackbird/I'm a Fool to Care/Star Dust/Blue, Turning Grey over You/Love Is a Many Splendoured Thing/Dream/You Always Hurt the One You Love/Have I Told You Lately That I Love You/Let the Rest of the World Go By

Beaucoups of Blues (Apple, 1970)
Beaucoups of Blues/Love Don't Last Long/Fastest Growing Heartache in the West/Without Her/Woman of the Night/I'd Be Talking All the Time/$15 Draw/Wine, Women, and Loud Happy Songs/I Wouldn't Have You Any Other Way/Loser's Lounge/Waiting/Silent Homecoming

Ringo (Apple, 1973)
I'm the Greatest/Hold On (Have You Seen My Baby?)/Photograph/Sunshine Life for Me (Sail Away Raymond)/You're Sixteen/Oh My My/Step Lightly/Six O'Clock/Devil Woman/You and Me (Babe)

Goodnight Vienna (Apple, 1974)
Goodnight Vienna/Occapella/Oo-Wee/Husbands and Wives/Snookeroo/All by Myself/Call Me/No No Song/Only You/Easy for Me/Goodnight Vienna (Reprise)

Blast from Your Past (Apple, 1975)
You're Sixteen/No No Song/It Don't Come Easy/Photograph/Back Off Boogaloo/Only You/Beaucoups of Blues/Oh My My/Early 1970/I'm the Greatest

Ringo's Rotogravure (Atlantic, 1976)
A Dose of Rock 'n' Roll/Hey Baby/Pure Gold/Cryin'/You Don't Know Me at All/Cookin' (in the Kitchen of Love)/I'll Still Love You/This Be Called a Song/Las Brisas/Lady Gaye/Spooky Weirdness

Ringo the 4th (Atlantic, 1977)
Drowning in the Sea of Love/Tango All Night/Wings/Gave It All Up/Out on the
Streets/Can She Do It Like She Dances/Sneaking Sally Through the Alley/It's No
Secret/Gypsies in Flight/Simple Love Song

Bad Boy (Portrait, 1978)
Who Needs a Heart/Bad Boy/Lipstick Traces (on a Cigarette)/Heart on My Sleeve/
Where Did Our Love Go/Hard Times/Tonight/Monkey See, Monkey Do/Old Time
Relovin'/A Man Like Me

Stop and Smell the Roses (Boardwalk, 1981)
Private Property/Wrack My Brain/Drumming Is My Madness/Attention/Stop and
Take the Time to Smell the Roses/Dead Giveaway/You Belong to Me/Sure to Fall (in
Love with You)/Nice Wau/Back Off Boogaloo

Time Takes Time (Private Music, 1992)
Weight of the World/Don't Know a Thing (About Love)/Don't Go Where the Road
Don't Go/Golden Blunders/All in the Name of Love/After All These Years/I Don't
Believe You/Runaways/In a Heartbeat/What Goes Around

Vertical Man (Mercury, 1998)
One/What in the . . . World/Mindfield/King of Broken Hearts/Love Me Do/Vertical
Man/Drift Away/I Was Walkin'/Le De Da/Without Understanding/I'll Be Fine Any-
where/Puppet/I'm Yours

I Wanna Be Santa Claus (Polygram, 1999)
Come On Christmas, Christmas Come On/Winter Wonderland/I Wanna Be Santa
Claus/The Little Drummer Boy/Rudolph the Red-Nosed Reindeer/Christmas
Eve/The Christmas Dance/Christmas Time Is Here Again/Blue Christmas/Dear
Santa/White Christmas/Pax Um Biscum (Peace Be with You)

Ringo Rama (Koch, 2003)
Eye to Eye/Missouri Loves Company/Instant Amnesia/Memphis in Your Mind/
Never Without You/Imagine Me There/I Think, Therefore I Rock 'n' Roll/Trippin
on My Own Tears/Write One for Me/What Love Wants to Be/Love First/Elizabeth
Reigns/English Garden

Choose Love (Koch, 2005)
Fading In Fading Out/Give Me Back the Beat/Oh My Lord/Hard to Be True/Some
People/Wrong All the Time/Don't Hang Up/Choose Love/Me and You/Satisfied/The
Turnaround/Free Drinks

■

In late 2005, Razor & Tie released *This Bird Has Flown: A 40th Anniversary Trib-
ute to The Beatles'* Rubber Soul, an uneven collection by such diverse artists as
Nellie McKay, Sufjan Stevens, Dar Williams, Mindy Smith, Cowboy Junkies, and
Ben Harper.

Credits

Grateful acknowledgment is made for permission to reprint the following copy-righted works:

"Beatlemania" from *Newsweek*, November 18, 1963. Copyright © 1963 by Newsweek, Inc. All rights reserved. Reprinted by permission.

Vincent Bugliosi with Curt Gentry: Excerpt from *Helter Skelter: The True Story of the Manson Murders* by Vincent Bugliosi with Curt Gentry. Copyright © 1974 by Curt Gentry and Vincent Bugliosi. Used by permission of W. W. Norton & Company, Inc.

Robert Christgau: "Secular Music," *Esquire*, December 1967. Used by permission of the author.

Maureen Cleave: "How Does a Beatle Live? John Lennon Lives Like This," *Evening Standard* (London), March 4, 1966. Reprinted by permission by Solo Syndication.

Ray Coleman: Excerpt from *Lennon: The Definitive Biography* by Ray Coleman. Copyright © 1985, 1992 by Definitives, Ltd. Reprinted by permission of HarperCollins Publishers.

Robert Deardorff: "Ringo Starr: Domesticated Beatle," *Redbook*, September 1965. Reprinted by permission of the publisher.

Paul Du Noyer: "They Were the Most Brilliant, Powerful, Lovable Pop Group on the Planet . . . But Now They're Really Important," *Q Magazine*, December 1995. Used by permission of the author.

Walter Everett: "The First EMI Recordings (September 1962–February 1963): New Drummer Ringo Starr," from *The Beatles as Musicians: The Quarry Men Through Rubber Soul* by Walter Everett. Copyright © 2001 Oxford University Press, Inc. Used by permission of Oxford University Press, Inc.

Simon Frith: "Something to Be—John Lennon," from *Music for Pleasure: Essays in the Sociology of Pop* by Simon Frith (Routledge) Copyright © Simon Frith. Used by permission of the author.

Allen Ginsberg: "Portland Coliseum," from *Collected Poems 1947–1980*. Copyright © 1984 by Allen Ginsberg. Reprinted by permission of HarperCollins Publishers.

Philip Glass: "George Harrison, World-Music Catalyst and Great-Souled Man: Open to the Influence of Unfamiliar Cultures," *The New York Times*, December 9, 2001. Copyright © 2001 by The New York Times Co. Reprinted with permission.

Martin Goldsmith: Excerpt from *The Beatles Come to America* by Martin Goldsmith. Copyright © 2004 by Martin Goldsmith. Reprinted with permission of John Wiley & Sons, Inc.

Richard Goldstein: "We Still Need the Beatles but . . . ," *The New York Times*, June 18, 1967. Copyright © 1967 by The New York Times Co. Reprinted with permission.

Adrian Henri: "New York City Blues (for John Lennon)," from *Collected Poems 1967–1985* by Adrian Henri (Allison & Busby, 1986). Copyright © Estate of Adrian Henri. Reprinted by permission of Rogers, Coleridge & White Ltd., 20 Powis Mews, London W11 1JN.

Mark Hertsgaard: "The Breakup Heard 'Round the World," from *A Day in the Life: The Music and Artistry of the Beatles* by Mark Hertsgaard (Delacorte Press). Copyright © 1995 by Mark Hertsgaard. Reprinted by permission of Ellen Levine Literary Agency/Trident Media Group.

Elliot J. Huntley: Excerpt from *Mystical One: George Harrison* by Elliott J. Huntley. Copyright © 2004 Elliot J. Huntley and Guernica Editions. By permission of the publisher.

Paul Johnson: "The Menace of Beatlism," *New Statesman*, February 28, 1964. Copyright © News Statesman, 1964. All rights reserved.

Larry Kane: from *Ticket to Ride: Inside the Beatles' 1964 Tour That Changed the World* by Larry Kane. Copyright © 2003 by Larry Kane. Reprinted by permission of Running Press, a member of Perseus Books, L.L.C.

Jim Kirkpatrick: "The WFRX Interview," from *Before He Was Fab: George Harrison's First American Visit* by Jim Kirkpatrick. Copyright © Jim Kirkpatrick, 2000. Reprinted by permission of Quick Publishing/DBA Cache River Press.

Cynthia Lennon: "The Liverpool Scene," from *A Twist of Lennon* by Cynthia Lennon (Star Books, 1978). Reprinted by permission of the author.

John Lennon: "The Mysterious Smell of Roses," from *Skywriting by Word of Mouth* by John Lennon. Copyright © 1986 Yoko Ono. Used by permission. All rights reserved.

Paul McCartney: "Here Today," from *Blackbird Singing: Poems and Lyrics 1965–2001* by Paul McCartney (W. W. Norton). Copyright © 2002 by MPL Communications, Ltd. Reprinted by permission of the author.

William Mann: "The Beatles Revive Hopes of Progress in Pop Music," *The Times* (London), May 29, 1967. Reprinted by permission of NI Syndication Ltd.

William Mann: "What Songs the Beatles Sang . . . ," *The Times* (London), December 23, 1963. Reprinted by permission of NI Syndication Ltd.

Greil Marcus: "Another Version of the Chair," from *The Rolling Stone Illustrated History of Rock and Roll,* edited by Anthony DeCurtis et al. Copyright © 1976, 1980 by Rolling Stone Press. Used by permission of Random House, Inc.

Jim Miller: "Paul McCartney Looks Back," *Newsweek*, May 3, 1982. Copyright © 1982 by Newsweek, Inc. All rights reserved. Reprinted by permission.

Philip Norman: "The Great Freedom," from *Shout!: The Beatles in Their Generation* by Philip Norman (Simon & Schuster). Copyright © 1981 by Philip Norman. Reprinted by permission of SLL/Sterling Lord Literistic, Inc.

Geoffrey O'Brien: "Seven Fat Years," from *Sonata for Jukebox: Pop Music, Memory, and the Imagined Life* by Geoffrey O'Brien. Copyright © 2004 by Geoffrey O'Brien. Reprinted by permission of Counterpoint Press, a member of Perseus Books, L.L.C.

Jim O'Donnell: "Late Afternoon," from *The Day John Met Paul* by Jim O'Donnell.

Copyright © James O'Donnell, 1994, 1996. Used by permission of Penguin Books, a division of Penguin Group (USA) Inc.

Andy Peebles: Excerpts from *The Last Lennon Tapes: John Lennon and Yoko Ono Talk to Andy Peebles, December 6, 1980* (Dell, 1983). Copyright © Yoko Ono Lennon. Reprinted by permission.

Christopher Porterfield: "Pop Music: The Messengers," *Time*, September 22, 1967. Copyright © 1967 Time Inc. Reprinted by permission.

Andru J. Reeve: Excerpt from *Turn Me On, Dead Man: The Beatles and the "Paul-Is-Dead" Hoax* by Andru J. Reeve (Popular Culture, 1994). Copyright © Andru J. Reeve, 1994. Used by permission of the author.

Ned Rorem: "The Beatles," *The New York Review of Books*, January 18, 1968. Used by permission of the author.

Andrew Sarris: "A Hard Day's Night," *The Village Voice*, August 27, 1964. Used by permission of the author.

David Sheff: Excerpt from the *Playboy* Interview: John Lennon and Yoko Ono, *Playboy* magazine, January 1981. Copyright © 1980 by Playboy. Reprinted by permission. All rights reserved.

David Simons: "The Unsung Beatle: George Harrison's Behind-the-Scenes Contributions to the World's Greatest Band," *Acoustic Guitar*, February 2003. Used by permission of the author.

Bob Spitz: Excerpt from *The Beatles: The Biography* by Bob Spitz. Copyright © 2005 by Bob Spitz. By permission of Little, Brown and Co., Inc.

Gloria Steinem: "Beatle with a Future," *Cosmopolitan*, December 1964. Used by permission of the author.

Jon Wiener: Excerpt from *Gimme Some Truth: The John Lennon FBI Files* by Jon Wiener. Copyright © 2000 by The Regents of The University of California. Reprinted by permission of The University of California Press.

Jon Wiener: "May '68: Rock Against Revolution," from *Come Together: John Lennon in His Time* by Jon Wiener (Random House). Copyright © Jon Wiener 1984. Used by permission of the author.

Jon Wilde: "McCartney: My Life in the Shadow of the Beatles," *Uncut*, July 2004. Used by permission of the author.

David Wojahn: "Fab Four Tour Deutschland: Hamburg, 1961," from *Mystery Train* by David Wojahn. Copyright © 1990, 1992 by David Wojahn. Reprinted by permission of the University of Pittsburgh Press.

Ken Womack: "Ten Great Beatles Moments," *The Morning News*, May 17, 2002. Used by permission of the author.

The following works were specially commissioned for this volume:

Wyn Cooper: "Girls, Screaming." Copyright © Wyn Cooper, 2006.

Anthony DeCurtis: "Crossing the Line: The Beatles in My Life." Copyright © Anthony DeCurtis, 2006.

Steve Earle: "The Ten Most Important Beatles Songs." Copyright © Steve Earle, 2006.

Colin Hall: "Inside Mendips." Copyright © Colin Hall, 2006.

Ashley Kahn: "All You Need." Copyright © Ashley Kahn, 2006.

Greg Kot: "Toppermost of the Poppermost." Copyright © Greg Kot, 2006.

Paul Mariani: "Remembering the Beatles." Copyright © Paul Mariani, 2006.

Tom Piazza: "Where You Once Belonged." Copyright © Tom Piazza, 2006.

Touré: "Too Late for the Show." Copyright © Touré, 2006.

Selected Bibliography

To list everything written about the Beatles and the post-Beatles would take up several volumes. Here's but a sample of what's out there.

Aldridge, Alan. "A Good Guru's Guide to the Beatles' Sinister Songbook." *Observer Magazine*, November 26, 1967.

Als, Hilton. "The Ballad of John." *The New Yorker*, August 29, 2005.

Anderson, Jack. "Beatle Lennon May Get to Stay in U.S." *The Washington Post*, June 14, 1975.

Aquila, Richard. "Why We Cried: John Lennon and American Culture." *Popular Culture and Society* X/1 (1985).

Associated Press. *John Lennon: Nothing's Gonna Change My World*. New York: Spotlight, 2005.

Baker, Glenn A., with Roger Dilernia. *The Beatles Down Under: The 1964 Australia & New Zealand Tour*. Ann Arbor, Mich.: Pieran Press, 1985.

"Bards of Pop." *Newsweek*, March 21, 1966.

The Beatles Anthology. San Francisco: Chronicle, 2000.

The Beatles: 10 Years That Shook the World. Foreword by Brian Wilson. New York: DK Publishing, 2004.

Bernstein, Richard. "Memories of Hamburg, Enough to Build a Dream On." *The New York Times*, April 8, 2006.

Best, Pete. *Beatle! The Pete Best Story*. New York: Dell, 1985.

Black, Johnny. "Paul McCartney." *Mojo*, May 2003.

———. "A Tale of Two Cities" from "1,000 Days of Beatlemania: The Early Years— April 1, 1962, to December 31, 1964," *Mojo*, Special Limited Edition, 2002.

Braun, Michael. *Love Me Do: The Beatles' Progress*. London: Penguin Books, 1964.

Brown, Peter, and Steven Gaines. *The Love You Make: An Insider's Story of the Beatles*. With a new foreword by Anthony DeCurtis. New York: New American Library, 2002.

Buckley, William F. "The Beatles and the Guru." *National Review*, March 12, 1968.

Bugliosi, Vincent, with Curt Gentry. *Helter Skelter: The True Story of the Manson Murders*. New York: Norton, 1974.

Carvell, Tim. "Sir Paul's Playbook." *The New York Times*, February 3, 2005.

Christgau, Robert. "John Lennon." *The Village Voice*, December 10, 1980.

Clayson, Adam. *Hamburg: The Cradle of British Rock*. London: Sanctuary Publishing, 1998.

———. *The Quiet One: A Life of George Harrison*. London: Sanctuary Publishing, 1996.

————. *Ringo Starr: Straight Man or Joker.* New York: Paragon House, 1992.

Cleave, Maureen. "How Does a Beatle Live? John Lennon Lives like This," *Evening Standard,* March 4, 1966.

Cocks, Jay. "The Last Day in the Life." *Time,* December 22, 1980.

Coleman, Ray. *Lennon: The Definitive Biography.* Updated and with a new introduction. New York: HarperPerennial, 1992.

Coles, Robert. "On the Death of John Lennon." *Mademoiselle,* June 1981.

Connolly, Ray. "Why Them? Why Then?" *Daily Telegraph,* November 18, 1995.

Cording, Robert, Shelli Jankowski-Smith, and E. J. Miller Laino, eds. *In My Life: Encounters with the Beatles.* New York: Fromm International, 1998.

Corliss, Richard. "A Beatle Metaphysic." *Commonweal,* May 12, 1967.

Cott, Jonathan, and Christine Doudna. *The Ballad of John and Yoko.* Garden City, NY: Rolling Stone Press Book/Dolphin Books Doubleday, 1982.

Coupland, Douglas. *Eleanor Rigby.* New York: Bloomsbury, 2004.

Crowther, Bosley. "A Hard Day's Night." *The New York Times,* August 16, 1964.

Davies, Hunter. *The Beatles: The Authorized Biography.* New York: McGraw-Hill, 1968.

Deardorff, Robert. "Ringo Starr: Domesticated Beatle." *Redbook,* September 1965.

DeCurtis, Anthony. "You Say It's My Birthday?" *AARP Magazine,* May–June 2006.

————, and James Henke with Holly George-Warren. *The Rolling Stone Illustrated History of Rock & Roll.* New York: Random House, 1992.

Delaney, Mark. *Pepperland.* Atlanta: Peachtree Publishers, 2004.

Difford, Chris. "To Be as Good." *Rolling Stone,* February 16, 1984.

DiLello, Richard. *The Longest Cocktail Party.* New York: Canongate, 2000.

Dowdling, William J. *Beatlesongs.* New York: Fireside, 1989.

Drumming, Neil. "Think Hip-Hop Started in the Bronx? Ha! Rappers Give Props to the Notorious B.E.A.T.L.E.S." *Entertainment Weekly,* February 13, 2004.

Du Noyer, Paul. "Across the Universe." In "Days of Beatlemania: The Early Years—April 1, 1962, to December 31, 1964," *Mojo,* Special Limited Edition, 2002.

————. *Liverpool: Wondrous Place—Music from Cavern to Cream.* Foreword by Sir Paul McCartney. London: Virgin Books, 2002.

————. *We All Shine On: The Stories Behind Every John Lennon Song, 1970–1980.* New York: HarperPerennial, 1997.

————. "Remembering Shea." *TV Guide,* August 14–20, 2005.

Epstein, Brian. *A Cellarful of Noise: The Autobiography of the Man Who Made the Beatles.* With a new introduction by Martin Lewis. New York: Byron Preiss Multimedia Company/Pocket Books, 1967, 1998.

Everett, Walter. *The Beatles as Musicians: The Quarry Men through Rubber Soul.* New York: Oxford University Press, 2001.

————. *The Beatles as Musicians: Revolver through the Anthology.* New York: Oxford University Press, 1999.

Fitzgerald, Jon. "Lennon-McCartney and the 'Middle Eight.'" *Popular Music and Society,* vol. 20, no. 4 (Winter 1996).

Flanagan, Bill. "Boy, You're Gonna Carry that Weight." *Musician,* May 1990.

Flippo, Chet. *Yesterday: The Unauthorized Biography of Paul McCartney.* New York: Doubleday, 1988.

Freed, Richard D. "Beatles Stump Music Experts Looking for Key to Beatlemania." *The New York Times,* August 13, 1965.

Freeman, Robert. *Yesterday: The Beatles 1963-1965.* New York: Holt Rinehart & Winston, 1983.

Freund, Charles Paul. "Still Fab: Why We Keep Listening to the Beatles." *Reason,* June 2001.

Frith, Simon. "Something to Be—John Lennon." In *Music for Pleasure: Essays in the Sociology of Pop.* London: Routledge, 1988.

Gambaccini, Paul. "A Conversation with Paul McCartney." *Rolling Stone,* July 12, 1979.

———. "Paul McCartney." *Rolling Stone,* January 31, 1974.

———. "Ringo Remembers." *Rolling Stone,* November 18, 1976.

Garbarini, Vic. "When We Was Fab." *Guitar World,* January 2001.

Garbarini, Vic, and Brian Cullman with Barbara Graustark. Special introduction by Dave Marsh. *Strawberry Fields Forever: John Lennon Remembered.* New York: Bantam, 1980.

Gilmore, Mikal. "Why This Band Plays On." *The New York Times,* August 24, 2005.

Ginsberg, Allen. "Portland Coliseum." In *Collected Poems 1947-1980.* New York: HarperCollins Publishers, 1984.

Goldsmith, Martin. *The Beatles Come to America.* New York: Wiley, 2004.

Goldstein, Richard. "We Still Need the Beatles, but . . .", *The New York Times,* June 18, 1967.

Golson, G. Barry, ed. *The Playboy Interviews with John Lennon and Yoko Ono.* New York: Playboy Press, 1981.

Gordinier, Jeff. "The 100 Greatest Entertainers." *Entertainment Weekly,* Winter 1999.

Gottfridsson, Hans Olof. *The Beatles from Cavern to Star-Club: The Illustrated Chronicle, Discography & Price Guide 1957-1962.* Stockholm: Premium Publishing, 1997.

Graustark, Barbara. "The Real John Lennon." *Newsweek,* September 29, 1980.

Gruen, Bob. *John Lennon: The New York Years.* New York: Stewart, Tabori, and Chang, 2005.

Guiliano, Geoffrey. *Dark Horse: The Private Life of George Harrison.* New York: Dutton, 1990.

Hamill, Pete. "John Lennon's Long Night's Journey into Day." *Rolling Stone,* June 5, 1975.

Harrison, George. *I, Me, Mine.* London: W. H. Allen, 1981.

Harrison, Olivia, and Brian Roylance, eds. *Concert for George.* Introduction by Paul Theroux. San Francisco: Chronicle Books, 2005.

Harry, Bill. *Mersey Beat: The Beginnings of the Beatles.* London: Omnibus Press, 1977.

Henke, James. *Lennon Legend: An Illustrated Life of John Lennon.* San Francisco: Chronicle Books, 2003.

Hertsgaard, Mark. *A Day in the Life: The Music and Artistry of the Beatles.* New York: Delacorte Press, 1995.

Huntley, Elliot J. *Mystical One: George Harrison—After the Break-up of the Beatles.* Toronto: Guernica, 2004.

Ingham, Chris. *The Rough Guide to the Beatles: The Story, the Songs, the Solo Years.* London: Rough Guides, 2003.

"Is Beatlemania Dead?" *Time,* September 2, 1966.

Jones, Ron. *The Beatles' Liverpool: The Complete Guide.* Liverpool: Ron Jones Associates, 2000.

Kael, Pauline. "Metamorphosis of the Beatles." *The New Yorker,* November 30, 1968.

Kane, Larry. *Ticket to Ride: Inside the Beatles' 1964 Tour That Changed the World.* Philadelphia: Running Press, 2003.

———. *Lennon Revealed.* Philadelphia: Running Press, 2005.

Kempton, Murray. "Mark David Chapman." *Rolling Stone,* October 15, 1981.

Kirchherr, Astrid, and Klaus Voorman. *Hamburg Days.* Foreword by George Harrison. Guildford, England: Genesis Publications, 1999.

Kirkpatrick, Jim. *Before He Was Fab: George Harrison's First American Visit.* Vienna, Ill.: Cache River Press, 2000.

Kozinn, Allan. *The Beatles.* London: Phaidon Press, 1995.

———. "They Came, They Sang, They Conquered." *The New York Times,* February 6, 2004.

———. "Going Back to Abbey Road By Way of Memory Lane." *The New York Times,* November 12, 1995.

Lahr, John. "The Beatles." *The New Republic,* December 2, 1981.

Larkin, Philip. "Fighting the Fab." *The Observer,* October 9, 1983.

Latham, Lewis. *With the Beatles.* Hoboken, N.J.: Melville House, 2005.

Leigh, Spencer. *Let's Go Down to the Cavern.* London: Vermilion, 1984.

Lennon, Cynthia. *A Twist of Lennon.* New York: Avon, 1978, 1980.

———. *John.* Foreword by Julian Lennon. New York: Crown, 2005.

Lennon, John. *In His Own Write.* London: Jonathan Cape, 1964.

———. *Skywriting by Word of Mouth.* London: Jonathan Cape, 1986.

———. *A Spaniard in the Works.* London: Jonathan Cape, 1965.

Lewis, Frederick. "Britons Succumb to 'Beatlemania.'" *The New York Times Magazine,* December 1, 1963.

Lewisohn, Mark. *The Beatles Live! The Ultimate Reference Book.* New York: Henry Holt, 1986.

———. *The Beatles Recording Sessions.* New York: Harmony Books, 1988.

———. *The Complete Beatles Chronicle.* New York: Harmony Books, 1992.

———. "I Wanna Be Your Fan." In "1,000 Days of Beatlemania: The Early Years—April 1, 1962 to December 31, 1964." *Mojo,* Special Limited Edition, 2002.

- ate133333333333333333

McCartney, Paul. *Blackbird Singing: Poems and Lyrics 1965–1999*. New York: Norton, 2001.

MacDonald, Ian. *Revolution in the Head: The Beatles Records and the Sixties*. New York: Henry Holt, 1994.

McGrath, Campbell. "Everybody Knows John Lennon Is Dead." In *Pax Atomica: Poems*. New York: Ecco Press, 2005.

McKeen, William. *The Beatles: A Bio-Bibliography*. New York: Greenwood Press, 1989.

McKinney, Devin. *Magic Circles: The Beatles in Dream and History*. Cambridge, Mass.: Harvard University Press, 2003.

Mann, William. "The Beatles Revive Hopes of Progress in Pop Music." *The Times* (London), May 29, 1967.

———. "What Songs the Beatles Sang." *The Times* (London), December 23, 1963.

Marks, J. "No, No, No, Paul McCartney Is Not Dead." *The New York Times*, November 2, 1969.

Martin, George. *All You Need Is Ears*. New York: St. Martin's Press, 1979.

———. *With a Little Help from My Friends: The Making of Sgt. Pepper*. Boston: Little, Brown, 1994.

Mellers, Wilfrid. *Twilight of the Gods: The Music of the Beatles*. New York: Schirmer Books, 1973.

Menand, Louis. "When They Were Fab." *The New Yorker*, October 16 and 23, 2000.

Mendips. Booklet. Text by Oliver Garnett. London: The National Trust, 2003.

Michaelis, David. "Sgt. Pepper's Words." *The American Scholar*, vol. 7, no. 4 (Autumn 2002).

Miles, Barry. *Paul McCartney: Many Years from Now*. New York: Henry Holt, 1997.

Miller, James. *Flowers in the Dustbin: The Rise of Rock and Roll, 1947–1988*. New York: Fireside/Simon & Schuster, 1989.

Miller, Jim. "Melancholy Masterpiece." *Newsweek*, May 3, 1982.

———. "Paul McCartney Looks Back." *Newsweek*, May 3, 1982.

Mitchell, Adrian. "Beatles." *The Listener*, October 3, 1968.

Moore, Allan F. *The Beatles: Sgt. Pepper's Lonely Hearts Club Band*. New York: Cambridge University Press, 1997.

Morris, James. "The Monarchs of the British Empire." *The Saturday Evening Post*, August 27, 1966.

Muldoon, Paul. "THE BEATLES: The Beatles." In *Hay: Poems*. New York: Farrar, Straus and Giroux, 1998.

Mulhern, Paul. "Paul McCartney." *Guitar Player*, July 1990.

Murakami, Haruki. *Norwegian Wood*. New York: Vintage, 2000.

Neises, Charles P., ed. *The Beatles Reader*. Ann Arbor, Mich.: Pierian Press, 1984.

NME Originals. "Beatles: The Solo Years 1970–1980," vol. 2, issue 3.

Norman, Philip. *Shout! The Beatles in Their Generation*. Rev. and updated. New York: Fireside/Simon & Schuster, 2003.

————. "Yesterday and Today, Beatles Are the Ultimate Show Business Tale." In *Forever Fab: Commemorative Newspaper from The New York Times,* 2005.

O'Brien, Geoffrey. *Sonata for Jukebox: Pop Music, Memory, and the Imagined Life.* New York: Counterpoint Press, 2004.

O'Donnell, Jim. *The Day John Met Paul: An Hour-by-Hour Account of How the Beatles Began.* New York: Penguin Books, 1996.

O'Grady, Terence J. *The Beatles: A Musical Evolution.* Boston: G. K. Hall, 1983.

————. "Rubber Soul and the Social Dance Tradition." *Ethnomusicology* XXIII/1, January 1979.

O'Hagan, Andrew. "Back in the US of A." *The New York Review of Books,* May 27, 2004.

"The 100 Greatest Songs of All Time." *Mojo,* Songwriters Special, August 2000.

"1,000 Days of Beatlemania: The Early Years—April 1, 1962, to December 31, 1964." *Mojo,* Special Limited Edition, 2002.

Ono, Yoko, ed. *Memories of John Lennon.* New York: Harper Entertainment, 2005.

Packard, Vance. "Building the New Beatle Image." *The Saturday Evening Post,* March 21, 1964.

Pank, Philip. "Beatle's Quiet Songwriting Genius." *The Guardian,* November 30, 2001.

Pareles, Jon. "At Age 20, Sgt. Pepper Marches On." *The New York Times,* May 31, 1987.

Partridge, Elizabeth. *John Lennon: All I Want Is the Truth.* New York: Penguin, 2005.

Pawlowski, Gareth. *How They Became the Beatles.* New York: E. P. Dutton, 1989.

Peebles, Andy. *The Last Lennon Tapes: John Lennon and Yoko Ono Talk to Andy Peebles December 6, 1980.* New York: Dell, 1981.

Pichaske, David R. *Beowulf to the Beatles: Approaches to Poetry.* New York: The Free Press, 1972.

Poirier, Richard. "Learning from the Beatles." *Partisan Review* 34 (Fall 1967).

Pond, Steve. "Being There." *TV Guide,* August 14–20, 2005.

Porterfield, Christopher. "Pop Music: The Messengers." *Time,* September 22, 1967.

Quantick, David. *Revolution: The Making of the Beatles' White Album.* Chicago: A Cappella Books, 2002.

Rappaport, Doreen. *John's Secret Dreams: The Life of John Lennon.* New York: Hyperion, 2004.

Reeve, Andru J. *Turn Me On, Dead Man: The Beatles and the "Paul-Is-Dead" Hoax.* Bloomington, Ind.: Author House, 2004.

Riley, Tim. *Tell My Why: A Beatles Commentary.* New York: Knopf, 1988.

Rockwell, John. "Leader of a Rock Group that Helped Define a Generation." *The New York Times,* December 9, 1980.

Rolling Stone, eds. *Harrison.* Foreword by Olivia Harrison. New York: Simon & Schuster, 2002.

Rolling Stone's 500 Greatest Albums of All Time. Introduction by Steven Van Zandt. New York: Wenner Books, 2005.

Roos, Michael E. "The Walruses and the Deacon: John Lennon's Debt to Lewis Carroll." *Journal of Popular Culture* XVIII/1 (1984).

Rorem, Ned. "The Music of the Beatles." *The New York Review of Books,* January 18, 1968.

Salewicz, Chris. *McCartney.* New York: St. Martin's Press, 1986.

Sarris, Andrew. "A Hard Day's Night." *The Village Voice,* August 27, 1964.

Schaffner, Nicholas. *The Beatles Forever.* New York: McGraw Hill, 1978.

Schaumburg, Ron. *Growing Up with the Beatles: An Illustrated Tribute.* New York: Pyramid Books, 1976.

Shames, Lawrence. "John Lennon, Where Are You?" *Esquire,* November 1980.

Shankar, Ravi. "A Childlike Simplicity, Full of Love and Fun." *The New York Times,* December 9, 2001.

Sheff, David and Victoria. "The Betrayal of John Lennon." *Playboy,* March 1984.

Shotten, Pete. *John Lennon: In My Life.* New York: Stein and Day, 1983.

Sinclair, Tom. "Do the Beatles Still Matter?" *Entertainment Weekly,* February 13, 2004.

Smith, Elliott. "Learning to Play in the Womb: A Songwriter on John Lennon as a Songwriter." *Spin,* January 2001.

Smith, Peter. *Two of Us: The Story of a Father, a Son, and the Beatles.* New York: Boston: Houghton, Mifflin Company, 2004.

Solt, Andrew, ed. *Imagine: John Lennon.* Preface by Yoko Ono. New York: Macmillan/Sarah Lazin Books, 1988.

Spitz, Bob. *The Beatles: The Biography.* New York: Little, Brown, 2005.

———. "He May Be Sir Paul, but He's Still a Beatle." *The New York Times,* May 25, 1997.

Stark, Steven D. *Meet the Beatles: A Cultural History of the Band that Shook Youth, Gender, and the World.* New York: HarperEntertainment/HarperCollins Publishers, 2005.

Stokes, Geoffrey. *The Beatles.* New York: Rolling Stone Press, 1983.

Strauss, Neil. "Beatles as Birthright: 3 Generations and Counting." *The New York Times,* November 12, 1995.

Sullivan, M. "'More Popular than Jesus': The Beatles and the Religious Far Right." *Popular Music* 6 (1987).

Terry, Carol D. *Here, There, and Everywhere: The First International Beatles Bibliography, 1962–1982.* Ann Arbor, Mich.: Popular Culture, 1985.

Tetsuya, Fujita, Yuji Hagino, Hajime Kubo, and Goro Sato. *The Beatles Complete Scores.* New York: Hal Leonard, 1993.

Theroux, Paul. "Why We Loved the Beatles." *Rolling Stone,* February 16, 1984.

Thomas, John D. "All the Lonely People: PW Talks with Douglas Coupland." *Publishers Weekly,* November 15, 2004.

Thomson, Elizabeth, and David Cutman, eds. *The Lennon Companion: Twenty-five Years of Comment.* New York: Schirmer Books, 1988.

Trynka, Paul, ed. *The Beatles: 10 Years that Shook the World.* Preface by Brian Wilson. New York: DK, 2004.

Turner, Steve. *A Hard Day's Write: The Stories behind Every Beatles Song.* New York: HarperPerennial, 1994.

———. *The Gospel According to the Beatles.* Louisville, Ky.: Westminster John Knox, 2006.

20 Forthlin Road. Booklet. Introduction by Paul McCartney. Text by Oliver Garnett. London: The National Trust, 1998.

Tyrangiel, Josh. "Do We Still Need Him?" *Time,* September 12, 2005.

Vowell, Sarah. "John Lennon: Musical Genius, Cultural Rebel, Total Goofball." *Spin,* January 2001.

Weinberg, Max, with Robert Santelli. *The Big Beat: Conversations with Rock's Great Drummers.* Chicago: Contemporary Books, 1984.

Wells, Simon. *The Beatles: 365 Days.* New York: Abrams, 2005.

Wenner, Jan. *Lennon Remembers: The Rolling Stone Interviews.* San Francisco: Straight Arrow Books, 1971; reprinted, Verso, 2001.

Wiener, Jon. *Come Together: John Lennon in His Time.* Urbana, Ill.: University of Illinois Press, 1991.

Wilde, Jon. "My Life in the Shadow of the Beatles." *Uncut,* July 2004.

Williams, Alan. *The Man Who Gave the Beatles Away.* London: Coronet, 1976.

Williams, Richard. "Please Please Me: The Immaculate Reception." In "Days of Beatlemania: The Early Years—April 1, 1962, to December 31, 1964." *Mojo,* Special Limited Edition, 2002.

Wojahn, David. "Fab Four Tour Deutschland: Hamburg, 1961." In *Mystery Train.* Pittsburgh: University of Pittsburgh Press, 1992.

Wolfe, Tom. "Beatles! More than Just a Word to the Wild." *New York Herald Tribune,* February 8, 1964.

———. *Electric Kool-Aid Acid Test.* New York: Bantam, 1968.

———. "A Highbrow under All that Hair?" *Book Week,* May 3, 1964.

Womack, Kenneth, and Todd F. Davis, eds. *Reading the Beatles: Cultural Studies, Literary Criticism, and the Fab Four.* Albany: State University of New York Press, 2006.

Wooler, Bob. "The Roving I." Mersey Beat 1 (October 5–19). In *Mersey Beat: The Beginnings of the Beatles,* ed. Bill Harry. New York: Quick Fox, 1977.